An Uncertain Glory

JEAN DRÈZE AND AMARTYA SEN

An Uncertain Glory
India and Its Contradictions

PRINCETON UNIVERSITY PRESS
Princeton & Oxford

Published in the United States and Canada by
Princeton University Press,
41 William Street, Princeton, New Jersey 08540

In the United Kingdom, published by the Penguin Group,
Penguin Books Ltd, 80 Strand, London WC2R ORL, England

press.princeton.edu

ISBN: 978-0-691-16079-5
LCCN: 2013942038

This book has been composed in Sabon LT Std

Printed on acid-free paper. ∞

Printed in the United States of America

1 2 3 4 5 6 7 8 9 10

Contents

Preface

This book goes to press at a time of considerable stir in Indian society and politics. There are many discussions and debates about the country's policy priorities, involving a great diversity of participants and viewpoints. Lively arguments and agitations have also developed around a wide range of issues that had been neglected for a long time, such as corruption, administrative failure, capital punishment, violence against women and democratic reforms. There are also spirited arguments about India's economic achievements and failures.

This abundance of questioning and arguing, facilitated by a vibrant media and robust democratic institutions, can be a great strength for the country. It is compromised, however, by a powerful bias in public discussions towards focusing mainly on the lives and concerns of the relatively privileged, including not only the very privileged but also others who are not right at the top but are certainly much more privileged – in affluence, education, health care, cultural opportunities and social standing – than the bulk of the Indian people. The issues that affect the lives, and even survival, of those who have been comprehensively left behind tend to receive remarkably little attention.

It is a very positive development that violence against women has, at last, become a big political issue in India, starting with the public outrage that followed a horrific incident of gang-rape in December 2012. The debate around this issue has drawn attention to many aspects of gender discrimination (including, but not only, the callous attitude of the police towards complaints of sexual violence), which had been grossly neglected for a long time. But it is also worth noting that the protests, which were hugely overdue and have become strongly – and appropriately – vocal, could be sparked off by an incident that involved a victim (a medical student) with whom the Indian middle classes could easily identify. Similar brutalities have happened in the lives of economically and socially downtrodden Dalit women for years, without getting much attention in the mainstream media or causing a significant public outcry.

To take another example (which we will discuss more fully later), consider the occasion when half the country suffered suddenly from a gigantic power failure on 30–31 July 2012, and 600 million people had no electricity. The country was rightly inflamed about the inefficiency of administrative arrangements in India. The failure of responsibility and accountability was certainly enormous, and India has good reason to ask how this problem can be urgently addressed and eliminated. What was not, however, much discussed at all was the fact that 200 million of those 600 million without electricity had never had any electricity at all, since these non-affluent people were not – and had never been – connected to power.

Issues of economic development in India have to be seen in the larger context of the demands of democracy and social justice. During the last twenty years, the Indian economy has done very well in terms of the growth of GDP (about 6 per cent per year in real terms in the 1990s, rising to more than 7 per cent in the last decade). India became the second fastest-growing large economy over the last two decades, next only to China. For a low-income economy which had been mired in near-stagnation through centuries of colonial rule and which made slow progress in the decades following independence, this is surely a major achievement. As discussed in the book, there is an urgent need for paying more attention to the environmental damage that has accompanied this rapid growth, but India's new economic dynamism makes it possible to pursue more responsible environmental policies along with reasonably high rates of growth.

However, the achievement of high growth – even high levels of *sustainable* growth – must ultimately be judged in terms of the impact of that economic growth on the lives and freedoms of the people. Over this period of rapid growth, while some people, particularly among the privileged classes, have done very well, many more continue to lead unnecessarily deprived and precarious lives. It is not that their living conditions have not improved at all, but the pace of improvement has been very slow for the bulk of the people, and for some there has been remarkably little change. While India has climbed rapidly up the ladder of economic growth rates, it has fallen relatively behind in the scale of social indicators of living standards, even compared with many countries India has been overtaking in terms of economic growth. For example, over the last two decades India has expanded its lead over Bangladesh in terms of average income (it is now about twice as rich in income per capita as Bangladesh), and yet in terms of many typical indicators of living standards (other than income per head), Bangladesh not only does better than India, it has a considerable lead over it (just as India had, two decades ago, a substantial lead over Bangladesh in the same indicators). The history of world development offers few other examples, if any, of an economy growing so fast for so long with such limited results in terms of reducing human deprivations.

A huge part of the current discontent in the Indian media has been concerned with the bad news that India's rate of GDP growth has slipped over the last couple of years. The fact that India's high growth rate has fallen certainly deserves serious attention, even though such slowing has happened in the same period across the world (including in China, and also in Brazil, South Korea and elsewhere), and even though India's new GDP growth rate of 5 or 6 per cent per year still places it among the world's fastest-growing economies. The concern is important because economic growth can certainly help to improve people's lives (not only by raising per capita incomes but also by generating public revenue that can be used for purposes of social advancement of the people), and also because a deeper analysis of the relation between economic growth and social progress is seriously overdue in India. What is remarkable is not the media's interest in growth rates, but its near-silence about the fact that the growth process is so biased, making the country look more and more like islands of California in a sea of sub-Saharan Africa.

In earlier works, we have argued that development is best seen in terms of an expansion of people's basic freedoms, or human capabilities. In this perspective, we have to recognize the importance of the two-way relationship between economic growth and the expansion of human capability, while also keeping in mind the basic understanding that the expansion of human freedom and capabilities is the goal for which the growth of GDP, among other factors, serves as important means. Growth generates resources with which public and private efforts can be systematically mobilized to expand education, health care, nutrition, social facilities, and other essentials of fuller and freer human life for all. And the expansion of human capability, in turn, allows a faster expansion of resources and production, on which economic growth ultimately depends.

This two-way relationship has been a central feature of the so-called 'Asian economic development', beginning with Japan immediately after the Meiji restoration, extending gradually to South Korea, Taiwan, Thailand and elsewhere, and ultimately making China the world leader both in raising economic growth and in expanding human capability. Those who dream about India becoming an economic superpower, even with its huge proportion of undernourished children, lack of systematic health care, extremely deficient school education, and half the homes without toilets (forcing half of all Indians to practise open defecation), have to reconsider not only the reach of their understanding of the mutual relationship between growth and development, but also their appreciation of the demands of social justice, which is integrally linked with the expansion of human freedoms.

This book is to a great extent about how to make effective use of the understanding of these interdependences, on which the progress of living standards and well-being, and ultimately also economic growth, depend. If that empirical connection motivates one part of our analysis, its bearing on social justice in India is the central motivation for writing this book. Of course, a great deal more than economic growth is involved in the pursuit of a less deprived and less unjust India. We go into the various 'social connections' as well as the more economic ones in some detail. For example, there is much evidence to suggest that Bangladesh's rapid progress in living standards has been greatly helped by the agency of women, and particularly the fact that girls have been rapidly educated and women have been widely involved – much more than in India – in the expansion of basic education, health care, family planning and other public services as well as being a bigger part of the industrial labour force. Experiences of other countries, and indeed from particular regions within India as well, offer similar lessons. Given the extent and forms of gender disparity in India, there is an urgent need to focus not only on what can be done for Indian women (important as it is), but also on what Indian women can ·do for India – helping to make it a very different country.

Well-functioning public services, especially (but not only) in fields such as education and health, are also critical in fostering participatory growth as well as in ensuring that growth leads to rapid improvements in people's living conditions. Some Indian states (such as Kerala, Himachal Pradesh and Tamil Nadu) have done reasonably well in this respect, reaping as they have sown, and there have also been positive, if partial, initiatives in some other states in the recent past. Nevertheless, the general state of public services in India remains absolutely dismal, and the country's health and education systems in particular have been severely messed up. While the privileged are able to take refuge in private arrangements (expensive as they tend to be), the rest are deprived of essential facilities that ought to be available to all as a matter of right. Aside from diminishing the country's prospects for participatory growth and broad-based development, India's highly privatized and compartmentalized health and education systems (with very different opportunities for different social groups) also perpetuate social disparities – instead of reducing them, in contrast with what health and education systems as well as other forms of public support have tended to do around the world. Beyond the specific – and very important – cases of health and education, India also faces larger issues of accountability in the public sector as a whole. The future of the country depends a great deal on more effective democratic engagement with these momentous issues.

An overarching theme of this book is the necessity for the lives, needs, rights and demands of underprivileged people to command greater attention in public discussion and policy making, and in democratic politics. Indian democracy is seriously compromised by the extent and form of social inequality in India, particularly since democracy stands not just for electoral politics and civil liberties but also for an equitable distribution of power. While some aspects of social inequality in India have diminished in the recent past, new imbalances have developed, including heightened economic inequality and the growth of corporate power. Nevertheless, it would be a mistake to think that privileged interests are bound to override and overwhelm all attempts at sharing power more equitably.

Indeed, even in this compromised state, Indian democracy offers significant opportunities for popular movements to flourish and resist the concentration of power and the neglect of the interests of the deprived. We have discussed ways and means of expanding the reach of public reasoning (through discussion as well as agitation), and of urgently addressing the needs of the underprivileged. The book is, thus, contingently optimistic, even though the investigation of what India has so far failed to do has to be an integral part of this forward-looking approach.

The empirical material used in the book, though cited in the respective chapters, is also presented separately in the Statistical Appendix, where reasonably detailed information on development in India as a whole and in India's major states can be found. We hope that the broad-based statistics included in this Appendix will also be useful for purposes other than those for which we have drawn on them.

We are most grateful to Sabina Alkire, Arudra Burra, Aashish Gupta, Reetika Khera and Emma Rothschild for detailed comments on earlier drafts. The book has also greatly benefited from useful advice, comments and suggestions from the following: Ankita Aggarwal, Isher Ahluwalia, Montek Singh Ahluwalia, Manzoor Ahmed, Sudhir Anand, P. Arokiasamy, Izete Pengo Bagolin, Pulapre Balakrishnan, J. Balasubramaniam, Nirmala Banerjee, Pranab Bardhan, Francesca Bastagli, Kaushik Basu, Akansha Batra, Bela Bhatia, Robert Cassen, Ha-Joon Chang, Lincoln Chen, Deepta Chopra, Mushtaque R. Chowdhury, Diane Coffey, Flavio Comim, Gurcharan Das, Monica Das Gupta, Gaurav Datt, Harishwar Dayal, Anuradha De, Arjan de Haan, Angus Deaton, Meghnad Desai, Sonalde Desai, Swati Dhingra, Albina du Boisrouvray, Jesus Felipe, Francisco Ferreira, Pedro H. G. Ferreira de Souza, Raghav Gaiha, Subhash Gatade, Haris Gazdar, Jayati Ghosh, Kaveri Gill, Srinivas Goli, M. Govinda Rao, Ramachandra Guha, Paranjoy Guha Thakurta, Stephen Howes, Arjimand Hussain, Clément Imbert, Rownaq Jahan, Anurodh Lalit Jain, Devaki Jain, Monica Jain, Raji Jayaraman, Ravi Kanbur, Sowmya Kidambi, Geeta Gandhi Kingdon, Stephan Klasen, Atul Kohli, Ashish Kothari, Ashok Kotwal, Gabrielle Kruks-Wisner,

Sanjay Kumar, Utsav Kumar, Robert LeVine, Ian MacAuslan, Guru Prasad Madan, Ajay Mahal, Simeen Mahmud, Wahiduddin Mahmud, Manabi Majumdar, Harsh Mander, Silvia Mangatter, Karthik Muralidharan, Rinku Murgai, Karuna Muthiah, Poonam Muttreja, Deepa Narayan, Sudha Narayanan, Christian Oldiges, S. R. Osmani, Felix Padel, Brijesh Pandey, John Papp, Lant Pritchett, Vinod Raina, Jairam Ramesh, Anita Rampal, Kumar Rana, Bhaskara Rao, Martin Ravallion, Rammanohar Reddy, Vivek S., Meera Samson, K. M. Sathyanarayana, Gita Sen, Mitu Sengupta, A. K. Shiva Kumar, Rukmini Shrinivasan, Abhay Shukla, Ben Siegel, A. K. Singh, Prerna Singh, Shekhar Singh, Amarjeet Sinha, Dipa Sinha, F. V. Soares, Rehman Sobhan, Dean Spears, Nicholas Stern, Aya Taketomi, Vito Tanzi, Dennis Tao Yang, Alessandro Tarozzi, Yoshifumi Usami, Fabio Veras, Vinod Vyasulu, Michael Walton, Yanyan Xiong and Yogendra Yadav.

We have benefited greatly from many editorial suggestions from Stuart Proffitt of Penguin Books, whose counsel has been extremely important for the presentation of our arguments and evidence. We would also like to thank Richard Mason for his careful copy-editing of our rather unwieldy manuscript, and Richard Duguid for his oversight of the book through the press.

The Department of Economics at Allahabad University and the Centre for History and Economics at Magdalene College, Cambridge, have served as very efficient bases for this work. The research facilities and administrative arrangements provided by the Cambridge Centre for History and Economics have been assisted by a generous grant from the Ford Foundation. We are most grateful also to Aashish Gupta and Aditya Balasubramanian for excellent research assistance, supplemented very effectively by Meghna Brahmachari, Kirsty Walker and Neesha Harman. The Centre's administrative help has been provided most effectively by Inga Huld Markan, and by Mary-Rose Cheadle. We are much indebted to them all.

Last but not least, parts of this book draw on collaborative work with the Pratichi Trust research team, led by Manabi Majumdar and Kumar Rana, from which we have learned a great deal.

Jean Drèze and Amartya Sen
Santiniketan, 15 February 2013

I

A New India?

'O, how this spring of love resembleth/The uncertain glory of an April day,' says Proteus in *The Two Gentlemen of Verona*. The recent achievements of modern, democratic India are not inconsiderable, and have been widely recognized across the globe over the last decade or more. India's record in pioneering democratic governance in the non-Western world is a widely acknowledged accomplishment, as is its basic success in maintaining a secular state, despite the challenges arising from its thoroughly multi-religious population and the hugely problematic history of violence around the ending days of the Raj. To this can be added the achievement of rapid economic growth in the last decade, when India became the second fastest-growing large economy in the world.

And yet – despite these great achievements – if the much talked-about glory of today's India is deeply uncertain, it is not because an unblemished sunny day stands in danger of being ruined by a freshly arriving shower, as was feared by Proteus of Verona. The uncertainty arises, rather, from the fact that together with the sunshine, there are dark clouds and drenching showers already on the scene. It is important and urgent that we try to evaluate both the achievements and the failures that characterize India today. To what extent have India's old problems been eradicated? What remains to be done? And are there new problems that India has to address?

In historical perspective, the accomplishments are large indeed, especially in light of what the country was at the time of independence in 1947. India emerged then from an oppressive colonial rule, enforced by dogged imperial rulers; there was little devolution of real power until the British actually left, and it was not unnatural at that time to doubt India's capacity to run a functioning democracy. A second challenge was to avoid the danger of chaos and conflict, or even a violent break-up of the country. There is a long history – stretching over thousands of years – of cultural affinities across India, and the struggle for independence generated a great deal of popular unity. And yet the diversities and divisions within India – of many languages, religions, ethnicities – gave sceptics good reason to worry about the possible break-up of the country in the absence of authoritarian rule. More immediately, the chaotic partitioning of pre-independent India into two countries – India and Pakistan – gave justified cause for anxiety about whether further violent splintering might occur.

Supplementing and in some ways overshadowing all these concerns, the poverty of India was perhaps the most well-known fact about the country – with little children in Europe and America being asked by their parents not to leave food on their plates because of the moral necessity to 'think of the starving Indians'. And indeed, in 1943, just four years before colonial rule ended, India did actually have a gigantic famine in which between 2 and 3 million people died.

India had not always been a symbol of poverty and hunger – far from it – and we shall turn, in the next chapter, to the question of how the country became so poor. What is not in doubt is that the economy of British India was remarkably stagnant, and that living conditions around the time of independence were appalling for a large proportion of the Indian population, and not just in famine years.*

---

* An investigation of world-wide health and anthropometric data, recently completed, brings out just how appalling the nutritional and physical conditions were in India at the time the colonial Raj came to an end in 1947: 'It is possible that the deprivation in childhood of Indians born around mid-century was as severe as any large group in history, all the way back to the Neolithic Revolution and the hunter-gatherers that preceded them. Life expectancy in India in 1931 was 27, also reflecting extreme deprivation . . . death and deprivation kept the population in check, but even for the survivors, the conditions of life were terrible.' See Angus Deaton (forthcoming), *The Great Escape and the Origins of Inequality*, Chapter 4.

ACHIEVEMENTS AND OPPORTUNITIES

Despite that grim beginning, newly independent India rapidly went on to have a cluster of significant political and economic successes. Its bold decision to go straight from centuries of colonial rule to resolutely democratic government, without a pause, has proved to be sound and sustainable. In India as in other democratic countries around the world, democracy in the full sense of the term (that of 'government of the people, by the people, for the people') has not been achieved, and there remain many gaps to fill in Indian democracy.[1] Nevertheless, after more than sixty years of largely successful democratic governance, India has earned its status as a leading democratic country. The army has not moved to take over civilian affairs as has happened in many newly independent countries in the world – not least in South Asia. The country has also shown quite powerfully how democracy can flourish despite a multitude of languages, religions and ethnicities. There are, it must be noted, confined departures from democratic norms, for example in the use of military power ordered by the civilian government at the centre to quell discontent at the periphery (on which more later), and there is need for change there – and not just on the periphery. But taking everything together, there are good reasons for seeing a major accomplishment in the broad success of secular democracy in India. Also, the relatively healthy state – overall – of democratic institutions in the country provides significant opportunities for reasoned solutions to the problems that remain as well as for further extending the reach and quality of democratic practice.

On the economic front, even though the growth of the Indian economy was quite slow – about 3.5 per cent annually – for several decades after independence, this slow growth was nevertheless a very large step forward compared with the near-zero growth (and at times even economic decline) that occurred in the colonial days. This prolonged economic stagnation ended as soon as the country became independent. However, to reverse a zero-growth performance can hardly be adequate, and there is much to discuss about the real as well as imagined reasons for the forces that held India back for decades after independence. Happily, things have changed in that respect as well over the recent decades, and India has now been able to establish a new position as one of the fastest-growing economies in the world. Table 1.1 presents a summary picture of the growth of the gross domestic product (GDP), from the colonial time to now.

Table 1.1
Growth Rates of India's GDP at Constant Prices
(% per year)

	GDP	Per capita GDP
Colonial period		
1900–1 to 1946–7	0.9	0.1
Early post-independence period		
1950–1 to 1960–1	3.7	1.8
1960–1 to 1970–1	3.4	1.2
1970–1 to 1980–1	3.4	1.2
Recent decades		
1980–1 to 1990–1	5.2	3.0
1990–1 to 2000–1	5.9	4.0
2000–1 to 2010–11	7.6	6.0

Sources: Sivasubramonian (2000) and Government of India (2012a); for details, see Chapter 2, Table 2.1.

There has been some slackening of the growth rate of the Indian economy very recently – partly related to the global slump (there has been a similar slowing in China as well, though from a higher base). India is still – even with its diminished growth rate below 6 per cent per year – one of the fastest-growing economies in the world. While that bit of reality check is useful, it is also important to consider the policy changes that could make India's growth performance perk up more. The country's growth potential remains strong and robust and it can be a major source of strength for India – particularly if the fruits of economic growth are well utilized for the advancement of human lives and the development of human freedom and capabilities (a subject on which there will be much to say as the book proceeds). We shall take up the 'growth story of India' more fully in the next chapter.

After two hundred years of colonial domination, combined with almost total economic stagnation, the economy seems well set to remedy the country's notorious and unenviable condition of poverty. The fact that there has also been, at the same time, maintenance and consolidation of democracy in one of the poorest countries in the world, makes India's achievements particularly noteworthy. India has also established itself as an innovative centre of some significant departures in the world economy, not just in the application of information technology and related activities, but also – no less significantly – as the great supplier of inexpensive but reliable modern medicine for the poor of the world. As the *New York Times* put it in a recent editorial, since 'India is the world's largest supplier of generic medicines', in the pharmaceutical field, 'its policies potentially affect billions of people around the world'.[2]

Along with economic progress, there has also been significant social change. Life expectancy in India today (about 66 years) is more than twice what it was in 1951 (32 years); infant mortality is about one fourth of what it used to be (44 per thousand live births today as opposed to 180 or so in 1951); and the female literacy rate has gone up from 9 per cent to 65 per cent. There have certainly been major improvements in the miserable levels of social indicators that prevailed at the time of India's independence (see Table 1.2).[3] All this is in contrast with the predictions of doom, gloom and famine that were often made about India in the 1950s and 1960s. It is also a substantial political achievement that many of the leaders of democratic politics have tended to come from neglected groups – women, minorities and disadvantaged castes. As we will discuss, enormous inequalities remain, and many divisions have not diminished at all, but the fact that some significant changes have occurred even in the political arena of hierarchy must be a reason to believe that more – *much* more – should be possible. B. R. Ambedkar, the champion of the socially and economically discriminated (who did not shy away from challenging the Indian nationalist leaders for their absence of engagement with 'economic and social democracy'), insisted that we have reason to pursue, rather than lose faith in, the power to 'educate, agitate and organize'.[4] Since India's political democracy allows plenty of room for that engagement, its absence or its timidity cannot be blamed on any prohibition imposed by 'the system'.

Table 1.2
India: Then and Now

	1951	2011
Gross domestic product (GDP) at constant prices (1951=100)	100	1,766
Per capita net national product at constant prices (1950–1=100)	100	511
Estimated life expectancy at birth (years)	32	66
Estimated infant mortality rate (per 1,000 live births)	≈ 180	44
Total fertility rate (children per woman)	5.9	2.4
Literacy rate[a] (%)		
Female	9	65
Male	27	82
Estimated proportion (%) of the population below the poverty line[b]		
Rural	47	22[c]
Urban	35	20[c]
Proportion (%) of households owning:		
Bicycle	≈ 0.4	46[d]
Radio	≈ 0.9	27[d]
Sewing machine	≈ 0.1	19[d]

[a] Age 5 years and above for 1951, 7 years and above for 2011.
[b] Based on national poverty lines applicable prior to Tendulkar Committee Report (Rs 49 and Rs 57 per person per month at 1973–4 prices in rural and urban areas, respectively).
[c] 2004–5.
[d] 2007–8.

Source: See Statistical Appendix, Table A.5. The fertility rate estimate for 1951 (strictly speaking, 1950–5) is from the United Nations Population Division (2011). In the last row, the 2007–8 figures are from the International Institute for Population Sciences (2010a), Table 2.8, and the 1951 figures are estimated from census data presented in Vaidyanathan (1983), Table 13.3.

In this context we have reason to rejoice in the massive expansion of a free media that has taken place since independence. We shall argue, as the book progresses, that there are nevertheless huge failings of the Indian media, but these limitations do not arise from governmental censorship nor from the absence of a sufficiently large network of print or oral or visual journalism. India can be proud of its huge circulation of newspapers (the largest in the world), and a vast and lively stream of radio and television coverage, presenting – among other things – many different analyses of ongoing politics (many of them round the clock). This is surely something of a triumph of democratic opportunity – at one level – that adds much force to the working of other democratic institutions, including free, multi-party elections.

The failings of the media, which we will discuss presently, concern a lack of serious involvement in the diagnosis of significant injustices and inefficiencies in the economic and social lives of people; and also the absence of high-quality journalism, with some honourable exceptions, about what could enhance the deprived and constrained lives of many – often most – people in the country, even as the media presents a glittering picture of the privileged and the successful. There is surely a need for political and social change here, which we will discuss (particularly in Chapters 7–9). By enriching the content of the coverage and analyses of news, the Indian media could certainly be turned into a major asset in the pursuit of justice, equity, and efficiency in democratic India.

AN UNFINISHED AGENDA

The record of India's achievements is not easy to dismiss, but is that the whole story? An agreeable picture of a country in a rapid march forward towards development with justice would definitely not be a comprehensive, or even a balanced, account of what has been actually happening: indeed far from it. There are many major shortcomings and breakdowns – some of them gigantic – even though privileged groups, and especially the celebratory media, are often inclined to overlook them. We also have to recognize with clarity that the neglect – or minimizing – of these problems in public reasoning is tremendously costly, since democratic rectification depends crucially on public understanding and widespread discussion of the serious problems that have to be addressed.

Since India's recent record of fast economic growth is often celebrated, with good reason, it is extremely important to point to the fact that the societal reach of economic progress in India has been remarkably limited. It is not only that the income distribution has been getting more unequal in recent years (a characteristic that India shares with China), but also that the rapid rise in real wages in China from which the working classes have benefited greatly is not matched at all by India's relatively stagnant real wages. No less importantly, the public revenue generated by rapid economic growth has not been used to expand the social and physical infrastructure in a determined and well-planned way (in this India is left far behind by China). There is also a continued lack of essential social services (from schooling and health care to the provision of safe water and drainage) for a huge part of the population. As we will presently discuss, while India has been overtaking other countries in the progress of its real income, it has been overtaken in terms of social indicators by many of these countries, even within the region of South Asia itself (we go into this question more fully in Chapter 3, 'India in Comparative Perspective').

To point to just one contrast, even though India has significantly caught up with China in terms of GDP growth, its progress has been very much slower than China's in indicators such as longevity, literacy, child undernourishment and maternal mortality. In South Asia itself, the much poorer economy of Bangladesh has caught up with and overtaken India in terms of many social indicators (including life expectancy, immunization of children, infant mortality, child under-nourishment and girls' schooling). Even Nepal has been catching up, to the extent that it now has many social indicators similar to India's, in spite of its per capita GDP being just about one third. Whereas twenty years ago India generally had the second-best social indicators among the six South Asian countries (India, Pakistan, Bangladesh, Sri Lanka, Nepal and Bhutan), it now looks second worst (ahead only of problem-ridden Pakistan). India has been climbing up the ladder of per capita income while slipping down the slope of social indicators.

Given the objectives of development and equity that India championed as it fought for independence, there is surely a huge failure here. It is not only that the new income generated by economic growth has been very unequally shared, but also that the resources newly created have not been utilized adequately to relieve the gigantic social deprivations of the underdogs of society. Democratic pressures, as we will discuss in later chapters, have gone in other directions rather than rectifying the major injustices that characterize contemporary India. There is work to be done both in making good use of the fruits of economic growth to enhance the living conditions of the people and in reducing the massive inequalities that characterize India's economy and society. Maintaining – and if possible increasing – the pace of economic growth will have to be only one part of a larger – much larger – commitment.

POWER AND INFRASTRUCTURE

If the continuation of huge disparities in the lives of Indians from different backgrounds is one large problem on which much more public discussion – and political engagement – are needed, a far-reaching failure in governance and organization is surely another. Indians face this problem, in one form or another, every day, even if global awareness of the extent of this systemic failure comes only intermittently, as when on 30–31 July 2012 a power blackout temporarily obliterated electricity from half of the country, wreaking havoc with the lives of 600 million people. Intolerable organizational chaos joined hands with terrible inequality: a third of those 600 million never have any electricity anyway (an illustration of the inequality that characterizes modern India), whereas two-thirds lost power without any warning (an example of the country's disorganization).

There is a gigantic inadequacy in the running of the power sector in India, of which the blackout was an obvious manifestation. Persistent power failures (or 'load shedding', the name given to 'organizing' the failures rather than curing them) occur day in, day out, in a great many places across the country, without getting much notice outside the community of sufferers, for whom they are not any less important

9

than the gigantic blackout of 2012 that drew the attention of the world. And, as noted, nearly a third of the population of India is not connected with electricity at all – compared with a mere 1 per cent in China.[5]

The dismal state of the power sector is only one part of the serious failure in India to address the need for good physical infrastructure. Similar deficiencies can be seen in water supply, drainage, garbage disposal, public transport, and in a number of other fields. In general, the physical as well as social infrastructure of the country is in a mess, and no great solution seems to be waiting to be implemented (we take up this question more fully in Chapter 4, 'Accountability and Corruption'). The contrast with China in this respect too could not be sharper. These days India seems to be full of invocations that the country should follow China and get rid of the problems associated with poor infrastructure (and there is indeed so much to learn from China), but while this advice rings everywhere, the advisors often imagine and portray a China that does not, in fact, exist. For example, it is often argued that the Indian government should get out of the power sector altogether, allegedly as the Chinese government has done, and then India too can 'privatize and flourish!' Private enterprise can, in fact, play a useful role in the generation, transmission and distribution of power (especially when competition exists), but that does require coordination and involvement by the state, taking into account the fact that there may be little – or no – money to be made from some of the tasks that the power sector has to perform (such as establishing connections in remote areas at heavy cost).

More immediately, leaving the power sector to private enterprise is not in fact what has been done in China. Both in China and in India the power sector is state-controlled, and both countries make use of the private sector to get part of the job done. The difference lies elsewhere – in the way state enterprises and planning operate in China, and in the fact that China has long been investing much more in the power sector than India, both in absolute terms and (more than twice as much) as a percentage of GDP. A similar point applies to many other infrastructural activities: the main contrast between China and India lies more in the effectiveness and accountability of public management than in the extent of privatization.

At the risk of oversimplification, it can be argued that the main respects in which the agenda for 'political, economic and social democracy' (much emphasized when India became independent) remains unfinished relate to two areas: (1) continued *disparity* between the lives of the privileged and the rest, and (2) persistent *ineptitude and unaccountability* in the way the Indian economy and society are organized. Depending on our fuller political vision, we may, of course, have other concerns too, and believe much more to be possible today and in the future.* But the urgent need to address these huge disparities and deficiencies would be hard to deny no matter how a commentator defines his or her exact political position.† We shall be much concerned with the identified deficiencies in the chapters to follow.

THE PRACTICE OF DEMOCRACY

The India-China comparison is particularly important to study in the context of China's lead over India in many of the central areas of development – including its much greater success in developing a social and physical infrastructure that contributes tremendously to economic and social development. There is surely much to interest Indians in what is happening in China. In fact, comparisons of standard social indicators that are widely used for international comparisons, such as those that are covered in the *Human Development Reports* of

---

* For a helpful discussion of the relation between one's 'goals' and 'visions', see Noam Chomsky (1999), Chapter 4.

† The pursuit of justice as a practical exercise has to be distinguished from a more theoretical search for a perfectly just world here and now (on this see *The Idea of Justice*, Sen 2009). Agreements on the need for the 'abolition of slavery' emerged in the late eighteenth and early nineteenth centuries, in line with arguments presented by Condorcet, Adam Smith, Mary Wollstonecraft, and others, though all the advocates accepted that even after that big step the world would still be far from ideally just. The feasibility of some changes that are seen to be justice-enhancing provide a strong argument for making those changes, without blocking off further changes that may be needed in pursuit of greater justice and which may become feasible in the near future or in the long run. Further, we can agree on the correctness of some changes as being justice-enhancing, even when different people have rather different visions of an ideally just society that they respectively seek.

the United Nations, or in the list of Millennium Development Goals, tend to be almost entirely in favour of China rather than India, and this contrast – and not merely China's lead over India in the growth of GDP per capita – does tell us something of considerable importance for development efforts in India.

However, there is a need for some caution here as well, since many concerns that Indians do have – and the Chinese too – are not included in the comparative tables of social indicators or growth rates. Most Indians seem to value the democratic structure of the country, including multi-party politics, systematic free elections, a largely uncensored media, a substantial guarantee of free speech, and the independent standing of the judiciary, among other characteristics of a lively democracy.[6] Those who are still critical of the functioning of India's democratic institutions (and we are certainly among them) cannot deny that there is a big contrast between what India has already been able to achieve and what many countries, including China, have accomplished so far in the practice of democracy.

Not only is access to the Internet and world opinion uncensored and unrestricted in India, there is a vast multitude of media presenting widely different points of view, often very critical of the government in office.[7] As already mentioned, India's newspapers also reflect enormously contrasting political perspectives, even though there are important gaps that still need addressing. Economic growth has greatly helped to expand people's access to mass communication (including radio, television and the Internet) across the country, in rural as well as urban areas, nicely complementing the availability of uncensored news and unrestrained critical discussion.

Freedom of expression has its own value, and it is something that most people enjoy. But it is also an important instrument for democratic politics, which strengthens people's potential – and actual – participation. The interest in political and social participation now seems to stretch even to the poorest parts of the Indian population.[8] There are other issues too around political and legal differences between India and China, such as the use of trial and punishment, including capital punishment, sanctified by law. China has often executed more people in just one week than India has since independence in 1947.[9] If our focus is on comprehensive comparisons between the quality of life in India and China, we have to look beyond the traditional social indicators. And here there are reasons to be appreciative of what India has been able to achieve, even as we demand more from the practice of democracy in the country.

We must, however, look also at what India has not achieved, and ask whether democratic freedoms are compatible with extending the achievements to cover those gaps. For instance, there has been a good deal of discussion and agitation recently about the widespread prevalence of corruption in India. This is certainly a big failure, but it would be silly to attribute the defect to democracy – indeed many non-democratic countries (including China) suffer from massive corruption. Nor can the problem be eradicated by the pursuit of undemocratic means of summary justice (such as hastily arranged severe punishment for the corrupt), as is sometimes proposed. We do not have to abandon due process in order to meet the demands of most Indians for democratic accountability to be extended in a more comprehensive way to those guilty of corruption (more on that in Chapter 4).

The media can contribute hugely to this important challenge, by helping to highlight the genuine complaints of the people, rather than largely neglecting the violations of rules and norms, as used to be the case until quite recently (and still very often happens when the transgressions occur far from the limelight). There is also the important issue of the susceptibility to corruption of particular systems of administration, by which government officers and business bosses have the power to offer favours for some reward, without being exposed or penalized for their infractions. In this respect, the so-called 'licence Raj' was a huge promoter of a culture of corruption. Many of these problems can be dealt with by institutional reforms, but there is a need also for some change in behavioural norms to eliminate the acceptability – to oneself and to others – of corrupt practice. And that too is a matter in which a socially conscious media has a role to play. We shall have more to say on these issues later on in this book: the point here is to draw attention to the problem of corruption that makes the delivery of public services as well as the operation of markets – and of course the exercise of democratic rights – more vulnerable than they need be.

The India-China comparison also raises another question, on which we should briefly comment, before ending this introductory chapter. Since China has done much better than India, by and large, in using economic growth for the advancement of public services and social infrastructure, it could be asked whether India's democratic system is actually a barrier to using the fruits of economic growth for the purpose of enhancing health, education and other features of 'social development'. In answering this question, it is hard to avoid a sense of nostalgia. When India had very low rates of economic growth, as was the case until the 1980s, a common argument used by the critics of democracy was that it was hostile to fast economic growth. It was hard to convince those critics that fast economic growth depends on the support of the economic climate, rather than on the fierceness of political systems. That debate on the opposition between democracy and economic growth has now ended (not least due to the high growth rates of democratic India), but how should we assess the alleged conflict between democracy and the *use* of the fruits of economic growth for social advancement?

What a democratic system achieves depends largely on what issues are brought into political engagement. Some issues are extremely easy to politicize, such as the calamity of a famine (recurrence of which tends to stop abruptly with the institution of a functioning democratic political system), whereas other issues – less spectacular and less immediate – provide a much harder challenge. Using democratic means to remedy non-extreme undernourishment, or persistent gender and caste inequalities, or the absence of regular medical care for all, is much more difficult, and success or failure here depends significantly on the range and vigour of democratic practice.[10] There has, however, been considerable progress in dealing with some of these issues, such as particular features of gender inequality, through somewhat improved practice of democracy in recent years. But there is still a long way to go to take on all the social disadvantages and injustices from which many Indians persistently suffer.

In China, the process of decision-making depends largely on decisions at the top, taken by political leaders, with relatively little scope for democratic pressure from below. The fact that the Chinese leaders, despite their scepticism of the values of democracy and liberty, have been strongly committed to eliminating hunger and illiteracy, has certainly helped China's economic and social advancement. There exists, however, a serious fragility in this process, since there is little remedy when the government leaders change their priority in a counterproductive direction. The reality of that danger revealed itself in catastrophic form in the Chinese famine of 1959–62, which killed at least 30 million people, when the regime failed to understand what was going on and there was no public pressure against its policies, as would have arisen in a functioning democracy. The policy mistakes continued throughout these three years of devastating famine. The fragility was seen again with the economic reforms of 1979, which greatly improved the efficiency of Chinese agriculture and industry, but also involved a huge retreat from the principle of universal health care coverage, especially in rural areas. As the axe fell on the 'rural cooperative medical system', the proportion of the rural population covered by free or heavily subsidized health care crashed to 10 per cent or so within a few years.

Such fragilities are inescapable in an authoritarian system where supportive and protective policies can suddenly change, depending on power politics at the top. An established right to health care could not have been so easily – and so swiftly – withdrawn in a functioning democracy. The withdrawal of universal entitlement to health care sharply reduced the progress of longevity in China, and China's large lead over India in life expectancy dwindled over the following two decades – falling from a 14-year lead to one of just 7 years. However, the Chinese authorities did eventually come to recognize the value of what had been lost, and reintroduced social health insurance on a large scale (under new arrangements, including the 'new cooperative medical scheme') from around 2004.[11] China now has a much higher proportion of people with guaranteed health care (more than 90 per cent) than does India. The gap in life expectancy in China's favour has been rising again, and the reach of health coverage is clearly central to the difference.

Given its political system, India has to cultivate democratic engagement in demanding universal health care and addressing this long-standing neglect. This means putting pressure on the government in office, but also making these priorities a part of the demands of the opposition, since governments, especially one made up of a coalition such as the present government in New Delhi, have to respond to the priorities set by political pressures and public demands, which can take widely diverse forms and which all compete for governmental attention and resources. Cultivating democratic engagement can be a harder task than convincing a handful of political leaders of the need for a policy change. On the other hand, if a norm of this kind is democratically established, it is less subject to the fragility to which all authoritarian decisions remain vulnerable. In order to match China in health coverage and surpass it in resilience, India has to make much greater use of the democratic system than it already has. The same can be said for the priority of basic education for all.

In dealing with India's multitude of problems, there may well be a temptation – but not a serious reason – for India to give up or reduce its long commitment to democracy, for which so many people have fought and out of which so much good has already come to the country. It is deeply disappointing that more use has not been made of the opportunities offered by a political democracy and a free society to solve the problems that so many Indians continue to face. What is important to recognize is that the success of a democracy depends ultimately on the vigour of its practice, and that will be one of the main points of focus in this book.

Ambedkar's invitation to 'educate, agitate and organize' (which we quoted earlier) is possible in a democracy in a way that is not in the absence of one. But, as Ambedkar also argued, organization and agitation have to be based on good and informed reasoning. The first item in his call – 'educate' – is important here. As will be clear as the book proceeds, we are much inspired by Ambedkar's vision of informed and reasoned public engagement. The important task is not so much to find a 'new India', but to contribute to making one.

2

Integrating Growth
and Development

In June of 2012, one of us was asked by two journalists to comment on economic growth in two different parts of the world. One of the journalists, from Paris, asked for a reaction to 'the wonderful fact' that the Eurozone had zero economic growth in the first quarter of 2012 (stopping the fall in GDP of the region in the preceding quarter); the other, from New Delhi, was seeking a response to 'the dismal growth figures' for India – 'only 6.2%' expansion over the preceding year. While the 'good news of zero growth' in the Eurozone was being loudly applauded in Europe, the Indian media was busy worrying about the 'alarming' slowness of economic growth in India – declining from the previous rates of 8 or 9 per cent per year to a figure a few percentage points lower. 'Dismal' is clearly a relative concept.

The moderating of economic growth, if we may call it that, has been a spectacular feature of the world economy in the recent past, and it certainly has not left India untouched, adding to the internal problems within the country which have also contributed to the slowdown. During 2011–12 (the last complete year as we finish this book), India remained the second fastest in terms of economic growth among all the large economies in the world (approximately equalled by Indonesia), trailing only a little behind the leader of the pack – China – which had also experienced a decline in its growth rate. India and Indonesia were followed in the growth league by Japan, Mexico, Russia and South Korea, among the other large economies of the world (Europe, not surprisingly, is at the other end of the scale, with the United States only a little higher). Growth in Brazil, a star performer in the economic field at one time (and more recently in other fields, on which more in the next chapter), has now fallen to 0.8 per cent.[1]

Still, there are good grounds for taking the slowdown of Indian economic growth to be a cause for concern. Even though 'dismal' is hardly an apt description, it is right to think afresh about what can be done over time to remedy this comparative sluggishness. Economic growth is indeed important, not for itself, but for what it allows a country to do with the resources that are generated, expanding both individual incomes and the public revenue that can be used to meet social commitments. Had European countries gone for growth rather than ill-timed austerity at the height of a recession, the public revenue so generated would have helped them to put their public finances in order without massively compromising the great European commitment to provide essential public services, which has been an inspiration for other parts of the world – from Singapore to Brazil. India, like Europe, carries a sizeable deficit, but it has resolutely – and we believe rightly – not fallen for the siren call of immediate austerity, thereby keeping its economy expanding fast and its financial standing relatively high.[2] In the long run, of course, India's public finances need fixing, which it should be able to do, making use of the financial freedom that high growth yields. What is, however, important to recognize is that in India public services call for far-reaching expansion (as will be presently discussed), and it is also critical to raise the individual incomes of the poor.

From both perspectives, maintaining a high-growth economy is an important objective, along with ensuring good use of the public revenue generated by economic growth. It is also essential, of course, to pay attention to the character of the growth process, including its equity and sustainability; we shall return to this presently.

A SHORT HISTORY OF FAST GROWTH

How long a history of fast economic growth does India have? India is, in fact, a new entrant on the sprinting field. Pablo Picasso once remarked, 'One starts to get young at the age of sixty.' Something rather like that seems to have been happening to the Indian economy in recent years. There are many more signs of life in the Indian economy today than could be seen when political independence was granted to the ancient land in 1947, after which its straitlaced economy moved at a resiliently slow pace – about 3.5 per cent per year – for nearly three decades. It was sometimes called 'the Hindu rate of growth', even though Hinduism had nothing to do with it – public policy had.* The feebleness of the economic pace was in sharp contrast to the speed with which political change took place in the newly established republic: overnight India became what the movement for independence had fought for, that is, a democracy – the first poor country in the world to be a full-scale democracy. It soon emerged to be a really functioning democracy.

As was noted in the last chapter, since Indian GDP preceding independence was mainly stagnant and sometimes declining, even economic growth of 3.5 per cent per annum in the decades immediately following independence was, in fact, a big leap upwards. But the fact remains that 3.5 per cent per year (translating, at that time, into something like 1.5 per cent per year in per capita terms) is painfully slow for the purpose of rapid development and poverty reduction. The modesty of Indian economic growth, which lasted from the 1950s through the 1970s, gave way to considerable quickening in the 1980s, with a higher rate of expansion at 5 per cent per year. And then, following the economic reforms of the early 1990s (led by Manmohan Singh, then Finance Minister and now Prime Minister of India), the economy settled down to faster progress, establishing a new norm of rapid growth, very near the top of the world league. The robustness of high growth in India is undoubtedly connected with the economic reforms of the 1990s, which have built a solid foundation for continuing economic growth. After hovering between 5 and 6 per cent, the growth rate took a further hike upwards to 7 per cent and then further up, even crossing 9 per cent for several years (between 2005 and 2008). Given India's long-standing income poverty, a phase of fast economic growth was certainly needed, and despite the recent slowdown (which still leaves India as the second fastest-growing large

* The seeming constancy of the growth rate (at around 3.5 per cent annually) during these three decades applies only when the growth rates are considered by decade. Taken yearly, it did vary a great deal, and it was also a little higher in the first half of these three decades than in the second half, especially if the growth rates are considered in per capita terms (see also Table 2.1).

economy in the world), India clearly has made huge progress in this respect.

The need for rapid growth is far from over, since India, after two decades of rapid growth, is still one of the poorest countries in the world. Indeed, as will be discussed in the next chapter, India's real income per head is still lower than that of most countries outside sub-Saharan Africa. The picture is even worse if we focus on the quality of life of the underprivileged part of the Indian population, hundreds of millions of whom continue to lack the essential requirements of satisfactory living, from nutritious food to health care, decent work conditions, and warm clothes in the winter. Growth alone is unlikely to end these problems, at least not within a reasonable time frame, but it is certainly much easier to remedy such deficiencies in a growing economy. India's potential for high economic growth is certainly a major asset for the country's development, and efforts to enhance its performance must remain an important priority, along with making sure that growth is used to improve people's living standards.

THE PAST AND THE PRESENT

How did India get to be so poor, indeed one of the poorest countries in the world? The irony is that one does not have to invoke some mythical golden age from an imagined past to think of a time when India was not – nor taken to be – poorer than most other countries. Indeed, far from it. Adam Smith thought that India in general, particularly Bengal, was one of the most prosperous regions on the globe, and he devoted some time in *The Wealth of Nations* (1776) to explaining the roots of India's comparative prosperity, which he attributed mostly to its flourishing system of trade, utilizing its navigable rivers. There were indeed long-established trading connections, stretching back nearly two thousand years, within the land and beyond it. Among other accounts, we have the interesting description of the trade-based prosperity of the region presented by Claudius Ptolemy, the pioneering geographer of the second century AD, who wrote about parts of the Indian economy in some detail, and identified a number of towns and cities that were engaged in thriving commerce within the country and were also active in trade with other countries. Pliny the Elder too provided descriptions of the open and flourishing economy of this region.[3]

When the East India Company initiated, through the battle of Plassey in Bengal in 1757, what would gradually become Britain's vast Indian empire, the region was famous for its industrial exports, particularly of textiles of various kinds. Even though Adam Smith noted that Bengal was 'the province of Indostan, which commonly exports the greatest quantity of rice', he went on to say that it 'has always been more remarkable for the exportation of a great variety of manufactures, than for that of its grain'.[4] Upstream from the settlements of the East India Company on the Ganges, there were other trading centres where merchants from Portugal, the Netherlands, France, Denmark, Prussia and other European nations were busily involved, among other channels of commerce, with exporting Indian manufactures to Europe and elsewhere. The competitiveness and quality of Indian exports was a cause of concern for native European manufacturers, and in Britain in particular, before the establishment of British rule in India, there were several acts of Parliament prohibiting the wearing of Indian textile products.

Did the Indian workers in industrial establishments enjoy a living standard commensurate with India's formidable reputation as a star exporter? It is hard to settle an issue of this kind given the paucity of data and the complexity of comparisons between living standards. But comparisons of wage rates and prices seem to indicate that the real wages of Indian labour – and of course of skilled artisans – in economically active regions were not lower, indeed sometimes higher, than those then enjoyed by the corresponding occupation groups in many European countries. For example, Prasannan Parthasarathi's comparison of real wages in the mid-eighteenth century, in terms of grain equivalent, indicates that weaving wages varied between 40 and 140 pounds of grain per week in Britain, but the corresponding wages of Indian weavers were between 55 and 135 pounds of grain per week in Bengal, and between 65 and 160 pounds of grain per week in South India.[5]

Just as it is unnecessary to invent some imaginary golden age to acknowledge the relative prosperity of pre-colonial India, one does not have to be an aggressive nationalist to recount the rapid decline of the relative position of the Indian economy during the British Raj. Adam Smith attributed the beginning of the economic decline of the British domain in India to 'some injudicious restraints imposed by the servants of the East India Company', to which he attributed even the Bengal famine of 1770.[6] The decline continued throughout the nineteenth century, along with many other changes taking place in British India (including some that were very positive, such as the development of a modern press, and the sharing of the new scientific knowledge emanating from the European Enlightenment). Economic descent and decline were quite relentless right into the first half of the twentieth century.

Indeed, in long periods during the epochal British rule the per capita real income of India actually *declined*. When there was growth, it was so moderate that falling behind other countries was not a hard feat. S. Sivasubramonian's detailed study of 'the national income of India in the twentieth century' places the annual growth rate of India's per capita income at about 0.1 per cent between 1900–1 and 1946–7. Growth was positive (though barely so) in this period because the dismal – and here we do mean 'dismal' – GDP growth of 0.9 per cent was counterbalanced by a low population growth rate (0.8 per cent), reflecting the high mortality rates that characterized British India.[7] And this was occurring over the centuries in which the changes initiated by the Industrial Revolution were elevating real incomes and transforming living standards in Europe and America, and even of some parts of Asia and Latin America.

GROWTH SINCE INDEPENDENCE

Given this history, it is not hard to understand why the post-independence growth rate of 3.5 per cent or so per annum seemed like a positive change (see Table 2.1). And yet, the economic policies of the early post-independence period did not succeed either in accelerating the growth rate or in bringing about a major transformation of people's living conditions. In fact, available evidence suggests that

Table 2.1
Growth Rates of GDP by Sector, at Constant Prices

	Primary sector	Secondary sector	Tertiary sector	GDP[a]
1900–1 to 1946–7	0.4	1.5	1.7	0.9 (0.1)
1950–1 to 1960–1	2.8	6.1	4.1	3.7 (1.8)
1960–1 to 1970–1	2.1	5.4	4.4	3.4 (1.2)
1970–1 to 1980–1	2.0	4.2	4.5	3.4 (1.2)
1980–1 to 1990–1	3.5	5.5	6.6	5.2 (3.0)
1990–1 to 2000–1	3.3	6.2	7.5	5.9 (4.0)
2000–1 to 2010–11	3.2	8.5	8.9	7.6 (6.0)

[a] In brackets, growth rate of per capita GDP (calculated by subtracting population growth rate from GDP growth rate).

Sources: Sivasubramonian (2000), Table 7.3, for the pre-independence period. The post-independence growth rates were calculated (by semi-log regression) from data on GDP at constant 2004–5 prices presented in Government of India (2012a), Tables A3 and A5. Sivasubramonian (2000), Table 9.3, presents similar figures for the early post-independence period based on an earlier GDP series, at constant 1948–9 prices.

there was virtually no reduction of poverty, especially rural poverty, in India for most of the three decades that followed the launch of the First Five Year Plan in 1951.[8]

This was certainly a major failure, and we have to ask what exactly went wrong in the initial period of Indian post-independence planning.[9] The point is sometimes made that India's problems arose from its 'socialist' planning. Interpretations of 'socialism' are, of course, many and various, but if that diagnosis is meant to suggest that India was following the kind of planning model that characterized the Soviet Union and other Communist countries, that would reflect a huge confusion. One thing that Communist countries – from the USSR and pre-reform China to Vietnam or Cuba – were committed to achieving, despite all the political indoctrination and dogmatism, was to ensure free and universal school education without delay. Indeed, when Rabindranath Tagore went to the Soviet Union in 1930, he already noticed the rapid progress that was being made in schooling the population, even in 'distant' Soviet Asia: 'In stepping on the soil of Russia, the first thing that caught my eye was that in education, at any rate, the peasant and the working classes have made such enormous progress in these few years that nothing comparable has happened even to our highest classes in the course of the last hundred and fifty years.'* Did 'socialist' India go that way? The answer is that it did nothing of the sort, so that three decades of planning brought about very little advancement in the schooling opportunities of Indian children.

In fact, the first Five Year Plan, initiated in 1951 – even though sympathetic to the need for university education which it strongly supported – argued against regular schooling at the elementary level, favouring instead a so-called 'basic education' system, built on the hugely romantic and rather eccentric idea that children should learn through self-financing handicraft.† It went on to say that 'the tendency to open new primary schools should not be encouraged and, as far as possible, resources should be concentrated on basic education and the improvement and remodeling of existing primary schools on basic lines'.[10] Not surprisingly, the idea of replacing proper schooling by so-called 'basic education' failed to resonate with the public. This did not, however, prevent the second Five Year Plan (initiated in 1956) from reasserting that 'the whole of elementary education has to be reoriented on basic lines'. Over time, the government had to yield to the public's demand for a proper schooling system, but the conceptual confusion over what schools should do added a further regressive force to the under-allocation of public money to make the country literate and numerate.

In this respect, Indian planners were at the opposite pole from planners in all the Communist countries – whether in Moscow and Beijing

---

* Rabindranath Tagore, *Letters from Russia* (1931, English translation 1960), p. 108. The English version of Tagore's letters was banned by the British Raj soon after its publication – a ban that would not be lifted until after Indian independence.

† The 'basic education' project was inspired by Mahatma Gandhi's pedagogic ideas. In his own words: 'The core of my suggestion is that handicrafts are to be taught, not merely for productive work, but for developing the intellect of the pupils.' He argued that teaching reading and writing to children before handicrafts 'hampers their intellectual growth'. See Gandhi (1937a, 1937b).

(even in the pre-reform period) or in Havana and Ho Chi Minh City.* They all valued universal standard school education, which was seen as a fundamental socialist commitment (clearly stated in the Communist Manifesto), and none of them allowed large proportions of children to remain out of school for decades on end (despite the mess they created in some other fields of economic policy in the name of socialism, not to mention the suppression of civil and political liberties). To see the huge neglect of school education in India's planning in that period as having resulted from its 'socialist' planning would be to miss altogether the indigenous nature of this Indian folly. It was indeed a home-grown folly, to a great extent reflecting an upper-class – and upper-caste – bias against the education of the masses.

It is also worth noting in passing that even India's economic planning in the early post-independence period was not particularly 'socialist', and it was certainly not Soviet-style planning as is sometimes suggested. India was attempting the sort of state-led development strategy that was also being pursued, in various forms, by many other countries around that time, with varying outcomes, and had also been used earlier in many European countries. Most of the economy (with the main exception of what were seen as 'essential services' such as railways, power and water) was firmly in the private sector, and while the government did intervene in many ways, there was no sweeping nationalization of industries, let alone major land reforms.[11] This is not to say that the planning of that period was a success – it was not. But the nature of the folly or eccentricity involved cannot be diagnosed simplistically as 'socialist'.

The early economic planning failed more completely in terms of social infrastructure and tertiary industries than it did in the fields of primary and secondary production. In fact, the growth rates of the primary and secondary sectors (roughly, agriculture and manufacturing respectively) were slightly *higher* in the 15 years that followed the launch of the first Five Year Plan in 1951 than in the 15 years that

---

* Interestingly, they were also ignoring the advice of economists of a very different persuasion, such as Milton Friedman, who submitted an enlightening 'memorandum to the government of India' in 1955 where he emphatically argued that Indian planning was giving too much importance to physical capital and grossly neglecting 'human capital' (Friedman, 1955).

followed the launch of economic reforms in 1991.[12] The growth rate of the tertiary sector was slower in the first period, as was that of GDP – but the GDP growth rate of around 4 per cent per year in that early period reflected some real overall progress, particularly in what classical economists used to call 'material production'. The growth could, of course, have been much faster with a more sensible economic strategy, as it was, for instance, in East Asia at that time, but the common notion that planning had brought the Indian economy to a halt in the Nehruvian period is no easier to substantiate than the belief that he pursued some kind of 'socialist' economic policy.

The period of sustained moderate growth came to an abrupt end in the mid-1960s (more precisely, in 1965–7), when India was hit by the worst successive droughts in the twentieth century, just after fighting a costly war with Pakistan in 1965. Agricultural production crashed, and GDP growth turned negative, as it often did at that time in drought years. Further calamities were not far off: another war with Pakistan in 1971, and another spell of devastating droughts in 1971–3. During this troubled ten-year period, from 1965–6 to 1974–5, per capita GDP stagnated and per capita agricultural production declined.

This was also a period of significant change in the politics of economic policy. Nehru, who died in May 1964, had been Prime Minister for 17 years more or less unchallenged – the Congress Party had no significant rival, nor did he. But his daughter, Indira Gandhi (Prime Minister from 1966 to 1977, her first term), had to fight fierce political battles both within and outside the party, battles in which economic policies increasingly came to play an instrumental role.[13] For instance, the nationalization of commercial banks in 1969, chosen clearly for political reasons (whether or not it could have been justified on other grounds), placed a huge apparatus of patronage at governmental command. Similarly, import quotas and industrial licences were freely used for the purpose of 'rewarding supporters, punishing opponents and winning over the uncertain'.[14] Things came to a point where, as Bimal Jalan puts it, 'even the most inconsequential economic activity required specific government approval'.* This

---

* Bimal Jalan (2012), p. 282. As the author notes, in this period, 'politics was the primary driver of Indira Gandhi's economics' (p. 283).

had disastrous effects, including stifling economic initiatives as well as encouraging corruption and abuse of power. Whether all this was the natural – and logical – outcome of the dirigiste framework put in place from Nehru's time, or an avoidable corruption of Nehruvian policies that had been reasonably effective earlier (despite the blindness about school education), is a matter of judgement. The fact remains that the economy, and the people, paid a heavy price for this transformation.

The outlook improved in the 1980s, when India experienced its second phase of growth acceleration, helped by a major recovery in the agricultural sector. The so-called Hindu rate of growth (whatever that meant) became a thing of the past, with the steady growth of the GDP rising to around 5 per cent per year in this decade. Further, this was also a period when growth was relatively balanced and equitable. The Green Revolution, launched after the 1965–7 droughts to reduce dependence on foreign aid, but delayed by further droughts in the early 1970s, began to show results: yields shot up by about 30 per cent in the 1980s (compared with barely 10 per cent in the 1970s), and the agricultural sector grew faster than ever before – at more than 3 per cent per year. Also, significantly for poverty reduction, agricultural wages grew at an unprecedented rate of about 5 per cent per year in real terms.[15] And for the first time in decades, there was a sustained decline in poverty, in urban as well as rural areas.[16]

The 1980s, however, were also a period of growing fiscal deficits, trade deficits and foreign debt. These imbalances turned into a major crisis in 1990, partly due to rising oil prices and the disruption of remittances from the Persian Gulf. India ran out of foreign exchange reserves, to the extent of having to pawn gold to the Bank of England to avoid defaulting on its sovereign debt. A structural adjustment programme followed, initially (in 1991–3) on a tight leash from the International Monetary Fund, and thereafter, on the Indian government's own terms: an anticipated follow-up loan was turned down as it was felt that 'the IMF's demands on fiscal prudence were more than India could deliver'.[17]

With the IMF at bay, shock treatment (for instance, across-the-board cuts in public expenditure including social spending) gave way to more gradual economic reforms. In terms of economic growth, the results were certainly impressive. While the growth rate of GDP was not much higher in the 1990s as a whole than in the 1980s (see Table 2.1 on p. 23), it picked up after the phase of economic stabilization (ending in 1993), and rose substantially in the years that followed. The impact of the reforms on economic growth in these years was certainly a significant achievement.

The process of economic reform has been quite slow. Some reforms, such as greater openness to international trade and the relaxation of internal controls, happened relatively early. Others occurred much later. And some are still being debated, including the privatization of particular public enterprises, extensive labour reforms, the permissibility of foreign direct investment in specific sectors, to give only a few examples. This gradualism is often seen as irritating by the champions of economic reform, but it is to be expected in a democratic system – many of these reforms, even when appropriate, require informed public debate. Unfortunately, the discussions often proceed along very conventional lines related to the commentators' *general* 'pro-market' or 'anti-market' predispositions, when the resolution of particular policy issues demands a specific, case-by-case assessment of arguments in favour and against. Most importantly, the case for specific reforms must ultimately be judged not just by their impact on economic growth, but also – indeed principally – by their effects on people's lives. We would argue that one of the main problems with the economic reforms of the 1990s lies not so much in what they tried to do (indeed with much success) as in what they did not even attempt to achieve, extending in the process some of the deeper biases of the pre-reform period.

In recent years, there has also been growing recognition of the need for wide-ranging reforms of a different kind – aimed for instance at eradicating corruption, restoring accountability in the public sector, fostering social equity, and improving the effectiveness of administrative, judicial and legislative processes. These wider programmes are not usually seen as being closely linked with economic reform, but ultimately both are part of a larger need to revitalize the country's economic and social institutions and ensure that they contribute more to the improvement of people's lives. These concerns – and the problems they pose, the opportunities they offer – will be taken up in the chapters to follow.

GROWTH OF WHAT?

India's record of rapid economic growth in recent decades, particularly in the last ten years or so, has tended to cause some understandable excitement. The living standards of the 'middle classes' (which tends to mean the top 20 per cent or so of the population by income) have improved well beyond what was expected – or could be anticipated – in the previous decades. But the story is more complex for many others such as the rickshaw puller, domestic worker or brick-kiln labourer. For them, and other underprivileged groups, the reform period has not been so exciting. It is not that their lives have not improved at all, but the pace of change has been excruciatingly slow and has barely altered their abysmal living conditions.

To illustrate, according to National Sample Survey data average per capita expenditure in rural areas rose at the exceedingly low rate of about 1 *per cent per year* between 1993–4 and 2009–10, and even in urban areas, average per capita expenditure grew at only 2 per cent per year in this period.[18] The corresponding growth rates of per capita expenditure for poor households in both areas would have been even lower, since there was growing inequality of per capita expenditures in that period.[19] Similarly, there has been a major slowdown in the growth of real agricultural wages in the post-reform period: from about 5 per cent per year in the 1980s to 2 per cent or so in the 1990s and virtually *zero* in the early 2000s (see also Table 2.2). It is only after 2006, when the National Rural Employment Guarantee Act (NREGA) came into force, that the growth of real agricultural wages picked up again, especially for women.[20]

The growth of real wages in other parts of the economy has also been relatively slow, especially for casual or (so-called) 'unskilled' workers. The contrast with China in this respect is really striking. According to comparable international data from the International Labour Organization, real wages in manufacturing in China grew at an astonishing 12 per cent per year or so in the first decade of this century, compared with about 2.5 per cent per year in India.[21] There is some possibility of exaggeration in the official Chinese figures, but many independent studies corroborate the fact that real wages in China have been rising rapidly over the last twenty or thirty years (see Figure 2.1).[22] In India, by contrast,

Table 2.2
Estimates of the Growth Rate of Real Agricultural Wages

Reference period	Estimated growth rate of real agricultural wages	
	Men	Women
1983–4 to 1987–8	5.1	–
1987–8 to 1993–94	2.7	–
1993–4 to 1999–2000	1.3	–
2000–1 to 2005–6	0.1	–0.05
2005–6 to 2010–11	2.7	3.7

Source: The pre-2000 figures are from Himanshu (2005), based on data presented in *Agricultural Wages in India* series (see also Drèze and Sen, 2002, Table A.5). The post-2000 figures are calculated from Usami (2012), based on the follow-up *Wage Rates in Rural India* series (for further details, see explanatory note in the Statistical Appendix). For similar patterns based on National Sample Survey data, see also Himanshu (1995), Himanshu et al. (2011), and National Sample Survey Office (2011a).

the growth rate of real wages has been much lower than that of per capita GDP over the same period. Consistently with this, there has been a steep decline in the share of wages in value added (see Figure 2.2).[23]

These facts may surprise some of those who are used to looking at official poverty estimates to assess how poor people are doing. For instance, according to the Planning Commission, the 'head-count ratio' of rural poverty (the proportion of the rural population below the poverty line) declined from about 50 per cent in 1993–4 to 34 per cent in 2009–10.[24] This looks like a big improvement. How does it square with the fact that the growth of real per capita expenditure has been so low? The clue lies in the so-called 'density effect': the fact that many people are just a little below the official poverty line, so that a small increase in per capita expenditure is enough to 'lift' them above the line. And the density effect, in turn, reflects the fact that the official poverty line is abysmally low (we shall return to this in Chapter 7).

The point is well illustrated by calculations presented in a recent paper by Ashok Kotwal, Bharat Ramaswamy and Wilima Wadhwa (2011), based on National Sample Survey data for 1983 and 2004–5.[25] Over that period, the head-count ratio (for rural and urban areas

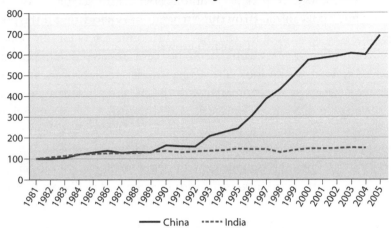

Figure 2.1 Real Wages in China and India, 1981–2005

Sources: Calculated from Tao Yang et al. (2010), Fig. 5(a).

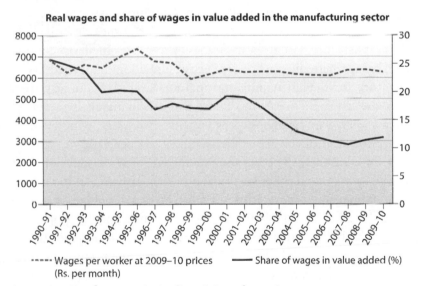

Figure 2.2 Real Wages in Indian Manufacturing, 1990–2010

Source: *Handbook of Statistics on the Indian Economy*, Tables 33 and 40 (Reserve Bank of India, 2012). Money wages have been deflated using the Consumer Price Index for Industrial Workers, from the same source. The left-hand vertical axis applies to real wages, and the right-hand axis to the share of wages in value added.

combined) declined from 45 per cent to 28 per cent based on the official poverty line applicable at that time.[26] The authors show that if the poverty line were to be doubled (though still to quite a low cut-off point), the corresponding figures would be 86 per cent in 1983 and 80 per cent in 2004–5. That would look like a very moderate improvement, over more than twenty years, compared with the steep decline based on official poverty lines. More recent work also shows that, no matter where one draws the poverty line, the rate of poverty decline has been much slower in India than in developing countries as a whole in the last twenty years or so, in spite of economic growth being much faster in India.

We shall return, later in this book, to these and related aspects of the lopsided nature of the growth process in India. For now, the main point to note is that questions about the nature and reach of economic progress in India demand much greater attention than they tend to receive. One of these questions is why has economic growth in India led to so little increase in wages and incomes for the poorer sections of the population. It is not difficult to see that this is associated with a failure to generate adequate employment, sometimes described – a little simplistically perhaps – as 'jobless growth'.[27] In sharp contrast with China, where the post-reform economic boom happened first in agriculture and then in manufacturing, India's rapid economic growth during the last twenty years or so has been driven mainly by 'services'. This is a very heterogeneous category, but there is growing evidence that a good deal of the growth in services has been heavily concentrated in skill-intensive sectors (such as software development, financial services and other specialized work), rather than more traditional labour-intensive sectors. While this has enabled the more educated section of the labour force to earn much higher wages and salaries, the bulk of the workforce is marooned in agriculture and other sectors (including the 'informal sector', which employs more than 90 per cent of India's labour force) where wages and productivity are – and tend to remain – very low.* Many other factors have also

* A particular issue related to this problem was discussed in our first book on Indian development, published in 1995: 'even if India were to take over the bulk of the world's computer software industry, this would still leave its poor, illiterate masses largely untouched. It may be much less glamorous to make simple pocket knives and reliable alarm clocks than to design state-of-the-art computer programmes, but the

contributed to a lack of any participatory character in India's growth process, but this certainly appears to be an important one.[28]

Aside from addressing this problem, there is also a powerful need to examine what is going on about the availability – and quality – of public services. In fact the two problems may well be closely related, since the lack of progress in education and health care limits the freedom that people have to enter and flourish in general manufacturing jobs. These links have to be further examined, but it is also important to see the lack of progress in public services as a huge barrier to improving the quality of life of people. Indeed, the sluggish growth of real per capita expenditure is only one aspect of the disappointing progress of people's living conditions in the last twenty years or so. As we will discuss in Chapter 3, there is also a sharp dissonance between India's performance measured in terms of incomes, on the one hand, and the progress of living standards, on the other, involving longevity, health security, literacy, educational opportunities, child undernourishment, social status, and so on.

Just to give one example, there has been very little improvement in India's nutrition indicators during the last twenty years or so. Nutrient intakes (calorie, protein, micronutrients – almost anything except fat) have *decreased*, for reasons that are not altogether clear, but are unlikely to obviate the need for concern.[29] Anthropometric indicators, for their part, have improved very slowly. In fact, according to the latest National Family Health Surveys, there was virtually no improvement in children's weights between 1998–9 and 2005–6, and the incidence of anaemia *increased* in that period. While there is much scope for debate about different ways of measuring undernourishment, what is not in doubt is that India still has a higher proportion of undernourished children than almost any other country in the world, even after thirty years of rapid economic growth. Many countries have been able to achieve big improvements in the health and nutrition status of their respective populations in a shorter time, even with lower rates of economic growth. We shall have more to say on this issue in the chapters to follow.

---

former gives the Chinese poor a source of income that the latter does not provide – at least not directly – to the Indian poor.' (Drèze and Sen, 1995, p. 39)

DEVELOPMENT, INSTITUTIONS
AND HUMAN CAPABILITY

The relation between growth and development – their differences as well as their complementarity – is central to the theme of this book. While the literature on that distinction is rather limited (even though the approach of 'human development' championed by Mahbub ul Haq and others has drawn attention to the possible dissonance between the two), there is a fast-growing literature on the causation of growth, or of growth and development seen together. Some of these writings are based on extensive empirical research on the comparative experiences of different countries in the world, and are clearly relevant to our study.

One summary finding that has been much supported is the importance of institutions, broadly defined, that secure and encourage economic initiatives and operations.[30] The development of growth-friendly institutions can be hindered both by social barriers and by imposed styles of governance. In their book *Why Nations Fail*, Daron Acemoglu and James Robinson illustrate both types of handicap in their brief account of what kept India in check even in the pre-colonial period, but particularly during the period of colonial rule:

> In India, institutional drift worked differently and led to the development of a uniquely rigid hereditary caste system that limited the functioning of markets and the allocation of labor across occupations much more severely than the feudal order in medieval Europe ... Though Indian merchants did trade throughout the Indian Ocean, and a major textile industry developed, the caste system and Mughal absolutism were serious impediments to the development of inclusive economic institutions in India. By the nineteenth century, things were even less hospitable for industrialization as India became an extractive colony of the English.[31]

Caste has indeed been a major barrier to social progress in India, and not just in the form of a counterproductive division of labour, but more importantly, as Dr Ambedkar argued with great clarity, as a pernicious division of human beings into iron-curtained compartments.* Colonialism, for its part, is a barrier that India shared with other economies of Asia and Africa. Japan escaped that fate by going into its shell, and prohibiting the trade-related foothold through which colonialism developed in India, China, Indonesia, Malaysia and elsewhere. Following the Meiji Restoration in 1868, the Japanese leadership, armed with the freedom of action that it had, took a well-considered initiative in fostering economic development. As Acemoglu and Robinson note, unrestrained by colonial rule, Japan was well served by the development of 'more inclusive political institutions and much more inclusive economic institutions'.[32]

There is a particularly central role to be played by education, and the formation of knowledge and skills, in the process of economic and social development. In his book, *The Gifts of Athena*, Joel Mokyr has provided a striking analysis of the critical importance of the accumulation of knowledge in transforming pre-modern Western countries into modern economies. Similarly, Elhanan Helpman has discussed the role of institutional change in the accumulation of knowledge in his book called *The Mystery of Economic Growth*, which shows, among other things, why economic growth through increasing total-factor productivity, especially helped by education and expansion of knowledge, need not be a mystery.[33]

In Chapter 5 we shall take up this important subject, including how Japan utilized its freedom from colonization to pursue a programme of economic development, giving education a central role in that nationalist programme. The Fundamental Code of Education, issued in 1872 (four years after the Meiji Restoration), expressed a public commitment to make sure that there must be 'no community with an illiterate family, nor a family with an illiterate person'. Kido Takayoshi, one of the leaders of Japanese reform, explained the basic idea: 'Our

---

* See particularly *The Annihilation of Caste* (Ambedkar, 1936). The stifling effects of the caste system were also well expressed by Rammanohar Lohia, another committed opponent of the caste system: 'Caste restricts opportunity. Restricted opportunity constricts ability. Constricted ability further restricts opportunity. Where caste prevails, opportunity and ability are restricted to ever-narrowing circles of the people.' Quoted in Agrawal (2008), p. 212.

people are no different from the Americans or Europeans of today; it is all a matter of education or lack of education.'

The foundational role of education and other ways of expanding human capability form a solid connection in development thinking, and are also central themes of this book. This does not, of course, undermine the need for proper institutional structures for an economy. However, as Glaeser, La Porta, Lopez-de-Silanes and Shleifer have argued in their sceptical paper, 'Do Institutions Cause Growth?', the development of human capital may be a more worthwhile pursuit – no matter what its instrumental basis is – than the setting up of some pre-specified list of 'necessary' institutions.[34] Recognition of the crucial role of institutions has to be distinguished from any formulaic adherence to important institutions identified by historical studies as a blueprint for the future. Intelligent and informed policy analysis has to be responsive to the general need for good institutions, appropriate to particular circumstances, while bearing in mind the foundational connections between economic growth and the expansion of education and human capital.

While the importance of institutions can hardly be denied, the exercise of institutional reform cannot be reduced to fulfilling the demand of a 'checklist' of 'needed' institutions. As Trebilcock and Prado judiciously remark after an extensive review of the empirical literature: 'In sum, while much empirical evidence supports the view that institutions matter for development, we know very little about which institutions matter, and what specific institutional characteristics within classes of institutions matter for development.'[35] We shall not proceed with a checklist, but that is not an invitation to ignore what can be broadly called 'the institutional perspective'. Rather, the broadness of connections brought out by empirical work shows the need to assess and scrutinize specific institutional needs in particular circumstances. We shall have more to say on the importance of different kinds of institutions for India as this book proceeds. We have to consider both (1) institutions that are important for growth and development seen together (as in the literature just reviewed), and (2) the specific institutional needs of translating the achievements in growth into the broader perspective of development and flourishing of human beings. The institutional needs of fast economic growth have to be supplemented by specific instruments and organizations for enhancing the living standards of people.

MUTUAL SUPPORT OF GROWTH AND DEVELOPMENT

The impact of economic growth on the lives of people is partly a matter of income distribution, but it also depends greatly on the use that is made of the public revenue generated by economic expansion. The fact, for example, that China devotes 2.7 per cent of its GDP to government expenditure on health care, compared with India's relatively miserable 1.2 per cent, is directly relevant to the much greater health achievements of China compared with India, including, for instance, its much higher life expectancy (about eight years higher than India's).

One result of the relatively low allocation to public health care in India is the development of a remarkable reliance of many poor people across the country on private doctors, many of whom have little, if any, medical training. Since health is also a typical case of 'asymmetric information', when – in particular – the patients may know very little about what the ailments are and what medicine is being given and why, the possibility of defrauding the families of patients is very large, in the absence of alternative public health care to which the patients can go for assistance and advice.* We shall return to the problems of health and health care in India in Chapter 6.

India has moved towards reliance on private health care without developing the solid rock of support of basic public health facilities that has been the basis of almost every successful health transition in the history of the world – from Britain to Japan, from China to Brazil, from South Korea to Costa Rica. Even within India, there is some experience, particularly in Kerala in the south-west, of a major expansion of public health services being accomplished before any large-scale surge

---

* Many empirical studies have revealed cases of severe exploitation of poor patients' ignorance of what they are being given to make them part with badly needed money to receive treatment that they do not end up getting. See e.g. Pratichi Trust (2005) and Das et al. (2012).

of private medical care. The effectiveness of the public route is sometimes missed by the advocates of reliance on private health care who point to the plentiful presence of the private sector in medicine in Kerala today. Kerala's health transition initially proceeded on the solid foundations of universal coverage provided by the state, and only later on, the use of private health care developed fast, particularly for the newly rich people: Kerala experienced a rapid increase in incomes – not unrelated to the development of human capabilities (on which more in the next chapter) – which ultimately supported private health care. There is, in fact, a world of difference between (1) allowing – and even encouraging – the auxiliary facilities of private health care to enrich a reasonably well-functioning state system (as happened in Kerala), and (2) trying to rely on private health care when the state provides very little in terms of health facilities (as in many other states, particularly in north India). There is also a word of caution in the professional economic literature on asymmetric information about trying to make up the gap by subsidizing private health care or private health insurance, since the problem of profit-seeking market transactions with very unequal knowledge of medical conditions is not a matter only of economic poverty.* A similar set of problems arise with Indian educational planning, particularly involving school education (as will be discussed in Chapter 5).

The central point to appreciate here, as has already been emphasized, is that while economic growth is an important tool for enhancing living conditions, its reach and impact depend greatly on what is done with the fruits of growth. The relation between economic growth and the advancement of living standards depends on many factors, including economic and social inequality in general, and no less importantly, on what the government does with the public revenue that is generated by economic growth. The importance of economic growth can be adequately understood only in this broader context. It is necessary to recognize the role of growth in facilitating development in the form

---

* Two classic papers in economic theory which establish the limitations of private provision of education and health care, because of the 'public goods' characteristic of these provisions and because of asymmetric information in the market economy, are Paul Samuelson (1954) and Kenneth Arrow (1963).

of enhancing human lives and freedoms, but it is also necessary in this context to appreciate how the growth possibilities of a country depend in turn on the advancement of human capabilities (through education, health care and other facilities), in which the state can play a very constructive part.[36]

When India began undertaking a sustained programme of economic reform in the early 1990s, the country faced two gigantic failures of economic governance. The first was a failure to tap the *constructive role of the market*, particularly in terms of fostering initiative, promoting efficiency, and coordinating complex economic operations. The so-called 'licence Raj' – making it necessary to have governmental permission for private initiatives – made economic enterprise extremely difficult and put it at the mercy of bureaucrats (large and small), thereby powerfully stifling initiative while nurturing corruption considerably. This particular failure has been partially remedied in the post-reform period – the removal of arbitrary controls and greater openness to international trade has helped India to achieve a solid basis for high rates of economic growth. There is more to be done, both in simplifying or removing counterproductive *regulations* (since arbitrary restrictions and bureaucratic power continue to constrain Indian economic expansion) and in ensuring that *regulation* (an essential aspect of any modern economy) is well-aimed, effective, transparent, and not easily amenable to corruption.

However, there was also an urgent need to address another failure – a resounding failure to harness the *constructive role of the state* for growth and development. While there was plenty of government intervention in the pre-reform period, it was mainly of a negative or restrictive kind, neglecting, at the same time, huge fields of activity where constructive public action could have achieved a great deal. There has been a sluggish response to the urgency of remedying India's astonishingly underdeveloped social infrastructure and of building a functioning system of accountability and collaboration for public services. To this can be added the neglect of physical infrastructure (power, water, roads, rails), which required both governmental and private initiatives. Large areas of what economists call 'public goods' have continued to be neglected.

The radical changes in the 1990s did little to remedy the second of these failures. If things have begun to change here too (though rather slowly), part of the credit for ushering in that change must go to India's democratic politics. There is a growing recognition of the electoral relevance of unfulfilled basic needs of people (related to schools, health care, water supply and accountable administration), and various social movements as well as sections of the media have also been able to bring greater attention to elementary human rights as well as freedom from corruption.

So where does India stand now after all this? The economic growth rate is, of course, agreeably high (even at its current lower level, after having hovered above 8 per cent for five out of six years from 2005–6 onwards), but the sharing of its benefits is still remarkably unequal. Poverty rates have come down, but not close to what could have been achieved had the distributional side (including the provision of essential services) got more attention. Some failures are huge, like widespread undernourishment in general and child undernutrition in particular – India is among the world's worst performers in this respect (even compared with many countries that are considerably poorer in terms of real GDP per head). Another big failure remains the provision of public health care to the bulk of the population. And there is also the continuing scandal of a quarter of the population (including nearly half the women) remaining effectively illiterate in a country with such high-tech achievements in education based on excellent specialized training and practice. A democratic country can hardly want to become part California and part sub-Saharan Africa.

Looking ahead, two major problems facing the Indian economy can be summed up as follows: (1) removing the sharp disparities that divide the country into the privileged and the rest, while continuing to encourage overall economic growth and expansion, and (2) bringing more accountability to the running of the economy, particularly in the delivery of public services and the operation of the public sector. In the next chapter we discuss in comparative terms the huge penalties of large disparities in stifling India's economic and social progress, and in Chapter 4 we address some institutional problems that have been constraining and restraining social and economic change in India, including the problem of accountability, and in that context, the seemingly ubiquitous prevalence of corruption. Both these are crucial parts of the unfinished agenda of growth and development in India today.

SUSTAINABLE DEVELOPMENT

One other issue that must be part of the concern of Indian economic development is that of making the process sustainable. Sustainability is not a new subject. The security of human lives has always to some degree been understood to depend on the strength and resilience of the natural world we inhabit. However, the so-called 'human predicament', including our mortality and our fragility, has typically been understood as the plight of the individual, a condition frequently contrasted with the strength and durability of humanity as a collective entity; indeed, throughout history people have tended to take for granted the robustness of nature, and a secure place for us in it. The frailty of individual lives (including their ultimate cessation) has typically been seen as an individual predicament that did not apply to mankind in general. In recent decades, all over the world, these perceptions have dramatically changed, and indeed it is hard to think of a subject that generates as much concern today among reflective people everywhere as the serious vulnerability of the environment in which we live. People are deeply worried about how human lives can continue to prosper, even perhaps continue at all in the form that we know them, if the depletion of our environment continues as fast as it is right now.

In India, we have huge reasons to be worried about our treatment of the environment and its implications for the lives people can lead in this increasingly polluted and environmentally devastated country. Indeed, the acceleration of economic growth in recent decades has coincided with unprecedented environmental plunder. Groundwater has been extracted with abandon, leading to a sharp fall in water tables in many areas. Majestic rivers have been reduced to a trickle, or to sewage drains. Mining activities (often illegal) have spread with few safeguards, destroying forests and displacing communities. Air pollution has risen so far that India is now rated as the most polluted among 132 countries for which comparable data are available.[37]

India's 'natural wealth' is estimated to have shrunk by about 6 per cent in value terms (more than 30 per cent on a per capita basis) between 1990 and 2008.[38] And all this might be no more than just a harbinger of things to come: many types of environmental damage are likely to accelerate in the near future, with, for instance, hundreds of dams being planned on the Ganges river and its tributaries alone.[39]

The basic challenge of environmental sustainability has been sidelined in the single-minded concentration on the current growth rate of the GDP, which seems to get the lion's share of attention in the media and even in policy discussions about how India should pursue growth and development. And this lack of attention to the environment seems to have grown sharply in recent years. As Ramachandra Guha notes:

> After economic liberalization . . . environmental safeguards have been systematically dismantled. The ministry of environment and forests has cleared destructive projects with abandon. Penalties on errant industries are virtually never enforced. Although by law every new project has to have an Environmental Impact Assessment (EIA), these, as the then environment minister Jairam Ramesh candidly admitted in March 2011, are a 'bit of a joke', since 'under the system we have today, the person who is putting up the project prepares the report'.[40]

This devastation is often seen as a symptom of the conflict between 'environment' and 'development'. But this interpretation is thoroughly misleading. If development is about enhancing human freedoms and the quality of life – an important understanding for which we have argued – then the quality of the environment is bound to be part of what we want to preserve and promote. In fact, this broader view of development can help not only to integrate development and environmental concerns but also to achieve a better understanding of our environmental challenges, in terms of the quality and freedom of human lives – today and in the future.[41]

It is important to understand that caring about the environment need not undermine the commitment to development and the removal of poverty and deprivation. In the broader perspective of seeing development in terms of promoting substantive human freedom, fighting poverty and being responsible about the environment cannot but be closely linked. Development is not merely the enhancement of inanimate objects of convenience, such as a rise in the GDP (or in personal incomes); nor is it some general transformation of the world around us, such as industrialization, or technological advance, or social modernization. Development is, ultimately, the progress of human freedom and capability to lead the kind of lives that people have reason to value.

If we are ready to recognize the need for seeing the world in this broader perspective, it becomes immediately clear that development cannot be divorced from ecological and environmental concerns. For example, since we value the freedom to lead a pollution-free life, the preservation of a pollution-free atmosphere must be an important part of the objectives of development. Especially for poorer people, who tend to spend a much higher proportion of their daily lives in the open – sometimes even sleeping on the streets – the quality of air is a critically important influence on the level of deprivation of their lives. Similarly, if substantial parts of India – not to mention the Maldives or large sections of Bangladesh – were to be submerged by a rising ocean (as seems very possible if global warming continues further), the people who would suffer most would be the poorer people in the affected regions, with very little access to alternative opportunities of a viable economic and social living. Indeed, as Nicholas Stern has argued, the risks of climate change may affect the lives of people across the world in very diverse ways, making the exacerbation of inequity one of the primary concerns about the consequences of unchecked climatic developments.[42]

If development is about the expansion of freedom, it has to embrace the removal of poverty as well as paying attention to ecology as integral parts of a unified concern, aimed ultimately at the security and advancement of human freedom. Indeed, important components of human freedoms – and crucial ingredients of our quality of life – are thoroughly dependent on the integrity of the environment, involving the air we breathe, the water we drink, and the epidemiological surroundings in which we live. The opportunity to live the kind of lives that people value – and have reason to value – depends among other things on the nature and robustness of the environment. In this sense, development has to be environment-inclusive, and the belief that development and environment are on a collision course cannot sit comfortably with the recognition of the manifest interdependence and complementarity between the two.

3

India in Comparative Perspective

'The first thing I ever learned about India,' Anand Giridharadas notes in his excellent book *India Calling*, 'was that my parents had chosen to leave it.' 'My parents had left India in the 1970s, when the West seemed paved with possibility and India seemed paved with potholes. And now, a quarter century after my father first arrived as a student in America, I was flying east to make a new beginning in the land they had left.'[1] That perspective of a rapidly changing India, re-establishing itself on the world stage, is both engaging and exciting. It is not only that the ancient – and dilapidated – land, traditionally short of opportunities for young men and women, is humming with new and exciting things to do in business and professional lives, but also that the country is full of new energy in the creative fields of literature, music, films, science, engineering, and other areas of intellectual and artistic pursuits. India is certainly calling, with much to offer.

Life can indeed be exciting in the rapidly reshaping India, and the picture of a new and dramatically changed India is both accurate and important. And yet, as was discussed in the earlier chapters, the majority of Indian people have been left behind in the enhancement of living standards. Many of the new freedoms and fresh opportunities can be enjoyed only by a minority of Indians – a very large number of people but still only a minority. In comparing India with the rest of the world to see how India is doing, the results depend greatly on which sections of the Indian population we look at.

Comparisons of India with other countries are often made for the purpose of checking where the country fits in the international 'league'. The focus, quite often, is on India's 'rank' (for example, in terms of GDP per capita). That is not a bad way to proceed, and the

Indian obsession with the rank of the country in the world league can be a useful way to start. But much depends on the variable chosen for the ranking. As should be clear from the hype around the growth rate of GDP or GNP per head, this is one league in which India is doing rather well. That high-achievement story, however, conflicts somewhat with India's mediocre performance in the progress of quality of life, as reflected in the standard social indicators.

The minority of people in India who have been prospering well enough is large in absolute numbers. Even though estimates of the size of this minority vary, they certainly far exceed 100 million or so – making them a larger group than the population of most countries in the world. And yet in the statistics involving the total Indian population of more than 1.2 billion, the fortunate group is still too small to swing the average figures for the Indian population as a whole in terms of most social indicators. In what follows we shall compare the Indian average with the averages of other countries, but we must bear in mind the fact that even the low averages reflected in the Indian numbers exaggerate what the Indians not in the privileged group actually enjoy. This would apply to other countries too, but it is particularly relevant for India, given the enormity of class, caste and gender inequalities in Indian society – we shall return to this issue in Chapters 8 and 9.

COMPARISONS WITH THE NON-AFRICAN POOR

In a previous book, we noted that human deprivation was heavily concentrated in two regions of the world: South Asia and sub-Saharan Africa.[2] That has been true for many decades now, and it is still largely true today. For instance, most of the countries with a low 'human development index' are in South Asia or sub-Saharan Africa. Cambodia, Haiti, Papua New Guinea and Yemen are among the few exceptions of countries with high levels of extreme poverty in other global regions.

Even though South Asia and sub-Saharan Africa share problems of high incidences of poverty, they are not, of course, similarly placed in every respect. Living conditions are now, in many ways, considerably better in South Asia (including India) than in sub-Saharan Africa, partly reflecting a faster rate of improvement during the last twenty years or so. For instance, per capita income is now about 50 per cent higher in South Asia than in sub-Saharan Africa, unlike in 1990, when it was much the same in the two regions. More importantly, life expectancy is estimated to be about ten years longer in South Asia than in sub-Saharan Africa, and child mortality is almost twice as high in sub-Saharan Africa compared with South Asia.*

It is worth noting, however, that the advantage of South Asia over sub-Saharan Africa in living standards is by no means uniform: indeed some social indicators are not much better – if at all – in South Asia than in sub-Saharan Africa. For instance, female literacy rates are still much the same in both regions, not only among adult women (50 per cent and 55 per cent respectively) but also in the younger age groups (e.g. 72 per cent and 67 per cent, respectively, in the age group of 15–24 years).[3] Despite some progress in recent years, both regions continue to share a severe problem of mass illiteracy and lack of school education, especially among women, which sets them apart from all other major regions of the world. Further, in at least one field – that of nutrition and especially child nutrition – South Asia fares distinctly worse than sub-Saharan Africa. More than 40 per cent of South Asian children (and a slightly *higher* proportion of Indian children) are underweight in terms of standard WHO norms, compared with 25 per cent in sub-Saharan Africa (the corresponding figure, incidentally, is less than 12 per cent in every other region of the world).[4]

Leaving sub-Saharan Africa aside, India is not well placed at all in international comparisons of living standards. Contrary to the increasingly used rhetoric which suggests that India is well on its way to becoming an economic 'superpower', this is far from the real picture, even in terms of per capita income. In fact, despite rapid economic

---

* The figures cited in this section are taken from the World Bank's *World Development Indicators* (online, 1 January 2013). This is also the main source used throughout the book for purposes of international comparisons of development indicators. For India, we are using the WDI for international comparisons, and the latest figures available from national statistical sources otherwise. For further discussion, see the Statistical Appendix.

expansion in recent years, India remains one of the poorest countries among those outside sub-Saharan Africa. According to the World Bank, only 15 countries outside sub-Saharan Africa had a 'gross national income per capita' lower than India's in 2011: Afghanistan, Bangladesh, Burma, Cambodia, Haiti, Kyrgyzstan, Laos, Moldova, Nepal, Pakistan, Papua New Guinea, Tajikistan, Uzbekistan, Vietnam and Yemen. India does indeed have a large gap in world living standards to overcome, as was discussed in the last chapter. What is disturbing, given the past, is not India's comparatively low position in terms of income per head among the countries in the world outside sub-Saharan Africa, but how badly India does in terms of *non-income* features of living standards even within this group of poorest non-African countries, as can be readily seen in Table 3.1.

India has, by the choice of our cut-off point, the highest GDP per capita in this particular group, with the rank of being number 1 among these sixteen countries. Aside from GDP per capita, as the last column indicates, India's rank among these 16 poor countries is 10th or worse in most cases. Not only are India's figures worse than the average for the other 15 countries for all social indicators presented here (except for the total fertility rate and male literacy rate), its rank in this group is an inglorious 10th for child mortality, 11th for female literacy and mean years of schooling, 13th for access to improved sanitation and DPT immunization, and absolutely the worst (along with Yemen) in terms of the proportion of underweight children.*

We argued in the last chapter that the common characterization of India's current economic growth rate of around 6 per cent per year as 'dismal' is hard to justify because India's rate of economic growth, though reduced, is still among the fastest in the world (as it would still be, even if the prediction of a 5 per cent growth rate by some agencies proved to be true). But 'dismal' would indeed be a very good adjective to describe the picture of comparative living standards, as Table 3.1 reveals.

Table 3.2 gives the detailed information on which the summary presented in Table 3.1 is based. Some of these comparisons are quite

* Similarly, in terms of the 'multi-dimensional poverty index' (MPI), discussed further in this chapter, India ranks 11th out of 14 countries for which estimates are available in this group (Sabina Alkire, personal communication).

Table 3.1
Selected Indicators for the World's 16 Poorest Countries, Outside Sub-Saharan Africa

	India	Average for other poorest countries[a]	India's rank among 16 poorest countries[b]
GDP per capita, 2011 (PPP, constant 2005 international $)	3,203	2,112	1
Life expectancy at birth, 2011 (years)	65	67	9
Infant mortality rate, 2011 (per 1,000 live births)	47	45	10
Under-5 mortality rate, 2011 (per 1,000 live births)	61	56	10
Total fertility rate, 2011 (children per woman)	2.6	2.9	7
Access to improved sanitation, 2010 (%)	34	57	13
Mean years of schooling, age 25+, 2011	4.4	5.0	11
Literacy rate, age 15–24 years, 2010 (%)			
Female	74[c]	79	11
Male	88[c]	85	9
Proportion of children below five years who are undernourished, 2006–10[d] (%)			
Underweight	43	30	15
Stunted	48	41	13
Child immunization rates, 2011 (%)			
DPT	72	88	13
Measles	74	87	11

[a] Population-weighted average of country-specific indicators. In two cases of missing data for a particular country (e.g. literacy rates for Afghanistan), the average was taken over the remaining countries.
[b] Based on ranking from 'best' to 'worst'. In case of 'ties', India was ranked first.
[c] 2006.
[d] Latest year for which data are available within 2006–10.

Sources: See Table 3.2. This table focuses on 16 countries with per capita GDP lower than or equal to India's, outside sub-Saharan Africa. These are: Afghanistan, Bangladesh, Burma, Cambodia, Haiti, India, Kyrgyzstan, Laos, Moldova, Nepal, Pakistan, Papua New Guinea, Tajikistan, Uzbekistan, Vietnam and Yemen.

instructive. For instance, Vietnam fares enormously better than India in terms of all these indicators, in spite of being poorer than India. So, incidentally, does Nicaragua, with virtually the same per capita GDP as India (just a little higher, so that Nicaragua is not included in Table 3.2). Uzbekistan, too, is far ahead of India in many respects, with, for instance, universal literacy in the younger age groups, universal access to improved sanitation, and (nearly) universal immunization of children – all goals that are nowhere near being achieved in India. Another striking contrast is between India and Nepal, which has much the same social indicators as India, with barely *one third* of India's per capita income (the last makes Nepal one of the very poorest countries outside Africa, along with Afghanistan and Haiti).

It could be argued that one would expect India not to fare as well, in many ways, as other countries at a similar level of per capita income, because India is growing quite fast and it takes time for higher per capita incomes to translate into better social indicators. In a country growing at 7 per cent per year in per capita terms, per capita income would double in ten years, but it could quite possibly take longer, even with significant efforts, to bring social indicators level with those of countries that were once twice as rich. That is a point worth noting, and is itself a good reason not to rely on income growth alone to bring about a transformation of living conditions (which is one of the main points we are trying to make). The basic concern remains that, for whatever reasons, India is not doing well at all in many respects even in comparison with some of the poorest countries in the world. This is not to disparage India's achievements, but to put them in perspective, and to focus on the deficiencies that plague India most and which have to be overcome.

INDIA'S DECLINE IN SOUTH ASIA

One indication that there is something defective in India's 'path to development' arises from the fact that India is falling behind every other South Asian country (with the exception of Pakistan) in terms of many social indicators, even as it is doing spectacularly better than

Table 3.2: Poorest Countries, Outside Sub-Saharan Africa (Part 1)

	India	Vietnam	Moldova	Uzbekistan	Laos
GDP per capita (PPP), 2011	3,203	3,013	2,975	2,903	2,464
Life expectancy at birth, 2011	65	75[d]	69	68[d]	67
Infant mortality rate, 2011	47	17	14	42	34
Under-5 mortality rate, 2011	61	22	16	49	42
Total fertility rate, 2011	2.6	1.8[d]	1.5	2.5[d]	2.7
Access to improved sanitation, 2010 (%)	34	76	85	100	63
Mean years of schooling, age 25+, 2011	4.4	5.5	9.7	10	4.6
Literacy rate, age 15–24, 2010 (%)					
Female	74[a]	96	100	100	79[b]
Male	88[a]	97	99	100	89[b]
Undernourishment among children below 5, 2006–10[e]					
Underweight	43	20	n/a	4	31
Stunted	48	31	n/a	19	48
Child immunization rates, 2011 (%)					
DPT	72	95	93	99	78
Measles	74	96	91	99	69

Table 3.2: Poorest Countries, Outside Sub-Saharan Africa (Part 2)

	Pakistan	Papua NG	Kyrgyzstan	Cambodia	Yemen	Tajikistan
GDP per capita (PPP), 2011	2,424	2,363	2,119	2,083	2,060	2,052
Life expectancy at birth, 2011	65[d]	63	69[d]	63	65	68
Infant mortality rate, 2011	59	45	27	36	57	53
Under-5 mortality rate, 2011	72	58	31	43	77	63
Total fertility rate, 2011	3.4[d]	3.9	2.9[d]	2.5	5.1	3.2
Access to improved sanitation, 2010 (%)	48	45	93	31	53	94
Mean years of schooling, age 25+, 2011	4.9	3.9	9.3	5.8	2.5	9.8
Literacy rate, age 15–24, 2010 (%)						
Female	61[c]	72	100[c]	86[c]	74	100
Male	79[c]	65	100[c]	88[c]	96	100
Undernourishment among children below 5, 2006–10[e] (%)						
Underweight	31	18	2	28	43	15
Stunted	42	43	18	40	58	39
Child immunization rates, 2011 (%)						
DPT	80	61	96	94	81	96
Measles	80	60	97	93	71	98

Table 3.2: Poorest Countries, Outside Sub-Saharan Africa (Part 3)

	Burma	Bangladesh	Nepal	Haiti	Afghanistan
GDP per capita (PPP), 2011	n/a	1,569	1,106	1,034	1,006
Life expectancy at birth, 2011	65	69	69	62	48[d]
Infant mortality rate, 2011	48	37	39	53	73
Under-5 mortality rate, 2011	62	46	48	70	101
Total fertility rate, 2011	2.0	2.2	2.7	3.3	6.3
Access to improved sanitation, 2010 (%)	76	56	31	17	37
Mean years of schooling, age 25+, 2011	3.9	4.8	3.2	4.9	3.1
Literacy rate, age 15–24, 2010 (%)					
Female	96	78	78	70[a]	n/a
Male	96	75	88	74[a]	n/a
Undernourishment among children below 5, 2006–10[e] (%)					
Underweight	23	41	39	18	33
Stunted	35	43	49	29	59
Child immunization rates, 2011 (%)					
DPT	99	96	92	59	66
Measles	99	96	88	59	62

[a] 2006.
[b] 2005.
[c] 2009.
[d] 2010.
[e] Latest year for which data are available within 2006–10.

Source: *World Development Indicators* (online, 1 January 2013). Mean years of schooling from *Human Development Report 2013* and child undernutrition data from UNICEF (2012). The countries in the table (other than India) are all those with per capita GDP lower than India in 2011, ranked in descending order of per capita GDP. In the absence of updated data, Burma (or Myanmar, as the military rulers of Burma now insist on calling it) has been placed in the same position as that in which it appears (in terms of per capita GDP) in *World Development Indicators 2011*.

these countries in terms of the growth of per capita income. The comparative picture is presented in Table 3.3.

The comparison between Bangladesh and India is a good place to start. During the last twenty years or so, India has grown much richer than Bangladesh: India's per capita income, already 60 per cent higher than Bangladesh's in 1990, was estimated to be about double that of Bangladesh by 2011. However, during the same period, Bangladesh has *overtaken* India in terms of a wide range of basic social indicators, including life expectancy, child survival, enhanced immunization rates, reduced fertility rates, and even some (not all) schooling indicators. For instance, life expectancy was more or less the same in both countries in 1990, but was estimated to be four years higher in Bangladesh than in India by 2010 (69 and 65 years respectively). Similarly, child mortality, a tragic indicator, was estimated to be about 20 per cent higher in Bangladesh than in India in 1990, but has fallen rapidly in Bangladesh to now being 25 per cent *lower* than in India by 2011. Most social indicators now look better in Bangladesh than in India, despite Bangladesh having less than half of India's per capita income.

No less intriguing is the case of Nepal, which – with all its problems of politics and governance – seems to be catching up rapidly with India, and even overtaking India in some respects. Around 1990, Nepal was far behind India in terms of almost every development indicator. Today, as Table 3.3 illustrates, social indicators for both countries are more similar (sometimes a little better in India still, sometimes the reverse), in spite of per capita income in India being about three times as high as in Nepal.[5]

Even the comparison with Pakistan, though favourable to India in general, is not comprehensively flattering. Between 1990 and 2011, real per capita income at constant prices increased by about 50 per cent in Pakistan and 170 per cent in India (see Table 3.3, first row). But the gap in social indicators (initially in favour of India in some respects, but in favour of Pakistan in others) has not been fundamentally altered in most cases. And in some respects, such as immunization rates, things seem to have improved more in Pakistan than in India.

To look at the same issue from another angle, Table 3.4 displays India's 'rank' among South Asia's six major countries respectively around 1990 and today (more precisely, in the latest year for which

Table 3.3: South Asia: Selected Indicators (1990 and latest)

				South Asia				China
		India	Bangladesh	Bhutan	Nepal	Pakistan	Sri Lanka	
GDP per capita, PPP:	1990*	1,193	741	1,678	716	1,624	2,017	1,121
(constant 2005 international $)	2011	3,203	1,569	5,152	1,106	2,424	4,929	7,418
Life expectancy at birth:	1990*	58	59	53	54	61	70	69
(years)	2011	65	69	67	69	65^f	75^f	73^f
Infant mortality rate:	1990*	81	97	96	94	95	24	39
(per 1,000 live births)	2011	47	37	42	39	59	11	13
Under-5 mortality rate:	1990*	114	139	138	135	122	29	49
(per 1,000 live births)	2011	61	46	54	48	72	12	15
Maternal Mortality Ratio:	1990	600	800	1,000	770	490	85	120
(per 100,000 live births)	2010	200	240	180	170	260	35	37
Total fertility rate:	1990*	3.9	4.5	5.7	5.2	6.0	2.5	2.3
(children per woman)	2011	2.6	2.2	2.3	2.7	3.4^f	2.3^f	1.6^f
Access to improved sanitation (%):	1990	18	39	n/a	10	27	70	24
	2010	34	56	44	31	48	92	64
Infant immunization (DPT) (%):	1990*	59	64	88	44	48	86	95
	2011	72	96	95	92	80	99	99
Infant immunization (measles) (%):	1990*	47	62	87	57	50	78	95
	2011	74	96	95	88	80	99	99

(Continued)

Table 3.3: (Continued)

	South Asia						China
	India	Bangladesh	Bhutan	Nepal	Pakistan	Sri Lanka	
Mean years of schooling, age 25+:							
1990	3.0	2.9	–	2.0	2.3	6.9	4.9
2011	4.4	4.8	2.3[e]	3.2	4.9	9.3	7.5
Female literacy rate, age 15–24 (%):							
1991[a]	49	38	–	33	–	93	91
2010[b]	74	78	68	78	61	99	99
Proportion (%) of underweight children:							
1990[c]	59.5	61.5	34	–	39	29	13
2006–10[d]	43	41	13	39	31	21	4

* Three-year average centred on the reference year (e.g. 1989–91 average when the reference year is 1990).

[a] 1990 for China; the Sri Lanka figure is an interpolation between 1981 and 2001 figures.

[b] 2006 for India, 2005 for Bhutan, 2009 for Pakistan.

[c] 1988 for Bhutan, 1991 for Pakistan, 1987 for Sri Lanka.

[d] Latest year for which data are available within this period.

[e] 2002–2012.

[f] 2010.

Sources: Mean years of schooling from *Human Development Report 2013*, online; other indicators from *World Development Indicators*, online (1 January 2013). Some of the country-specific figures for 1990 are subject to a significant margin of error; the focus is best kept on broad patterns rather than exact numbers.

Table 3.4
India's Rank in South Asia

Indicator	India's rank among six South Asian countries (Top = 1, Bottom = 6)	
	In 1990	Around 2011
1. GDP per capita	4	3
2. Life expectancy	4	5
3. Infant mortality rate	2	5
4. Under-5 mortality rate	2	5
5. Maternal mortality ratio	3	4
6. Total fertility rate	2	4
7. Access to improved sanitation	4–5[a]	5
8. Child immunization (DPT)	4	6
9. Child immunization (measles)	6	6
10. Mean years of schooling, age 25+	2–3[a]	4
11. Female literacy rate, age 15–24	2–3[a]	4
12. Proportion of underweight children	4–5[a]	6

[a] Ambiguous rank due to missing data for Bhutan (or Nepal, in the case of 'underweight children').

Source: See Table 3.3. The six countries considered here are Bangladesh, Bhutan, India, Nepal, Pakistan and Sri Lanka.

comparable international data are available as we write this book). As expected, in terms of the absolute level of per capita income, India's rank has improved – from fourth (after Bhutan, Pakistan and Sri Lanka) to third (after Bhutan and Sri Lanka). In terms of the rate of expansion of income per head, India is now at the top of this group (as it is of most groups of countries in the world). But in most other respects, India's rank has worsened, in fact quite sharply in many cases. Overall, only one country in South Asia (Sri Lanka) clearly had better social indicators than India in 1990, but now India looks second worst, ahead of only trouble-torn Pakistan.

The comparative perspectives in South Asia tend to be commonly overlooked in development studies, especially in India. Yet there is a great deal to learn from looking around us within South Asia. For instance, many development experts in India, increasingly keen on using the private sector for school education, would be interested to learn that in Sri Lanka, with its huge lead over India in social indicators and particularly schooling and literacy (see Table 3.3), private schools are virtually absent – and have in fact been prohibited since the 1960s. A similar remark applies to the fact that in Sri Lanka 'few people live more than 1.4 km away from the nearest health centre'.[6] Many other policies and achievements in neighbouring countries merit attention from Indian planners – and the Indian public generally. Notwithstanding its enormous size and rapid economic growth compared with its neighbours, India may have much to learn from them.

BANGLADESH'S PROGRESS AND THE ROLE OF WOMEN

Bangladesh has come a long way in the last four decades. In the first half of the 1970s, the country endured a lethal cyclone (estimated to have killed up to half a million people in 1970), a popular rebellion and a fully fledged 'war of liberation' (eventually leading to the country's independence in 1971), and a large-scale famine (in 1974, when 6 per cent of the population had to depend for their survival on the distribution of free food in *langarkhanas*, or feeding centres). Few observers at that time expected Bangladesh to make rapid social progress in the next few decades. In fact, the famine of 1974 appeared to vindicate the prophets of doom, some of whom had even dismissed Bangladesh as a 'basket case' country that should not even be assisted because it was sure to lose in the race between population and food.

Today, Bangladesh is still one of the poorest countries in the world, and large sections of its population continue to lack many of the bare essentials of good living. And yet Bangladesh has made rapid progress in some crucial aspects of living standards, particularly in the last twenty years – overtaking India in terms of many social indicators in spite of its slower economic growth.

Some particular features of the Bangladeshi experience are of special relevance to India. Bangladesh is not a model of development by any means. In spite of much recent progress, it remains one of the most deprivation-ridden countries in the world, and many of the policy biases discussed in this book with reference to India apply to Bangladesh as well. With per capita GDP half as high in Bangladesh as in India, and public expenditure a mere 10 per cent or so of GDP in Bangladesh (again about half as much as in India), public services in Bangladesh are inevitably restrained, and whatever is already in place suffers from serious accountability problems, much as in India.[7] Democratic institutions in Bangladesh are also in some trouble, maintaining a tradition by which opposition parties do not seem to attend Parliament. And yet there are also features of astonishing achievement in Bangladesh that cannot but excite interest, curiosity and engagement.

The roots of Bangladesh's social achievements are not entirely transparent, and deserve much greater scrutiny than they have received so far.[8] However, some likely clues are immediately worth noting. Perhaps the most important clue is a pattern of sustained positive change in gender relations. As Table 3.5 shows, many gender-related indicators are now much better in Bangladesh than in India. For instance, women's participation rate in the workforce is almost twice as high in Bangladesh as in India (57 per cent and 29 per cent, respectively). This, along with greater female literacy and education, is recognized across the world as a powerful contributor to women's empowerment, and Bangladesh has made much greater use of this avenue of change than has India.[9] In the field of elementary education, Bangladesh has made remarkable strides towards gender equality, so much so that school participation rates and literacy rates of Bangladeshi girls are now *higher* than those of boys, in contrast with India where a substantial gender bias (against girls) persists. Indeed, Bangladesh is now one of the few countries in the world where the number of girls exceeds the number of boys in school. Even the share of women in Parliament, while much below one half in both countries, is higher in Bangladesh than in India.[10]

Table 3.5
Gender-related Indicators in India and Bangladesh

	India	Bangladesh
Female labour force participation rate, age 15+, 2010 (%)	29	57
Female-male ratio in the population, 2011		
(females per 1,000 males)		
All ages	940	997
Age 0–6 years	914	972[a]
Ratio of female to male death rates, 2009[b]		
Age 0–1	1.01	0.89
Age 1–4	1.55	1.25
Ratio of female to male school enrolment, 2010 (%)		
Primary	100[c]	104[d]
Secondary	92	113
Literacy rate, age 15–24 years, 2010 (%)		
Female	74[e]	78
Male	88[e]	75
Proportion of adults (age 25+) with secondary education, 2010 (%)		
Women	27	31
Men	50	39
Women's share of seats in national Parliament, 2011 (%)	11	20
Total fertility rate, 2011 (children per woman)	2.6	2.2

[a] Age 0–4 years.
[b] 2007 for Bangladesh.
[c] 2008.
[d] 2009.
[e] 2006.

Sources: *World Development Indicators* (online, 1 January 2013), unless started otherwise. *Human Development Report 2011*, p. 141, for adults with secondary education. Female-male ratios in the population from Census of India 2011 (Government of India, 2011b, p. 88) and Population and Housing Census 2011 (Bangladesh Bureau of Statistics, 2011, p. 7); ratio of female to male death rates from *Sample Registration System Statistical Report 2009* and Bangladesh Demographic and Health Survey 2007 (National Institute of Population Research and Training, 2009, Table 8.3, p. 104).

To what extent women's agency and gender relations account for the fact that Bangladesh has caught up with, and even overtaken, India in many crucial fields during the last twenty years calls for further investigation. But it certainly looks like an important factor, in the light of what we know about the role of women's agency in development. For instance, the fact that both female literacy and women's participation in the workforce play an important role in the 'demographic transition' (from high to low mortality and fertility rates) is fairly well established.[11] The subjugation of women in South Asia has also been plausibly invoked in the past as a major explanation for the 'South Asian enigma' – the fact that child undernutrition rates are higher in this region than in many countries that are much poorer. It is thus entirely plausible that Bangladesh's recent progress has been significantly driven by positive changes in gender relations and by the new role of women in Bangladeshi society. Some of its achievements, in fact, build in a fairly direct and transparent way on women's agency. For instance, very large numbers of Bangladeshi women have been mobilized as front-line health workers (both by NGOs and by the government).[12] In this and in many other areas of activity involving Bangladeshi women, it looks as if the country would have been a very different place – and far less successful – but for the positive role played by its women.

No comparable change can be observed in India as a whole, and especially in its 'northern heartland'.[13] There, women's participation in the workforce has been stagnating at very low levels for decades, in sharp contrast not only with Bangladesh but also with many other Asian countries, where large numbers of women have entered remunerated employment. Similarly, India continues to have a serious problem of gender bias in childcare (reflected for instance in much higher mortality rates and lower school participation rates for girls than for boys), which has even acquired new manifestations in the recent past, such as sex-selective abortion. As will be discussed in Chapter 8, these biases against the girl child are reflected in a low female-male ratio among children: only 914 girls per 1,000 boys in India in 2011, compared with 972 in Bangladesh, suggesting much less gender discrimination in childcare there as well as a relative absence of sex-selective abortion (see Table 3.5).* None of this detracts from the fact that Bangladesh, like India, is a traditionally male-dominated society and continues to be very patriarchal in many ways even today. But at least there are strong signs of transformational change in Bangladesh, much more so than in India as a whole.

A second pointer, particularly relevant to health achievements, is Bangladesh's apparent ability to focus on the basic determinants of health care and elementary education in ways that have not happened in India. Bangladesh's endeavours have been helped by flourishing NGO activities, from comprehensive development efforts to specialized micro-credit initiatives (led by organizations such as BRAC and Grameen Bank). There have also been sensible moves in the public sector with an eye to basic living requirements. Even though the overall size of public expenditure on health is still very low in Bangladesh, and many of the governance issues that have plagued India's health care system also seem to apply to Bangladesh, nevertheless the country has made very substantial progress with essential, low-cost measures, particularly related to public health. The point is easily seen in the information presented in Table 3.6. Taking the data in Tables 3.5 and 3.6 together, the contrast between the two countries is very sharp: elementary good-health practices such as the use of sanitation facilities, full immunization of children, and oral rehydration therapy (to treat diarrhoea) have become widely accepted social norms in Bangladesh, but are still confined to only a section of the Indian population, leaving large gaps in coverage.

The sanitation figures are worth noting. Only 56 per cent of Bangladeshi households have access, at their homes, to facilities – such as modern toilets – that meet the World Development Indicators' standards of 'improved sanitation' (with an even lower figure, 34 per cent, for India – see Table 3.3). However, a much higher proportion – more than

* There are major contrasts in gender relations, including the prevalence of sex-selective abortion, among different regions within India, and the comparison of Bangladesh's figures with the average numbers for India can be rather deceptive (some of the regional contrasts will be discussed later on in this chapter and in Chapter 8). However, for the same reason, some regions of India compare much more unfavourably with Bangladesh than the comparison between country averages indicates.

Table 3.6
India and Bangladesh: Selected Indicators of Public Health

	India (2005–6)	Bangladesh (2007)
Proportion of households practising open defecation (%)	55	8.4
Proportion of children aged 12–23 months who are fully immunized (%)	44	82
Proportion of children who started breastfeeding within 24 hours of birth (%)	55	89
Proportion of children aged 9–59 months who received Vitamin A supplements[a] (%)	18	88
Proportion of the population with sustainable access to an improved water source (%)	88	97
Proportion of diarrhoea-affected children treated with 'oral rehydration therapy' (%)	39	81

[a] Age 6–59 months for India.

Sources: Bangladesh Demographic and Health Survey 2007, for Bangladesh; National Family Health Survey 2005–6, for India. These two surveys (DHS and NFHS respectively) are very similar in terms of questionnaires and survey methods – both are variants of the worldwide DHS household surveys.

90 per cent – of households in Bangladesh do have access to some sanitation facilities, including rudimentary latrines and washing facilities, so that only 8.4 per cent have to resort to 'open defecation' (see Table 3.6). In India, a full 50 per cent of households had to practise open defecation in 2011, according to the latest population census – a higher proportion than in almost any other country for which data are available. Open defecation is not only a major health hazard, but also a source of enormous hardship, particularly for women who are often constrained to rise before dawn and have no convenient way of relieving themselves after that.[14] This hardship passes largely unnoticed, and indeed, the need for universal access to basic sanitation facilities has not been a major concern in Indian planning until very recently. Bangladesh, meanwhile, has been quietly building toilets around the country over the years,

sparing the vast majority of the population from the hardships and hazards of open defecation. Even if some of these facilities are quite rudimentary, they are at least laying foundations for adequate sanitation.[15] This is also a good illustration of the possibility of effective health initiatives even with a great shortage of public resources.

Another area of particular interest is family planning in the two countries. Bangladesh has implemented a fairly effective, non-coercive family planning programme which has led to a dramatic reduction of fertility in a relatively short time – from around 7 children per woman in the early 1970s to 4.5 in 1990 and 2.2 in 2011 (very close to the 'replacement level' of 2.1). As one commentator put it to us, family planning is now as familiar to Bangladeshi women as 'dal-bhat' (rice and lentils – the staple foods of the country). This is also reflected in survey data (e.g. from the Bangladesh Demographic and Health Survey), showing high levels of awareness of family planning matters among Bangladeshi women, and a much higher use of modern contraceptive methods than in India. Just to cite one more example, Bangladesh has also made early strides in the development and distribution of low-cost generic drugs through public or non-profit institutions.[16] It is partly by focusing on these and other 'basics' that the country has been able to improve people's health in spite of its very low per capita income.

A third pointer relates to the importance of social norms in health, education and related fields, and to the role of public communication and community mobilization in bringing about changes in social norms. Most of Bangladesh's relatively successful programmes in these fields have built in one way or another on these social factors.[17] Tens of thousands of grass-roots health and community workers (mobilized by the government as well as by NGOs) have been going from house to house and village to village for many years facilitating child immunization, explaining contraception methods, promoting improved sanitation, organizing nutrition supplementation programmes, counselling pregnant or lactating women, and much more. India, of course, has also initiated programmes of this sort, but it still has much to learn from Bangladesh, both about the required intensity of these communication and mobilization efforts, and about the need to overcome the social barriers that often stand in the way of such initiatives.

INDIA AMONG THE BRICs

While the South Asian perspective has been much neglected in India, another group of countries is commonly seen as comprising its 'peer group': Brazil, Russia, India and China (also known as the BRIC countries). These nations do have some important features in common, starting with their gigantic populations.

As Table 3.7 illustrates, however, India is actually an exception within this group, in important ways. For instance, while every country in the set has achieved universal or near-universal literacy in the younger age groups, India is still quite far from this elementary foundation of participatory development: one fifth of all Indian men in the age group of 15–24 years, and one fourth of all women in the same age group, were unable to read and write in 2006. Similarly, child immunization is almost universal in every BRIC country except India. In fact, as we saw earlier, India's immunization rates are abysmally low even in comparison with those of other South Asian countries including Bangladesh and Nepal. India also stands out dramatically in terms of the extent of undernourishment among children. This terrible problem has largely disappeared in other BRIC countries, but is still rampant in India, where more than 40 per cent of all children below the age of five are underweight, and an even higher proportion (close to 50 per cent) are stunted.

To some extent, this pattern reflects the fact that India is still much poorer than other BRIC countries: India's per capita GDP (adjusted for 'purchasing power parity') is less than half of China's, one third of Brazil's, and one fourth of Russia's. But clearly, much more needs to be done to fill these massive gaps than just 'catching up' in terms of per capita income. For instance, rapid economic growth has not achieved much on its own, during the last twenty years or so, to reduce India's horrendous levels of child undernourishment, or to enhance child immunization rates. Similarly, making a swift and decisive transition to universal literacy in the younger age groups would take more than just waiting for the growth of per capita incomes to make it easier for parents to send their children to school.

In others words, the required 'catching up' pertains not only to per

Table 3.7
Selected Indicators for 'BRIC' Countries

	India	China	Brazil	Russia
GDP per capita (PPP, 2005 constant international $), 2011	3,203	7,418	10,279	14,821
Life expectancy at birth, 2010				
Female	67	75	77	75
Male	64	72	70	63
Infant mortality rate, 2011	47	13	14	10
Under-5 mortality rate, 2011	61	15	16	12
Total fertility rate, 2010	2.6	1.6	1.8	1.5
Access to improved sanitation, 2010 (%)	34	64	79	70
Mean years of schooling, age 25+, 2011	4.4	7.5	7.2	11.7
Literacy rate, age 15–24, 2010 (%)				
Female	74[a]	99	99[c]	100
Male	88[a]	99	97[c]	100
Undernourishment among children below 5, 2006–10[b] (%)				
Underweight	43	4	2	n/a
Stunted	48	10	7	n/a
Child immunization rates, 2011 (%)				
DPT	72	99	96	97
Measles	74	99	97	98
Public expenditure on health, 2010:				
As a proportion of total health expenditure (%)	29	54	47	62
As a proportion of GDP (%)	1.2	2.7	4.2	3.2
Per capita (PPP, 2005 constant international $)	39	203	483	620
Public expenditure on education as a proportion of GDP, 2010 (%)	3.3	n/a	5.6[c]	4.1[d]

[a] 2006.

[b] Latest year for which data are available within this period.

[c] 2009.

[d] 2008.

Source: *World Development Indicators* (online, 1 January 2013). Mean years of schooling from *Human Development Report 2013* and child undernutrition from UNICEF (2012). Countries are ranked in increasing order of GDP per capita.

capita incomes but also – very importantly – to public services, social support and economic distribution. It is, in fact, worth noting that among these four countries, India is the only one that has not (at least not yet) gone through a phase of major expansion of public support or economic redistribution. China made enormous progress (especially in comparison with India) very early towards universal access to elementary education, health care and social security – much *before* embarking on market-oriented economic reforms in 1979. While there were some setbacks in some of these fields in the 1980s and 1990s, notably in the field of health care, China's growth-oriented policies during that period benefited a great deal from the solid foundations of human development that had been laid earlier, and also retained that commitment in many ways, for instance through guaranteed and equitable access to land in rural areas. Further, as discussed in Chapter 1, the undoing of socialized health care in the 1980s and 1990s, for which China paid a heavy price, was reversed again from around 2004.[18] The principle of universal health coverage has reappeared in China's health planning, and rapid progress has been made in that direction: it appears that nearly 95 per cent of the people are now covered by the revamped, publicly funded health system.

Russia, too, had put in place a comprehensive system of social protection and public services during the Communist period. As in China, the system came under heavy stress after economic reforms – of a more extreme variety – were introduced in the early 1990s. In Russia, however, the breakdown was far more serious, and compounded by an economic catastrophe (possibly the worst economic recession in modern history, lasting for the best part of a decade), not unrelated to the lethal advice of Western experts who kept predicting an imminent 'economic miracle' in a newly marketized Russia even as the economy kept sinking.[19] There was, eventually, an economic take-off of a limited sort (in the 2000s), but only after the economy and social infrastructure had been substantially ruined, or handed over to business magnates. This prolonged economic crisis was associated with an equally catastrophic deterioration of the health of the Russian population, particularly men, who now have the same sort of life expectancy as Indian men (see Table 3.7). Even then, some of the social achievements of the earlier period remained, including universal basic education, involving schooling well beyond literacy. And as in China, there have been major efforts to rebuild public services and the social security system in Russia in recent years, with help from sustained economic growth from the turn of the century.[20]

To some extent, similar events have taken place in various parts of the former Soviet Union and Eastern Europe. It is often forgotten that, before the break-up of the Soviet Union in 1991, patterns of social spending in Western and Eastern Europe were not vastly different – most countries in both regions had a well-developed welfare state and spent a large proportion of their GDP on health, education, social security and related purposes.[21] It was after the break-up of the Soviet Union, and the economic catastrophe that followed in much of Eastern Europe, that social spending also came under enormous strain in many countries of that region (especially those with weak democratic institutions). The damage still remains partially unrepaired.

In Brazil, progressive social policies are comparatively recent, and followed a period of rapid economic growth, instead of preceding it as in China; it is perhaps interesting that the social indicators of Brazil and China look quite similar today (see Table 3.7), even though they reached a similar situation through very different routes. For a long time, Brazil combined rapid economic growth with repressive governance, massive inequality and endemic deprivation. However, as discussed in the next section, this picture has radically changed during the last twenty years, a time of ambitious and wide-ranging initiatives in the fields of health, education and social security (largely driven by the democratic upsurge that followed the end of military dictatorships), and the results have been impressive.

THE OLD AND NEW BRAZIL

Along with our analysis of the scope for 'growth-mediated' development, in an earlier book, we also discussed the pitfalls of 'unaimed opulence' – the indiscriminate pursuit of economic expansion, without paying much attention to how it is shared or how it affects people's lives.[22] At that time (in the late 1980s), Brazil was in many ways a fitting illustration of this pattern. In the 1960s and 1970s, it had one of the fastest-growing economies in the world, but living conditions remained deplorably low for large sections of the population. Commenting on this again in the mid-1990s, in contrast with a more equitable and participatory growth pattern in South Korea, we wrote that 'India stands in some danger of going Brazil's way, rather than South Korea's'.[23] Recent experience vindicates this apprehension about the path that India might be following – there is a fair amount of unaimed opulence in India today.

Interestingly, over the last couple of decades, Brazil has substantially changed course, and adopted a more inclusive approach based on active social policies. This change has been largely driven by the flourishing of democracy that followed the promulgation of a democratic constitution in 1988, soon after the end of a long spell of military dictatorships. Notable aspects of this new orientation include a strong commitment to free and universal health care, bold programmes of social security and income support, and major efforts to expand the reach and quality of elementary education. It is, of course, the case that many significant imperfections remain, but these problems are subjects of powerful critiques and public discussions in Brazil today.[24]

The right to health was included in the new democratic constitution, not in the non-binding mode of the 'directive principles' of the Indian constitution, but as a matter of justiciable right. In pursuance of this state obligation, Brazil created the 'Unified Health System', aimed at providing free health care to everyone without discrimination, and also launched an ambitious Family Health Programme. The system involves both public and private health care providers, but is publicly funded. It has led to a major expansion of access to health care, particularly for the underprivileged – according to the World Health Organization, 75 per cent of the population 'rely exclusively on it for their health care coverage'.[25] Today, Brazil's health indicators are reasonably good, with, for instance, universal immunization of children, an infant mortality rate of only 14 per 1,000 (compared with 47 in India), and only 2 per cent children below five being underweight (compared with a staggering 43 per cent in India).

A special feature of Brazil's new health care project is that it is rooted in strong popular movements. The Unified Health System itself was largely conceived by health activists as part of a larger 'social policy project designed by social movements', strongly associated with 'the transformation of the state and society into a democracy'.[26] Interestingly, this project is known in Brazil as 'health sector reform' – a useful reminder that 'reform' has many possible connotations, and need not be taken to mean, as it is often assumed in India, a retreat from state action. Brazil's experience also reminds us that, in a democracy, health care can be a lively political issue, as it is in the experience of Western Europe (and to some extent, more recently, even of the United States). As discussed in Chapter 6, there is a very important lesson here for India, where health care is still way down on the list of issues that catch the imagination of political leaders, opposition parties or talk-show hosts.

Programmes of income redistribution and social security, also in line with Brazil's new democratic constitution, have had substantial results as well. In an insightful study, Martin Ravallion (2011) compares the speed and causes of poverty reduction in Brazil, India and China between 1981 and 2005. During the second half of this period (between 1993 and 2005), Brazil's per capita GDP grew at just 1 per cent or so, compared with nearly 5 per cent in India. Yet, the rate of poverty reduction (in terms of annual percentage reduction of the 'head-count ratio') was much larger in Brazil, where this was also a period of substantial redistribution, in contrast with India where economic inequality went up.[27] Further investigations, based on updated data series extending to the late 2000s, corroborate the role of economic redistribution in Brazil's recent experience of poverty reduction.[28]

The redistribution initiatives relevant to poverty included various social assistance programmes (including large pension schemes), minimum wage policies, and, from 2003 onwards, the well-known *Bolsa Família* programme of targeted cash transfers, which covers about one fourth of the population – mainly those outside the formal sector of the economy.[29] These programmes have had a limited impact on the extent of *inequality* in Brazil – indeed, Brazil is still one of the most unequal countries in the world (along with India, China and South Africa). But they certainly had a major impact on poverty, especially extreme poverty.[30]

Less well known than *Bolsa Família* or *Fome Zero* (Zero Hunger, Brazil's food security initiative), but no less important, is the sustained expansion and improvement of Brazil's schooling system during the last twenty years or so.[31] Even in Brazil's highly unequal society, the proportion of children attending private schools at the primary level (about 10 per cent) is much smaller than in India (nearly 30 per cent), and unlike in India, it does not seem to be growing.[32] Government schools, for their part, have gone through major reforms. For instance, municipalities have started assuming the main responsibility for school management; a 'funding equalization law' has been enacted to ensure a fair distribution of education funds; pupil achievements have been carefully monitored through regular, standardized country-wide school tests; conditional cash transfers (initially *Bolsa Escola*, and later *Bolsa Família*) have been used to promote school attendance; and (very importantly) Brazil has invested heavily in pre-school education, which has been extended to more than 80 per cent of young children.[33]

The results have been impressive. At least three major educational improvements have been well documented. First, there was a large increase in school attendance and schooling attainment in the younger age groups. By 2009, school attendance in the age group of 6–14 years was 98 per cent, and literacy in the age group of 15–24 years was also 98 per cent.[34] Second, this period also saw a sharp reduction in educational *inequality*. For instance, the Gini coefficient of years of schooling dropped from 0.41 in 1995 to 0.29 in 2009.[35] Education reforms, including the funding equalization policy, also helped the lagging regions (such as the north-east) to catch up with the rest of the country. Third, pupil achievements (as measured by test scores) dramatically improved, albeit from what was, in an international perspective, a low base. In fact, between 2000 and 2009, Brazil had one of the fastest rates of improvement of student test scores among all those included in the Programme of International Student Assessment (PISA).[36] To view the speed of progress in these different dimensions from another angle, by 2009 the average schooling opportunities of children from the *poorest* income quintile in Brazil were not far from those enjoyed by children from the *richest* income quintile were receiving just 16 years earlier.[37]

Social spending as a proportion of GDP is now higher in Brazil (about 25 per cent) than in any other Latin American country except Cuba (about 40 per cent), and about four times the corresponding ratio in India (a measly 6 per cent or so).[38] As in many other Latin American countries, a substantial proportion of this social expenditure (especially social security expenditure) has regressive features, in the sense that it disproportionately benefits comparatively well-off sections of the population.[39] But recent initiatives have firmly extended the reach of social support to the underprivileged, and corrected the earlier biases to a significant extent. These achievements and the speed of change – most of this happened within twenty years of a democratic constitution being promulgated – are important facts from which encouraging lessons can be drawn.

COMPARISONS WITHIN INDIA AND THE INTERNAL LESSONS[40]

While India has much to learn from international experience, it also has a great deal to learn from the diversity of experiences *within* this large country. The regional records are very diverse indeed, and if some states were separated out from the rest of India, we would see a very different picture from the average for the country taken together. A number of Indian states – Kerala and Tamil Nadu, for example – would be at the top of the South Asian comparisons if they were treated as separate countries, and others – Uttar Pradesh and Madhya Pradesh, for example – would do enormously worse. But what is most powerfully apparent from these interstate comparisons within India is just how much this diverse country can learn from the experiences of the more successful states within it.

These contrasts are indeed sharp. For instance, whereas female life expectancy is 77 years in Kerala, it is still below 65 years in many of the large north Indian states. Further, these contrasts reinforce, in many ways, the lessons of comparative international experiences for development strategy. In particular, the Indian states that have done well tend to have been those which had laid solid foundations of participatory development and social support early on, and actively promoted the expansion of human capabilities, especially in terms of education and health.

The interstate disparities are illustrated in Table 3.8, which presents a sample of basic development indicators relating to education, health and poverty.* We also present in Table 3.9 two summary indexes of deprivation: a standard 'human development index', which gives equal weight to the nine indicators given in Table 3.8, and the proportion of the population estimated to be living in 'multi-dimensional poverty'.[41]

Seven major states (with a combined population of 545 million in 2011, about half of India's population) have had poor social indicators for a long time, as well as high levels of poverty: Bihar, Chhattisgarh, Jharkhand, Madhya Pradesh, Odisha, Rajasthan and Uttar Pradesh.[42] The dismal nature of living conditions in these states, for large sections of the population, is evident from Table 3.8. These figures show, for instance, that less than half of all children aged 8–11 years are able to pass a very simple reading test (going a little beyond liberal definitions of 'literacy') in some of these states, only 23 per cent of young children are fully immunized in Uttar Pradesh, and more than half of the population in Bihar lives below the Government of India's extremely low poverty line.

In international perspective, some of these states are not very different from the poorer countries of Africa in the intensity of human deprivation. This is reaffirmed by the recent work on multi-dimensional poverty. For instance, computations of the 'multi-dimensional poverty index' (MPI) place states like Bihar and Jharkhand in the same category as some of the poorest African countries – countries like Mozambique and Sierra Leone.[43] Further, in terms of MPI, the seven states mentioned earlier (Bihar, Chhattisgarh, Jharkhand, Madhya Pradesh, Odisha, Rajasthan and Uttar Pradesh) are more or less on a par – taken together – with the 27 poorest countries of Africa, and have roughly the same population.[44] What the multi-dimensional poverty figures suggest, roughly speaking, is that *living conditions in*

---

* A wider range of state-specific indicators are presented in the Statistical Appendix, Tables A.3 and A.4, not only for the major states but also for the smaller states of the north-eastern region. Some of these smaller states, such as Sikkim (and, in some respects, Manipur, Mizoram and Tripura), have done comparatively well in various dimensions of human development. These experiences deserve more attention than they have received so far.

Table 3.8: Selected Indicators for Major Indian States, 2005

	Education-related indicators			Health-related indicators			Poverty-related indicators		
	Female literacy, age 15–49 years, 2005–6 (%)	Proportion of children aged 6–14 attending school, 2005–6 (%)	Proportion of children aged 8–11 who pass a simple reading test, 2004–5 (%)	Under-5 mortality rate, 2005–6 (per 1,000)	Proportion of young children fully immunized, 2005–6 (%)	Proportion of adult women with low BMI, 2005–6 (%)	Proportion of population below the poverty line, 2004–5 (%)	Proportion of population in India's lowest wealth quintile, 2005–6 (%)	Median per capita income, 2004–5 (Rs/year)
Andhra Pradesh	49.6	81.4	50	63.2	46.0	33.5	29.6	10.8	6,241
Assam	63.0	84.4	72	85.0	31.4	36.5	34.4	19.8	6,000
Bihar	37.0	62.2	44	84.8	32.8	45.1	54.4	28.2	3,530
Chhattisgarh	44.9	81.1	61	90.3	48.7	43.4	49.4	39.6	5,306
Gujarat	63.8	83.0	64	60.9	45.2	36.3	31.6	7.2	6,300
Haryana	60.4	84.1	65	52.3	65.3	31.3	24.1	4.1	9,443
Himachal Pradesh	79.5	96.2	83	41.5	74.2	29.9	22.9	1.2	9,942
Jammu & Kashmir	53.9	87.8	40	51.2	66.7	24.6	13.1	2.8	8,699
Jharkhand	37.1	71.7	59	93.0	34.2	43.0	45.3	49.6	4,833
Karnataka	59.7	84.0	53	54.7	55.0	35.5	33.3	10.8	5,964
Kerala	93.0	97.7	82	16.3	75.3	18.0	19.6	1.0	9,987
Madhya Pradesh	44.4	89.1	46	94.2	40.3	41.7	48.6	36.9	4,125

Maharashtra	70.3	87.2	66[a]	46.7	58.8	36.2	38.2	10.9	7,975[a]
Odisha	52.2	77.5	58	90.6	51.8	41.4	57.2	39.5	3,450
Punjab	68.7	85.3	66	52.0	60.1	18.9	20.9	1.4	9,125
Rajasthan	36.2	75.4	55	85.4	26.5	36.7	34.4	24.2	6,260
Tamil Nadu	69.4	93.9	79	35.5	80.9	28.4	29.4	10.6	7,000
Uttar Pradesh	44.8	77.2	39	96.4	23.0	36.0	40.9	25.3	4,300
Uttarakhand	64.6	90.4	63	56.8	60.0	30.0	32.7	6.0	6,857
West Bengal	58.8	79.7	51	59.6	64.3	39.1	34.2	25.2	6,250
India	**55.1**	**79.6**	**54**	**74.3**	**43.5**	**35.6**	**37.2**	**20.0**	**5,999**

[a] Including Goa.

Sources: Figures with 2005–6 as reference year are from the third National Family Health Survey (International Institute for Population Sciences, 2007, and state reports for school attendance); poverty estimates for 2004–5 are from the Tendulkar Committee Report (as reprinted in Government of India, 2012c); reading proficiency and median per capita income are from the India Human Development Survey (Desai et al., 2010). For further details, see Drèze and Khera (2012a).

Table 3.9
Human Development and Multi-dimensional Poverty:
Summary Indexes for Major Indian States

	Human Development Index, 2005[a]	Proportion of population 'multi-dimensionally poor', 2005–6[b] (%)
Kerala	0.970	12.7
Himachal Pradesh	0.846	29.9
Tamil Nadu	0.749	30.5
Punjab	0.742	24.6
Haryana	0.670	39.3
Jammu & Kashmir	0.655	41.0
Uttarakhand	0.612	39.5
Maharashtra	0.601	37.9
Gujarat	0.520	41.0
Karnataka	0.500	43.2
Andhra Pradesh	0.458	44.5
West Bengal	0.446	57.4
Assam	0.441	60.1
Rajasthan	0.301	62.8
Chhattisgarh	0.271	69.7
Madhya Pradesh	0.230	68.1
Odisha	0.229	63.2
Uttar Pradesh	0.212	68.1
Jharkhand	0.170	74.8
Bihar	0.106	79.3
India	0.400	53.7

[a] Based on National Family Health Survey (NFHS) data for 2005–6, National Sample Survey (NSS) data for 2004–5, and India Human Development Survey (IHDS) data for 2004–5.
[b] Based on National Family Health Survey (NFHS) data for 2005–6.

Sources: The human development index presented here is an unweighted average of normalized values for each of the 9 indicators presented in Table 3.8 (see Drèze and Khera, 2012a). On the multi-dimensional poverty figures, see Alkire and Seth (2012). The states are ranked in decreasing order of HDI for 2005.

the poorer half of India are not much better, if at all, than in the poorer half of Africa.

Looking at the other end of the scale, in Table 3.9, three major states distinguish themselves with relatively high levels of human development: Kerala, Himachal Pradesh and Tamil Nadu. Punjab and Haryana are not very far behind; in fact, in terms of 'multi-dimensional poverty', Punjab actually does a little better than both Himachal Pradesh and Tamil Nadu. There are, however, two particular reasons to give special attention to Kerala, Himachal Pradesh and Tamil Nadu. First, they do much better than Punjab and Haryana by gender-related and child-related indicators. Second, Kerala, Himachal Pradesh and Tamil Nadu are all states that were very poor not so long ago (say in the 1950s and 1960s) – unlike Punjab and Haryana, which have been relatively prosperous regions of India for a long time.[45] This adds to the interest of their recent achievements – their performance in enhancing living conditions as well as their success in raising per capita income along with the expansion of human capability.

Kerala's social achievements have a long history and have been widely discussed – including in our earlier work.[46] What is interesting is that Kerala continues to make rapid progress on many fronts, and that its lead over other states shows no sign of diminishing over time. Since the 1980s there have been regular warnings – coming mainly from commentators suspicious of state intervention – that Kerala's development achievements were unsustainable, or deceptive, or even turning into a 'debacle'.[47] As it turns out, however, the improvement of living conditions in Kerala has not only continued but even accelerated, with help from rapid economic growth, which in turn has been assisted by Kerala's focus on elementary education and other basic capabilities.

Like Kerala, Himachal Pradesh launched ambitious social programmes, including a vigorous drive toward universal elementary education, at a time when it was still quite poor – the early 1970s.[48] The speed of progress has been truly impressive: as Table 3.8 illustrates, Himachal Pradesh is now on a par with Kerala as far as elementary education is concerned, and other social indicators are also catching up. Within forty years or so, Himachal Pradesh has made the transition from severe social backwardness and deprivation (as the region was seen then) to a relatively advanced state with a widely shared freedom from abject deprivation.

Tamil Nadu is another interesting case of a state achieving rapid progress over a relatively short period, though it started from appalling levels of poverty, deprivation and inequality. Throughout the 1970s and 1980s official poverty estimates for Tamil Nadu were higher than the corresponding all-India figures, for both rural and urban areas (about half of the population was below the Planning Commission's measly poverty line).[49] Much as in Kerala earlier, social relations were also extremely oppressive, with Dalits (scheduled castes) parked in separate hamlets (known as 'colonies'), generally deprived of social amenities, and often prevented from asserting themselves even in simple ways like wearing a shirt or riding a bicycle. It is during that period that Tamil Nadu, much to the consternation of many economists, initiated bold social programmes such as universal midday meals in primary schools and started putting in place an extensive social infrastructure – schools, health centres, roads, public transport, water supply, electricity connections, and much more. This was not just a reflection of kind-heartedness on the part of the ruling elite, but an outcome of democratic politics, including organized public pressure. Disadvantaged groups, particularly Dalits, had to fight for their share at every step.[50] Today, Tamil Nadu has some of the best public services among all Indian states, and many of them are accessible to all on a non-discriminatory basis. Tamil Nadu's experience will be discussed again in Chapter 6, with special reference to health and nutrition.

While each of these experiences tends to be seen, on its own, as some sort of confined 'special case', it is worth noting that the combined population of these three states is well above 100 million. Tamil Nadu alone had a population of 72 million in 2011, larger than most countries in the world. Further, the notion that these states are just 'outliers' overlooks the fact that their respective development trajectories, despite many differences, have shared features of much interest. First, active social policies constitute an important aspect of this shared experience. This is particularly striking in the vigour of public education, but it also extends to other domains, such as health care, social security and public amenities.

Second, these states have typically followed universalistic principles in the provision of essential public services. This is especially noticeable in the case of Tamil Nadu, as will be further discussed in Chapter 6, but the point also applies to Himachal Pradesh and Kerala. The basic principle is that facilities such as school education, primary health care, midday meals, electricity connections, ration cards and drinking water should as far as possible be made effectively available to all on a non-discriminatory basis, instead of being 'targeted' to specific sections of the population. In fact, in many cases the provision of essential services and amenities has not only been universal but also free.*

Third, these efforts have been greatly facilitated by a functioning and comparatively efficient administration. The governments involved have delivered their services in traditional lines, and there has been little use of recently favoured short-cuts such as the use of para-teachers (rather than regular teachers), making conditional cash transfers, or reliance on school vouchers for private schools (rather than building government schools). The heroes in these successful efforts have been 'old-fashioned' public institutions – functioning schools, health centres, government offices, Gram Panchayats (village councils) and cooperatives. These traditional public institutions have left much room for private initiatives at a later stage of development, but they have laid the foundations of rapid progress in each of these cases.

Fourth, dealing with social inequality has also been an important part of these shared experiences. In each case, the historical burden of social inequality has been significantly reduced in one way or another. In Kerala and Tamil Nadu, principles of equal citizenship and universal entitlements were forged through sustained social reform movements as well as fierce struggles for equality on the part of underprivileged groups – especially Dalits, who used to receive abominable treatment and have to continue their battle to reverse the old handicaps altogether.[51] Himachal Pradesh benefited from a more favourable social environment, including relatively egalitarian social norms and a strong tradition of cooperative action. While substantial inequalities

---

* This approach is consistent with growing evidence of the strongly adverse incentive effects of 'user fees' (that is, charging beneficiaries) in the context of essential public services, especially related to health and education. These and other aspects of the delivery of supportive public services are discussed more fully in Chapter 7.

of class, caste and gender remain in each case, the underprivileged have at least secured an active – and expanding – role in public life and democratic institutions.

Fifth, these experiences of rapid social progress are not just a reflection of constructive state policies but also of people's active involvement in democratic politics. The social movements that fought traditional inequalities (particularly caste inequalities) are part of this larger pattern.[52] These social advances, the spread of education, and the operation of democratic institutions (with all their imperfections) enabled people – men and women – to have a say in public policy and social arrangements, in a way that has yet to happen in many other states.

Last but not least, there is no evidence that the cultivation of human capability has been at the cost of conventional economic success, such as fast economic growth. On the contrary, these states have all achieved fast rates of expansion, as indeed one would expect, both on grounds of causal economic relations and on the basis of international experience (including the 'east Asian' success story). While many of their big social initiatives and achievements go back to earlier times, when these states were not particularly well-off, today Kerala, Himachal Pradesh and (to a lesser extent) Tamil Nadu have some of the highest per capita incomes and lowest poverty rates among all Indian states (see Table 3.8). Economic growth, in turn, has enabled these states to sustain and consolidate active social policies. This is an important example of the complementarity between economic growth and public support, discussed earlier.

Not so long ago, Kerala was considered as an anomaly of sorts among Indian states. Its distinct social history and political culture appeared to set it apart, and to make it difficult for any other state to follow a similar route. Today, the situation looks a little different. Kerala is still ahead in many ways, but some other states have also made great strides in improving the quality of life – not in exactly the same way but in ways that share many interesting features with Kerala's own experience. Other states have good reason to learn from these positive experiences, even as India also learns from the successes and failures in the rest of the world.

4

Accountability and Corruption

On the shores of a man-made lake in Sonebhadra District (the Govind Ballabh Pant Sagar in Uttar Pradesh) there is a huge power plant operated by the National Thermal Power Corporation (NTPC). When one of us visited the NTPC headquarters, located on a pleasant green campus near the power plant, he found that a large number of air conditioners were switched on full blast throughout the day, even in the deserted lobby of the guest house (this was in the middle of the summer). Just outside the boundary walls of the campus, people from the Dom community (a scheduled caste), who have been working as 'sweepers' for the NTPC for twenty-five years, live in shacks, without any electric connections (or any other modern amenity). When asked, they said that they were afraid of losing their jobs if they complained about their predicament. A little further on, people who have been displaced by the power plant without any significant compensation are somehow trying to rebuild their lives. Like their Dom neighbours, they too have no electricity connections, and they are also afraid to complain.

The operation of the public sector is a matter of general interest in every country in the world, because all countries have one. The size and extent of the public sector do, of course, vary from country to country, but despite these variations, the problem of achieving accountability in the public sector arises everywhere. Particular to India is the combination of insistence – for entirely plausible reasons – on having a large public sector, combined with a fairly comprehensive neglect of accountability in operating this large sector. Given the size of the public sector and the crucial role it plays in the Indian development strategy, it is particularly important to ask how the accountability of the public sector should be developed and strengthened. The unfortunate fact is that the overwhelming focus of the public-private debate up to now has been on the extent to which the economy and the people 'need' a well-run public sector, rather than on exactly how the supposedly required public institutions should be run, and what would make the decision makers and operators involved accountable and responsible.

The presumption that there is something politically reactionary about raising the question of accountability in the public sector is far too common. It also reflects a serious confounding of two different questions:

1. In what areas can the public sector, given feasibly good arrangements, serve the interests of the public better than the private sector?
2. How can public sector institutions be made accountable so that they can serve well the purposes for which they are set up?

To insist on the legitimacy of the second question does not in any way undermine the relevance of the first.

On the first question, the case for going beyond private profit calculations in making economic decisions is strong, particularly in a country like India. The existence of what economists call externalities – like the pollution of air or water, or denuding of natural resources – tends everywhere to drive a wedge between private gains and social benefits. Similarly, asymmetric information between the buyers and sellers, and more generally a lack of adequate knowledge on the part of the uninformed or ill-informed to choose sensibly, can make the search for private profits diverge from the goals of social welfare. The absence of competition can also be a reason for worrying about artificially high prices of products that competition – had it been present – could have cut down.* A further reason for avoiding complete reliance on private-sector allocations is poverty and inequality. Since profitability is conditional on the ability of the purchaser, or the consumer, to pay,

---

* As John Vickers and George Yarrow noted in their classic work on 'privatization', relying on privatization can work well when there is competition – in a way it may not be able to when there is none, or little (Vickers and Yarrow, 1988).

private profits can often be a very inadequate guide to the priorities of public need. Some of these problems can be dealt with by instituting appropriate taxes and subsidies, but many of them, such as the difficulties of asymmetric information or of monopoly power (when they are strong), cannot be adequately addressed through those instruments.

The case for having well-run public enterprises can, thus, be strong, in addition to the need for well-delivered basic public services (they are typically delivered, across much of the world, by the government). There are also, of course, many areas in which the private sector has done excellent work already in India, and contributed to the country's general prosperity. We doubt that many Indians are pining for a public-sector take-over of the production and operation of mobile phones or information technology. The record of the public sector in many economic fields, from collectivist agriculture to state-run hotels, is by now fairly comprehensively tarnished across the world. And yet there are other areas (particularly in education, health care, nutrition, among others) where the need for a public sector can be very strong indeed, and where it can make a major contribution not only to the well-being of the people but also to the rest of the economy (including individual initiatives and the private sector). We shall return to this issue in subsequent chapters, particularly in the context of the need for public involvement in the provision of medical care, elementary and secondary schooling, and related facilities.

Having said this, the need to distinguish between the two questions posed earlier remains, and the answer to the first is obviously contingent on the second. It is difficult to deny that the operational record of public enterprises in India is rarely good and often disastrous. Of course, the private sector too can be very inefficient, but there is something of accountability there to the extent that ineptitude generates private losses, or reduces private profits, and would tend to be penalized by the logic of business operations and by the discipline of the market. It is, of course, true (as we have just discussed) that private costs and benefits may depart substantially, in many cases, from public interest and social costs and benefits, and that scepticism about the private sector being the solution to all problems cannot be dismissed just because that sector does have a system of accountability anchored within the limits of its own logic – that of profit-making. The adequacy of a system of accountability cannot be divorced from the goals being pursued. However, just because the pursuit of private profits may take us, in many cases, away from public interest, it should not be presumed that a public enterprise, by contrast, will do better, without a proper system of accountability and critical scrutiny.

The argument for public involvement is strongly dependent on the possibility of well-functioning and accountable delivery systems and public enterprises. The tragedy in India has been that most of the political debates have tended to avoid getting into the question of accountability of the public sector, *either* through rubbishing the public sector altogether, in contrast with the allegedly immaculate virtues of private enterprise, *or* through rubbishing the private sector, in contrast with an imagined world of dedicated public servants doing their social duties with admirable efficiency and humanity. We have to avoid being captivated by either of these fairy tales.

In emphasizing the critical importance of this question, we do not have to believe that a solution will emerge as soon as we look for it. But we do contend that a solution is unlikely to emerge *unless* we look for it.* That search has been a hugely missed priority in Indian political economy, and the issue is only just beginning to receive the attention it deserves. We shall return to this issue presently.

INFRASTRUCTURE AND POWERLESSNESS

The issue of accountability arises, at different levels, in coming to grips with infrastructure planning in India. The neglect of infrastructure in India – both physical infrastructure (power, roads, water supply, sanitation, and other physical facilities) as well as social (education, health care, and other contributors to the development of

---

* There is also a need for objective testing of the relative merits of different kinds of public intervention. Abhijit Banerjee and Esther Duflo have shown the possibility of using randomized trials to establish solidly researched conclusions in areas in which such empirical testing had been previously taken to be impossible or unusable; see their *Poor Economics* (Cambridge, MA: MIT Press, 2011).

human capability) – has been amazingly widespread. In addition to problems of accountability at the level of individual enterprises, there are serious issues at a higher level, dealing with rules of operation for whole sectors.

A telling example of failure of public delivery was the crippling power blackout across the country at the end of July 2012, which plunged half the country in darkness, and earned India the reputation of being 'the blackout nation' (as *The Economist* put it). How could this happen? Explanations are plentiful:

- The expansion of the productive capacity of electricity has not kept up with demand.
- Some states draw more power than their allocated quota without informing the central authorities that control the grids.
- There is no system by which states are prevented quickly enough from drawing more than their quota.
- A delayed monsoon in parts of the country led to a greater use of electricity, of which the authorities took little note.
- A large proportion of electricity supply is actually stolen or unaccounted for, and while those in charge know this, they are not inclined to engage with the problem as it can have significant political consequences.
- There is no effective early warning system to alert the authorities that something is beginning to go wrong.

There are many other 'mini-explanations' as well. There is some truth to most of them, and yet the signal which the massive blackout conveys exceeds the sum of the different identified parts.

If explanations of power blackout are plentiful, so are the proposals for instant solutions that would, allegedly, remedy the problems in no time. One idea is that because the problem arises from the fact that the power sector is in the hands of the government, it should simply be privatized, as allegedly it is in China. The Chinese power sector does indeed work quite well in comparison with its Indian counterpart, and the admiration for the Chinese achievements (including near-universal access to electricity) is largely well deserved. However, as was discussed in Chapter 1, this particular explanation for China's success in this field does not work very well, since the Chinese power sector is not actually privatized: power production and supply in both China and India are predominantly state-controlled. There are, to be sure, private power companies in China that are part of the total picture, but so there are in India (including Reliance Power, Tata Power and others). Where the Chinese score higher is in running a more efficient and in fact a more sensible state-led power sector.

Part of the difference lies in the fact that China has tended to invest more than twice as much as a proportion of GDP on the power sector than has India. China has built capacity in generating power, as its need expanded, in a way that India has not.[1] The Chinese also seem to generate a significant return on their investment in power, whereas the Indian power sector is perpetually in deficit, and – as Pranab Bardhan notes – the need for subvention of the State Electricity Boards by many state governments tends to exceed 10 per cent of the states' fiscal deficits.[2] Why are we in the grip of perpetual deficits in the power sector?

This too is ultimately a problem of accountability. Even at the highest levels, the central guardians of Indian power strategy seem to face little pressure to get things right, and are not asked to take responsibility for the terrible state of power planning in India. A basic lack of systems of control and accountability within Indian power generation and distribution was painfully obvious when the blackout occurred, and yet it seemed impossible to pin responsibility on any particular power boss. It is easy enough – and appropriate too – to ask for more competence in running the enterprises and the entire system of power generation and distribution, but the basic lacuna is the almost total absence of responsibility attributed to particular persons who take decisions and command what should be done, without having to face any consequences themselves if and when things go badly wrong.[3] That lack of responsibility seems to run through all the layers of hierarchy, and the calamity that occurred in July 2012 – smaller examples of which take place day in, day out – was made to look like an unexpected natural disaster (such as an earthquake), untouched by human hands. As this book goes to press, in early 2013, the power sector still has no proper system of accountability, and is also kept perpetually starved of cash and dependent on huge state-financed handouts that pull money away from other urgent social purposes.

A related reason for the limited reach and capacity of the Indian power sector is the practice of tolerating (and, in due course, underwriting) the huge losses accrued by state power utilities, which arise to a great extent from badly reasoned electricity subsidies, poor collection of electricity charges, power theft, transmission losses and other costs – largely for the benefit of heavy consumers who have the political clout to prevent any attempt to enforce cost-recovery measures. This odd system leads to a huge loss of public revenue, rather than strong incentives to invest in the power sector (as in China). In fact, when electricity is supplied at a loss, distribution companies have little to gain from extending the reach of electricity connections, or even from supplying power without interruptions.[4] While the vocal advocates of subsidized power get what they want, many of the poorest Indians, about a third of the population (around 400 million people), are not even connected to any electric supply. It is amazing how little hearing the 'perpetually powerless' receive compared with grievances – important as they are – of those who only lose electricity from time to time. In the unaccountable chaos of electricity planning in India the worst sufferers attract the least attention.

THE POLITICS OF SUBSIDIZING POWERFUL CONSUMERS

The bankruptcy of the power sector in India is part of a general political problem that has to be addressed at an overall level and involves the need to resist (or counter) the political influence of privileged pressure groups. Even though this difficulty manifests itself directly only at the end of the electricity chain – in the so-called 'last mile' of retail distribution when power is sold to the consumers – the large economic drain involved also influences the arrangements that can be made for the earlier stages of power generation and transmission.

India's power sector makes huge losses, by selling electricity below the cost of supply (and even providing free power for agriculture in some states) as well as through implicit subsidies associated with transmission losses, power theft, non-payment of bills and so on. These consumer subsidies, explicitly made or implicitly accepted, tend to be quite regressive, and have led to serious problems of loss and potential insolvency for the Indian power sector, reducing investment in power generation and transmission capacity, and to a continued absence of electric connections to hundreds of millions of people. They also divert very significant amounts of public resources to subsidizing the power consumption of relatively better-off consumers, using money that could have been utilized to help the expansion of education for the unschooled and provide health care for the medically deprived – or for that matter to extend electricity connections to those who are permanently without them. To stop that drain and face the pressure groups head-on are hard political tasks, and unless Indians – government servants, politicians, people at large – rise to this challenge, the Indian power sector will continue to fail (no matter who owns it), and there will continue to be transfers of money to the relatively affluent.* This too is an issue of accountability, fed by the bias of public discussion in the politics of India (which is one of the main themes of this book). Nothing is easier for the government than to let the present irrational and inequitable system of transfers continue unchallenged. There are protests on the streets from well-organized groups when the regressive consumer subsidies are cut, but none when those without electricity connection remain unconnected, nor when money is drawn from the pool of public resources that could have been used instead for more urgent or worthwhile social purposes.

Similar issues arise with the pricing policies of many other sources of power, such as petrol and diesel, with the same implicit priority being given to the relatively affluent, rather than those who have little

---

* We are not arguing against subsidizing any electricity consumption no matter what the circumstances. There may be a good case, for example, for subsidizing the power consumption of poorer households. Price discrimination and differentiated tariffs (including what are known in India as 'telescopic tariffs') are common features of electricity pricing in many countries, and are not difficult to implement if electricity consumption is properly metered. In some Indian states, differential pricing has been used with relatively good effect to enable poor households to use electricity. Our argument is that all such subsidies have to be carefully scrutinized and accountably assessed. There is no convincing justification for regressive consumer subsidies for privileged power users, resulting from pressures by users of electricity who wield influence across India today.

means – and no instruments – to make significant use of artificially cheapened fuel. Aside from privileged urban residents who enjoy the luxury of modern gadgets and affluent lifestyles at public expense, major beneficiaries of these power subsidies include telecom companies and air-conditioned shopping malls.[5] Attempted reductions of petrol or diesel subsidies tend to generate a huge outcry from the powerful lobbies of the biggest consumers, and are often abandoned within a few days. Keeping up these regressive subsidies placates the vocal people in relatively privileged positions – they are not tycoons, but they are affluent in a way the bulk of the population of India is not. Such placating may be politically very useful for the opposition parties to 'demand', and for the ruling government to 'accept', but it is a real misnomer to describe such concessions to the powerful as 'populist' policies (which they are sometimes called), since they are actually of little use to the bulk of the population.[6]

A similar point applies again to the fertilizer subsidy, which has been an enormous drain on India's public finances for a long time, costing about 1.5 per cent of the country's total GDP in 2008–9, when public expenditure on health (by central and state governments combined) was *less* than 1.5 per cent of GDP – a fairly transparent case of distorted priorities. While the fertilizer subsidy possibly played a useful role when it was introduced in the late 1970s (in the early days of the Green Revolution), it would be hard to justify today – certainly at that scale – given its distributionally regressive nature as well as its adverse environmental impact. It is regressive not only because it disproportionately benefits larger farmers, but also because the main beneficiaries have been powerful fertilizer companies.[7] While there has been some rationalization in recent years, the fertilizer subsidy remains very large – close to Rs 70,000 crores (about 0.8 per cent of India's GDP) in 2011–12.

None of this is to say that all subsidies are wrong or should be withdrawn. On the contrary, the case against regressive subsidies rests partly on the possibility of making much better use of the same resources for the benefit of the underprivileged. What is sorely lacking in current debates is a discriminating and objective assessment of who benefits from different types of subsidies.[8] For instance, very confusing use is often made of terms such as 'middle class' or 'aam aadmi' (the common man) to project relatively privileged groups as under-dogs (we shall have more to say on this in Chapter 9). The real underdogs, meanwhile, hardly figure in the entire debate.

The pernicious role of regressive subsidies applies not only to those that are visibly and explicitly given, such as subsidies on diesel or fertilizer, but also to implicit subsidies, notably those arising from what the Finance Ministry calls 'revenue forgone'– tax revenue that could have been collected, but was forgone on account of various exemptions and incentives. Some of these exemptions and incentives could quite possibly be justified, but many others are nothing more than disguised handouts to powerful lobbies, especially corporate lobbies. The annual 'Revenue Forgone' statement released by the Finance Ministry estimates it to be an astounding Rs 529,432 crores in 2011–12, or more than 5 per cent of India's total GDP.[9] This includes more than Rs 57,000 crores of custom duties forgone on 'diamonds and gold' alone. We shall return, in Chapter 9, to the sad political fate of an attempt – a very small attempt – made in 2012–13 to achieve a marginal reduction in this implicit subsidy to jewellers and goldsmiths, which had to be promptly withdrawn as a result of vocal protests.[10]

As we have discussed earlier, and will scrutinize further on, the unequal power of the relatively privileged is a huge source of distortion of India's equitable development priorities, to which the country is meant – in theory – to be committed, going all the way back to the 'Directive Principles' of the Indian constitution. The challenge of accountability, which has many different aspects, is not ultimately detachable from the general problem of inequality of power between the relatively privileged and the rest, which is a pervasive feature of India's social landscape. This general problem will be the principal subject for examination in Chapters 8 and 9.

ENERGY COSTS, EXTERNALITIES AND UNCERTAINTY

If there are gross problems of operational efficiency and political accountability for the power sector in India, that sector also has to face problems of rational calculation in choosing between different forms of energy. The lines here are not so clearly drawn as they are in the case of the corruption of policy priorities related to the unequal power of different pressure groups. The choices over different sources of energy – coal, oil, gas, nuclear, solar and so on – demand technically informed attention, even though – as will be presently discussed – the interests of different groups of people are also involved in those choices.

India does have large coal reserves, even though the quantities that are actually being dug up at present by authorized organizations (primarily the state-owned Coal India) fall short, in terms of the immediate needs for power generation. The issue of digging is not, however, the only one to address here, and it may not even be the most significant, particularly in the long run. The environmental costs of relying on coal can be very damaging: this applies both to getting hold of the coal and to using it. Depending on its location and how the digging is undertaken, mining can be highly destructive of both trees and natural resources on the one hand, and human habitats on the other. Moving from mining coal to using it, coal burning generates major environmental adversities – both locally (through pollution) and globally (in terms of warming the atmosphere).

In addition to the short-run operational problem of providing vitally needed power, the long-run issue of rational choice between different forms of energy in India has to be addressed. The shortage of power, and even the kind of national blackout that India had in July 2012, may demand the digging of more coal and greater use of coal-based energy in the country, but there is also the larger social problem of its 'full cost', including the externalities generated by more digging and more burning of coal – for the country and for the world at large. The fact that India's power use is already quite significant as a proportion of power consumption in the world, and that it will very likely continue to expand fast given the growth of the Indian economy, makes it ethically unacceptable for India to worry only about the damage to its own local environment – bad enough as it is.

The market costs and social costs of power use tend to diverge because of externalities, including the emissions related both to the generation and the use of power. There are also social costs of mining, linked with dangers to human lives and the spoiling of local environments.

These externalities are not significantly controlled in any way at all in India. For example, there have been many cases of forcible and even brutal eviction of long-term residents from their land, often with little or no facility for resettlement or rehabilitation. The human costs of involuntary resettlement in India have been enormous, as environmental activists (among others) have pointed out.[11]

Market profits do not, of course, provide good social guidance here. Market decisions tend not to take externalities into account, unless the decisions are forced on them by law or public opinion, or unless they are influenced by taxes, subsidies, regulations or other tools of public finance. It would of course be more desirable if some major changes in human mentality made people think about the lives of others even when their own lives are not endangered, but given the values that dominate the market culture today in India, the likelihood of this happening any time soon is not very great.

This implies that market decisions on energy production will be typically based on incorrect social indicators of real costs and benefits, ignoring serious externalities. If we look at the cost of production of traditional types of energy, coal seems to be the cheapest, then fossil fuels of other kinds (including oil), with solar energy and wind power much more expensive as far as standard market calculations are concerned. One of the new forms of energy extraction in recent years has been the local excavation of shale gas, particularly in the USA, which we learn can be even cheaper than coal – though the process of fracking can have serious external costs for the neighbourhood. The costs of nuclear energy fall somewhere in between: here there are so many different cost estimates that it is hard to separate out science from advocacy. But there is considerable evidence that nuclear power can be produced at least more cheaply than power from oil, and could be less expensive than coal extraction as well (despite coal's lower market cost), once the externalities of emission and pollution of coal mining and use are included in the cost calculations.

Anti-emission activists, engaged in an all-out battle against global warming, often tend to take a relatively tolerant view of nuclear power for civilian use, for reasons that are easy to see. But it could be a very serious mistake to identify the externalities merely with carbon emissions and related pollution. Nuclear energy has its own externalities, which can be very large indeed – possibly even gigantic. It raises serious problems of waste disposal, something that could become more and more problematic as a country becomes increasingly dependent on nuclear power as a staple source of energy. In addition, there is the possibility of the theft of nuclear material by terrorists; there are dangers of nuclear accidents with catastrophic results; and there are risks of sabotage, possibly causing disastrous havoc.[12] The general recognition, based on cases of leak or scare (the latest at Fukushima Daiichi in 2011), that confident planning can go wrong – even in a country as well regulated as Japan – makes it hard to believe that the probability of an unforeseen mishap can be made zero or near-zero through precautionary steps. Like the notorious 'Indian blackout' of July 2012, the calamity may not be expected until it happens – when hindsight could offer plenty of reasons why it should have been expected.

The fact is that the Fukushima disaster occurred in a scientifically advanced country, with incomparably the most disciplined population in the world (evident, for instance, in Japan's remarkable ability to accomplish civil evacuation without a stampede); and yet the disaster caused some deaths and came close to creating far greater fatalities over a much larger region of Japan to which the nuclear clouds might have migrated (Tokyo too, we are told, could have been hit). This should be an alarm bell for energy planning across the world – even in France (despite the evident conviction there that nothing can go wrong with French measures of safety). There is such a web of secrecy around Indian nuclear power plants that reliable facts about them are hard to ascertain, but many commentators, including the International Atomic Energy Agency, have warned that there is enough evidence to suggest that the Indian civilian nuclear establishments are in fact particularly unsafe.[13] In general, this issue cannot but be a huge source of worry for the future of India – and for the world, as more and more countries fall increasingly for the apparent cheapness and environmental innocence of nuclear power. We have to take into account how widespread that danger may be as nuclear power becomes a staple source of energy across the world. Conglomerations of low probabilities can yield a very large sum (as J. B. S. Haldane made us understand almost a century ago), with horrifying prospects of an 'unexpected' decimation of human lives and habitats.

The environmental challenge seems now to be that we are caught between the old dangers of choking from traditional fuels (coal, oil and natural gas) and the new dangers of nuclear mishaps and contamination caused by accidents, but also possibly by sabotage and terrorist activities. The horns of a dilemma are clear enough here, but the solution need not be confined to choosing the lesser danger, after careful analysis of certainties and uncertainties (important as this must be in the short run). It also involves, ultimately, advancing the usability of other sources of energy (including solar energy and wind power) that do not produce either of the two large energy externalities (atmospheric pollution and the risk of nuclear disasters) which threaten the world today.

Externalities – even if estimated in probabilistic terms – are crucial. Given the market signals, alternative sources of power generation like wind and solar energy will never proceed very far without public support, which is quite limited as things stand – especially in contrast with India's lavish subsidies for conventional forms of energy, discussed earlier. We need powerful and well-assessed systems of incentives – through taxes and subsidies – to encourage the market to respond to the social needs, in addition to what state-supported research can achieve in public and private institutions. Solar energy and wind power may not have been adequately harnessed yet, but the technology will have to be developed with the creativity that human beings are capable of achieving. There is no reason why India, with its scientific talents and achievements, should not be a leading country exploring newer technology in this area of the greatest importance to the contemporary world.

CORRUPTION AND INSTITUTIONAL CHANGE

The issue of accountability relates closely to that of corruption, which has received a great deal of attention recently in Indian political debates. In the absence of good systems of accountability, there may not only be serious neglects of duties, but much temptation for officials to deliver at high 'prices' what they are actually supposed to deliver freely, as part of their job. This 'reward', aside from being an example of corruption based on official privilege, can also deflect a facility from those for whom it was meant to others who have the means and the willingness to buy favours. Corruption has become such an endemic feature of Indian administration and commercial life that in some parts of the country nothing moves in the intended direction unless the palm of the deliverer is greased.

It is good that this long-standing problem has become a widely discussed issue in recent years, generating a good deal of public discontent. This is as it should be, for corruption is a huge drag on the economy – and more immediately on the lives of the people of the country. However, democracy demands not only that grievances about terrible practices be widely aired, but also that this leads to serious *reasoning* about what can be sensibly done to remove the problem. The temptation to 'end corruption' by summary punishment delivered outside the Indian legal procedures, which seems to attract many people (not surprisingly, given their frustration with the existing legal actions), may be hugely counterproductive. Aside from the possibility of penalizing the accused (which could be erroneous), rather than the tried and the guilty, the procedures of instant summary justice generate the illusion – a costly illusion – that something is being done to change a corrupt system that generates corrupt practices. We have to seek real remedies that work, rather than pleasing retribution meted out to the guilty – or the accused. Corruption is fostered and nurtured by the absence of systems of accountability, which cannot be generated by the favoured gross means of retribution under summary justice. Even establishing some kind of super-powerful ombudsman, with draconian powers that are not tempered by judicial procedures (as in some versions of the proposed 'Lokpal Bill'), can generate more problems than it helps to solve. When a system is faulty, and gives people the wrong kind of incentives – to neglect one's duty and to reap illicit earnings without systematic penalties – what has to be amended is the system itself. For example, any system that leaves government officers effectively in sole command – or oligarchic dominance – over giving licences (say, import or mining licences), without checks and invigilation, can become a minefield of corrupt practices.*

What kind of institutional change could be considered and pursued? At least three different issues are central to the prevalence of corruption in public services. First, corruption flourishes in informational darkness: by nature, it is a secretive affair. An institutional change that fosters transparency and accessibility of information can be a real force in spoiling the prevalence of bribery and embezzlement. Second, corruption survives in a social environment of tolerance of misdeeds no matter how 'moral' people tend to see such misdeeds. A general belief that corruption is 'standard behaviour' and has to be tolerated unless the misdeeds are fully exposed and are unusually blatant can generate a situation where bribe-seekers are not under much pressure to reform, whether from others or from their own conscience. Third, corruption can be curtailed through a realistic threat of prosecution and sanction. But prosecution can be difficult to secure in the absence of witnesses prepared to speak out or of documentary evidence, and this can be a major barrier to suing or punishing a bribe-taker, which in turn tends to give a sense of immunity to the civil servants who seek – and get – bribes. There are also other issues involved (some of which were discussed earlier in this chapter), but the trio of informational lacuna, social leniency and prosecutional difficulty are among the factors that help to sustain a culture of corruption.

So what can be done about each of these underlying factors? There has been some genuine progress in tackling the first of these problems – that of hidden information. The Right to Information Act of 2005 has been a major step toward greater transparency and accessibility of information, making governmental affairs much more open to the

---

* See Gurcharan Das's (2012) *India Grows at Night* for an insightful analysis of the contribution of the 'license Raj' to generating corruption. Das is quite correct when he says, 'The lesson is to raise the capacity of the state or to limit its ambition' (p. 438). For reasons discussed extensively in this book, including the critical importance of well-functioning public services, the former cannot but remain a critically important engagement in India. That there is no inherent impossibility here is evident from the fact that most of the countries rated as 'least corrupt' in international comparisons (on which see Das, p.226), such as Sweden, Denmark, Canada and Singapore, have a significantly larger public sector as a proportion of the economy than India has.

public and helping to foster accountability as well as reduce corruption. Though very widely used already, the Act still has enormous further potential, notably through wider enforcement of norms of 'pro-active disclosure' as well as of mandatory penalties in the event of non-compliance. Other technological and social innovations, including the rapid spread of information technology and (in some states) the institutionalization of social audits, have also consolidated this trend toward transparency.[14] Here again, there are significant achievements as well as an enormous scope for further gains.

The second issue – that of social leniency – is also indirectly helped by greater transparency of information. For instance, the use of 'naming and shaming' demands naming before shaming can be attempted. Vigorous public campaigns and skilful use of the Right to Information Act, combined with constructive use of the media (including 'social media'), can be of great help in this respect, as well as in altering public perceptions of what is acceptable and what is not. This approach has already been used with good effect in various contexts, from public scrutiny of the backgrounds, including possible criminal records, of electoral candidates to the analysis of tax returns or business deals of public personalities, and can be taken much further than it has been so far. Underlying the reluctance to make larger use of this remedial measure is both what can be called an 'inertia of social norms' (a subject which we will take up presently) and a belief – often implicit – that norms cannot change much until and unless some prominent prosecution with punitive judgement draws heralded attention to the transgression involved.

It is on the third front – effective prosecution– that very little has been done so far. It is, of course, not surprising that acts of corruption are often difficult to expose and establish with sufficient confidence to justify prosecution. But even a relatively small number of cases of successful prosecution, if they are stringent and well publicized, could have important deterrent effects on the incidence of corruption.[15] Yet conviction rates are so 'ridiculously low' (as the Law Commission of India put it in its 160th report, submitted in 1999) that the Prevention of Corruption Act has not even achieved this minimal objective. The problem goes well beyond the routine difficulties of establishing guilt in corruption cases.

One aspect of the problem is the reluctance of witnesses to testify in court, or generally to provide evidence. In this connection, Kaushik Basu has argued for exempting bribe-givers from any punishment in cases where they are the victim of a so-called 'harassment bribe', that is, when a bribe is extracted from them for something to which they are entitled in the first place (for instance, getting a passport or residence certificate). This exemption would give such bribe-givers an incentive to report the bribe, and, knowing this, bribe-takers might hesitate to demand one in the first place.[16] As it happens, the Prevention of Corruption Act can already be read to have this exemption as a feature, but since the relevant sections of the Act (Sections 12 and 24) are actually open to different interpretations, there is perhaps a case for greater clarity about the immunity of a bribe-giver in the specific case of harassment bribes.[17]

Basu's proposal is certainly worth investigating, but there are also serious problems to consider. First, would the legalization of bribe-giving encourage morally upright people to give bribes which they would not have done otherwise? Second, would it be difficult to distinguish in practice between harassment bribes and other kinds of bribes where the bribe-giver is seeking to get an advantage to which he or she may *not* be entitled? Third, would the government undermine its credibility by doing something that looks like condoning an evil practice, particularly since the practical reasoning on the basis of which the distinction in culpability is made – between the bribe-giver and bribe-taker – would be missed by many people? These are the sorts of doubts and concerns that would have to be examined if the proposal were to be pursued beyond the exemption provisions already included in the Prevention of Corruption Act.[18]

More importantly perhaps, there are many other barriers to successful prosecution, including the inefficiencies of the legal system, political patronage of corrupt elements, lack of protection arrangements for whistle-blowers, and the general reluctance of state authorities to allow the prosecution of government employees. The last point is particularly important, since the ongoing rule is (amazingly) that no government employee can be prosecuted for dereliction of duty without the prior permission of the government, which is rarely granted. The Prevention of Corruption Act itself (Section 19) clearly states that 'previous sanction' of the concerned government is required even just to 'take cognizance' of any violation of the Act on the part of a public servant. This is, surely, an outrageous piece of bureaucratic safeguard that demands immediate repeal. There are similar, sweeping immunity provisions for government ministers and other elected representatives, and even when prosecution is allowed, the prosecution agencies (such as the Central Bureau of Investigation) are generally under the control of the government, making independent and impartial proceedings very difficult. Not surprisingly, Members of Parliament have been reluctant to dismantle this system of immunity and impunity, despite numerous demands and proposals for change. As A. G. Noorani, the eminent constitutional lawyer, aptly puts it: 'Despite their loud rancorous exchanges, political parties join hands against greater measures for accountability.'[19]

This is one illustration of a general difficulty in restoring accountability and eliminating corruption: the success of the battle depends a great deal on government initiatives to put in place the required safeguards, but the government has little incentive to make itself accountable to the people. This is one reason why efforts to secure the enactment of legislation aimed at restoring accountability (including the Right to Information Act) have often met with tremendous resistance. Overcoming this resistance is a major challenge for democratic practice.

CHANGE IS POSSIBLE

One of the biggest obstacles to restoring accountability is the hugely pessimistic impression that nothing can change in this respect, except possibly for the worse. This impression tends to be created by a fairly sustained experience of *declining* accountability in many areas of government activity and public life in India in recent decades. There is no reason, however, why these trends cannot be reversed. In fact, in some respects they have already started to be reversed, and there are several reasons to be hopeful.

First, people are becoming more vocal and demanding, partly due to rising levels of education. Evasion of duty is a form of exploitation, sometimes gross exploitation – as when government officers repeatedly ask helpless applicants to 'come tomorrow'. Education and self-confidence help to resist this abuse of power, both individually as well as through collective action.

Second, legislative and institutional changes can make a big difference. The most dramatic demonstration of this in the recent past is the Right to Information Act, mentioned earlier. India's Right to Information Act is one of the strongest in the world, and it has led to fairly radical changes, not only in terms of access to information for the public but also in terms of building a culture of transparency in public life and curbing abuses of state power. The Act guarantees unrestricted access to virtually any government document (in fact, not just 'documents' but also information in a much wider sense), to be given – within 30 days – to any citizen who applies for it. It also places on all public authorities an obligation of 'pro-active disclosure' of all essential information (that is, an obligation to place that information in the public domain without waiting for someone to ask for it). Any civil servant who fails to provide the requested information within 30 days is liable to be fined. These rights and obligations are actively guarded by powerful and independent 'information commissioners'. Perhaps the most encouraging feature of the Right to Information Act is its enormous popularity and widespread use: more than a million applications for information are being submitted each year under the Act, and a large proportion of them are successful in terms of obtaining the information being sought.[20]

The Right to Information Act is just one of a series of recent legislative and institutional initiatives aimed at curbing corruption and restoring accountability in public life. The much-debated Lokpal Bill is another well-known example, but there are many others, including laws or proposed laws dealing with redressal of grievances, judicial accountability, public procurement, electoral reforms, corporate lobbying, protection of whistle-blowers, and people's 'right to public service'. Many of these legislations are still pending, or have been passed in a diluted form, and some of them (including the Lokpal Bill) have serious flaws as things stand. Nevertheless, these initiatives represent an important development in Indian politics, and hold much promise.

Third, there is enormous scope for better use of modern technology in preventing corruption as well as dereliction of duty. Computerization is one obvious example. Several states, for instance, have been able to reduce embezzlement in the Public Distribution System (PDS) by computerizing the system, and others are moving rapidly in that direction.[21] Mobile phones have made it much easier to reach civil servants who used to be conveniently 'out of station' most of the time. Smart-cards make it possible to generate tamper-proof records, and biometrics can be a useful tool against identity fraud. All these innovations have their own limitations, and they can also be misused, or cause significant short-term disruption even when they help in the longer term.[22] They call for critical evaluation and public debate, but this does not detract from the possibility of putting these technical innovations to constructive use. An important challenge is to harness these new technologies for social purposes and not just private gain (as they are widely deployed already).

Fourth, the decentralization of power and decision-making is still at a very early stage. Most states have yet to build effective institutions of local governance such as Gram Panchayats and Gram Sabhas (Kerala is one notable exception). The head of a Gram Panchayat may not be intrinsically more people-friendly than a Block Development Officer, but at least he or she is more accessible as well as more answerable to the electorate. Also, there are reserved seats for women and disadvantaged communities in Panchayati Raj Institutions (PRIs), and there is some evidence that this 'assists in adequate delivery of local public goods to disadvantaged groups'.[23] There are also indications that, in states with active PRIs, people are learning quite quickly to use these institutions to voice their demands. For instance, one recent survey of 2,000 households in 105 villages of Rajasthan (not one of the most 'progressive' states in India) reported that three-quarters of the respondents 'engage public officials to demand services', and that in nearly two cases out of three, Gram Panchayat members are the first to be approached.[24] Here again, there are important possibilities for the future, even if the achievements so far are limited.

Fifth, all these developments, and other forms of democratic engagement with accountability issues (including media exposés and public debates), could lead to significant changes in social norms, habits of thought and work culture. This has, in fact, already happened to some extent. For instance, any civil servant who marks a file 'confidential' (as used to be done as a matter of routine, even when trivial information was at stake) is likely to be ridiculed today, unless the file pertains to something like national security. The discipline of transparency has been grudgingly accepted by the bureaucracy, but it is there to stay. It is not unreasonable to hope that, one day, a bureaucrat who asks for a bribe will also be ridiculed, admonished or reported, because it will just not be 'the done thing' by then, as it is today. It is when the thought of using public resources for private gain *stops occurring* to most people that the battle for corruption will really have been won.

Last but not least, the politics of public sector accountability are changing. Until recently, there was no organized constituency for the restoration of accountability in the public sector. On the political left, there was little acknowledgement of the problem – government employees have been the stronghold of India's mainstream Communist parties, who rarely entertained the idea that a government employee could be an obstacle to the pursuit of public welfare. On the hardened political right, the public sector was more or less written off anyway – a little more or a little less inefficiency was hardly an issue. The right-wing agenda was to privatize, not to improve, the public sector. All this produced an odd left-right 'coalition of apathy' towards public sector accountability.

This apathy, however, is beginning to subside as people are learning to demand greater accountability, and also in response to a variety of public initiatives and social movements that give expression to this demand.[25] Some of these initiatives are more inspiring than others, but the fact that elected representatives and civil servants are under much greater public scrutiny than they used to be is certainly a step forward. The legislative reforms mentioned earlier have happened largely in response to this growing popular movement for accountability in public life.

There is tentative evidence that some of these forces of change are beginning to make a difference. If one were to go by media reports, one would get the impression that corruption is increasing by leaps and bounds. And certain types of corruption, notably corporate-driven corruption, have indeed acquired unprecedented proportions. But it is also to some extent the case that corruption has become more *visible*, because of growing public scrutiny as well as the new powers to expose corruption (notably due to the Right to Information Act). There is little evidence that the public's general exposure to corruption in daily life is growing. In fact, according to the Centre for Media Studies' latest *India Corruption Study*, the proportion of Indians who felt that corruption had 'increased' in the previous year came down from 70 per cent in 2005 to 45 per cent in 2010; the proportion who felt it had 'decreased' rose fivefold, from 6 per cent to 29 per cent. More importantly perhaps, the proportion of rural households that had paid bribes during the previous year had also come down sharply, from 56 per cent in 2005 to 28 per cent in 2010.[26] There is no ground for smugness here, since both surveys point to rampant corruption, as well as to a still-dominant perception of rising corruption; nevertheless, it is important to take note of some significant signs of improvement, particularly the apparent decline in the proportion of households actually having to pay bribes.

It would be naive to assume that the battle for transparency and accountability is about to be won, but at least there is a serious battle taking place. Not so long ago, any attempt to build a campaign against corruption would have been seen as a case of hopeless romanticism. Today, millions of people are part of this battle in one way or another. Its outcome has a crucial bearing on the prospects for a more constructive influence of – and help from – the state in the lives of Indian citizens.

BEHAVIOUR AND SOCIAL NORMS

In addition to reform of systems, there is, of course, the important role of behavioural change, bringing norms of behaviour a little closer to the demands of accountability and public service. It cannot be denied that reform of the ways people behave is very difficult to bring about through policy decisions or public advocacy only. It takes time, and there is often a gap between intellectual persuasion and actual conduct. Scepticism for these reasons is well justified, but that scepticism need not suggest a fatalistic acceptance of the prevailing ways of behaving. What can lead to fatalism and cynicism in this field is the implicit and oft-repeated belief that human behaviour is basically self-centred and entirely oriented toward personal gain, no matter what social values are sacrificed in the process.

There is, however, plenty of evidence from every sphere of economic, political and social behaviour that various self-imposed behavioural rules are implicitly accepted by human beings in shaping their conduct, and people do make room for concerns other than narrow self-interest, in different ways, in actual human conduct. Even criminals bent on making money typically follow rules of good 'gang behaviour', and 'honour among thieves' is not just empty rhetoric. Much depends on what the established rules of behaviour are in a particular society. As Adam Smith discussed in his *The Theory of Moral Sentiments*:

> Many men behave very decently, and through the whole of their lives avoid any considerable degree of blame, who yet, perhaps, never felt the sentiment upon the propriety of which we found our approbation of their conduct, but acted merely from a regard to what they saw were the established rules of behaviour.

The trouble in India today is that in commercial dealings and in public life, the established rules of behaviour have progressively deteriorated, making illicit financial extraction a part of what is taken for granted. And yet the converse of a vicious circle is a virtuous circle, so that increased observation of standard rules of economic behaviour begets further compliance of those very rules.*

In proposing socially useful codes of conduct what is attempted is not the conversion of thoroughly self-centred people into fully altruistic human beings. It is a question of some shift of focus in multiple-objective behaviour that characterizes most human choices. That 'extra' element is present in every type of human behaviour related to social relations – involving family, friends, colleagues,

---

* On this see Adam Smith, *The Theory of Moral Sentiments* (1759, 1790). The quotation from Smith comes from page 162. See also the essays included in Sen (2002a).

political allies, fellow businessmen, other gang members and even all human beings.

However, efforts to change behavioural norms and practices, important as they are, cannot be a substitute for institutional reforms of other types. Organizing the economy and establishing rules governing the connection between business and politics demand legal and institutional attention, and attempts to advance that must not be given up in the hope of behavioural reform. Indeed, the institutional reforms and behavioural codes have to be seen as complementary to each other, and each can reinforce the other very substantially.

Finally, the activism of the media has a definite role to play both in demanding and encouraging institutional reforms, and in influencing human behaviour. Human beings respond to incentives. To want to do well for oneself is not the same as cupidity, and there is no dishonour to humanity in accepting that completely selfless behaviour is very rare. Incentives include not only financial gains and profits, but also public admiration and praise as a positive influence, and naming and shaming as a potential deterrent. Adam Smith noted that it is 'praise-worthiness' that should move us most in our moral thinking, but also recognized that it is actual praise that tends to encourage human beings (just as actual blame restrains them).[27] The media can play a major role here.

However, no system of media vigilance, important as it is, can be in itself a sufficient force to establish accountability or eliminate corruption. Nor can reasoned public discussion, on its own, make an adequate difference, despite the impact it may have on making people's intolerance of corrupt behaviour heard loud and clear. Nor can institutional reforms, through moving the pattern of incentives sharply away from the profitability of crooked behaviour towards 'normal' conduct, make the change on their own. But all these initiatives, undertaken together, can produce a substantial, if gradual, movement to changing a climate of tolerance of crookery, moving a society to a different set of – in Adam Smith's words – 'established rules of behaviour'.

There is no 'magic bullet' that can single-handedly bring more accountability into practice. We have to look, instead, to a combination of moves that have to include reforming the administrative and investigative systems, changing the incentive structure, making appropriate legal reforms, reducing the social tolerance of financial dishonesty, expanding the use of provisions already codified in the Right to Information Act and related legislations, and making investigative journalism aim at reporting unaccountable misbehaviour in a systematic way. The resulting progress may start only rather slowly, but the properties of a virtuous circle of behavioural shift can gather momentum to generate unexpected speed – judging from the experience of other countries in the world, such as Italy, which was caught, not long ago, in what used to be called a 'deontological crisis'.* The world has seen again and again that what appears hopelessly beyond reform may not be quite so hopeless.

---

* One of us had the privilege of serving as an official advisor to the Italian Parliament's 'Anti-Mafia Commission', chaired by Luciano Violante, in 1992–4, dealing, among other things, with the causation of rampant corruption and its connection with the world of crime. It was striking to see how the justifications of crooked financial behaviour that were most frequently offered by the perpetrators were (1) 'everyone does it – not just me', and (2) 'I could not survive in a competitive world unless I too follow the same kind of behavioural rules as others do.' As the behavioural norms moved on, the spread of compliance to reformed behaviour proved to be considerably faster than had been feared, even in a country with a continuing reputation for the presence of corruption.

5

The Centrality of Education

In a powerful diagnosis, Rabindranath Tagore said: 'in my view the imposing tower of misery which today rests on the heart of India has its sole foundation in the absence of education'.[1] The remark is somewhat extreme, in separating out just one factor among many problems that India faces. And yet Tagore offers a judgement that is deeply insightful.

The role of basic education in the process of development and social progress is very wide and critically important. First, the capability to read and write and count has powerful effects on our quality of life: the freedoms we have to understand the world, to lead an informed life, to communicate with others, and to be generally in touch with what is going on. In a society, particularly in the modern world, where so much depends on the written medium, being illiterate is like being imprisoned, and school education opens a door through which people can escape incarceration.

Second, our economic opportunities and employment prospects depend greatly on our educational achievements and cultivated skills. The ability to understand written information and to keep track of the numbers involved in particular tasks can be necessary qualifications for even simple jobs, especially with increasing specialization in production and distribution. The need for education has particularly expanded in the world of globalized trade and commerce, and the success of economies like China has been based substantially on the ability of a reasonably well-educated workforce to meet the demands of quality control and skill formation involved in producing goods and services for the world at large.

Third, illiteracy muffles the political voice of people and thus contributes directly to their insecurity. The connection between voice and security is often underestimated. This is not to deny that democracies can be effective even when many people are still illiterate: that point certainly needs emphasizing because it is missed in the deeply reactionary argument which is often aired, that an illiterate population has no use for democratic rights. It is nevertheless the case that the reach of people's democratic voice can be much greater when political opportunities are combined with social empowerment, including the ability to read newspapers, periodicals and books, and to communicate with each other. The issue is not whether democracies can be at all effective, but how much more effective they can become if the voices of people muffled by illiteracy can be liberated from the smothering that inadequate school education produces.

Fourth, basic education can play a major role in tackling health problems in general and public health in particular. It is easy to see the importance of specialized health education (for example, about the ways in which infections spread and how diseases can be prevented). But even general education can develop an individual's capacity to think, and can generate social understanding in ways that may be extremely important in facing epidemiological problems. Indeed, some studies suggest that general school education can have a bigger impact on health than specialized health education itself. School education also tends to facilitate the implementation of public health measures, related for instance to immunization, sanitation or the prevention of epidemics.

Fifth, educational development has often been the prime mover in bringing about changes in public perceptions of the range and reach of what can be called human rights, broadly defined.[2] For example, the educational development in Kerala – and more recently in Himachal Pradesh – has been a major factor in the increased demand for health care, based on a clearer perception of the importance of health and the role of the society in providing health facilities and services. The understanding of what can be seen as human rights – and health care would certainly figure in the global perception of human rights today – tends to be much sharpened by the spread of school education and literacy.

Sixth, education can also make a difference to the understanding and use of legal rights – the already legislated rights that people may already have, but which they are, sometimes, not able to utilize. When people are illiterate, their ability to understand, invoke and use their legal rights can be very limited. This applies in particular to women, as Salma Sobhan brought out many years ago in the context of Bangladesh, where illiteracy was one of the major barriers to the realization of women's rights.[3] Lack of schooling can directly lead to insecurities by distancing the deprived from the ways and means of resisting the violation of established legal rights.

Seventh, there is now extensive evidence that the schooling of young women can substantially enhance the voice and power of women in family decisions. Aside from the general importance of equity within the family, the voice of women can also lead to many other social changes. One of the most important to consider relates to the fact that women's empowerment tends to have a strong downward impact on the fertility rate. This is not surprising, since the lives that are most affected by the frequent bearing and rearing of children are those of young women, and anything that enhances their voice and increases the attention that their interests receive tends, in general, to prevent over-frequent childbearing. Furthermore, women's education and literacy tend to reduce the mortality rates of children. There is, indeed, considerable evidence of a close relationship between female literacy and child survival in many countries.[4]

Eighth, even though education is no magic bullet against class barriers, it can make a big contribution to reducing inequalities related to the divisions of class and caste. As was discussed in Chapter 1, stratification remains a major barrier to India's economic and social development, and the spread of education is one of the important means for tackling that debilitating feature of Indian society.

Last but not least, learning and studying can be immensely enjoyable and creatively engaging activities, if they are well arranged and well supported, and the process of schooling itself can add greatly to the quality of life of young people, quite apart from the long-run benefits they receive from it. This may not be obvious to the average Indian schoolchild, who often studies in a drab or hostile environment, and may be exposed, in many cases, to physical punishment. And yet, for most children, schooling not only is greatly preferable to child labour, domestic work, or other alternatives, but it can also make their lives fun as well as rewarding.

The difference that basic education can make to human life is easy to see. It is also readily appreciated even by the poorest of families. Contrary to a common anecdotal story that Indian parents are often uninterested – or even opposed – to the schooling of their children, especially girls, it is striking to see how easily the importance of education for all children is perceived even by the poorest and the most deprived of families in India. This was one of the main findings of the *Public Report on Basic Education* (known as the 'PROBE report'), published in 1999, and also of more recent investigations, for example by the Pratichi Trust.[5] And contrary to claims often made, systematic empirical studies have not found any serious reluctance by parents to send their children – daughters or sons – to school, provided that affordable, effective – and safe – schooling opportunities actually exist in their neighbourhood. In those cases in which some reluctance exists, it tends to come from the nature of the schooling arrangements, for example concern about the safety of children, particularly of girls, when the schools are located at a considerable distance from where the parents work, or when the school has only one teacher who may, on some days, be absent.[6]

DEVELOPMENT AND EDUCATION

The connection between education and development, including the crucially important role of public services in bringing about an educational transformation, was very clearly seen more than two hundred years ago by Adam Smith, who provided the classic analysis of how the market mechanism can work successfully. He wanted much greater use of state resources for public education and argued:

> For a very small expence the publick can facilitate, can encourage, and can even impose upon almost the whole body of the people, the necessity of acquiring those most essential parts of education.[7]

The experiences of Europe and America, which have been extensively studied, bring out most forcefully the pervasive role of education, led typically by governmental initiatives, in facilitating and sustaining economic and social development.

Those lessons also inspired the rising economic powers in Asia from the nineteenth century onwards. Already in the mid-nineteenth century, the transforming role of school education was seen with remarkable clarity in Japan – the pioneering country to undertake modern economic development in Asia.[8] At the time of the Meiji restoration in 1868, Japan already had a higher level of literacy than Europe, even though the country had not yet undergone any industrialization or modern economic development, which Europe had experienced for a century. As we noted in Chapter 2, the Fundamental Code of Education issued in 1872 expressed an unequivocal public commitment to make sure that there must be 'no community with an illiterate family, nor a family with an illiterate person'. It was the constructive – if authoritarian – state that powerfully led the universalization of schooling in Japan.

The focus on education was intense in the early period of Japanese development, during the Meiji era (1868–1912). For example, between 1906 and 1911, education consumed as much as 43 per cent of the budgets of the towns and villages, for Japan as a whole.[9] In this period, the progress of elementary education was particularly rapid, and the recruiting army officers were impressed by the fact that whereas in 1893 one third of the army recruits were illiterate, already by 1906 there was hardly anyone in that condition. By 1910 Japan was almost fully literate, at least for the young, and by 1913, though still very much poorer than Britain or America, Japan was publishing more books than Britain and more than twice as many as the United States. The concentration on education determined, to a large extent, the nature and speed of Japan's economic and social progress.

The fact that human development in general and school education in particular are first and foremost allies of the poor, rather than only of the rich and the affluent, is an understanding that has informed the Japanese strategy of economic development throughout its entire modern history. Later on, South Korea, Taiwan, Singapore, Hong Kong and of course China followed similar routes and firmly focused on basic education, largely delivered by the state. In explaining the rapid economic progress of East Asia, its willingness to make good use of the global market economy is often and rightly emphasized. But that process was greatly helped by the achievements of these countries in public education. Widespread participation in a global economy would have been hard to accomplish if people could not read or write.

INDIA LEFT BEHIND

Oddly enough, despite the strong pro-education rhetoric in the Indian national movement, the expansion of school education has been remarkably slow in India – much slower than in East Asia. Indeed, India has been lagging behind East Asia by a long margin, as Table 5.1 illustrates. The deficit is particularly striking for Indian women, including young women, a large proportion of whom are illiterate even today, in sharp contrast with East Asia – including, for instance, Indonesia, which was earlier on (even in 1960) not performing much better in this respect than India, but where literacy is more or less universal in the younger age groups today.

To be sure, the different parts of India have disparate records in this field. The state of Kerala (which was formed after independence by putting together two 'native Indian states', Travancore and Cochin, allowed by the British Raj to have their own domestic policies) did have a history of pro-education policy – much more so than the rest of India. This pro-education outlook was continued and intensified after independence, under a left-wing political leadership, placing Kerala substantially ahead of the rest of India in school education. A small part of new Kerala, Malabar, which came from the old state of Madras in British India, and had a more backward educational history before India's independence, soon caught up with the rest of Kerala in educational development. But Kerala was the exception in the otherwise educationally backward post-independent India, just as Sri Lanka was also an exception, with its own history of rapid expansion of schooling.[10] The bulk of India had astonishingly little schooling – for India as a whole, when the British left, the adult literacy rate was only around 18 per cent. And as we have discussed in Chapters 2 and 3, this neglect of school education continued solidly through the post-independence years, until quite recently.

About 20 per cent of Indian children between the ages of 6 and 14 years were not attending school even in 2005–6, and about 10 per cent of children of that age group had never been enrolled in any school at all.[11] The neglect is particularly strong for Indian girls, nearly half of whom were out of school in large parts of India (e.g.

Bihar) in the same year. In this respect, South Asia (including India) has remained very much closer to sub-Saharan Africa than to the rest of Asia. And even within South Asia, India is not doing particularly well. Bangladesh, despite being much poorer than India, has caught up with – and in some ways overtaken – India in the education of girls, as was discussed in Chapter 3. Nepal is even poorer, and had less than half of India's literacy rates as recently as 1980, but has almost caught up with India too, in the younger age groups (see Table 5.1).

Table 5.1
Literacy Rates in Selected Asian Countries

Country	Adult literacy rate (% of literate persons in the age group of 15 years and above)			Youth female literacy rate (% of literate women in the age group of 15–24 years)	
	1960	1980[a]	2010[b]	1980[a]	2010[b]
South Asia					
India	28	41	63	40	74
Bangladesh	22	29	57	27	78
Nepal	9	21	60	15	78
Pakistan	15	26	55	24	61
Sri Lanka	75	87	91	90	99
East Asia					
China	n/a	65	94	82	99
Indonesia	39	67	93	82	99
Malaysia	53	70	93	87	98
Philippines	72	83	95	93	98
Thailand	68	88	94	96	98
Vietnam	n/a	84	93	94	96

[a] 1981 for Bangladesh, India, Nepal, Pakistan, Sri Lanka; 1979 for Vietnam; 1982 for China.
[b] 2006 for India; 2009 for Indonesia and Pakistan; 2008 for Philippines; 2005 for Thailand.

Sources: *World Development Report 1980*, Table 23, for 1960 data. *World Development Indicators* (online, 1 January 2013) for other years. Age-specific literacy rates from India's 2011 census are not available at the time of writing; for persons aged 7 and above, the census estimate is 74 per cent.

And even the literacy gap between India and Pakistan looks much smaller today (though it is still to India's advantage) than it did thirty years ago. There is an alarming story here of sustained neglect of elementary education, and especially of girls' education, which is a central necessity in the process of economic and social development.

CHALLENGES OF HIGHER EDUCATION

There are many problems to be addressed at different educational levels in India – starting from pre-school education to the highest levels of higher education. In this book, we concentrate mostly on the neglected state of schools – and schooling – in India, not only because these deficiencies are critically important in themselves, but also because they influence what can or cannot be achieved in post-school education. Since the intake into colleges and universities is severely compromised by the exclusion at the school stage of a significant part of the population, and an even larger exclusion from acceptably good school education, it is difficult for higher education to achieve anything near its potential. However, there are special problems of higher education that originate elsewhere, and it is useful to look briefly at the state and quality of higher education in India as a whole.

First, a few words on tradition. Europe and North America have been the dominant centres of organized higher education for nearly a thousand years. It is in Bologna in Italy that the oldest extant university in the world was created in 1088. Paris followed three years later, in 1091. Other citadels of higher learning soon emerged in different countries in Europe, including Oxford University in 1167 and Cambridge University in 1209. There is a tendency across the world – reflected in India as well – to assume that higher education is somehow a quintessentially Western contribution to the world. The history of the last millennium tends to confirm that understanding, and yet it is important in this context to remember – and be inspired by – the fact that India has, in some ways, an even longer heritage of higher education.

Consider Nalanda University, which served as a pan-Asian university (it drew students from all over Asia), run by a Buddhist foundation – to which others, including Hindu kings, contributed support. When the oldest European university, Bologna, was founded in 1088, Nalanda was already more than six hundred years old.* Nalanda was an ancient centre of advanced learning that attracted students from many countries in the world, for example China, Korea, Japan, Thailand, Indonesia, and the rest of Asia, but a few also from as far in the West as Turkey. At its peak, Nalanda, a residential university, had ten thousand students in its dormitories, in the seventh century.

The subjects that were taught in Nalanda are still being investigated, as the old university is being re-established under a joint initiative of the East Asia Summit; it is not an easy search, since the documents in Nalanda were indiscriminately burnt by Bakhtiyar Khilji and his conquering army at the end of the twelfth century. Contemporary accounts tell us that Nalanda's large and distinguished library – apparently housed in a nine-storeyed building – burnt for three days in the flames of destruction. While Nalanda lingered on for some time more after it had regrouped and reorganized itself following the devastation, it would never regain its former size, quality or reputation. But putting together all the accounts we have, especially the memoirs of former students of Nalanda (particularly from China), we do know that the subjects taught and researched there included religion, history, law, linguistics, medicine, public health, architecture and sculpture, as well as astronomy (with a tall observatory that Xuangzang, a Chinese scholar who studied in Nalanda in the seventh century, described as towering majestically over the fog on misty mornings). There is circumstantial evidence that mathematics must have been taught too, closely linked as it is to astronomy, and this would have been natural given the proximity of Nalanda to the old

---

* There was an earlier Buddhist establishment in Takshila, in what is now Pakistan, but while it offered religious instruction and some education related to Buddhism, it did not develop the kind of pedagogic reach and liberality that Nalanda managed to evolve. In this respect Takshila was more similar to Al Azhar, an early and very distinguished Muslim university in Egypt, which was initiated about a couple of hundred years after Nalanda, and which developed a regular system of pedagogic instruction, closely related to religion, and became justly renowned across the world.

haunt of Indian mathematicians in Kusumpur at Pataliputra – what is now Patna.

The interest in medicine and public health was particularly important, and Yi Jing, another student at Nalanda, from China, had the distinction of being the first author in the ancient world who wrote a comparative assessment of medical systems in two countries – China and India. Incidentally, in the history of ancient China, Nalanda is the only academic institution outside China where any Chinese scholar received higher education. It is hard to think of a better acknowledgement of the quality of higher education in Nalanda than that. It is also important to recognize that while Nalanda was the pioneer of higher education in India – and in the world – it was not unique, since other centres of higher education emerged in India in the first millennium, often inspired by Nalanda. Of these, Vikramshila, also in what is now Bihar, and which was also a Buddhist foundation, came to compete with Nalanda in terms of educational offerings and reputation for excellence.

But all this was a long time ago, and while all Indian universities today, including the newly re-establishing Nalanda University, can be inspired by the long history of higher education in India, the fact remains that the achievements of contemporary Indian universities are rather limited. The quality of higher education is hard to judge (and cannot but raise controversies), but if we go by the list of 200 top-ranking universities prepared by *The Times Higher Educational Supplement* in October 2011, an overwhelming proportion of the leading institutions of higher education in the world are based in the United States. Indeed, the top five are all in America: Harvard, Caltech, MIT, Stanford and Princeton, in that order. The British follow just behind, and in the top ten we also find Cambridge, Oxford and Imperial College, London.

What is, however, really arresting in the list is the preponderance of Western establishments in the entire list of 200 top universities.[12] There are none from Asia in the top 20, and while some elite universities in Asia do get in below that, including Hong Kong, Tokyo, Pohang, Singapore, Peking, Hong Kong University of Science and Technology, Kyoto, Tsinghua, and a few others, together they form only a small minority of the top universities on the globe. It is particularly striking that there is not a single university in India in this list of the top 200 in the world.

Since the whole world benefits from the availability of first-rate higher education in the West, non-Western nations have no reason to grudge the excellence of the West in this critically important field. This is so particularly because the doors of all Western universities are open to students from anywhere in the world – provided they can afford to pay the fees, which can, of course, be prohibitively high (unless the incoming students manage to receive a scholarship or other academic support from these universities or elsewhere). But given India's academic potential, and its long history in higher education, it would be natural to expect a much better performance from the Indian university sector than we actually see today.

To make that judgement, we do not have to go only by the ranking presented by *The Times Higher Educational Supplement*, which could be, it has been alleged, culturally biased. There is plenty of other evidence pointing to the same conclusion. Even the assessment by students themselves, in particular which universities they try to get into, tend to confirm an important problem of quality deficiency. Indian students do spectacularly well once they enter any of the leading universities in the world, in a way that is hard for them to achieve within the confines of Indian universities. The situation can certainly be changed, and may, to some extent, already be changing. Many of the leading Indian universities have excellent areas of instruction and training in particular subjects, even when the overall achievement of the particular universities is pulled down by the low or indifferent quality of other departments. The quality of higher education offered in specialist institutions (such as the Indian Statistical Institute, or the Indian Institutes of Technology, or some Institutes of Management) has, by and large, been very high, and there is a maintenance of quality in them that the Indian universities in general do not have.

The problems of Indian universities, including academic arrangements and facilities, recruitments and emoluments, can be critically assessed – and should be. The limitation of intake is, however, a major drag on the reach and performance of Indian higher education, and to improve this it is crucially important to reform, indeed to remake, the entire system of school education in the country.

ACHIEVEMENTS AND DEFICIENCIES

It is encouraging that in recent years the neglect of school education in India has been partially addressed. But there is a long way to go to remedy this long-standing neglect. It is important to ask: what progress has there been, and what failures remain? India's official statistics show a steady increase in school enrolment – for both girls and boys – and in the facilities available in schools. Governmental decisions as well as orders of the Supreme Court have contributed to these developments, and the enactment of the Right to Education Act in 2010, uncertain as its impact may be, is certainly an attempt to move things forward. The all-India Sarva Shiksha Abhiyan ('campaign for universal education'), implemented by state governments with central government support, has also been of great help in expanding and improving school facilities across the country.

The progress that has come about is apparent not only in the government's own reports (there is considerable scepticism among the public about the reliability of some of these reports), but also in independent studies. These include, for instance, a recent re-survey of 200 randomly selected villages initially studied by the PROBE Team in 1996, located in seven large states of northern India (Bihar, Chhattisgarh, Jharkhand, Madhya Pradesh, Rajasthan, Uttar Pradesh, Uttarakhand) where school participation and educational levels are comparatively low.[13] Even in these states, the school enrolment ratio for children between the ages of 6 and 12 years moved up from 80 to 95 per cent between 1996 and 2006.[14] Progress was particularly rapid for disadvantaged communities: by 2006, the school enrolment rates of Dalit, Muslim and (to a lesser extent) Adivasi children in the same age group had nearly caught up with the average of 95 per cent for the sample population as a whole. Though far from complete, the rapid movement towards universalization of primary-school enrolment across social groups is nevertheless impressive.

School amenities in the PROBE villages had also improved. By 2006, 73 per cent of the sample schools had at least two all-weather rooms, compared with 26 per cent in 1996. Also, by 2006, 60 per cent of the schools had their own toilets and nearly three-fourths of them had drinking water facilities. Free uniforms were given to the students in more than half of the schools (up from 10 per cent in 1996), and free textbooks were distributed in nearly all schools by 2006 (up from less than half in 1996). At least as significantly, provisioning of cooked midday meals (very important on nutritional grounds as well as for preventing the distraction of children from studies because of hunger), which were introduced between the two survey dates, were functioning in 86 per cent of the schools by the end of the period.[15]

And yet the functioning of the schools remains seriously – perhaps even disastrously – deficient. Only two-thirds of the pupils were present on the day of the survey, according to the school registers, and even fewer according to the field investigators' direct observations. There is considerable absenteeism among teachers as well, in addition to widespread late arrival and early departure. The proportion of schools with only one appointed teacher is still significant – about 12 per cent. There is a chronic shortage of regular teachers, largely due to the reluctance of public authorities to make appointments at what have now become, after the reports of successive Pay Commissions, fairly substantial salaries by Indian standards. The gap is sometimes met by 'contract teachers', hired at considerably lower salaries, but whose teaching performance is unclear – as is the sustainability of this dualist and discriminatory treatment of the teaching cadre.

In addition to the shortage of appointed teachers, however, absenteeism contributes to the one-teacher characteristic of many schools. Indeed, in the 2006 survey, 21 per cent of the sample schools were operating as single-teacher schools on the day of the survey, either because they had a single teacher appointed or due to teacher absenteeism. Additionally there is a shocking lack of teaching even by those teachers who do bother to show up. In fact, half of the schools had no teaching activity *at all* at the time of the investigators' unannounced visit – both in 1996 and in 2006.* This is certainly not a picture that inspires confidence about school education in areas where it is most

---

* Another recent study, based on a random sample of more than three thousand schools across the country, came to similar conclusions: fewer than half of the teachers were engaged in teaching activity on an average day (Kremer et al., 2005). The PROBE findings, related to northern India, were actually worse (no teaching activity in a school means that *all* the teachers are doing something else). Teacher absenteeism rates

needed. While much of the rest of the world, and even a significant part of the rest of the country, were humming with teaching activities, half of the schools in these states did next to nothing to impart education to children, neglecting their duties as well as ignoring the right of the young students to receive elementary education and to join the modern world.

Without even taking note of the low quality of teaching, the toll of this catastrophic breakdown of regularity and order in the schooling system can be appreciated by considering the implications of these survey findings for the number of active teaching days a child enjoys over the school year. In the PROBE states, the official number of school days per year is around two hundred. But with a teacher absenteeism rate of around 20 per cent, and a pupil absenteeism rate of about 33 per cent, the combined probability of a child *and* his or her teacher being present on an average day is only just above 50 per cent. This brings down the number of teaching days effectively to one hundred days or so. But this is not the end of the story, because the survey also suggests that even during those hundred days, about half of the time is bereft of any teaching activity. So the actual teaching time is more like fifty days – about *one fourth* of what would happen in a well-functioning schooling system.

EDUCATIONAL STANDARDS

School education in India suffers from two principal deficiencies: firstly, limitation of coverage, and secondly, poor standards of the education that is offered and received. While there has been some progress in the former, the quality of education in Indian schools seems to be exceptionally low over a wide range of institutions. Teaching methods are quite often dominated by mindless rote learning, including repetition – typically without comprehension – of what has been read, and endless chanting of multiplication and other tables. Children

---

in the national sample varied from 15 per cent in Maharashtra to 42 per cent in Jharkhand, with a national average of 25 per cent.

often learn rather little in these schools, and in tests conducted in 2006 as part of the survey mentioned in the preceding section, it was found that nearly half of the pupils in Classes 4 and 5 could not do single-digit multiplication, or a simple division by 5. Their knowledge of important facts is also, in general, dismally poor. This was a relatively small survey, but the findings on pupil achievements are broadly consistent with those of a whole series of other studies, as Table 5.2 illustrates.

Lack of quality characterizes the education offered in most ordinary schools, but it appears that it is widely present even in what are considered to be 'top schools' in the larger Indian cities, such as Delhi, Mumbai, Chennai, Kolkata and Bangalore. In fact, in 83 such 'top schools' studied jointly by WIPRO, a leading informational enterprise, and Educational Initiatives (EI), the students' knowledge as well as skills seemed to be very limited. For example, only a third of these 'top school' students in Class 4 knew who was the alive person in a list of four: Mahatma Gandhi, Indira Gandhi, Rajiv Gandhi and Sonia Gandhi (a small number thought, interestingly enough, that it was Mahatma Gandhi who was still alive). About two-thirds of the students in Class 4 could not master the measurement of the length of a pencil with a ruler. There was also a noticeable lack of awareness of social issues among the sample students.[16]

Even though Indian authorities have resisted the country's inclusion in international comparisons of pupil achievements, some recent studies make it possible to compare Indian students with others, such as the 'PISA Plus' survey conducted in 2009. Indian performance comes out very much at the bottom of the 74 countries or economies included in this survey.[17] And this is the case even though the two Indian states that participated in PISA Plus happened to be two of the better-schooled states, Tamil Nadu and Himachal Pradesh. In a comparison of overall reading ability of 15-year-old students in these 74 countries or economies, both Indian states figure among the bottom three (in the company of Kyrgyzstan). In other tests, including writing, science education and mathematics, Indian students are similarly disadvantaged compared with students from other countries included in the PISA survey.

Table 5.2: Pupil Achievements in Primary School: Recent Findings

Source	Basis	Sample findings
India Human Development Survey, 2004–5	Large, all-India random sample	• Only half of all children aged 8–11 years enrolled in a government school are able to read a simple paragraph with three sentences. • Less than half (43 per cent) of these children are able to subtract a two-digit number from another two-digit number. • More than one third (36 per cent) are unable to write a simple sentence such as 'My mother's name is Madhuben.'
ASER Survey, 2011	Large, all-India representative survey of schoolchildren in rural areas	• Only 58 per cent of children enrolled in Classes 3 to 5 can read a Class-1 text. • Less than half (47 per cent) are able to do a simple two-digit subtraction. • In Classes 5 to 8, only half of the children can use a calendar.
PROBE Revisited, 2006	Random sample of 284 rural government-school pupils in the Hindi-speaking states	• Only 37 per cent of children enrolled in Class 4 or 5 can 'read fluently'. • Less than half (45 per cent) are able to divide 20 by 5. • One third are unable to add with carry-over.

CORD-NEG Village Studies, 2010–11	Random sample of children in government schools of 9 villages in peripheral districts of Bihar, Jharkhand and Odisha	• Out of 110 children enrolled in Class 4 or 5, only half were able to recognize a two-digit number. • Less than one fourth of these 110 children were able to subtract a two-digit number from another two-digit number.
WIPRO-EI Quality Education Study 2011	Survey of more than 20,000 students in 83 'top schools' in five metro cities (Bangalore, Chennai, Delhi, Kolkata and Mumbai)	• Reading and maths skills of Class 4 pupils in India's 'top schools' are below the international average. • Only 16 per cent of Class 4 pupils could master the measurement of the length of a pencil with a ruler. • Only 22 per cent of Class 6 pupils could understand that crumpling a paper does not alter its weight.

Sources: Desai et al. (2010), p. 93; Pratham Educational Foundation (2012), p. 58; Pratham Educational Foundation (2012), p. 68; De et al. (2011), p. 57; De et al. (2010), pp. 94–7 and Samson and Gupta (2012), pp. 145–8; Educational Initiatives (2011), pp. 4, 34 and 36.

The point is sometimes made that these tests – PISA and others – are culture-related, and reflect 'Western' biases. It is hard to understand why reading, writing and elementary mathematics should be seen as uniquely Western abilities, but perhaps it is worth noting that the world-beaters in these tests tend to be Asians, rather than only Europeans: the top three spots in the comparison of reading ability are in fact occupied by Shanghai (China) and South Korea, along with Finland. The top five also include Hong Kong and Singapore. What India seems to suffer from is not a problem of being excluded from the West, or one arising from a cultural problem of being in Asia rather than Europe or America: it is specifically an Indian – and South Asian – failure to benefit from the insight about the role of quality education that has informed the development experiences of much of Asia, Europe and America.

In addition to the general adversity of low-quality education that Indian school students have to settle for, there is the further problem of wide variations in the educational accomplishments of Indian schoolchildren between different regions. As Table 5.3 shows, the two states included in the PISA study (Himachal Pradesh and Tamil Nadu) have some of the best pupil achievement levels among all major Indian states. While their educational standards are seriously deficient from an international perspective, the performance of students in other parts of India tends to be worse – in fact, much worse. It is horrifying, for instance, to learn that in seven large Indian states, accounting for *half* of India's population, the proportion of children aged 8–11 years enrolled in a government school who can pass a very simple reading test (going only a little beyond what passes for official 'literacy') varies between one fourth and one half.*

* These findings on pupil achievements need to be seen in light of the fact that a large proportion of the children going to elementary schools are first-generation learners. The parents of these students can offer little or no help to their children about education, and the lack of any educational tradition in those families makes the problem of generating interest and concentration much harder. Since the development of aspiration is a very important part of improving educational achievement (on which see Hart, 2012), the need for paying particular attention to the low aspiration levels of first-time school-goers is part of the task on which a rapidly expanding schooling system has to focus. None of this, of course, detracts from the shocking nature of recent findings on pupil achievements and the quality of education in Indian schools.

Table 5.3
Pupil Achievements in Major States, 2004–5

	Proportion of children aged 8–11 years enrolled in a government school who are able to:		
	Read[a]	Subtract[b]	Write[c]
Himachal Pradesh	81	64	77
Kerala	80	64	84
Tamil Nadu	78	67	82
Assam	73	45	97
Maharashtra, Goa	65	53	71
Haryana	63	58	61
Gujarat	60	36	64
Chhattisgarh	58	31	46
Odisha	58	48	73
Punjab	54	61	65
Uttarakhand	53	35	62
Jharkhand	51	54	56
West Bengal	51	56	72
Rajasthan	50	37	53
Karnataka	45	48	76
Andhra Pradesh	44	46	62
Bihar	40	43	65
Madhya Pradesh	39	25	38
Uttar Pradesh	29	22	51
Jammu & Kashmir	26	50	67
India[d]	50 (69)	43 (64)	64 (79)

[a] At least a simple paragraph with three sentences.
[b] Two-digit number from two-digit number, with borrowing.
[c] A simple sentence, with two or fewer mistakes.
[d] In parentheses, the corresponding percentages in private schools.

Source: Desai et al. (2010), p. 94, based on the India Human Development Survey (IHDS). Indian children generally join primary school at the age of 6 years, or (sometimes) 5 years. States are ranked in descending order of reading abilities.

Recent research points to other worrying aspects of pupil achievements (in terms of basic skills such as simple arithmetic or the ability to read and write) in India.[18] First, aside from being extremely low, they *improve very slowly* as children progress through the schooling system. One recent review of pupil achievements, for instance, suggests that among children who are unable to pass a very simple test (such as a single-digit vertical addition), the proportion who are *still unable* to pass the same test after another year of schooling is typically somewhere between 80 and 90 per cent.[19] This is consistent with the common observation that teachers often tend to focus mainly on children who are doing better, and to neglect those who actually need special attention. Second, low pupil achievements are not confined to government schools. In fact, differences in test scores between government and private schools are not particularly large, especially after taking into account differences in the socio-economic background of the pupils (see also Table 5.3, last row).[20] Even in expensive private schools, pupil achievements leave much to be desired, although they are certainly better than in an average school. Last but not least, there is little evidence of any general improvement in pupil achievements over time, at least in the recent past. In fact, the ASER surveys (initiated in 2005) suggest, if anything, a deterioration of average pupil achievements during the last few years.[21]

This is a very discouraging picture, which is yet to receive adequate recognition in education debates in India. The cognitive achievements of schoolchildren, and more broadly, the quality of education, matter a great deal. As was discussed earlier, education plays a very central role in a wide variety of fields – economic, social, political, cultural and others – and it can also play an enormously important part in reducing the force of inequalities of class, caste and gender. Recent research also brings out, more specifically, the importance of cognitive achievements for economic growth and participation. Indeed, learning achievements seem to have far more explanatory power than just 'years of schooling' as drivers of growth and development.* The enormous burst of economic activities in East and Southeast Asia, including

---

* As one review puts it: '. . . there is strong evidence that the cognitive skills of the population – rather than mere school attainment – are powerfully related to individual

an active role for women, owes a lot to the educational achievements of these countries, compared with India. If this connection is comparatively neglected in Indian discussions, this failure possibly reflects inadequate attention being paid to the nature of the economic expansion based on human capability development that Japan initiated and which has been followed with great success in East Asia, and to some extent even in Southeast Asia. More recent experience elsewhere, including Latin America, reinforces earlier evidence that standards of school education matter, both for economic growth and for the quality of life. As the boundaries of education research expand, the enormity of the price India is paying for its failure to put in place a well-functioning schooling system is becoming increasingly clearer.

PRIVILEGED EXCELLENCE AND SOCIAL DIVISIONS

There is, however, an interesting conundrum in the low quality of Indian education and the high praise that well-trained Indians often get across the world. Indian education, despite its huge limitations, often receives spectacular acclaim from abroad. This raises an interesting question of epistemology (what gives the Indian education system its international plaudits?), but also has practical implications in terms of creating a false sense of satisfaction that things are, by and large, fine enough in Indian education.[22] We are told that well-trained Indian experts are taking away good jobs from previously unthreatened Westerners – this was an important part of the rhetoric of even the recent campaigns for the presidential election in the United States. Leading American newspapers have carried articles urging improvements of the education and training systems in the USA, in order to keep up with that learned lot from distant Asia, India included, who are said to be as accomplished as they are keen on snatching good employment opportunities away from simple Americans.

Is this the India that has such a terrible record of school education?

---

earnings, to the distribution of income, and to economic growth' (Hanushek and Woessmann, 2008, p. 607).

What can the story be? Certainly, a large number of Indians – a minority but still quite numerous – receive excellent education in India. There are elite schools, advanced centres of higher learning, and a society that values educational excellence and honours it. Even in second-rate schools, the leading students often get very helpful attention and instruction. As we noticed earlier in this chapter, the institutes of higher education, such as the Indian Institutes of Technology (IITs) and Indian Institutes of Management (IIMs), can offer teaching and guidance of the highest quality in the world, and so do particular departments of a number of Indian universities. Well trained and confident, a lot of Indians are extremely successful abroad, and lead the businesses and professions in which they enter. In addition, Indian firms can handle outsourced business from America and Europe with competitive excellence and economy – not just low- to medium-skilled work (as in the so-called Call Centres), but sometimes jobs involving complex technical problems of programming and design.

The fact is that the Indian educational system is extraordinarily diverse, in a peculiar way, with a comparatively tiny group of children from the privileged classes enjoying high – often outstanding – educational opportunities, and the bulk of the population being confined to educational arrangements that are, in many different ways, poor or deficient. The facilities that students get vary enormously from their early school days to their specialized education, and place a small proportion of students – though a large group in absolute numbers – on the highest step of the ladder, whereas others are confined way down below. The Indian educational system – taking the social, economic and organizational elements together – does seem to make sure, in line with the general division between 'the privileged and the rest' in Indian society, that a few young people, out of a huge pool, manage to get an excellent education. The picking is done not through any organized attempt to keep anyone out (indeed far from it), but through differentiations that are driven by economic and social inequality related to class, caste, gender, location and social privilege.

The privileged by and large do very well – to their credit, they typically don't waste opportunities. Their success comes, first, in the educational establishments themselves, and then in the world at large, impressing Indians and foreigners alike. The country then celebrates with abandon the 'nation's triumphs'. Furthermore, not only do these 'first boys' (and, increasingly, 'first girls') do well in life, they can also relish – of course with becoming modesty – the homage that they receive for having 'done their country proud'. Meanwhile, the last boys, and particularly the last girls, can't even read or write, not having had the opportunity of any kind of decent education.

We should make clear that we have nothing against the first boys themselves. The country certainly needs them for many different purposes: for the academia to flourish, for the economy to prosper, for science and technology to move on, for medicine to progress, and indeed, for tackling with better effect the multitude of economic, social, administrative and environmental challenges that India faces. Our concerns do not arise from any sense that the first boys are letting us down. What goes wrong is the system in which the success of the educational enterprise is judged by the performance of a small (and largely self-contained) elite, ignoring the rest, and in which there is remarkable social insensitivity to the unfairness and injustice of such gross disparities, contributing to the persistence of a hugely stratified Indian society.

The recognition that we have to seek is that, despite the great successes of the first boys, India's education system is tremendously negligent both in coverage and quality. The steep educational hierarchy that has come to be tolerated in India is not only terribly unjust, but also extraordinarily inefficient in generating the basis of a dynamic economy and progressive society. It is in that structural perspective, combining considerations of efficiency with equity, that we can best understand how – and how much – the country loses through its extraordinary concentration on some, while neglecting the vast majority of Indians hampered by economic disadvantage, caste divisions, class barriers, gender inequalities and social gaps related to ethnicity and community.

SCHOOL MANAGEMENT AND
THE TEACHING PROFESSION

The spread of literacy across the world has been achieved overwhelmingly through state education. This applies to all the major regions of the world where basic educational developments have led to literate and numerate societies. State action was the main basis of educational transformation in Europe and America in the nineteenth century, matched by the progress of Japan thereafter, followed by the rapid expansion of schooling under Communist rule in the Soviet Union (including Soviet Asia), China, Cuba, Vietnam and elsewhere, and strongly championed with great success by East Asia (despite the strong commitment there to develop a privatized market economy in general). It is difficult to see how India can achieve the same educational results without a similar level of commitment and effort by the state, and yet – as it happens – there is much championing of reliance on private schools among some development thinkers in India. We shall argue that while it is easy to see what is so attractive about reliance on the private sector for the growth of Indian school education, the real scope for that unusual path to educational transformation is rather limited. But before we discuss the problems of over-reliance on private schooling, we must look at the huge problems that state education has faced since independence and the difficulties that remain to be overcome right now. If the *solution* offered by privatized education to the gigantic problems faced by public education in India is unreal (as we believe it largely is), the *problems* are real enough.

The classic problem of school education in India has been underfunding by the state. This was, of course, the case in British India right up to India's independence (when the British left India, more than four-fifths of Indians had not been touched by schooling), but it was followed by public policies of the newly independent India which continued gross underfunding despite rousing rhetoric claiming exactly the contrary, with such slogans as 'Education is our first priority.' That problem of underfunding remains today, but it is certainly much reduced by now – the limited progress discussed earlier in this chapter builds on a substantial heightening of financial support for school education. But even as the funding limitations are being, at least partially, remedied, other problems of public education in India have become increasingly more limiting and powerfully regressive.

Foremost among these problems is that of accountability in the delivery of school education. We mentioned earlier the incidence of absenteeism by teachers, which is very large indeed in some parts of the country, and on top of that, as was also discussed, in many regions the teachers who do show up seem reluctant to teach. There is something quite chilling in the thought that a large proportion (possibly as high as half) of the country's children are sitting idly in classrooms on an average school day – eager to learn, but deprived of any guidance, and condemned in many cases to leaving the schooling system without even being able to read or write. Most of the children are, of course, perfectly able not only to acquire basic literacy or mathematical skills, but also to study well beyond the constitutionally guaranteed minimum of eight years.[23] The schooling system's failure to respond to these aspirations and abilities is a manifest and colossal injustice, and yet it has remained unaddressed for many decades.

Could the laid-back attitude of many schoolteachers have something to do with their salaries being too low? The salaries used to be low (and one of us recollects joining protest marches on the streets of Calcutta, as a college student in the early 1950s, voicing demands for 'a decent salary for our teachers'). But that was a long time ago. It is difficult to defend that line of explanation today, given the steep rise in the salaries of schoolteachers, based on the recommendations of successive Pay Commissions, which have boosted the salaries of teachers (and other government employees) beyond levels that could have been reasonably imagined only a few decades ago. In fact, the salaries of government teachers in India are now well out of line with private-sector norms as well as with international patterns.

Just to use one possible benchmark, consider primary-school teacher salaries as a ratio of per capita GDP.[24] In 2001 this ratio of teacher salary to the GDP per head was estimated to be around one in China, somewhere between one and two in most OECD countries, and a little higher in developing countries, but not higher than three for any of the countries (except India) for which data were available. More recent data suggest similar ratios of teacher salaries to GDP in 2005 and

2009.[25] For instance, the OECD average hovered around 1.2 between 2000 and 2009. In India, however, it seems that the corresponding ratio was already around three before the Sixth Pay Commission scales came into effect (in 2009, with retrospective effect from 2006), and shot up to around 5 or 6 after that (see Table 5.4). The state-specific ratios are even higher – much higher – in some of the poorer and more educationally deprived states (e.g. around 17 in Uttar Pradesh), if we use the state's per capita GDP as the denominator. Whatever may be the source of the problem of low teaching efficiency, the blame cannot be placed on any alleged lowness of salary of schoolteachers.

There is also, it appears, little evidence to suggest that high salaries are of particular help in raising teaching standards.[26] High salaries make it possible to select teachers from a larger pool of applicants, or to raise the minimum qualifications. On the other hand, they also transform teaching posts into plum jobs that attract anyone with the required qualifications – including those who have no interest whatsoever in teaching. But perhaps more importantly, high salaries also increase the social distance between teachers and parents. In many Indian states today, the salary of a primary schoolteacher is more than *ten times* what an agricultural labourer would earn, even if he or she were successful in finding employment every day at the statutory minimum wage. This social distance that has grown over the years, partly related to huge earning gaps, does not help to foster mutual cooperation between teachers and parents from most rural families, which could have been very important for the success of school education.

The relatively high salaries of schoolteachers have also had the effect of making the expansion of school education immensely more expensive in a country with a large pool of people qualified to teach and eager to do so. It is important to recognize that the problem of comparatively high salaries of teachers is part of the general problem of public sector salaries in India. The country has an odd system of pay fixation based on periodic reviews by appointed Pay Commissions that recommend salary scales for public sector employees without bearing any specific responsibility to offer enlightenment on how the financial burden of the wage structure would be financed, and more importantly, what the implications of the salary increases would be on the lives of those whose wages are *not* determined by Pay

Table 5.4
Estimates of Primary-School Teacher Salaries
as a Ratio of Per Capita GDP

Country/state	Reference year	Estimated ratio of teacher salary to:	
		Per capita GDP	Per capita SDP
OECD *average*	2009	1.2	–
Asian *countries*			
China	2000	0.9	–
Indonesia	2009	0.5	–
Japan	2009	1.5	–
Bangladesh	2012	≈ 1	–
Pakistan	2012	≈ 1.9	–
India			
Nine major states[a]	2004–5	3.0	4.9
Uttar Pradesh[b]	2006	6.4	15.4
Bihar	2012	5.9	17.5
Chhattisgarh	2012	4.6	7.2

GDP = Gross Domestic Product.
SDP = State Domestic Product (for Indian states).

[a] Andhra Pradesh, Bihar, Gujarat, Jammu & Kashmir, Madhya Pradesh, Maharashtra, Rajasthan, Uttar Pradesh, West Bengal. Figures in this row refer to *all* primary-school teachers (including 'contract teachers', who earn much lower salaries than regular teachers), *before* the Sixth Pay Commission.
[b] Based on Sixth Pay Commission scales (fixed in 2009 with retrospective effect from 2006).

Note: The international figures apply to 'statutory salaries of teachers' after 15 years of service, at the primary level. Unless stated otherwise, Indian figures refer to regular teachers (as opposed to contract teachers). For more detailed information at the country level, see OECD (2011), Table D3.4.

Sources: OECD average, Indonesia and Japan: OECD (2011), Table D3.4, p. 419. China: Ciniscalco (2004), Figure 4 and data appendix, page 3. Bangladesh and Pakistan: Our informal estimates, based on data kindly provided by BRAC University (Dhaka) and the Collective for Social Science Research (Karachi), respectively. India: 'nine major states', calculated from Kingdon (2010), Table 1, based on population-weighted averages of her state-specific figures. Uttar Pradesh: Re-calculated from Kingdon (2010), using *Economic Survey* data on per capita GDP and SDP. Bihar and Chhattisgarh: Our estimates, based on enquiries about teacher salaries from the concerned Education Departments and Planning Commission data on per capita SDP.

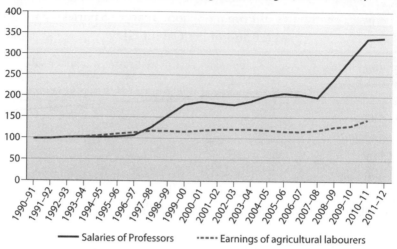

Index of university salaries and agricultural wages (1993–94 = 100)

—— Salaries of Professors   ····· Earnings of agricultural labourers

Figure 5.1: Earnings of University Professors and Agricultural Labourers

Sources: Index of university salaries applies to the average consolidated salary of Delhi School of Economics professors, deflated by the Consumer Price Index for Industrial Workers. Index of agricultural wages is based on linking two real-wage series: a series based on *Agricultural Wages in India* presented in Drèze and Sen (2002), and a new series based on *Wage Rates in Rural India* from Usami (2012), using 1999–2000 as the link year. For further details, see the Explanatory Note in the Statistical Appendix.

Commissions.* The members of the Pay Commission have little incentive to disappoint those whose salaries they are entrusted to determine (themselves included), without having any particular responsibility towards others, from rural labourers to the urban proletariat. Figure 5.1 compares recent trends in agricultural wages and public sector salaries (specifically, those of university professors),

---

* The Central Pay Commission reports are, technically, advisory in nature, but the pay recommendations are typically endorsed wholesale by the central government, and emulated within a short period of time by state governments. The entire process goes largely unopposed, and tends to be treated with passive acceptance as an inevitable event by the mainstream media as well as by the academic profession, which is among the main beneficiaries of it.

and the extent to which economic inequality has been enhanced over time by this bizarre system of fixing pay is truly astonishing.

Faced with the cost escalation involved in these salary hikes, many states have stopped recruiting regular teachers and have increasingly come to rely on hiring 'contract teachers' to do the teaching.[27] The salaries of contract teachers are typically a fraction (as low as one fifth or so, in many cases) of what the regular teachers earn. They also typically have lower formal qualifications and less training than regular teachers. In fact, a large proportion of contract teachers are fairly untrained, or trained through dubious techniques such as *en masse* correspondence courses. On the other hand, they are expected to be more accountable, because they have renewable contracts, sometimes conditional on the approval of local communities or Gram Panchayats. Limited evidence suggests that, in terms of imparting basic skills such as reading and writing, contract teachers do no worse than regular teachers – at a much lower cost.[28] 'No worse', however, is not good enough, in view of what was discussed earlier about the remarkably low quality of school education in India, compared with the rest of the world. The contract approach has certainly facilitated a rapid expansion of the schooling system by lowering the unit costs, but it could easily become a major barrier against the improvement of teaching standards.

The result of all this is an oddly dualistic teaching cadre, where professional but often laid-back 'permanent teachers' work side by side with informal but more active 'contract teachers' hired at a fraction of the former's salary. It would have been nice to see some sort of middle path emerging from this dualism: new terms and conditions for the teaching profession, with decent salaries, good qualifications and some security of employment, but not unconditional, permanent plum jobs that undermine work incentives and ruin the integrity of the profession. Interesting proposals have also been made for integrating contract and permanent teachers in a common 'career ladder' that would help to spot and promote the best teachers.[29] However, there has been little space for exploring these and other alternatives in the polarized debate 'for or against' contract teachers, which tends to pose the question as an all-or-nothing choice between contract and permanent teachers.

The implementation of the recently enacted Right to Education Act may be an opportunity for constructive rethinking of the terms and conditions of employment of teachers in India. The Act prescribes not only a higher density of schools but also a pupil-teacher ratio no higher than 30:1 in every school. Further, all teachers are supposed to have minimum qualifications prescribed by the central government. Meeting these norms by expanding the cadre of permanent teachers on Sixth Pay Commission scales would be financially ruinous, especially in poor states with large shortfalls.[30] On the other hand, meeting them by hiring untrained contract teachers would become, strictly speaking, illegal. Many states, therefore, are constrained to seek a middle path between these unsatisfactory extremes. Failing that, accelerated privatization of schooling (as disgruntled parents pull their children out of government schools) is unfortunately a possible – even likely – scenario.

PRIVATE SCHOOLING AS AN ALTERNATIVE

It is not hard to see why the various problems faced by school education in the public sector would encourage commentators to think about going for privatization of school education. How viable is that as an allegedly superior alternative? Private schools do offer an alternative opportunity, but one which cannot, in any way, take over the role that state schools are meant to play and have played in the educational transformation of most countries in the world.

There is, first of all, a major problem of affordability, since substantial fees are inescapably linked with the profitability of private schools. This is not how children of poor families and disadvantaged communities are likely to get schooled and educated in India.

Second, even if the problem of affordability is somehow removed (based, say, on a system of private-aided schools or school vouchers), other problems remain. School education is a quintessential territory of informational limitation, particularly for parents of first-time school-goers, and there is also a huge presence of asymmetric information in so far as school authorities, or private-school entrepreneurs, know a lot more about what they are able (and intend) to offer than do the families of potential students. This is hardly the ideal territory for the working of a voucher system which tries to eliminate the problem of unaffordability by backing the supposedly informed choice of parents with the economic might of the vouchers.[31]

Third, in the absence of competition, as is very often the case in the Indian rural areas, private schools can be very extractive money-making machines with modest educational offerings. The role of competition in making markets function well cannot be overlooked when it comes to school education. There are, of course, many well-meaning efforts to expand non-government schools by collecting some fees for the sake of the viability of such efforts. But the recent experience of private schools in Indian education offers examples both of dedicated successes and of money-grabbing enterprises, with a reputation, often well deserved, for offerings not matched by performance. The fact that private schools in India do not seem to be doing much better than government schools, as mentioned earlier, in terms of average pupil achievements, indicates that there may not be an easy solution lying in wait to use here.

Fourth, school education, as has been widely noted across the world, has many features of what Paul Samuelson (1954) called 'public goods'. There are externalities of school education, as well as indivisibilities of acquired knowledge. All this makes markets potentially very defective in terms of operation and delivery. This is not to indicate that these defects must necessarily outweigh the problems that the public sector has, but there is a clear need for hard-headed testing and checking of what the private schools are actually delivering (particularly in comparison with what they promise to deliver). That is, of course, the central problem in the monitoring of government schools as well. There is no automatic exemption from such continuous assessment when it comes to private schools.

Perhaps the most hidden penalty of greater reliance on private schools is that it tends to take away from state schools the children of precisely those parents who are likely to contribute most to the critiques and demands that could make state schools more responsible and accountable. Reliance on private schools can make the problems of state schools much greater, by providing a way out for the more prosperous and more vocal families who suffer from low-quality school education in the state sector.[32] The private schools are likely to remain a part of the picture of Indian school education, but the need for carrying out major reforms of state schools as well as for relying on them is not going to disappear merely because of the existence of the private option for those who can afford it.

THE EVALUATION GAP

Among the organizational issues that have to be faced in reforming school education in India is the difficult one of pupil evaluation and school assessment. At the moment, the entire system of school tests is in a state of dangerous disarray. Under the Right to Education Act of 2010, 'automatic promotion' from one class to the next is guaranteed, irrespective of what a child has learnt, and Board Examinations are prohibited until Class 8. The Act does not prohibit school tests (as opposed to Board Examinations), but it does not encourage them either. Instead, it prescribes a system of 'comprehensive and continuous evaluation'. The details of this method, however, are far from clear, and some states have already complained that the new approach to evaluation effectively translates, on the ground, as 'no evaluation'.[33]

There is an urgent need to restore some clarity on this whole issue. No doubt, the traditional examination system in India had many flaws, and often ended up in large-scale cheating, excessive pressure on children, dumbing-down of teachers, and a reinforcement of crude teaching methods such as rote learning.[34] On the other hand, abolishing standardized tests of any kind in a system where pupil achievements are so low and teacher supervision is so scanty can hardly be a sound idea.

The main purpose of standardized tests is not so much to put pressure on children to learn – something many educationists understandably oppose – but to find out what kinds of help, attention or encouragement particular children or schools need. If a large proportion of children learn virtually nothing for years on end in a particular school, it is important to know it, well before they are sent for slaughter in the Board Examination (if indeed they reach the end of Class

8 without dropping out). This recognition is not a ground for the rejection of comprehensive and continuous evaluation, but for having adequate information about pupil achievements, which the alternative to standardized tests does not seem to provide.[35] An inadequately reasoned rejection of such tests without a viable and effective alternative is hardly what Indian schoolchildren need today.

The importance of information about pupil achievements is, of course, immediate for teachers, headmasters, inspectors, or administrators, but it applies also to the parents of the concerned children and the community around them. The disempowerment of parents is not the least reason for lack of accountability in the schooling system, and the difficulty they have in assessing what their children are learning (and what is going on in the school) plays a very important part in that disempowerment. Generating useful information on pupil achievements and placing it in the public domain (if only in anonymous or statistical formats) could be of great help in enabling parents and others to hold the system accountable.

The nature and content of the tests, of course, need considerable thought. For instance, it is possible to design standard tests that evaluate the competencies of a child (say, the ability to comprehend – not just read – a simple text), rather than his or her ability to memorize. Similarly, 'open book' tests can help to shift the focus of tests from memorization to comprehension or competency. But the first step is to recognize the need for reform: the current evaluation gap is alarming.

UNIVERSALIZATION WITH QUALITY

School education in India is in a terrible state, and given the wide-ranging individual and social roles of education, this failure has played no small part in a whole gamut of social problems discussed in this book – from the lack of participatory growth and poor health achievements to problems of public accountability, social inequality and democratic practice. While the centrality of education to development is better recognized in India today than it used to be, and even though some progress has been made in extending the coverage and infrastructure of the schooling system, there is an urgent need to go beyond these elementary steps, and in particular, to give much greater attention to the *quality* of education.

The task of restoring accountability in the schooling system must certainly be an important part of the larger educational agenda. Since salaries of schoolteachers are fixed from outside (as was discussed earlier), the present system of teacher payment in government schools cannot be said to have any built-in system of financial incentives at all. However, incentives can come in some other forms, since the rewards of teachers include reputation and respect as well as general recognition as good teachers, and there is evidence that such non-financial incentives can indeed sway the work of schoolteachers in a substantial way.[36]

There are other concerns as well, since the quality of education also depends on many further factors (for instance, the school curriculum and pedagogy, the competence of teachers, and the good health of children). But accountability is clearly a central issue at this time – not just teacher accountability, but the accountability of the entire schooling system.

As discussed in Chapter 4, one of the principal obstacles against restoring accountability in the public sector, in general, is the fatalistic notion that nothing can be done about it. This applies to the schooling system as well. During the last ten years, even as so much was done to put in place schooling facilities, pupil incentives, and even a Right to Education Act, accountability issues were largely ignored or sidestepped.[37] And yet, much could be done if the sort of energy and resources that have been spent on expanding the reach of schooling facilities are now also aimed at improving the quality of education.

It is not difficult to see, for instance, that a school without a head teacher is unlikely to function much better than a ship without a rudder. And yet, the survey of schooling facilities mentioned earlier in this chapter found that half of the schools were bereft of a head teacher at the time of the investigators' unannounced visits – due either to absenteeism, or, in one fifth of the sample schools, because no head teacher had been appointed at all. There is absolutely no reason to tolerate this gap, since it is easy enough to ensure that every school has a head teacher and to prevent absenteeism. Similarly, an active system of school inspection (not necessarily of a punitive kind) is clearly an essential component of any schooling system, and there is indeed some evidence that regular inspections make a difference to teaching standards.[38] And yet, the very term 'inspection' seems to be treated as a dirty word in Indian education policy. It is not mentioned in the National Policy on Education, except once, to say that it is expected to be gradually replaced with 'a developed system of school complexes', without much explanation of what this system would be (that was in 1992).[39] Nor is it mentioned in the Right to Education Act of 2010.

As discussed in the preceding section, a better system of pupil evaluation and school evaluation would also be of great help in enabling parents and others to hold the system accountable. Many other levers can be activated to create accountability – teacher selection, promotion rules, parent-teacher associations, grievance redressal facilities, among others. None of them is likely to suffice on its own, but taken together, they can make a big difference.

A related issue of some importance is the need to seek the cooperation of teachers' unions to assist in improving the work culture in the schooling system. More generally – not confined only to school education – there is a strong case for treating the unions as helpers rather than as sources of hindrance in enhancing accountability in the public sector. The attitude to unions and their own views have become too narrowly politicized in India. Free-market activists tend to treat the unions as just a nuisance, while the union-oriented Left seems most reluctant to criticize the narrowly self-centred priorities of some of the unions. All this has detrimental effects on the interests and well-being of pupils as well as, at least in the long run, of the teachers themselves. It is really important to try to get the unions to recognize their social responsibilities and, on the other side, to see them as collaborators rather than as obstacles that need to be eliminated – or comprehensively weakened. There are different ways of approaching the issue of social collaboration.* Treating the unions as pure adversaries is not one of them.

---

* The Pratichi Trust has been working for some years now jointly with the All Bengal Primary Teachers Association and other unions of primary-school teachers in West

These are just some among a long list of issues that need much greater discussion and wider attention if questions of school accountability and of the quality of education are to receive the consideration they truly need. India does need a radical change in the force and cogency of public debates on school education, with much more focus on quality. This is one aspect of the case made in this book for a broadening of public discussion on development matters.

The distinct issues of increasing funding, restoring accountability, seeking the cooperation of teachers and teachers' unions in improving the quality of education, and many other remedial measures all demand attention, since there is no magic solution that is going to resolve all the problems from which Indian education in general – and school education in particular – suffer. One overarching priority, however, is the need for more active pursuit of quality in India's schooling system. Even as the much recognized problem of having many children out of school is remedied (and there is need for more speed in addressing that as well), the improvement of the shockingly low quality of Indian schooling must be a central concern of educational planning in India today. We have identified certain specific problems, and possible ways of remedying them, but the conquering of so great an adversity requires much greater attention in public discussion and social reasoning than it currently gets. It is hard to think of a more urgent challenge that India faces today than the reshaping of school education to achieve universal coverage with good-quality education for the children of India.

Bengal on the work responsibility of the teachers, and the results have been very positive and encouraging. On this see Kumar Rana (2012). See also Sarkar and Rana (2010) and Majumdar and Rana (2012).

6

India's Health Care Crisis

Sometimes the most important things in life are least talked about. For instance, it is hard to think of anything more important than health for human well-being and the quality of life. And yet, health is virtually absent from public debates and democratic politics in India.

To illustrate, the coverage of essential aspects of health and health care in the mainstream media is extremely limited. This applies not only to what can be called, without intending any disrespect, India's relatively lightweight newspapers, but also to the most seriously engaged parts of the media. In our previous book, we found that even in India's best newspapers – with a creditable record of coverage of social issues in general – issues of health were rarely discussed. For example, among more than three hundred articles published on the editorial page of one of India's finest dailies between January and June 2000, not one was concerned with health.* We examined this issue again recently, by scrutinizing all the articles (there were more than five thousand) published on the editorial pages of India's leading English-medium dailies during the last six months of 2012. There were some signs of improvement compared with the situation 12 years earlier, but the overall coverage of health issues in editorial discussions remains minuscule – about 1 per cent of the total editorial space (even if we adopt a very broad definition of health-related matters).

---

* See Drèze and Sen (2002), pp. 300–303. Out of interest, we repeated the exercise three years later, for the period January-June 2003. This time, we did find an article dealing with health issues – it was about the 'SARS crisis' in China as a 'potential threat to Asian economy'.

Most of the sample dailies did not publish more than one lead article on health on their editorial page over this period of six months. This is particularly striking considering that the second half of 2012 was a critical time for health policy, when there were real prospects of health becoming one of the main priorities of the Twelfth Five Year Plan, but also serious questions about the health policy framework outlined in the draft Plan (we shall return to this). While these questions were causing much concern among health activists and professionals, they did not become a matter of wide public discussion.

The low visibility of health issues in India's mainstream media and democratic politics applies also to child health, adding to the neglect of children in political discussions in general. For instance, a recent analysis of questions asked in the Indian Parliament found that only 3 per cent of these questions related to children (who constitute more than 40 per cent of the population). Further, of these children-related questions, less than 5 per cent were concerned with early childhood care and development. A similar analysis of recent media coverage of child-related issues shows that the interests of young children are virtually invisible in the mainstream media.[1]

A particularly telling illustration relates to child immunization. There is very little public awareness of the fact that India's immunization rates are among the lowest in the world. This is illustrated in Table 6.1, using comparable international data from UNICEF's latest *State of the World's Children* report. Except for the BCG vaccine, India's immunization rates are uniformly lower than the corresponding averages for sub-Saharan Africa, or for the 'least developed countries'. They are also uniformly lower (even for the BCG vaccine) than the corresponding estimates for every other South Asian country, including Nepal and Pakistan. In fact, outside sub-Saharan Africa, one has to go to conflict-ravaged countries like Afghanistan, Haiti, Iraq or Papua New Guinea to find lower immunization rates than India's.[2] In contrast, Bangladesh has achieved immunization rates of around 95 per cent for each vaccine. This contrast reflects the fact that child immunization rates in India increased very slowly in the 1990s and early 2000s, while Bangladesh closed most of the immunization gap over the same period, as Figure 6.1 illustrates.[3]

Table 6.1: Immunization Rates, 2012

	Proportion (%) of 1-year-old children who are immunized				
	BCG	DPT	Polio	Measles	Hep B
India	87	72	70	74	37
South Asia	88	76	75	77	51
Sub-Saharan Africa	84	77	79	75	74
Middle East & North Africa	92	91	92	90	89
Latin America & Caribbean	96	93	93	93	90
East Asia & Pacific	97	94	96	95	94
CEE/CIS	96	95	96	96	94
Industrialized countries	–	95	95	93	66
World Average	**90**	**85**	**86**	**85**	**75**
'Least developed countries'	84	80	80	78	78
Bangladesh	94	95	95	94	95
Number of countries doing worse than India[a]	26	16	13	25	0

(Continued)

Table 6.1: (*Continued*)

	Proportion (%) of 1-year-old children who are immunized				
	BCG	DPT	Polio	Measles	Hep B
Countries doing worse than India, outside Africa[a]	Afghanistan, Azerbaijan, Colombia, Costa Rica, Haiti, Iraq, Laos, Papua New Guinea, Tajikistan, Yemen	Afghanistan, Haiti, Iraq, Papua New Guinea	Afghanistan, Haiti, Iraq, Papua New Guinea	Afghanistan, Azerbaijan, Haiti, Iraq, Laos, Lebanon, Papua New Guinea, Yemen	–

CEE/CIS = Central and Eastern Europe/Commonwealth of Independent States.

[a] Among all countries (with a population of at least 2 million) for which data are available; there are approximately 150 such countries (for each vaccine).

Source: *UNICEF* (2012), Table 3, pp. 96–9.

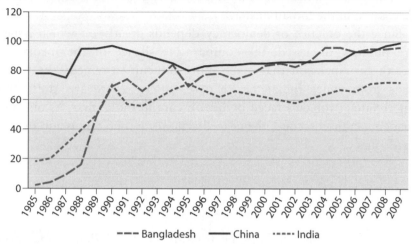

Proportion of children aged 12–23 months immunized with DPT (%)

--- Bangladesh   — China   ····· India

Figure 6.1: Immunization Coverage in India, China and Bangladesh (1985–2009)

Source: *World Development Indicators* (online, as on 1 January 2013). Very similar patterns apply to measles immunization data, available from the same source.

The issue is not only that India is doing very badly in child immunization, but also that this terrible record has remained unchallenged and virtually unaddressed. We found no evidence of any significant public debate having taken place on this issue in the last few years despite the enormity of the health problem involved.* The opposition to polio immunization in Pakistan by the Taliban does get attention (as it should), but India's lack of progress in critically important fields of immunization (despite some recent achievements,

---

* There are sporadic references to the problem in specialized publications, such as some professional medical journals (see e.g. Vashishtha 2009), but it seems to have been largely ignored in the general media. Measles alone is estimated to be responsible for more than 100,000 child deaths in India every year (John and Choudhury 2009). While many poor countries have achieved dramatic reductions in measles mortality in the 2000s, India's progress has been so slow that its share of global measles mortality is estimated to have increased from 16 per cent in 2000 to 47 per cent in 2010 (Simons et al. 2012). In this period, apparently, '[a]ll countries have implemented a measles mortality reduction strategy, except India' (Duclos et al. 2009).

including the eradication of polio), even without a Taliban, gets little discussion in the Indian media.[4]

Since the practice of democracy depends greatly on which issues are publicly discussed, the comparative silence of the media on health care makes it that much more difficult to remedy the problems from which Indian health care suffers. There are, thus, two interrelated problems faced by health care in India: first, its massive inadequacy, and second, the near-absence of public discussion of this inadequacy.

A HEALTH CHECK-UP

This silence would perhaps be tolerable if the Indian population enjoyed good health and adequate health services, but nothing could be further from the truth. We already noted, in Chapter 3, that India's health and nutrition indicators are very poor, and compare quite unfavourably with those of many other countries – both rich and poor. For example, despite the fact that India's GDP per head is about twice as high as that of Bangladesh, the latter has a higher life expectancy than India and lower child mortality rates. The lack of effective public involvement with health matters in India has played no small part in the resilience of India's health predicament.

Public expenditure on health in India has hovered around 1 per cent of the country's GDP for most of the last twenty years – very few countries spend less than that on health care, as a ratio of GDP. When the United Progressive Alliance (UPA) government came to office in 2004, one of the core commitments of the coalition government's National Common Minimum Programme was to raise public health expenditure to 'at least 2–3 per cent of the GDP over the next five years'. But the ratio actually declined, to 0.9 per cent of GDP in 2005, before rising very slowly again, partly due (in recent years) to salary increases in the public sector. At 1.2 per cent of GDP, public expenditure on health in India today is still exceptionally low in comparative perspective: only nine countries in the world have a lower ratio of public expenditure on health to GDP. India's 1.2 per cent compares with 2.7 per cent in China, 3.8 per cent in Latin America, and a world average of 6.5 per cent (including countries with a national health insurance, such as those in the European Union, where the average ratio of public health expenditure to GDP is around 8 per cent). In absolute terms, this translates (in terms of purchasing-power-parity 2005 international dollars) to $39 per person per year in India, compared with $66 in Sri Lanka, $203 in China and $483 in Brazil.

A related symptom of India's lack of governmental commitment to health care is that public expenditure on health accounts for less than one third of total health expenditure. Only a few countries (such as Afghanistan, Haiti and Sierra Leone) have a lower ratio of public health expenditure to total health expenditure. To put this in perspective, public expenditure accounts for 70 to 85 per cent of total health expenditure in most countries of the European Union and North America, with an average of 77 per cent in the European Union, and one notable outlier – the United States (just below 50 per cent), which remains a bit of a 'developing country' as far as public health care is concerned. Even the US ratio, however, is much higher than India's. The world average is 63 per cent, and even the averages for sub-Saharan Africa (45 per cent) and for the 'least developed countries' in the world (46 per cent) are also much higher than India's 29 per cent (see Table 6.2). These are some indications, among others, that India has one of the most commercialized health care systems in the world.

The unusual reliance on private health care in India results largely from the fact that the country's public health facilities are very limited, and quite often very badly run. Health facility surveys conducted by the International Institute for Population Sciences (Mumbai) in 2003 gave a chilling picture of the state of public health centres around the country. To illustrate, only 69 per cent of Primary Health Centres (PHCs) had at least one bed, only 20 per cent had a telephone, and just 12 per cent enjoyed 'regular maintenance'. These are national averages, and the corresponding figures for the poorer states are much worse. In Bihar, for instance, a large majority of PHCs had to make do without luxuries such as electricity, a weighing machine or even a toilet. It is worth remembering that a PHC is supposed to

Table 6.2
Public Expenditure on Health, 2010

	As a share of GDP (%)	As a share of total health expenditure (%)	In absolute terms (2005 PPP international dollars)[a]
India	1.2	29	39
South Asia	1.2	30	36
Sub-Saharan Africa[b]	2.9	45	66
East Asia & Pacific[b]	2.5	53	167
Middle East & North Africa[b]	2.9	50	199
Latin America & Caribbean[b]	3.8	50	424
Europe & Central Asia[b]	3.8	65	585
World Average	6.5	63	641
European Union	8.1	77	2,499

[a] Calculated from per capita expenditure on health and share of public health expenditure in total health expenditure.
[b] 'Developing countries' only.

Source: *World Development Indicators* (online, 1 January 2013).

be a health facility of some importance, serving a population of about fifty thousand persons on average (often many more – about 158,000 in Bihar).

Even when health facilities are available, their utilization leaves much to be desired. According to one recent study, absenteeism rates among health workers ranged between 35 and 58 per cent in different Indian states in 2002–3.[5] A similar picture emerges from another study of health services in Udaipur district (Rajasthan): more than half of the health sub-centres were found to be closed during regular opening hours, and even in the PHCs and Community Health Centres, 36 per cent of the personnel were absent on average. Meanwhile, local residents suffered from horrendous levels of morbidity: one third of all adults had a cold during the 30 days preceding the survey, 42 per cent had body ache, 33 per cent had fever, 23 per cent suffered from fatigue, 11 per cent had chest pains, and more than half suffered from anaemia. Close to one-third found it difficult to draw water from a well and one in five had difficulty standing up from a sitting position.[6]

The problem is, naturally, most intense for the poorer Indians, but the bias towards private facilities affects even the relatively well-off, who too often have rather limited access to decent and affordable health care. The technology and expertise are usually available, but public facilities are highly inefficient and disorganized, and private services are virtually unregulated, leaving patients at the mercy, often enough, of unscrupulous practitioners. Fraud, over-medication, exploitative pricing and unnecessary surgery seem to be quite common in the private health sector. To illustrate, a recent study of health services in Chennai found that 47 per cent of deliveries performed in the private sector end up with a Caesarean, which is much higher than the WHO norms of up to 15 per cent (the corresponding ratio in the public sector in Chennai was 20 per cent).[7] Another recent study of health care in Delhi and Madhya Pradesh found that both public and private health facilities offered very defective services, with simple diseases being inaccurately diagnosed and inappropriately treated in a majority of cases.[8] The need for reform applies not just to public services, or to the services available to poor households, but to the health sector as a whole.

THE PRIVATE INSURANCE TRAP

The rapid growth of India's GDP and public revenue during the last twenty years, discussed in Chapter 1, was an opportunity to launch major initiatives in the field of health policy. This opportunity, however, has been largely missed, despite some signs of positive change in recent years. The rate of progress in public health care has been astonishingly slow over the last two decades, even as the growth of GDP in India has been exceptionally high. The 1990s were largely a 'lost decade' for India as far as health is concerned, and much of the 2000s did little better.

As mentioned earlier, the Common Minimum Programme of the first UPA government promised a radical increase in public expenditure on health, which did not materialize. It did lead to one major initiative: the National Rural Health Mission (NRHM), launched in 2005–6. However, NRHM expenditure was below Rs 10,000 crores per year during the first five years (less than 0.2 per cent of the GDP) – far too little to make a major difference in the country. This is quite possibly a good programme (about which more presently), but it can only achieve so much without greater economic resources and political commitment – from the government and from the public.

Along with these faltering moves towards consolidation of India's public health services, there are also other developments, of a very different kind – towards even greater reliance on private provision of health care and private insurance of health risks. The Rashtriya Swasthya Bhima Yojana (RSBY), or 'national health insurance scheme', is one step in that direction. Under this scheme, launched in 2008, 'below poverty line' (BPL) families are enrolled with private health insurance companies. The government pays the insurance premium, which entitles them to Rs 30,000 of health care in an institution of their choice, to be picked from a list of accredited hospitals and health centres.

Not surprisingly, this move has been welcomed by the corporate sector. As *The Wall Street Journal* put it a few years ago in an upbeat article, praising this 'business model', the Rashtriya Swasthya Bhima Yojana 'presents a way for insurance companies to market themselves and develop brand awareness'. Private hospitals also get their due, as 'the program can increase the number of patients and potentially widen the client base'. RSBY is a convenient springboard for the private health insurance industry – one of the fastest-growing sectors of the Indian economy.

Subsidized private health insurance under RSBY may, of course, bring some relief to selected households.[9] It is certainly an improvement over the current 'out of pocket system' (OOPS), whereby the bulk of health care is purchased for cash from private providers. But what sort of health system is it supposed to lead to, or be part of? One interpretation is that private insurance is expected to become the backbone of India's future health system. The government will pay the insurance premium for BPL families, and others will buy health insurance from private companies on their own. People will then seek health care from accredited institutions, public or private, and the costs will be reimbursed by private health insurance companies.* Despite its attractive sound, there are very serious reasons to be deeply concerned about this health care model.

Efficiency issues: The limitations of private (more precisely, commercial) health insurance begin with a series of standard 'market failures', associated in particular with adverse selection and moral hazard. Briefly, adverse selection refers to the fact that health insurance is likely to attract people who are particularly prone to illness, and this would drive up insurance premiums, restricting the pool of willing buyers to high-risk clients. Insurance companies can try to protect themselves from this by 'screening' their clients, but this runs against basic principles of equity in health care. And it can turn the problem on its head, by restricting insurance to low-risk groups and excluding those who are in greatest need of health care.

Turning to moral hazard, one of its manifestations is the fact that the insured patients – and health care providers – have little incentive to contain the costs. Every 'solution' to this raises its own problems. For instance, incentives to contain the costs of health care can be created by reimbursing costs on some sort of 'presumptive' basis (e.g. fixed amounts for specific procedures such as a delivery or treatment of tuberculosis). But then the health care providers (doctors, hospitals and so on) have strong incentives to use the cheapest possible method for each procedure, even if it goes against the interests of the patient. They may also be tempted to indulge in 'cream-skimming', that is, focusing on patients who can be treated at low cost and turn away the rest. These are just some examples of the complex efficiency problems associated with private health insurance – problems that can, at best, be alleviated with strict and sophisticated regulation, of a kind that would be very hard to implement in India as things stand.

Distortion issue: Commercial health insurance tends to be geared

---

* This is not – at least not yet – an explicit policy, but as Gita Sen (2012) observes, 'there are many powerful forces that would like the health system to move (or continue to move) in the direction of an unregulated and lucrative private market, including for service provision, health insurance and medical education' (p. 52). There were further apprehensions of this sort among many observers during the process of preparation of the Twelfth Five Year Plan; see e.g. Gaitonde and Shukla (2012), Varshney (2012) and Varshney et al. (2012).

primarily to hospital care. A health system based on commercial health insurance is likely to be biased against preventive health services, and more generally, against non-hospitalized care. This would be a problem for any health system based on private insurance, but particularly so in India where a large part of the burden of ill health consists of communicable diseases.[10] It is also the case that health care for many types of non-communicable diseases such as diabetes, circulatory problems and cancer can be best dealt with by early – pre-hospitalization – treatment, against which a system focused primarily on hospitalization might be biased. This is an additional problem to the general undermining of public health and preventive services that can be expected to follow from increased reliance on schemes like RSBY. Quite likely, private health insurance would also end up promoting further privatization of health services and affect the resources, time, energy and commitment available to strengthen public health services, and this could undermine precisely the channel through which health transition has been brought about across the world – in Europe, Japan, East Asia, Latin America, Canada and even the USA. There are important lessons here from the global experience of successful health transitions from which India can learn, but which it seems to have ignored.[11]

Targeting issue: The idea that the government will pay the insurance premiums for poor households, to ensure that they are included in the system, raises all the problems associated with 'BPL targeting', including the unreliability and divisiveness of the BPL identification process (for further discussion, see Chapter 7). In the context of health, these problems are particularly serious, for two reasons. First, health contingencies can rapidly 'push' families into poverty. Thus, a family that was 'above the poverty line' yesterday may be below the poverty line today. BPL lists, for their part, are quite rigid (even renewing them every five years or so has proved extremely difficult in most states), and it is simply not possible to revise them as and when people fall into poverty due to health contingencies. So a BPL list can hardly serve the intended purpose well. The second reason is that taking into account people's health status creates problems for the entire logic of the BPL approach, based as it is on the per capita expenditure criterion and proxy indicators of it. For instance, a person with some disability but not severely low income may be severely deprived and in dire need of health insurance because of the costs and deprivations associated with that disability, and yet fail to qualify for the BPL list.* Thus, subsidizing the insurance premiums of BPL households is a very inadequate – and defective – way of ensuring universal health coverage.

Equity issue: A health system based on targeted insurance subsidies is very unlikely to meet basic norms of equity in health care, as four different sources of inequality reinforce each other: exclusion errors associated with the targeting process; screening of potential clients by insurance companies; the obstacles (powerlessness, low education, social discrimination, among others) poor people face in using the health insurance system; and the persistence of a large unsubsidized component in the health system, where access to health care is linked with the ability to pay insurance premiums.

Irreversibility issue: Last but not least, the private health insurance model can be, in effect, something of a one-way street – the health insurance industry can easily become a powerful lobby and establish a strong hold on health policy, making it very difficult to move away from that model if it proves ineffective. The current drift in India towards private health insurance, without developing a solid base of public health care, has that problematic feature – aside from others, just discussed.

The private health insurance model is essentially the American model, the lack of reach of which President Obama – and earlier the Clintons – tried hard to remedy (with some recent success).† Despite the excellent quality of top-level medical care in the USA, the country

* On the inescapable relevance of disability in understanding the demands of the justice of health care, see the section on 'Disabilities, Resources and Capabilities' in *The Idea of Justice* (Sen 2009, pp. 258–60).
† In the health care systems of other OECD countries, insurance also plays a major role in many cases (one notable exception is the United Kingdom, where the National Health Service directly provides universal health care free 'at the point of delivery'), but insurance is normally arranged by the state, or by regulated non-profit institutions (as in Germany and Japan). Very few of them rely significantly on profit-driven health insurance, and to the extent that they do, it is subject to very tight regulation. For a useful review of health care systems in 13 OECD countries, see The Commonwealth Fund (2010).

has paid a heavy price for taking this route, in terms of limited access to, and exclusions from, health care. The US health care system is one of the most costly and ineffective in the industrialized world: per capita health expenditure is more than twice as high as in Europe, but health outcomes are poorer (with, for instance, the US ranking 50th in the world in terms of life expectancy). This system is also highly inequitable, with nearly 20 per cent of the population excluded from health insurance, and terrible health conditions and risks among deprived groups. Further, attempts to reform the health care system in the US have proved extremely difficult, partly due to the power of the health insurance business, and partly due to deep-rooted political resistance to the idea of 'socialized' health care, which resistance has been much cultivated by private health insurance companies. The contrast with Canada, with so-called 'socialized medicine', which achieves more at far less cost than the USA for normal health care through state-provided health care, brings out some of the problems that the USA has to overcome before it can become a 'model' for the world – in particular India – to follow. This is not to say that Canada itself is a flawless model: its exclusion of private health insurance, except for very limited purposes, may be seen as too extreme (it is not clear why the rich should not be allowed to pay for extra health insurance while remaining quite free to spend money on expensive holidays or yachts), and surely there is much to learn also from the European system of reliance on national health services and social insurance without ruling out private health insurance.

The fundamental need for active public involvement with health care (including a strong foundation of public provision) in India was recognized at least as early as the Bhore Committee Report of 1946, and reaffirmed recently – in a somewhat different form – by the Report of the High Level Expert Group on Universal Health Coverage for India.[12] The actual trajectory of the health sector, however, has been very different, at times even diametrically opposite – moving more and more towards privatized health care and insurance systems that do not preclude exclusion of 'unprofitable patients'. The proposed regulations seem deeply inadequate to tame a profit-seeking health care system to serve the purposes of universalism and equity. Health policy today is in a somewhat confused state, with some positive initiatives towards the consolidation of public services (including the National Rural Health Mission, and, more recently, a move towards public provision of generic drugs), but also a steady drift towards greater reliance on private insurance (actively encouraged by the health industry), and very little clarity about the principles on which India's future health system should be based. Meanwhile, many other developing countries – not just China, but also Brazil, Mexico, Thailand, Vietnam, among others – have made decisive progress towards universal health coverage, based on clear commitments to publicly funded universal health coverage and well-functioning public health services.* This is an aspect of public policy where very important choices remain to be made in India.[13]

THE NUTRITIONAL FAILURE

India's nutrition indicators have significantly improved during the last 65 years, starting from abysmal levels that existed at the time of Indian independence (see Chapter 1). For instance, clinical signs of severe undernutrition (such as marasmus and kwashiorkor) are much less common now than they used to be, and there has been a slow but steady improvement in children's heights and weights. And yet, even today, the nutrition situation in India (and in much of South Asia) remains appalling – worse than almost anywhere else in the world.[14]

To illustrate, none of the countries for which recent nutrition data are available have a higher proportion of underweight children than India.[15] The Indian figure, 43 per cent, is close to the South Asian average, but much higher than the estimated averages for sub-Saharan Africa (20 per cent) or the 'least developed countries' (25 per cent), not to speak of other major regions of the world (less than 12 per cent

---

* Mexico has moved rapidly towards universal health coverage through its System of Social Protection in Health (SSPH), introduced in 2003, with a crucial role for a national health insurance programme ('Seguro Popular'), run by the state, to provide 'effective health care as a universal right based on citizenship'. By 2012, Mexico seems to have achieved – or nearly achieved – universal health coverage. See 'A Crucial Juncture for Health in Mexico', *The Lancet*, 14 July 2012; and Richard Horton (2012). For an excellent discussion of the way SSPH and Seguro Popular work, see Felicia Marie Knaul et al. (2012).

in each case – see Table 6.3). The latest estimate for China, 4 per cent, is about one tenth of the corresponding figure for India. The broad patterns are much the same for stunting (low height-for-age), although the contrasts in stunting rates are less sharp, and one or two countries (e.g. Burundi) do have a higher estimated proportion of stunted children than India's 48 per cent.

The Indian population – not just children – also suffer from massive micronutrient deficiencies, including iron deficiency (which affects a majority of women and children), but also shortages of many other essential nutrients, as Table 6.4 illustrates.[16] According to the National Nutrition Monitoring Bureau data, the ratio of average intake to 'recommended daily allowance' among children in the age group of 4–6 years was only 16 per cent for Vitamin A, 35 per cent for iron and 45 per cent for calcium in the early 2000s. The situation remains much the same today in this respect, partly due to the inadequate reach of supplementation programmes, also illustrated in Table 6.4. For instance, only one third of Indian children below the age of five years are covered by the Vitamin A supplementation programme, compared with near-universal coverage in every other South Asian country and even in much of sub-Saharan Africa.

A view is sometimes aired claiming that child undernutrition in India is a 'myth', because Indian children are genetically shorter, so that international anthropometric standards are not applicable to them. However, this recent reincarnation of the so-called 'small but healthy' hypothesis (and that is what it is – a hypothesis) is yet to receive any sort of scientific support.[17] It is also difficult to reconcile with a recent re-examination of the validity of applying the same anthropometric standards of height and weight to children across the world: the Multicentre Growth Reference Study (completed under the auspices of the World Health Organization), which found no evidence of Indian children being genetically shorter than other children.*

* The Indian component of this study focused on a large sample of children from well-off families in South Delhi, with at least one well-educated member (17 years of education) and other favourable conditions including intensive maternal and child-care. These privileged children, brought up in a favourable environment, were found to grow along the same 'curve' (in terms of height and weight at different ages) as children in the other countries included in the WHO study – Brazil, Ghana, Norway,

Table 6.3
Child Nutrition Indicators, 2006–10[a]

	Proportion (%) of children under 5 who are undernourished:		Proportion (%) of infants with low birthweight
	Weight for age	Height for age	
India[a]	43	48	28
South Asia	42	47	27
Sub-Saharan Africa	20	39	13
East Asia & Pacific	10	19	6
Middle East & North Africa	11	28	11
Latin America & Caribbean	4	15	8
'Least developed countries'	25	41	16

[a] Latest year for which data are available within that period.

Source: UNICEF (2012), Tables 2 and 3. The regional estimates are based on countries for which data are available, and pertain to 'developing countries' only.

But even if this hypothesis is correct to some extent, it would not invalidate the basic fact that undernutrition levels in India are extremely high – certainly among the highest in the world.[18]

The phenomenon of high levels of child undernutrition in South Asia (not only India), even compared with many sub-Saharan African countries that have poorer income and health indicators, is known as 'the South Asian enigma', following an influential article published in 1996 by a team led by Vulimiri Ramalingaswami, who was the Director of the All India Institute of Medical Sciences.[19] The original article drew attention to various aspects of the low status of women in South Asia as a possible explanation for this enigma, and this hypothesis is consistent with more recent work on this issue.[20] One of the connections between women's well-being and child nutrition works through low birthweights: women's poor nutritional status and other deprivations (especially during pregnancy) lead to poor

---

Oman and the United States. See WHO Multicentre Growth Reference Study Group (2006).

Table 6.4: Micronutrient Deficiencies and Supplementation

	Deficiencies (%)				Supplementation (%)	
	Proportion of pre-school age children with anaemia	Proportion of pregnant women with anaemia	Proportion of pre-school age children with Vitamin A deficiency	Proportion of school-aged children with iodine deficiency	Vitamin A supplementation coverage rate (age 6–59 months), 2010	Proportion of households consuming adequately iodized salt, 2006–10
South Asia						
India	74	50	62	31	34	51
Bangladesh	47	47	22	43	100	84[a]
Nepal	78	75	32	27	91	63[b]
Pakistan	51	39	13	64	87	n/a
Sri Lanka	30	29	35	30	85	92[a]
China	20	29	9	16	–	97
Sub-Saharan Africa	68[c]	56[c]	44[c]	41[c]	86	53

[a] Data differ from standard definition or refer to only part of the country.
[b] 2002–7 figure, based on Micronutrient Initiative and UNICEF (2009), Annex A.
[c] Population-weighted average of country-specific figures.

Source: Micronutrient Initiative and UNICEF (2009), Annex A, for 'deficiencies'. UNICEF (2012), Table 2, for 'supplementation'.

foetal growth and low birthweights, affecting children's nutrition status right from birth and even conception. The original article, for instance, suggested that weight gain during pregnancy may be only about half in South Asia (about 5 kgs on average) as in Africa (much closer to 10 kgs).

In this connection, it is worth recalling that not only children but also adult women are more undernourished in India (and South Asia) than almost anywhere else in the world. According to the Demographic and Health Surveys, the proportion of adult women with a 'body mass index' below 18.5 (a standard cut-off conventionally associated with chronic energy deficiency) was as high as 36 per cent in India in 2005–6 – higher than in any other country for which DHS data are available, and nearly three times as high as the corresponding estimate for sub-Saharan Africa (14 per cent).[21]

This is just a sample of the distressing facts that characterize the nutrition situation in India. As in the case of child immunization, discussed earlier, there is also a serious issue of lack of improvement over time. This was one of the main messages of the third National Family Health Survey ('NFHS-3'), conducted in 2005–6 – the most recent comprehensive household survey on health and nutrition in India at the time of writing. For instance, the proportion of underweight children was not much lower in 2005–6 than in 1992–3, the date of the first National Family Health Survey, and while child stunting rates seem to be improving a little faster, the overall picture is one of very limited progress over this period (see Table 6.5). Thirteen years may seem like a short time, but it is actually long enough to achieve major improvements in child nutrition based on bold interventions, as Thailand showed in the 1980s and China demonstrated in the 1960s and 1970s. The NFHS-3 data also point to very low rates of improvement in women's heights and body-mass index, and no improvement at all in the prevalence of anaemia. Like the stagnation of child immunization over the same period, these alarming trends have received astonishingly little attention outside specialized circles.*

* One of the casualties of this lack of concern with nutrition trends is the nutrition monitoring system itself. NFHS-3 data are already eight years old, and very little information is available (at the time of writing) on subsequent developments in the

Table 6.5
Trends in Child Nutrition

	Proportion (%) of children under the age of three years who are undernourished				
	Old NCHS Standards			New WHO Standards	
	1992–3	1998–9	2005–6	1998–9	2005–6
Weight-for-age					
Below 2 SD	52	47	46	43	40
Below 3 SD	20	18	n/a	18	16
Height-for-age					
Below 2 SD	n/a	46	38	51	45
Below 3 SD	n/a	23	n/a	28	22

SD = standard deviation (based on the reference population). Below 2/3 SD corresponds to moderate/severe undernourishment, respectively.

Source: International Institute for Population Sciences (2000), pp. 266–7, and International Institute for Population Sciences (2007a), p. 274, based on successive National Family Health Surveys (NFHS). The 2005–6 figures based on NCHS standards are from the 'National Fact Sheet' (International Institute for Population Sciences, 2007b). The National Centre for Health Statistics (NCHS) standards were used in NFHS surveys until the new WHO Child Growth Standards were released in 2006. For further details, see Deaton and Drèze (2009), Table 11.

CHILDCARE AS A SOCIAL RESPONSIBILITY[22]

Imagine how we would view a gardener who allows anyone to trample on the flowers he is growing, and then tries to rectify the neglect by giving the plants extra care and heavy doses of water and fertilizer. Something like this, however, is done by the state to Indian children on a regular basis, since very often public intervention does not begin until the children reach school-going age, when they are finally herded into school for education and attention (which they get if lucky). Yet the first

nutrition situation. The findings of NFHS-4 (yet to be conducted) are not expected to be available until 2015 at the earliest. This ten-year gap in nutrition statistics does not help to take timely and effective steps to address India's nutrition problems.

six years of life (and especially the first two) have a decisive and lasting influence on a child's health, well-being, aptitudes and opportunities.*

The long-standing neglect of childcare services in India arises partly from a common assumption that the care of young children is best left to the household. Parents are indeed best placed to look after their young children, and generally do take care of them. But parents often lack the resources, energy, power or time to take adequate care of their children, even when commitment and knowledge of what has to be done are not lacking. What they can do for their children depends on various forms of social support, including health services, crèche facilities and maternity entitlements. Further, many parents have limited knowledge of matters relating to childcare and nutrition. To illustrate, in a recent study in Uttar Pradesh, half of the sample children were found to be undernourished, yet 94 per cent of the mothers described their child's nutritional status as 'normal'. Folk wisdom on, say, breastfeeding can also be quite limited and even plain wrong, in spite of thousands of years of experience. For instance, the initiation of breastfeeding is often delayed based on the erroneous belief that a mother's first breast milk (colostrum) is harmful for the child, when exactly the opposite is true. In the same state of Uttar Pradesh, a majority of children are kept hungry for a full 24 hours after birth, and only 15 per cent are breastfed within an hour – the medically recommended practice.[23] What parents do for their children (for instance, whether they get them vaccinated, or how a pregnant woman is fed) also depends a great deal on social norms that lend themselves to positive influence through public action.

For all these reasons, the care of young children cannot be left to the household alone. Social involvement is required, both in the form of enabling parents to take better care of their children at home, and in the form of direct provision of health, nutrition, pre-school education and related services through public facilities.

In principle, there is much room for this under the Integrated Child

---

* There is a pervasive need here for taking into account what Sudhir Anand and his colleagues have called, inspired by an approach pioneered by Albina du Boisrouvray, the 'cost of inaction' (see Anand et al. 2012). The costs – or losses – generated by inaction can be large, and often very much larger than the cost of undertaking actions that would have prevented the loss from neglect.

Development Services – the only national programme aimed at children under six years of age. The aim of ICDS is to provide integrated health, nutrition and pre-school education services to children under six through local anganwadis (childcare centres). However, ICDS tends to be starved of resources, attention and political support. It is only in recent years that the programme has come to life, largely due to Supreme Court orders that have compelled the government to reframe it in a rights perspective: all ICDS services are now supposed to be available to all children under six as a matter of legal entitlement.[24]

The functioning of existing ICDS centres has been subjected to considerable criticism. Indeed some critics have even argued that to spend money on ICDS is to sink funds into a bottomless pit of a dysfunctional programme. There are surely many shortcomings of the ICDS programme as it now stands. And yet an impartial scrutiny of the available evidence does not support this defeatist assessment. The standards of implementation of ICDS have certainly been very low – so far – in many states, but this situation is neither universal nor immutable. The findings of the FOCUS Report, based on a survey of 200 anganwadis in six states (Chhattisgarh, Himachal Pradesh, Maharashtra, Rajasthan, Tamil Nadu and Uttar Pradesh) in 2004, shed some useful light on this matter.

These six states purposely included three (Himachal Pradesh, Maharashtra and Tamil Nadu) that have taken active interest in ICDS, and three (Chhattisgarh, Rajasthan and Uttar Pradesh) that have not – 'active states' and 'dormant states' respectively in Table 6.6, which presents a summary of the assessments of sample mothers. Aside from averages for the active and dormant states, the table also presents the corresponding figures for Tamil Nadu and Uttar Pradesh: the states with the best and worst ICDS programmes, respectively, among the six sample states.

The first point to note is that in every state an overwhelming majority (more than 90 per cent) of the anganwadis open regularly and have an active 'supplementary nutrition programme' (SNP). Bearing in mind that more than 90 per cent of villages in India today have an anganwadi, these findings point to a very important opportunity:

Table 6.6
FOCUS Survey: Perceptions of ICDS Among Sample Mothers

	Tamil Nadu	'Active States'[a]	'Dormant States'[a]	Uttar Pradesh
General perceptions of the sample mothers (% of affirmative responses)				
The local anganwadi opens regularly	100	99	90	87
Their child attends regularly[b]	86	75	52	57
Supplementary nutrition is provided at the anganwadi	93	94	93	94
Their child is regularly weighed at the anganwadi	87	82	47	40
Immunization services are available at the anganwadi[c]	63	72	49	44
Pre-school activities are taking place at the anganwadi[b]	89	55	41	36
ICDS is 'important' for their child's welfare	95	88	57	59
Perceptions about the supplementary nutrition programme[d] (% of affirmative responses)				
Food distribution is regular	100	95	72	54
Children get a 'full meal'	100	87	48	32
Quantity is inadequate	2	13	54	69
Quality of food is poor	7	15	35	55

[a] Active states: Himachal Pradesh, Maharashtra, Tamil Nadu. Dormant states: Chhattisgarh, Rajasthan, Uttar Pradesh.

[b] Among mothers with at least one child in the age group of 3–6 years (the relevant age group for this question).

[c] These figures are likely to underestimate the extent of immunization activities under ICDS, because immunization sessions often take place at the local health centre, with the anganwadi worker playing a facilitation role (e.g. by bringing the children).

[d] Among mothers who reported that supplementary nutrition was provided at the anganwadi.

Source: FOCUS Report (Citizens' Initiative for the Rights of Children Under Six, 2006), pp. 42 and 59. The figures are based on a random sample of women with at least one child under the age of six years, enrolled at the local anganwadi.

India already has a functional, country-wide infrastructure that makes it possible, in principle, to reach out to children under six.[25]

The standards of functionality, however, vary a great deal, as Table 6.6 illustrates. The picture is reasonably encouraging for the active states, and especially for Tamil Nadu, where ICDS has achieved exemplary standards (more on this presently). In the dormant states, however, many anganwadis have been reduced to feeding centres, and even the supplementary nutrition programme often works quite badly. An important message from the same report, however, is that in many cases the failures are not particularly difficult to diagnose or even cure.

Consider for instance the supplementary nutrition programme. There is much evidence that the best approach here is to combine nutritious, cooked food for children aged 3–6 years with well-designed 'take-home rations' (together with nutrition counselling) for younger children. Yet, at the time of the survey, many states were not even trying to take these simple steps to improve the nutrition component of ICDS. For instance, in Rajasthan and Uttar Pradesh, children aged 3–6 years were getting the same bland 'ready-to-eat' food (e.g. panjiri or murmura) day after day, and children under the age of three were getting nothing at all. It is no wonder that the mothers sampled in these states were often dissatisfied with the supplementary nutrition programme.

It is also worth noting that the resistance to replacing ready-to-eat food with locally cooked meals in some states is not unrelated to the powerful influence of food contractors, whose interests are directly involved. As will be discussed in Chapter 8, the last ten years have been a period of protracted battle against the invasion of commercial interests in child nutrition programmes.

The FOCUS report pointed to another very important role of cooked food for children aged 3–6 years: it is of enormous help in ensuring regular attendance. In this respect too, the provision of cooked food (as opposed to ready-to-eat mixtures) is a prime example of a simple but effective step to improve ICDS. Other interesting examples also emerged from the same study. For instance, it was found that the regularity of health workers' visits at the anganwadi was much greater when the health workers (e.g. the 'auxiliary nurse midwife', known as ANM) have a clear, fixed schedule of visits to different anganwadis than when they are allowed to 'drop by' at their convenience.

A recent analysis of National Family Health Survey data on ICDS corroborates the potential (and in some states, actual) effectiveness of the programme. The author, Monica Jain, found that daily nutrition supplements for children below the age of two years had a substantial positive effect on their height, particularly among girls. The effect was especially large (a gain of about two centimetres for girls) in states where daily feeding of young children under ICDS is a widespread practice, including the three 'active states' mentioned earlier. Jain also concluded, based on tentative cost-benefit calculations, that daily feeding of children under two was highly effective even in terms of plain economic returns – taking into account the links between nutrition, productivity and wages.[26] This is a useful reminder of the fact that while taking care of young children is imperative from the point of view of their own rights and well-being, it is also sound economics.[27]

Given all this, it is rather unfortunate that only a small minority (about 6 per cent) of children under two in the country-wide NFHS sample seem to have benefited from daily feeding under ICDS, most of them concentrated in a few states that have used the programme extensively. This is one reflection of the programme's general bias towards older children (within the age group of 0–6 years). Some of the active states mentioned earlier have demonstrated the possibility of correcting that bias, not just in the feeding programme but also in other aspects of ICDS.[28] The need for much greater attention to younger children is especially urgent in the light of mounting scientific evidence that much of their nutritional and health future is sealed by the age of two or three years.* Aside from nutrition supplements, this would also call for other interventions, both within as well as outside ICDS, relating for instance to nutrition counselling, safe water,

---

* The importance of prioritizing intervention at a very young age is one of the central messages of recent work by James Heckman and his colleagues on the early determinants of human capabilities, as well as of the growing literature on the economics of child development; see e.g. Heckman (2008), Conti and Heckman (2012), and earlier work cited there.

sanitation, immunization, maternity entitlements and crèche facilities, among other needs.

As far as ICDS is concerned, the main challenge is to break the vicious circle of low awareness, low expectations, weak demand and lethargic implementation. In a recent evaluation of ICDS by the Planning Commission, startling contrasts were found in women's awareness of children's food entitlements under the programme, ranging from 96 per cent in Kerala and 88 per cent in Tamil Nadu to less than 20 per cent in most of the poorer states, where the programme is desperately needed (e.g. 16 per cent in Bihar and 12 per cent in Uttar Pradesh).[29] Even then, interestingly, anganwadi workers report that one of their main difficulties is 'living up to the expectations of the communities who demand better quality services'. If anganwadi workers are responsive to the expectations of the community, and if awareness of entitlements is yet to rise from below 20 per cent to 80 per cent or more in the 'dormant states', perhaps there is hope for ICDS. A number of recent experiences across the country vindicate that hope – Tamil Nadu is one important example.[30]

INSIGHTS FROM PUBLIC SERVICES IN TAMIL NADU

Unlike most other Indian states, Tamil Nadu has a clear commitment to free and universal health care – not extending to every aspect of health care by any means, but covering a wide range of facilities and services. As discussed in our previous book, this commitment is evident in relatively good health services, and also translates into better health achievements than most other states.[31] Recent studies suggest not only that Tamil Nadu has made further rapid progress in this field during the last ten years or so, but also that these achievements fit into a larger pattern of comparatively active, creative and inclusive social policies.

In our earlier work, Tamil Nadu's lead in terms of health outcomes was brought out by comparing them with those of other states (e.g. the 'large north Indian states') that had similar levels of per capita income or per capita expenditure at that time.[32] Tamil Nadu is now significantly better-off, economically, than most of those states, because of its relatively high rate of economic growth in recent years. In terms of per capita expenditure, it is now in the same league as states like Gujarat, though still significantly poorer than, say, Haryana. As Table 6.7 illustrates, however, Tamil Nadu's health-related indicators are enormously better than those of both Gujarat and Haryana (for instance, its infant mortality rate and maternal mortality ratio are about half as high as the corresponding figures for those states). In fact, Gujarat and Haryana's health indicators are not very different from the all-India averages in most cases, while Tamil Nadu is much closer to Kerala in this respect – and getting closer year after year.

The foundation of Tamil Nadu's health care system is an extensive network of primary health centres, routinely visited by patients from diverse social backgrounds. A series of recent field studies indicate that these health centres are reasonably well organized, well staffed, and well supplied with basic medicines.[33] A fairly typical account is the following by Dipa Sinha:

> The Primary Health Centres (PHCs) in Tamil Nadu were very lively and vibrant. Someone was present whenever I went there to visit. In the mornings the PHCs were bustling with activity and there was a well-rehearsed routine of people queuing up for their tokens, then going to the doctor and from there moving on to the pharmacy or the 'injection room'. While this drill is on it is impossible to catch the attention of any of the PHC staff. Everyone is busy, everyone takes their work seriously and curious visitors like me are requested to wait . . . I asked all the people in the queue whether they had to pay for the medicines or for consultation or any other fee and invariably the answer was in the negative.*

These impressions are corroborated not only by other independent accounts but also, in some respects at least, by secondary data. For instance, National Sample Survey data indicate that the private costs of obtaining health care in public institutions are much lower in Tamil

---

* The author attempted similar enquiries at PHCs in Uttar Pradesh. But the Centres were closed most of the time and 'in the sample villages the respondents did not know where the nearest PHC was' (Dipa Sinha, 2013).

Table 6.7: Health-related Indicators for Selected States

	Kerala	Tamil Nadu	Gujarat	Haryana	India
Per capita consumption expenditure, 2009–10 (Rs per month)					
Rural	1,835	1,160	1,110	1,510	1,054
Urban	2,413	1,948	1,909	2,321	1,984
Infant mortality rate, 2011 (per 1,000 live births)	12	22	41	44	44
Maternal mortality ratio, 2007–9 (per 100,000 live births)	81	97	148	153	212
Life expectancy at birth, 2006–10 (years)					
Female	76.9	70.9	69.0	69.5	67.7
Male	71.5	67.1	64.9	67.0	64.6
Proportion (%) of children below age 5 who are undernourished, 2005–6					
Weight-for-age	22.9	29.8	44.6	39.6	42.5
Height-for-age	24.5	30.9	51.7	45.7	48.0
Proportion (%) of births assisted by skilled health personnel, 2005–6	99	91	63	49	47
Proportion (%) of women who gave (live) birth with specific types of maternal care, 2005–6					
At least one ANC visit/antenatal care	94	99	87	88	76
Post-natal check-up	87	91	61	58	41

Proportion (%) of children aged 12–23 months, 2005–6, with					
Full immunization	75.3	80.9	45.2	65.3	43.5
No immunization	1.8	0.0	4.5	7.8	5.1
Proportion (%) of children aged 12–35 months who had at least one dose of Vitamin A in the last 6 months, 2005–6	46.5	44.8	20.6	15.9	24.8
Proportion (%) of children under three years, 2007–8, who started breastfeeding:					
Within one hour of birth	64.6	76.1	48.0	16.5	40.5
Later than 24 hours after birth	3.2	6.6	22.2	44.6	29.1

Source: Statistical Appendix, Table A.3.

Nadu (even zero, in the case of outpatient care in rural areas) than in other states.[34] The geographical density of health centres, ratio of doctors and nurses to population, and share of women in health staff (including doctors), are also much higher in Tamil Nadu than in most other states, among other indicators of public commitment to health care.[35]

Tamil Nadu has also been able to concentrate on many of the health 'basics' that have been so neglected in much of India, as discussed in Chapter 3 (and also in this chapter). For instance, there has been a sustained focus on 'public health', in the technical sense of public activities that are aimed at preventing illness rather than curing it.[36] Among other results of this focus on the basics are high child immunization rates – the highest among all major Indian states, with more than 80 per cent of children fully immunized in 2005–6.[37] Similarly, to ensure timely supply of free medicines in government-run health centres, the state has set up a pharmaceutical corporation and developed a sophisticated supply chain with computerized records. This, again, is in sharp contrast with the situation prevailing in many other states, where patients in government health centres are typically given a prescription and told to buy their own drugs in the market – often from a nearby chemist (the charge that these chemists share their profits with the prescribing doctors is unfortunately quite common). In Tamil Nadu's health centres, the provision of free medicines is compulsory and doctors are not allowed to send patients away with a paper prescription.

Further evidence on the performance of ICDS centres in Tamil Nadu is presented in Table 6.8, based on the FOCUS survey discussed earlier. Whether we look at the ICDS infrastructure, child attendance rates, the quality of pre-school education, immunization rates, or mothers' perceptions, Tamil Nadu shines in comparison with other states, especially the northern states. Perhaps the best sign of real achievement is the fact that 96 per cent of the sample mothers in Tamil Nadu considered ICDS to be 'important' for their child's well-being, and half of them considered it to be 'very important'.[38]

A central feature of Tamil Nadu's experience with ICDS is initiative and innovation. Unlike many other states that have passively implemented the central guidelines, Tamil Nadu has 'owned' ICDS and

Table 6.8
Anganwadis in Tamil Nadu

	Tamil Nadu	Northern States[a]
Proportion (%) of Anganwadis that have:		
Own building	88	18
Kitchen	85	30
Storage facilities	88	58
Medicine kit	81	22
Toilet	44	17
Average opening hours of the Anganwadi (according to the mothers)	6½ hours a day	3½ hours a day
Proportion (%) of children who attend 'regularly'[b]		
Age 0–3	59	20
Age 3–6	87	56
Proportion (%) of mothers who report that:		
Pre-school education activities are taking place at the Anganwadi	89	48
The motivation of the Anganwadi worker is 'high'	67	39
The Anganwadi worker ever visited them at home	58	22
Proportion (%) of women who had at least one pre-natal health check-up before their last pregnancy[c]	100	55
Proportion (%) of children who are 'fully immunized'[d]	71	41
Average number of months that have passed since an Anganwadi worker attended a training programme	6	30
Proportion (%) of Anganwadi workers who have not been paid during the last three months	0	22

[a] Chhattisgarh, Himachal Pradesh, Rajasthan, Uttar Pradesh.
[b] Among those enrolled at the local Anganwadi; responses from mothers.
[c] Among those who delivered a baby during the preceding 12 months.
[d] Based on assessment of trained investigators.

Source: FOCUS Survey, 2004; see Drèze (2006a), Table 6, and Citizens' Initiative for the Rights of Children Under Six (2006).

invested major financial, human and political resources in it. For instance, anganwadis in Tamil Nadu are typically open for more than six hours a day, compared with an average of barely three hours a day in the northern states. Similarly, high child attendance rates in the age group of 0–3 years (see Table 6.8) show that many anganwadis in Tamil Nadu include crèche facilities for small children. Tamil Nadu has also developed sophisticated training programmes, involving the formation of active training teams at the Block level, joint trainings of ICDS and Health Department staff, regular refresher courses for anganwadi workers, inter-district exposure tours for ICDS functionaries, and more. Incidentally the entire ICDS programme in Tamil Nadu, from top to bottom, is run by women.[39]

Interestingly, this creative activism is also found in many other social programmes in Tamil Nadu. For instance, Tamil Nadu was the first state to introduce free and universal midday meals in primary schools. This initiative, much derided at that time as a 'populist' programme, later became a model for India's national midday meal scheme. Today, school children in Tamil Nadu (more precisely, those enrolled in government schools) get not only free midday meals but also free uniforms, textbooks, stationery and health check-ups. Creativity and initiative have also been observed, more recently, in other major social programmes, such as the Public Distribution System (PDS) and the National Rural Employment Guarantee Act (both programmes are discussed in more detail in the next chapter).[40] Tamil Nadu's PDS, like its midday meal scheme and anganwadis, has become a model for the country, with regular distribution, relatively little corruption, and a major impact on rural poverty.[41] The standards of implementation of the National Rural Employment Guarantee Act in Tamil Nadu are also among the best in the country.[42]

Tamil Nadu's capacity for innovation and creative thinking in matters of public administration is an important example for the entire country. Some of the initiatives that have been taken there to improve the functioning of anganwadis, or to plug leakages in the Public Distribution System, or to ensure timely supply of drugs in health centres, are truly impressive. It is not an accident that Tamil Nadu has been ranked first among India's major states in terms of the overall quality of public services.[43]

Another noteworthy feature of Tamil Nadu's experience, already mentioned in Chapter 3, is the commitment to comprehensive and universalistic social policies. The most striking example is Tamil Nadu's PDS: every household is entitled to a minimum quota (currently 20 kgs) of subsidized rice every month, aside from other essential commodities. When an attempt was made to 'target' the PDS in 1997, in pursuance of national policy, targeting had to be rolled back within a week 'following a spate of protests'.[44] The principle of universalism in Tamil Nadu also applies to public health, midday meals (and other school incentives), childcare, employment guarantee, public transport, and also basic infrastructure such as water and electricity. As a result, the incidence of deprivation of some of the basic necessities of life is remarkably low in Tamil Nadu, as Table 6.9 elucidates.

The question arises as to how and when Tamil Nadu developed this commitment to universal and well-functioning public services. Various interpretations have been proposed, focusing for instance on early social reforms (including the 'self-respect movement' founded by Periyar in the 1920s), the political empowerment of disadvantaged castes, the hold of populist politics, and the constructive agency of women in Tamil society. These and other aspects of the social history of Tamil Nadu, and their relevance to the state's contemporary achievements, remain a lively subject of research. What is interesting is that these different interpretations point, in one way or another, to the power of democratic action.

This includes the power of public reasoning and social action in elevating the visibility of health issues and opening new horizons. Visionary figures such as Dr K. S. Sanjivi, a pioneering proponent of social health insurance in Tamil Nadu, argued for public support for health care a long time before this became a more discussed issue in the country.* Tamil Nadu has had a major role, in general, in initiating

---

* Dr. Sanjivi's initiative in building a remarkable institution in the form of Voluntary Health Services, established in 1958, demonstrated how much could be achieved through social cooperation in health care (including income-based health insurance with a built-in progressivity), rather than leaving matters in the hands of doctors serving only those clients who could afford to pay the – often unaffordable – fees. See 'The Great "Little" Man', *The Hindu*, 23 December 2003.

Table 6.9
Access to Public Services in Tamil Nadu, 2005–6

	Tamil Nadu	India
Proportion (%) of households:		
With access to electricity	89	68
With improved water source	94	88
With a ration card[a]	94	83
Who find the PDS 'reliable' (2001)	73	23
Proportion (%) of adult women who:		
Get ante-natal care	99	76
Get tetanus vaccine during pregnancy	96	76
Give birth with help from skilled health personnel	91	47
Get a post-natal check-up	91	41
Proportion (%) of young children who:		
Are fully immunized	81	44
Are not immunized at all	0	5
Live in area covered by Anganwadi	97	81
Proportion (%) of government schools with:[b]		
Drinking water	100	92
Electricity	92	31
Midday meal	98	88
Health check-up	94	55
Proportion (%) of Primary Health Centres with:[c]		
Essential drugs	98	70
Medical officer	85	76
Pharmacist	94	69
Regular power supply	87	36
Functional operating theatre	90	61
Cold chain equipment	95	67

[a] 2004–5.
[b] 2009–10.
[c] 2007–8.

Sources: International Institute for Population Sciences (2007a), Table 8.22 (p. 220) for post-natal care, and Table 9.19 (p. 254) for anganwadi coverage; Desai et al. (2010), Table A.13.1.b (p. 206), for ration cards; Paul et al. (2006), p. 87, for reliability of PDS; for other indicators, see Statistical Appendix, Table A.3. Unless stated otherwise, the reference year is 2005–6.

public discussion of social issues. Health-related programmes, such as the provision of midday meals in schools, became subjects of lively public discussion quite early and were often implemented first in Tamil Nadu. These issues have continued to play an important role in election campaigns in the state, much in contrast with the rest of the country, particularly north India, where health (or other basic needs such as elementary education or child nutrition) does not seem to figure much on the political agenda.

The role of democratic action (at all levels, from small Dalit hamlets to state-wide social and political movements) in Tamil Nadu's health achievements emerges particularly clearly in Vivek Srinivasan's (2010) recent study of public services in Tamil Nadu. As the author notes, 'a culture of protest for public services in Tamil Nadu . . . developed over the last 30 years or so'.* Further, this development was closely linked with struggles for liberation from the oppressions of caste, class and gender. In the process, the provision of public services became highly politicized, much as had happened earlier in Kerala. This possibility of bringing democratic action to bear on the concerns of common people, and of linking collective demands for better public services with larger struggles for social equality, is perhaps the most important insight from Tamil Nadu's experience.

OVERCOMING THE HEALTH CRISIS

So what is the way out of the health crisis which is perhaps the biggest adversity facing India today? The problems are large, but rather than being overwhelmed by their enormity, we should identify the ways and means of overcoming this adversity, drawing both on the analyses, just presented, of the factors that have contributed to this crisis, and also – closely related to that investigation – on the lessons that have emerged from the experiences of other developing countries

* Srinivasan (2010), p. 156. A case study of a Dalit hamlet, in the same study, vividly illustrates the emergence and influence of this culture of protest: 'A series of petitions, demonstrations, protests and bargaining marked how each hand pump, street light, road and other services were secured' (p. 177).

which have dealt with these problems much better than India has. There is also much to learn from the better performance of those Indian states (Kerala and Tamil Nadu in particular) which have taken care of the health of the people a lot better than the rest of India. As far as the rest of the world is concerned, the countries that offer immediate lessons for India include – most importantly – China, but also Brazil, Mexico and Thailand, among others.

Perhaps the first – and the most crucial – thing to appreciate is the importance of the commitment to universal coverage for all in a comprehensive vision of health care for the country as a whole. Thailand, Brazil and Mexico have got there in recent years, and transformed the reach of health care for their people. China's experience is particularly interesting, since it attempted, first, to deny the necessity of this commitment when the economic reforms first occurred, in 1979, and by reversing the earlier universalism, China paid a heavy price for this denial in terms of the progress of longevity and general health (this was discussed in Chapter 1). China eventually realized the error in this denial and, from 2004, started moving rapidly back to universal commitment (China is already 95 per cent there), reaping as it is sowing. And contrary to what we often hear from alleged admirers of China who want India to follow China without being quite sure of what it is that the Chinese do, China does not leave the coverage of health in the hands of private health insurance – the state is the major player to ensure this.[45] These experiences are, as we have already discussed, entirely in line with what we would expect on grounds of economic reasoning, particularly because of (1) the 'public goods' character of the health of people, (2) the role of asymmetric information, and (3) the impact of inequality on the achievement of general health in a community and a nation.

The commitment to universal health coverage would require a major transformation in Indian health care in at least two respects. The first is to stop believing, against all empirical evidence, that India's transition from poor health to good health could be easily achieved through private health care and insurance. This recognition does not, of course, imply that there is no role at all for the private sector in health care. Most health care systems in the world do leave room for private provision in one way or another, and there is no compelling reason for India to dispense with it. Nor can health planning in India ignore the accountability issues and other challenges (discussed in Chapter 4) that affect the operation of the public sector – including the public provision of health care. Nevertheless, the overarching objective of ensuring access to health services and other requirements of good health 'to all members of the community irrespective of their ability to pay' (as the Bhore Committee aptly stated the core principle of universal health coverage many years ago) is intrinsically a public responsibility.[46] Further, given the limitations of market arrangements and of private insurance in the field of health care, public provision of health services has an important foundational role to play in the realization of universal health coverage.

Following on this, the second respect in which the proposed approach demands a change in India lies in the need to go 'back to basics' as far as public provision of health care services – both of a preventive and curative kind – is concerned, with a renewed focus on primary health centres, village level health workers, preventive health measures, and other means of ensuring timely health care on a regular basis. While RSBY (the newly established scheme of subsidized health insurance for poor households, discussed earlier) is a humane programme and much better than leaving the poor to die or suffer from neglected health care and unaffordable intervention, better results can be achieved at far less cost through early and regular health care for all (supplemented by providing expensive intervention if and when it is needed despite early and more systematic medical care for all).[47]

The need for public involvement is particularly strong in a range of activities aimed at preventing rather than curing disease, such as immunization, sanitation, public hygiene, waste disposal, disease surveillance, vector control, health education, food safety regulation, and so on (what is technically known, as mentioned earlier, as 'public health'). In general, the prevention of illness as opposed to curing disease tends to be identified as particularly the responsibility of society and the state.* Expanded collective action in these areas is

---

* The critical need for collective action in these fields arises partly from the fact that private incentives to promote public health tend to be very weak. Public health played an important role in the historical expansion of longevity in Europe, Japan, and the United States, as well as in more recent experiences of rapid increase in life expectancy in East Asia (including China), or, closer to home, in Sri Lanka. In India, however,

extremely urgent, especially given India's shockingly defective record in fields like immunization and sanitation, which we have also discussed.[48]

There have been limited but valuable attempts to revamp the public provision of health services in India (including some aspects of public health) in recent years, notably under the National Rural Health Mission (NRHM). And some of them, it seems, have already had positive results. For instance, the involvement of village-level 'accredited social health activists' (ASHAs) in vaccination programmes seems to have led to a significant increase in child immunization rates, ending a long period of virtual stagnation in this regard.[49] Similarly, the drive to promote institutional deliveries under the Janani Suraksha Yojana (maternal safety scheme) has led to a steep increase in the proportion of births attended by skilled health personnel.[50] There is even some tentative evidence of a more broad-based revival of public health facilities, and it may not be an accident that India's infant mortality rate declined by about 3 percentage points per year in the five years that followed the launch of the NRHM, compared with barely 1 percentage point per year during the preceding five years.[51]

The main message is not that the National Rural Health Mission is the solution to the crisis of India's health system. Indeed, the Mission is much too small for this (also, it was planned as a short-term programme, and was meant to end in 2012, though it has now been extended). Rather, the lesson here, as in the field of education and early childcare, is that well-planned efforts to improve public facilities – even some that have functioned rather poorly for a long time – can indeed lead to significant results. There is also an important confirmation in these achievements of the general possibility (also evident from a great deal of international experience) of promoting 'good health at low cost' – a very important lesson for poor countries in general and for India in particular.[52]

The challenge ahead is to consolidate these initiatives and build on

---

public health is one of the most neglected aspects of health policy. In fact, during the last fifty years or so, public health services have been, as has been rightly observed, 'gradually eclipsed by the medical services, which attract far more political and public attention' (Das Gupta et al. 2010, p. 48). On the general neglect of public health in India, see also Das Gupta (2005).

comparative lessons from the world as well as from within India. There is a need not only for better health delivery, through institutional change, but also for devoting much more resources, as a proportion of the GDP, to public expenditure on health (as all the countries mentioned earlier in this section do).[53] This has to go hand in hand with the cultivation of greater efficiency and accountability in public services in general – a subject on which there are many lessons already in the experiences of some states in India (including Tamil Nadu, Kerala and Himachal Pradesh).

Last but not least, issues of health and health care must be brought much closer to the centre of attention in democratic politics. As we saw, while health has had little place in public reasoning in India as a whole, democratic engagement with health issues has played a very important role in the transformation of health policies in countries like Thailand, Brazil and Mexico, and within India, in Tamil Nadu and Kerala.* Even the gigantic lessons emerging from the commitment of the state in health care in the more authoritarian polity of China can be replicated within India's multiparty democratic system only through making these lessons part of the democratic dialogue in India. Democracy gives India the freedom to learn from any country in the world, and there are excellent reasons for us to make much greater use of informed reasoning in the practice of democracy, rather than our being stuck in the hole in which we have placed ourselves, in the absence of systematic reasoning about the most important necessity of the people.

---

* Among other inspiring experiences in this regard, there is a great deal to learn from the 'Health Assembly' in Thailand (established under the National Health Act of 2007), which holds regular meetings where complaints as well as wide-ranging reviews are aired by citizens on the working of public policy in health care. Thailand has made huge and rapid progress in universal coverage of health care for all through radical health initiatives, helped by interactive reviews of the problems encountered by citizens at the receiving end as well as by public servants on the delivery aspects of health care.

7

Poverty and Social Support

'*Hamaree baat koi naheen manega – ham log lathi chalane wale naheen hai*': 'Nobody is going to listen to us – we are not the sort who wield sticks'. So said a tribal woman of Jhapar, a remote village of Sarguja District in Chhattisgarh. This was in October 2001. Her grudge was against the non-functional state of the Public Distribution System (PDS) in the area. The local ration shop was three hours away on foot, and this was just the first of a series of hurdles that people had to overcome in order to get their monthly quota of subsidized rice. Only a few succeeded, and much of the PDS rice ended up on the black market.

Another visit to Jhapar in June 2012 revealed a completely different picture. The ration shop was right in the middle of the village, and managed by local residents. Most families had a ration card, and were getting their full quota of 35 kgs of rice, virtually for free, regularly on the first day of each month. This assurance that there would be food in the house was clearly a great relief for them. But just a few kilometres away, across the border between Chhattisgarh and Uttar Pradesh, the situation was still much the same as it used to be in Jhapar a decade ago.

Well-functioning public services can make a big difference to people's lives. In the preceding chapters, we focused on education and health because of their central role in the formation of human capabilities and in expanding people's real freedom, which is what development is ultimately about. These are also areas of individual life and social relations in which the limitations of market incentives and the need for public action can be particularly strong, as has been well recognized in mainstream economic literature (even though in politically ideological debates the need for state institutions is resisted by many commentators). Similar considerations also apply to many other aspects of living conditions, related for instance to environmental preservation, expansion of employment, food security, and many other areas in which the efficiency and fairness of the uncontrolled market mechanism can be quite limited. In fact, it is hard to think of any important aspect of poor people's lives in a country like India that does not depend in one way or another on public policy, and especially on what is often called 'social policy' even though many of the activities involved – such as skill formation, health care and employment support – have economic as well as social aspects. An initiative can be called 'social' in the sense of drawing on many societal institutions – not just the market mechanism. It is social policy in this broad sense that is the subject matter of this chapter.

PUBLIC PROVISION AND SOCIAL RESPONSIBILITY

Depending on political allegiances, both 'market phobia' and 'market mania' have had some following in Indian debates – indeed in discussions across the world. Instinctive reactions to the market – either pro or against – are not, however, particularly useful in a world that requires many institutions of which the markets must be a part, but not at all the sole constituent.* In recent years, market phobia has subsided greatly in India, and while that is useful, it is important not to be gripped now by the market mania of wanting to marketize everything that can be handed over to the market. China went through a similar phase around 1979 when the economic reforms not only overthrew the exclusion of the market in areas in which it could do a lot of good (particularly in agriculture and industry) – and did so in the post-reform period – but also marketized fields in which the market is a very limited instrument (such as health care), with rather

* For a fuller discussion of the need for both market and non-market institutions, as well as of the pitfalls of market mania and market phobia, see Sen (1999) and Drèze and Sen (2002).

terrible results. China has moved out of that phase in a policy readjustment: for example, state arrangements for health insurance returned fairly comprehensively in the last decade, with excellent results (see Chapter 1). There is a real need for pragmatism here, and to avoid both the crushing inefficiency of market denial (well illustrated, for example, by the weakness of the Soviet economy) and the pathology of ideological marketization (illustrated by the economic and social catastrophe that visited Russia in the immediate post-Soviet phase with breathless marketization of everything).

Relying solely on the market has become a strongly advocated theme in India on the basis of highly exaggerated expectations, often based on a misreading of the conclusions of mainstream economics, which includes much scepticism of the performance of markets in the presence of externalities, public goods, asymmetric information and distributional disparities.[1] We do not have to look for any 'alternative economic paradigm' to see what the market cannot do, in addition to what it can do – and do very well.*

Some examples of indiscriminate extension of market principles to social policy have already been discussed in earlier parts of this book, including the sobering experience of abrupt privatization of the health system in China in the early 1980s (vastly reducing people's right to public health care), which was just mentioned. In India, democratic institutions provide some safeguards against this kind of sudden withdrawal of people's rights – when they exist – but there are, nevertheless, powerful tendencies toward the commercial delivery of health and education, as we saw in the preceding chapters.

There is also an influential view that, in so far as public support is required for basic services, it is better aimed at enabling people to purchase these services from the market than at providing them through collective arrangements. The basic argument is that private provision is more efficient than public provision, because competition creates a strong

---

* In this work we do not go into a more moral question, which can also be seen as important, about whether certain types of interpersonal relations should be marketized at all, even if the markets work well. The question was famously raised by John Stuart Mill in denying the moral acceptability of slavery even if the persons sold as slaves were willing partners in the transaction (see Mill, 1859, Chapter V). See also the important questions raised in Sandel (2012) and Skidelsky and Skidelsky (2012).

pressure to cut costs and improve quality. This is indeed often the case, but that approach also has serious limitations, as we have discussed earlier – particularly Chapter 5, in the context of the use of 'school vouchers'. We shall not revisit the case of school vouchers, but the general argument for facilitating the private purchase of basic services, instead of providing them through public institutions, is worth reconsidering.

One example of a situation where there is a strong case for activating the market, by creating purchasing power and enabling people to purchase what they need, instead of addressing their needs through direct public provision, is that of famine relief. In earlier writings, we have argued that 'cash relief' (for instance, through local public works, with wages being paid in cash) is a more effective method of famine relief, in many circumstances, than direct feeding or food distribution.[2] The decisive argument here is that in a situation of impending starvation and the unfolding of a famine, speed is critically important. Generating incomes in cash makes it possible to activate the logistic resources of private trade and distribution, instead of having to rely exclusively on public delivery, which may need initiation time and meet with organizational problems.

This is not a fail-safe approach, since private trade itself may be disrupted or ineffective in a famine situation (especially if there is an armed conflict in the same area, as has been the case with most recent famines), and there is always the danger of the traders profiting from establishing a kind of monopoly. However, the general argument in that direction is strong, and in fact it has worked relatively well on many occasions, including the bulk of India's own history of famine prevention since independence. Cash payments of wages also have a positive role to play in the creation of employment and purchasing power through public works projects (for example, under the National Rural Employment Guarantee Act, discussed later in this chapter). The use of cash is often much easier and less costly, and also – under appropriate governmental supervision – easier to monitor.

Reasoning on this issue must, however, also take into account many other factors that make the use of market-based provision far from universally useful, for example in the delivery of elementary education, health care, water supply, sanitation, immunization and a host of services for other 'basic needs'. Many of these difficulties are well recognized in mainstream economics (contrary to what many market fundamentalists seem to believe), and have already been discussed, in different contexts, earlier in this book. They include the pathologies of market allocation when there are pervasive asymmetries of information, for example, between patients who may know little about the treatment they need or are given, unlike the doctors who may know much more.[3] Another problem is the wide divergence between private and social costs – and benefits – in the presence of 'externalities' (e.g. those associated with communicable diseases and public health). There is the issue of 'distribution' as well, since purchasing power and wealth are unequally distributed, and there is extensive discussion in the welfare-economics literature of the frequently inequitable nature of market outcomes, leaving the poor behind. Further, there is sometimes a case for public fostering of changes in traditional practices and behavioural norms.

The last point deserves elaboration, since it has gained (or rather, regained) relatively slow recognition in economics. In parts of mainstream economics, somewhat exaggerated emphasis is often placed on so-called 'consumer sovereignty', that is, the idea that people are best judges of their own interests (a utilitarian argument, in the broad sense) and that their choices should, in any case, be accepted as they are (a libertarian argument, also in a broad sense): there are, thus, two distinct ideas, conflated in the notion of 'consumer sovereignty'. However, a century of economic literature, enriched recently by research in experimental and behavioural economics, has drawn attention to a host of ways in which people may fail to behave in their own – or their families' – best interest. For instance, parents may keep postponing the decision to vaccinate a child until it is too late, and regret it later on; a woman may neglect her own nutrition or health for the sake of other family members; many decisions may be influenced by conformism, herd behaviour, misplaced optimism, procrastination, and other psychological factors. And of course, even an intelligent and well-informed decision-maker, as Robert Aumann has observed, 'may be tired or hungry or distracted or cross or drunk or stoned, unable to think under pressure, able to think only under pressure, or guided more by his emotions than his brains'.[4] Thus, people can often benefit from assistance to make the choices that further their own goals, and also to re-examine their goals by reasoned scrutiny. Unaided market processes may not be particularly effective for this purpose, since they are driven by whatever choices people happen to make, frequently without reasoned scrutiny of these choices. In fact, some market-based processes, notably high-key advertising, can interfere with rather than promote enlightened decision-making.

In India, these issues have come to the fore quite sharply in the context of child feeding. As discussed in the previous chapter, effective child feeding depends on various forms of social support including maternal counselling and nutrition education. Commercial firms selling – and pushing – infant milk substitutes and related products have often been quite hostile to the nutritional well-being of babies and children, so much so that the public authorities have had to restrain these counterproductive pursuits of commercial interests through laws such as the Infant Milk Substitutes, Feeding Bottles and Infant Foods (Regulation of Production, Supply and Distribution) Act, better known as 'IMS Act'. The idea that 'consumer sovereignty' is the best bet in every field has to be firmly questioned, even when the violation of human well-being is less obvious than in this case.

To these – fairly standard – arguments must be added other, less obvious considerations. For instance, market-based operations may involve forgoing the opportunity of ushering in social results that public reasoning can demand but which cannot be easily accommodated in the individualistic transactional modes of standard market purchases. Some public activities in fields like health and education also have various process benefits that may be very difficult to replicate through market processes. To illustrate, consider the provision of cooked midday meals in primary schools, initiated in response to a sustained public campaign including a public interest litigation in the Supreme Court. When this activity is organized from the point of view of public purpose, it can serve many useful goals, simultaneously: promoting school attendance, improving the nutrition of children, helping to increase the attention span of children (hard to achieve on an empty stomach), generating employment for underprivileged rural women, enhancing classroom activities, imparting nutrition education, and reducing caste prejudices among schoolchildren through joint eating.[5] If it were just a matter of distributing food, the whole exercise could quite possibly be efficiently subcontracted to private agencies. But the promotion of other, related objectives could be hard to organize as a commercial activity, balancing the force of the different reasons behind such a programme. Similar remarks apply to many other policies concerned with health (particularly public health), nutrition, schooling and related matters.

The idea that health or education is best arranged by enabling people to buy it from private providers is entirely contrary to the historical experience of Europe, America, Japan and East Asia in their respective transformation of living standards. Closer to home, this is also not how Kerala and Sri Lanka have achieved great strides in these fields at an early stage of development, nor how Tamil Nadu and Himachal Pradesh are rapidly catching up with Kerala today. As discussed in Chapter 3, these experiences were not driven by private provision of health and education services, nor for that matter by public-private partnerships (PPPs), school vouchers, commercial health insurance or other market-based arrangements. Old-fashioned government schools, health centres, truant officers, public health inspectors, vaccination camps and sanitation campaigns were far more important.

It is equally important not to misread the recent history of conditional cash transfers in Brazil or Mexico or other successful cases today. In Latin America, conditional cash transfers usually act as a complement, not a substitute, for public provision of health, education and other basic services. As discussed further in this chapter, a conditional cash transfer is basically an incentive; but in these countries the incentives work for their supplementing purpose because the basic public services are well established there in the first place. In Brazil, for instance, basic health services such as immunization, antenatal care and skilled attendance at birth are virtually universal. The state has done its homework, as we saw in Chapter 3, and put in place functional and widely-used public facilities for health care. In this situation, providing monetary incentives to complete the universalization of health care may be quite sensible. In India, however, these basic services are still largely missing, and conditional cash transfers (useful as they may be for incentive purposes) cannot fill the gap.

None of this is to dispute the fact that direct provision of basic amenities by the state can be very inefficient and also exploitative. The case for public provision requires a reasonable assurance of functionality. A well-functioning public health centre can do enormously more to enhance the well-being of the people than profit-seeking nursery homes or private doctors, but a health centre that remains closed most of the time may do no better than a village quack. This reinforces the urgency, discussed in Chapter 4, of restoring accountability in the public sector. Privatization is an alluring short-cut, but it can have the effect of merely replacing one serious problem by another no less grave.

ON THE POVERTY LINE

India's official 'poverty line' has recently been a subject of lively debates. The controversy began with an affidavit submitted to the Supreme Court by the Planning Commission in September 2011, in response to a query (from the Court) concerning the method being used to determine the official poverty line as well as the feasibility of meeting minimum nutritional norms at that level of per capita expenditure.

The Planning Commission's affidavit clarified the official poverty estimation methodology, based on the Tendulkar Committee Report (2009). It also included the odd statement that the official poverty lines (Rs 32 per person per day in urban areas and Rs 26 per person per day in rural areas, at June 2011 prices) 'ensure the adequacy of actual private expenditure per capita near the poverty lines on food, education and health'. This ill-chosen observation caused an instant uproar, with one commentator after another pointing out that the official poverty line is actually a 'destitution line', which does not ensure anything above bare subsistence. The point was not difficult to illustrate. For instance, the reference budget associated with the urban poverty line includes princely sums of about ten rupees per month for 'footwear' and forty rupees per month for health care. The former would just about make it possible to get a sandal strap repaired once a month, and the latter might buy something like the equivalent of an aspirin a day. Similarly, the monthly allowance of thirty rupees for 'rent and conveyance' would not go further than a one-way, short-distance bus ticket every few days, with nothing left to travel back, let alone pay for any sort of rent.

These measly norms reflect the fact that poverty-line standards were set decades ago, at a time when even bare subsistence was far from assured for a large majority of the Indian population. The poverty line is, of course, regularly updated for price increases, but not for the enhanced requirements of dignified living. Understandably, the poverty line today looks quite out of tune with the bare minimum one would wish everyone must minimally have.

As the debate unfolded, a series of issues became confused. For instance, an impression developed that the official poverty line was so low because the Planning Commission had just lowered it. In fact, nothing of the sort had happened: the Tendulkar Committee Report led to an upward – not downward – revision of the rural poverty line. Incredible as it may seem, the poverty line was even lower earlier. Much confusion also grew around other issues such as the purpose of official poverty lines as well as the relation between poverty estimates and food entitlements under the Public Distribution System.

Aside from these confusions, the debate ended up missing the main point. What is really startling is not so much that the official poverty line is so low, but that *even with this low benchmark*, so many people are below it – a full 30 per cent of the population in 2009–10, or more than 350 million people. How are these people supposed to live? The shocking discovery that it is impossible to have anything like a dignified life on or below the official poverty line draws attention to the appalling living conditions of the Indian poor, which receive so little attention in public discussion and go largely unnoticed (in more privileged circles). This is at least partly because poor people have learnt to live precariously with such deprivations, and keep, rather fatalistically, a low profile. This basic message about the terrifying yet hidden nature of mass poverty – its enormous size – has been quite lost in the din of the recent debate.

This recognition makes it all the more important to explore possible ways of extending direct income support to poor families, without waiting patiently for economic growth to raise their wages and incomes. There is, in fact, growing evidence that various forms of income support, economic redistribution and social security can make a substantial difference to people's living standards without delay, even with the limited administrative and financial resources that are available in India today. These are no less important than the health and education policies discussed in the previous chapters. Indeed, these interventions complement each other in important ways – reducing intense human suffering as well as helping to build basic capabilities of people, which actually tends to contribute even to economic growth.

TARGETING VERSUS SOLIDARITY

Not so long ago, 'targeting' was a widely accepted principle of social policy in India. The idea is deceptively simple: focus public resources on the poor. This sounds like a common-sense way of ensuring that limited resources are well used, from the point of view of poverty reduction. In practice, however, there are serious problems with a targeting-based system of social support.

Targeting, of course, is not in general a bad idea, and it can be quite useful in many circumstances. For instance, as discussed in Chapter 2, targeted programmes of social support such as *Bolsa Família* have made an important contribution to poverty reduction in Brazil. One reason why *Bolsa Família* works relatively well is that there is a fairly well-identified target group: the poor in the informal sector who are not covered by the standard social security system. It is useful to remember that Brazil has an urbanization rate of around 85 per cent, with a large proportion of the population in the formal sector, and covered by extensive social security programmes. Further, a fairly sophisticated administration and large human resources are available to 'screen' applicants from the informal sector and determine what sort of support they need. In this context, targeting is quite possibly efficient as well as equitable.

India's experience with targeting, however, is far from encouraging. The notion of 'below poverty line' (BPL) households, initially introduced in the context of the Integrated Rural Development Programme, has been used from 1997 onwards to target the Public Distribution

System (PDS). That is, the PDS has been effectively restricted to BPL households, in most states ('APL' – above poverty line – households were effectively eased out of the PDS in 2001, by raising the APL issue prices). However, this move has turned out to be quite problematic , for two reasons.

First, identifying BPL households is extremely difficult, and typically involves large exclusion errors (assigning APL status to poor households) as well as inclusion errors (assigning BPL status to well-off households).The identification process is based on a 'BPL Census', which ranks households based on some sort of scoring system. For instance, the 2002 BPL Census had a scoring system involving 13 indicators (related to occupation, dwelling, education, etc.), with a scale of 0 to 4 for each indicator, so that the aggregate score varied between 0 and 52. This produced a ranking of households in terms of their score, and state-wise 'cut-offs' were then supposed to be applied to this ranking in such a manner that the number of poor households in each state matches the Planning Commission's official poverty estimates. For instance, if the official poverty estimate for Bihar is 55 per cent, the cut-off score for Bihar is supposed to be such that 55 per cent of households are below that cut-off. The poverty estimates, for their part, are based on applying the official poverty line (discussed earlier) to National Sample Survey data on household per capita expenditure. This entire method is a little disjointed: the Planning Commission uses one method to count the poor, and the BPL Census uses a different method to identify them. The conceptual confusion is compounded by major implementation problems, especially when the relevant indicators are unclear or non-verifiable, opening the door to cheating, errors and favouritism. Further, as mentioned in Chapter 6, poverty is not a static condition: someone who is not poor today may be poor next year (due to illness, crop failure, unemployment, extortion, or other reasons), and vice versa. The BPL list, for its part, often remains without change for as long as ten years. The bottom line is that the BPL identification process tends to be a hit-or-miss affair, with plenty of inclusion and exclusion errors. At least three independent national surveys (the National Family Health Survey, the National Sample Survey and the India Human Development Survey) show that about half of all poor households in India did not have a BPL card in 2005.[6]

Second, targeting (and especially hit-or-miss targeting) is very divisive. Since the coverage of the BPL list is supposed to match the Planning Commission's poverty estimates, BPL households are typically in a minority (though some states have departed from this entire approach, as will be presently discussed); it is also, on the whole, a disadvantaged minority, despite 'inclusion errors' whereby relatively well-off households are sometimes on the list. The bargaining power of BPL households therefore tends to be quite weak, in the absence of solidarity from APL households. In fact, BPL households can easily become a target of exploitation by vested interests. This absence of political clout, including the power to protest effectively, is one reason why social programmes and public services based on BPL targeting have tended not to work particularly well – the Public Distribution System is a prime example.

Both problems (exclusion and divisiveness) are exacerbated by the fact that official poverty lines are low, as discussed in the preceding section. It is difficult enough to justify the principle of excluding from social support any household that spends more than twenty-six rupees a day (in rural areas). The fact that these households are extremely difficult to identify, and that targeting undermines public solidarity, makes this principle even more problematic. This is not to say that targeting is always a wrong policy – but the circumstances where it is appropriate need careful evaluation, and, in the light of recent experience, seem to be more limited than they are often assumed to be.

Meanwhile, many public programmes based on alternative principles of universalism with 'self-selection' have done comparatively well. One interesting example, mentioned earlier, is India's school meal programme, whereby all children studying in a government or government-aided school are entitled (under Supreme Court orders, later incorporated in government policy) to a nutritious midday meal, free of cost. This programme, which covers more than 120 million children, is likely to look badly 'targeted' to someone who insists on restricting social benefits to households below the poverty line. However, these children come from a self-selected group of families that choose government schools over private schools, and tend to belong to relatively underprivileged sections of the population. Most of these children are in need of nutritional support as well as of better incentives to attend school, whether or not their households are 'below the poverty line'. Further, the inclusive nature of the school meal programme has greatly helped to make it a success. It is extremely doubtful that a targeted school meal programme would have done anywhere near as well.[7]

Another example is the National Rural Employment Guarantee Act (NREGA), also based on the principle of self-selection – anyone is entitled to apply for work, on the assumption that well-off households will voluntarily stay away from NREGA worksites. Interestingly, when the Act was being drafted and debated, the government attempted to restrict it to BPL households.[8] However, this misguided attempt to enforce targeting where it does not belong was abandoned, and in the final version of the Act every rural resident above the age of 18 is eligible for employment. As is discussed later on in this chapter, this self-selection principle seems to work quite well: NREGA workers typically do belong to underprivileged sections of the population.

Some interventions do not lend themselves so easily to self-selection. For example, not many households 'opt out' of the Public Distribution System when it supplies rice or wheat at a fraction of the market price. Various suggestions have been made to induce more self-targeting in the PDS (e.g. by distributing millets or fortified flour instead of rice and wheat), but whatever their merit, they have not convinced the authorities involved. On the other hand, BPL targeting has not worked well either. It is in the light of this sobering experience, and (in some cases) of popular resentment against targeting, that many states have recently moved towards a more inclusive or even 'universal' PDS – Andhra Pradesh, Chhattisgarh, Himachal Pradesh, Odisha, Rajasthan and Tamil Nadu, among others. Further, this new approach, combined with other PDS reforms, seems to have been of considerable help in making the PDS work better than it had earlier (we shall return to this).[9]

As discussed in Chapters 3 and 6, the social achievements of India's progressive states (such as Himachal Pradesh, Kerala and Tamil Nadu) are also built to a considerable extent on universalistic or inclusive social policies, taking a very different line of action from the tightly targeted approach. Universal coverage can, of course, be expensive, especially in those fields in which effective self-selection cannot be used. It is not a general formula for unconditional use, nor a principle that can be applied in every domain, especially at an early stage of development. But the regional experiences indicate that it can work well in many cases even in poor India – and this understanding demands more recognition than it seems to be getting at this time. The importance of universalism as a principle is supplemented by its easier – and often more efficient – implementability, and the Indian debates on the subject have to take more note both of the evidence in favour of universal coverage within present-day India as well as of the global literature on this central policy issue.*

TRANSFERS AND INCENTIVES

The case for public involvement in the provision of basic services and social security, discussed earlier, does not detract from the useful role that cash transfers can play in some circumstances – indeed it can be a constructive part of that involvement. For instance, many Indian states have initiated reasonably effective (though limited) schemes of social security pensions for widows, disabled persons and the elderly.[10] Similarly, scholarships for disadvantaged children can be of great help in enabling them to pursue their studies. These cash transfer schemes have much to contribute within their limited domain.

What we have to guard against is premature enthusiasm on the basis of underscrutinized expectations. Since conditional cash transfers (CCTs) have been a subject of growing interest in recent years, and are even seen, at times, as the 'wave of the future' for India's

---

* This includes the literature on the welfare state in Europe, where universalism has been a very influential principle of social policy. As Tony Judt pointed out, this principle has also been critical in securing the political support of the middle classes for the welfare state: 'In most cases [this] was achieved by the magic of 'universalism'. Instead of having their benefits keyed to income – in which case well-paid professionals or thriving shopkeepers might have complained bitterly at being taxed for social services from which *they* did not derive much advantage – the educated 'middling sort' were offered the same social assistance and public services as the working population and the poor: free education, cheap or free medical treatment, public pensions and unemployment insurance.' See Tony Judt (2010), p. 52.

social programmes, it is useful to place their role in perspective. The idea of CCTs is relatively simple – give people cash, conditional on constructive behaviour, such as sending children to school or getting them vaccinated. This helps to score two goals in one shot: poor people get some income support, and at the same time they take steps – like sending children to school – that help to lift them (and their families) out of poverty.

A conditional cash transfer is basically an incentive, and often enough it works very well: if people are paid to do something that benefits them anyway, they tend to do it. As mentioned earlier, however, the services (e.g. schools and health centres) that enable people to meet the conditions must be there (or must improve very rapidly), and work reasonably well, for this approach to make sense. CCTs are not a *substitute* for having these services available – or ready to be quickly developed. From one recent study, we learn that CCTs in India 'represent a shift in the government's approach of focusing on the supply-side to a demand-driven approach'.[11] This statement, if it is accurate as a reading of the government's perspective, reflects an exaggerated dichotomy between 'supply-side' and 'demand-driven' approaches, as if one could succeed without the other. Further, even when the demand can be met, in principle, through market institutions (despite their limitations in many areas of traditional social policy, including school education and elementary health care), the creation of these institutions may not be an easy exercise. We should not fall for the trap, which did such harm in Russia during the 1990s, of assuming that market institutions would instantly materialize as soon as pro-market incentives are in place. This issue is additional to the limitations of the market institutions themselves, discussed earlier.

The incentive role of conditional cash transfers can, of course, also be played by conditional 'in-kind' transfers. The midday meal programme in primary schools is one example: children get the meal only if they come to school, and as discussed earlier, the incentive effects seem to be quite powerful in encouraging pupils to attend school regularly, aside from other benefits to this programme (including the nutrition benefits, and the socialization aspects of joint eating).[12] Another interesting example of fairly encouraging experience with conditional in-kind transfers is the policy, introduced in several states, of giving free bicycles to girls who reach a certain stage (say Class 8) in the schooling system. These schemes are very popular, and while formal evidence of their incentive effects is limited as things stand, they are likely to be substantial.[13] The cycles also help girls to continue going to school *after* completing Class 8 (secondary schools are often much more distant than upper-primary schools), and give them valuable mobility and freedom. It is doubtful that a conditional cash transfer to the girl's parents (conditional on her attending school) would achieve similar social benefits.

Thus, while conditional cash transfers may be useful in many cases, there are also rival systems, including unconditional cash transfers (e.g. social security pensions for widows and the elderly) as well as transfers in kind, both conditional (e.g. midday meals in primary schools) and unconditional (e.g. the Public Distribution System). India can certainly learn something about the incentive value of CCTs from recent experiences elsewhere, notably in Latin America. But these lessons (both positive and negative) have to be integrated with those of other experiences of different types of transfers, within as well as outside India.

Recent lessons about the power of well-designed cash incentives also have to be integrated with their 'converse' – the negative effects of inappropriate charges. For instance, it is fairly well recognized by now that charging fees in primary schools tends to be a bad idea. Aside from violating the right to free education, it would amount to raising tiny sums of money at the risk of much greater damage in the form of lower school attendance. Recent research suggests that the same point often applies in the field of health: even tiny 'user fees' can have dramatic negative effects on the demand for health services or products such as deworming, insecticidal bednets or water purification.[14] This important finding, incidentally, can be seen as another example of the difficulties that people often have in realizing their goals, even when they are well defined, reinforcing the arguments discussed earlier for social support. If small user fees have big disincentive effects, and if subsidizing private provision is difficult (as it often is), then public provision may be the best option, if only by default.

Finally, it is also important to take note of the possible *counterproductive* role of cash incentives in specific circumstances. Cash rewards draw on people's motivation to do certain things to the extent that they are interested in getting money (for themselves or to share with others), and this is, of course, an important ground for choice. But in many situations, people have diverse motives, and attempts to draw on – and to reinforce – some motives can seriously conflict with other values. Most people have selfish as well as non-selfish motives, and appealing exclusively to people's selfish motives may sometimes run into conflict with their broader behavioural commitments.[15] There are, for instance, many examples of people *losing* their motivation to do something once they are paid for it, because they were doing it for other motives in the first place. As Richard Titmuss has observed, on the basis of empirical studies in Britain, cash rewards for blood donations can be counterproductive: people who would be happy to donate their blood out of public-spiritedness may not like the idea of 'selling' their blood (even as others step in to earn some cash).[16] Similarly, in some circumstances, cash incentives such as pay-for-performance schemes for government employees can undermine what is known as 'public service motivation'. As Samuel Bowles has observed, based on a generalization of the findings of many economic experiments: 'Experimental evidence indicates that incentives that appeal to self-interest may reduce the salience of intrinsic motivation, reciprocity, and other civic motives.'[17] This potentially counterproductive impact of cash incentives may or may not be a serious issue, depending on the context. But it is important not to lose sight of the sophisticated economic and social literature on incentives, taking instead a crude and simplistic view of how human beings are motivated and make their choices.

To illustrate, consider the recent introduction, in many Indian states, of schemes of cash incentives to curb sex-selective abortion.[18] The schemes typically involve cash rewards for the registered birth of a girl child, and further rewards if the girl is vaccinated, sent to school, and so on, as she gets older. These schemes can undoubtedly tilt economic incentives in favour of girl children. But a cash reward for the birth of a girl could also reinforce people's tendency to think about family planning in economic terms, and also their perception, in the economic calculus of family planning, that girls are a burden (for which cash rewards are supposed to compensate). Further, cash rewards are likely to affect people's non-economic motives. For instance, they could reduce the social stigma attached to sex-selective abortion, by making it look like some sort of 'fair deal' – no girl, no cash. The fact that the cash incentives are typically lower for a *second* girl child, and nil for higher-order births, also sends confusing signals. In short, it is not quite clear what sort of message these cash incentives are supposed to convey about the status and value of the girl child, and how they are supposed to affect social attitudes towards sex-selective abortion. As mentioned earlier, the working of social norms is critically important in this kind of area of values and actions, and it is important to think about the possible effects of cash transfers on social norms and their role, and not just about economic self-interest.

All this tends to reinforce the arguments presented earlier against market mania in social policy. Markets are typically praised for generating incentives, and indeed, they very often do just that. But there are contrary considerations related to the effectiveness and impact of cash incentives (on which there is an extensive global literature as well as considerable local experience in India). What is needed most of all is an objective scrutiny of the arguments and counter-arguments in each case, rather than being guided by a crudely simplistic view of human motivation and of the social consequences of different systems of incentives. It would be sad to be liberated from the near-absence of thinking about incentives in Indian planning only to be captured by the crudest model of incentives that the human mind can generate.

EMPLOYMENT AND EMPOWERMENT

The enactment of the National Rural Employment Guarantee Act (NREGA) in mid-2005 was a heady time. On 22–23 August the proposed Act was the subject of many stirring speeches in the Indian Parliament, well past midnight on the first day. After this long debate, there was a voice vote, and when the time came for the opponents to say 'nay', there was pin-drop silence.

Meanwhile, however, alarm bells were ringing in other quarters. 'Expensive gravy train', 'money guzzler', 'costly joke' and 'wonky idea' is just a small sample of the colourful terms that were used to disparage NREGA in financial journals and conservative editorials. One Minister, otherwise praised as the 'poster boy of economic reforms', was called a 'turncoat' for supporting NREGA – 'What is he smoking these days?' asked a dismayed columnist.[19]

In retrospect, the excitement was perhaps overdone on both sides. The high hopes of radical change in power relations, or of dramatic poverty reduction, have not quite materialized; nor did the doomsday predictions of financial bankruptcy or economic chaos. To some extent, this is because the implementation of the law has fallen short of its letter and spirit – but that was predictable enough. Even so, the enactment of NREGA was a very significant development in many ways.

The economics of the Act were not particularly new. Public works have been used for a long time as a means of social support in India, particularly in times of drought. This strategy builds on the principle of self-selection: anyone who joins the worksites is recognized to be in need of social support. It is also an opportunity to build useful assets in rural areas. While this approach has been used mainly in the context of famine relief, it can also be seen, in many circumstances, as a development strategy. For instance Sukhamoy Chakravarty, the distinguished Indian economist and planner, was a strong advocate of rural public works (along with agrarian reforms) as a means of combining economic redistribution with rural development.

The NREGA, however, did make a radical departure by recasting public works in the framework of justiciable rights – not only the right to work on demand, but also the right to minimum wages, payment within 15 days, essential worksite facilities, and so on.[20] Even this was not completely new, since the state of Maharashtra in western India had already implemented a legally binding 'employment guarantee scheme' from the early 1970s onwards.[21] But NREGA took the idea much further, building on Maharashtra's example, among other experiences.

The Act also built on a broad vision of the social objectives of employment guarantee, going well beyond the traditional objectives of providing employment and building rural assets. For instance, it was also seen as an opportunity to curb gender inequality and empower rural women, by enabling them to work outside the house, earn their own income, have their own bank account, learn to defend their rights, participate in Gram Sabhas (plenary village assemblies), and so on. Similarly, the Act was expected to energize the institutions of local governance, by giving them, for the first time, substantial resources and a clear purpose. Like Maharashtra's employment guarantee scheme, NREGA was also seen as a great organizational opportunity for rural workers, most of whom belong to the 'unorganised sector'.[22]

Last but not least, the Act sought to impart new principles and standards of governance in rural development schemes, under the law: participation, transparency and accountability, among others. NREGA works were to be planned by Gram Sabhas and implemented mainly by Gram Panchayats (elected village councils). All NREGA records were to be open to public scrutiny, and in fact, to be actively disclosed to the public in a convenient form.[23] Accountability provisions include the duty of the state government to pay an unemployment allowance when work is not provided, a right to compensation when wages are not paid on time, and a penalty clause whereby any officer who fails to do his or her duty under the law is liable to a fine.

For rural workers, the Act was a chance to put their foot in the door. As we saw in Chapter 2, during the period 1990–2005, rural workers were largely left behind. Agricultural production barely increased in per capita terms, the growth of real agricultural wages gradually ground to a halt, and rural employment stopped being anything like a policy priority. The enactment of NREGA in 2005 led to a serious reorientation of governmental priorities towards employment creation, and also, in the process, strengthened the bargaining power of rural workers.

Indeed, the first achievement of the Act, soon after it came into force in February 2006, was a massive expansion of rural public works programmes.[24] According to official data, about 50 million households have been participating in NREGA every year since 2008–9 (when the Act was extended to the whole country), with an average employment level of around forty person-days per household per year. Even after allowing for a substantial margin of exaggeration in the official figures, this is no mean feat.[25]

A second achievement, linked to the first, was a series of impressive changes in wage relations, particularly of casual labour, in rural areas, including actual payment of statutory minimum wages on public works, a major increase in people's awareness of minimum wages, and substantial increases in agricultural wages (particularly for women), ending the long spell of stagnation that preceded NREGA (see Table 7.1).[26] These developments, particularly the third, benefit *all* rural workers, not just those actually employed on NREGA, and significantly magnify the income-generation effects of the programme.[27]

NREGA workers, for their part, belong mainly to deprived sections of the rural population.[28] This is as one would expect, but it is still worth noting that the self-selection principle has worked fairly well (particularly in contrast with 'BPL targeting', discussed earlier), reinforcing the redistributive role of NREGA. One aspect of this self-selection process is that most NREGA workers belong to relatively poor households, but another, no less important, is that about half of them are women, and half belong to scheduled-caste or scheduled-tribe households.[29]

The gender dimension of NREGA deserves special emphasis. The share of women in total NREGA employment has been consistently around 50 per cent in the last few years, and perhaps more import-

Table 7.1
Growth Rates of Real Wages in Rural Areas
in the 2000s (% per year)

	2000–1 to 2005–6 (pre-NREGA)		2005–6 to 2010–11 (post-NREGA)	
	Men	Women	Men	Women
All rural labour	0.01	− 0.05	1.82	3.83
Agricultural labour	0.10	− 0.05	2.67	3.67
Non-agricultural labour	− 0.04	− 0.04	1.21	4.34
Unskilled labour	− 0.01	− 0.04	3.98	4.34

Source: Calculated from Usami (2012), based on wage data compiled by the Labour Bureau (Shimla), also published in *Wage Rates in Rural India*. For further details, see the explanatory note in the Statistical Appendix.

antly, the participation of women has risen steadily in most of the states where it used to be very low – Bihar, Himachal Pradesh, Uttarakhand, West Bengal, among others.[30] These are states where rural women have very few opportunities to earn an independent cash income, and in that respect among others, NREGA is a real step forward. One recent study of NREGA workers in six northern states, for instance, found that only 30 per cent of the women workers had earned any cash income other than NREGA wages in the preceding three months.[31] Many other studies bring out the special value of NREGA for rural women, especially in north India.[32]

These are some of the contributions that NREGA has made – at least so far – to poverty reduction and social equity. There are also other achievements, of varying strength, such as the creation of productive assets in rural areas (more on this presently) and the revival of Panchayati Raj Institutions including Gram Sabhas. All these achievements, of course, have varied a great deal across states, with some (e.g. Andhra Pradesh, Himachal Pradesh, Rajasthan, Tamil Nadu, Sikkim) achieving really impressive results whereas others (e.g. Bihar, Karnataka and Maharashtra) are yet to activate NREGA on a significant scale.

On the negative side, two major objections have been raised against NREGA. One is that most of the money allegedly goes 'down the drain' because of endemic corruption. The other objection is that the assets being created under NREGA are of little value.

The first objection can actually be turned on its head: NREGA is in fact a potential weapon against corruption. There was certainly a great deal of embezzlement in the early years of the programme, and the problem has not entirely gone away – far from it. Nevertheless, NREGA has also been a lively laboratory for anti-corruption efforts, involving a whole series of innovations that are now being gradually extended to other schemes as well: the use of the Internet to place all essential records (including every wage payment, worker-wise and worksite-wise) in the public domain, the payment of wages through bank accounts, and the practice of regular social audits, to mention a few. There is some evidence of a substantial reduction in the extent of embezzlement of NREGA funds over time (at least in the wage component of the programme, which accounts for the bulk of total expenditure), a significant achievement at a time when there is a wide public perception of growing corruption across the country.[33] Some states (notably Andhra Pradesh and Tamil Nadu) have shown the possibility of putting in place fairly effective safeguards against corruption in NREGA, and there is enough general experience now to have some confidence in the possibility of extending these achievements to other states.

The second objection is based on the myth that most NREGA works are useless (just 'playing with mud', as one critic put it). This myth has acquired a certain influence by sheer repetition, but it has little factual basis. Nor is this the perception of NREGA workers or village communities: several studies indicate that most of them have a positive view of the value of NREGA works.[34] This is not to say that all NREGA works are productive, or of adequate quality. Indeed, independent evaluations suggest a mixed record, with many examples of reasonably successful asset creation (involving, for instance, desilting of canals, digging of ponds, land levelling, roadside plantation, soil conservation and the construction of wells) as well as many other cases of unsatisfactory or even useless works.[35] This is a subject on which a great deal of further evidence is required. Meanwhile, the available evidence does not justify any sweeping condemnation of NREGA works as useless – indeed far from it. If anything, it suggests that NREGA has a great deal of productive potential, provided that adequate structures, including technical support, are in place.

While these objections to the very idea of NREGA are unconvincing, there are plenty of valid criticisms of the Act and the manner in which it is being implemented.[36] NREGA is a complex programme implemented by a fragile and lethargic system, and the results inevitably fall short of what could be achieved in other circumstances. For NREGA workers, these hurdles translate into routine violations of their legal entitlements, starting with work on demand. Prolonged delays in wage payments have also played havoc with the programme in recent years, and caused enormous hardship to NREGA workers.

Behind many of these problems is a partial failure to ensure accountability in the implementation of NREGA. An important reason for placing public works in a legal framework is to create accountability, and, as mentioned earlier, the Act includes specific provisions for this purpose, such as the unemployment-allowance clause, the compensation clause and the penalty clause. These provisions, however, have remained largely unused and dormant, partly because they are supposed to be enforced by the administrative machinery that is implementing the programme in the first place, and has no stake in making itself accountable to the people.[37] The future of NREGA depends a great deal on the activation of these accountability provisions and on the creation of effective mechanisms for grievance redressal.[38] Failing that, NREGA is likely to be gradually reduced to a lame top-down scheme, instead of a demand-driven, rights-based programme, as it has been envisaged.

At the time of writing, the future of NREGA looks a little uncertain. A worrying 'fatigue factor' seems to have set in, but there are also many opportunities for further growth (both quantitative and qualitative) of the programme: operational innovations, the activation of NREGA's accountability provisions, and better collective organization of NREGA workers, among others. There are vast possibilities for constructive work in what is now a well-identified and promising field.

THE PUBLIC DISTRIBUTION SYSTEM: A NEW LOOK?[39]

Aside from the National Rural Employment Guarantee Act, the largest programme of economic support in India today is the Public Distribution System (PDS). Under the PDS, households are entitled to subsidized commodities in accordance with the type of ration card that they possess. These commodities consist mainly of rice and wheat, although some states have started including other food items (such as pulses and edible oil) in the PDS.[40]

The central government provides wheat and rice to state governments to run the PDS. Allocations to states are based on official poverty estimates; some state governments supplement them with their own resources.[41] It is their prerogative to assign households to different types of ration cards – mainly APL and BPL (above and below poverty line), though some states have other categories too.[42]

In some states, the PDS is universal or near-universal, in the sense that all or most households have substantial PDS entitlements (not necessarily the same for every category). In other states, the PDS is effectively restricted to BPL households – APL households have negligible entitlements, if any.

At the risk of simplification, a distinction can be made between the 'old-style' PDS, the defects of which have become clearer over the years, and the 'new-style' PDS which seems to be in a formative phase. Basic features of the old-style PDS include narrow coverage (typically, BPL targeting), large exclusion errors (due to the unreliability of the BPL list, discussed earlier), erratic supply of food (often reflecting the disempowerment of the target group) and massive corruption. The new-style PDS is based on a focused effort to tackle these inter-related problems, and to achieve broad coverage, low exclusion errors, regular supply, and relatively small leakages. Underlying these differences is a contrast in PDS politics. At the risk of a slight exaggeration it can be said that the old-style PDS tends to be under the control of corrupt middlemen, but in the new-style PDS, end recipients matter much more than before. In practice, different states are on different grounds, and to some extent in different stages of the transition between an old-style and new-style PDS.

The old-style PDS used to be the dominant pattern in most states until a few years ago. It gave a bad name to the PDS system, which came to be widely seen (particularly among economists) as a very expensive and ineffective affair – a terminally dysfunctional operation that would be best phased out, or perhaps replaced with cash transfers.[43]

Contrary to this verdict, however, there has been a significant revival of the PDS in many states in recent years.[44] One of the pioneer states, here as in many other fields (as we have observed), was Tamil Nadu, where the PDS is universal, regular and relatively corruption-free. Other south Indian states have also made early moves towards a new-style PDS. But the big breakthrough happened in Chhattisgarh, where the PDS used to have all the defects of an old-style PDS (including massive corruption), and was widely thought to be beyond repair, and yet was 'turned around' in a few years – from the mid-2000s onwards – based on a firm political decision to make it work. Today, a vast majority (about 75 per cent) of rural house-holds in Chhattisgarh receive 35 kgs of rice from the PDS every month at a symbolic price (one or two rupees a kilo, depending on the type of ration card).[45] Many recent reports indicate that food distri-bution in Chhattisgarh is now quite regular, with most cardholders getting the prescribed quota every month at the correct price.[46] Thirty-five kgs of rice per month (about two-thirds of the foodgrain requirements of an average family of five) is not the end of poverty by any means, but for people who are constantly struggling to make ends meet, it does make a difference. In 2011 this monthly rice quota had roughly the same value as a week's wages under NREGA – without having to work.

The PDS turnaround in Chhattisgarh is particularly significant because it took place in the 'northern heartland' (generally known for poor governance, as discussed in Chapter 3), and in a state where the PDS had the reputation of being extremely corrupt and 'virtually non-functional'.[47] This is the sort of situation that still prevails in many states, including Bihar which is undergoing a number of signifi-cant reforms, but where the PDS is still largely unreformed. This contrast between Bihar's old-style PDS and Chhattisgarh's new-style PDS is illustrated in Table 7.2. It is perhaps not an accident that, in this survey of BPL households conducted in May–June 2011, the pro-portion of respondents who reported having skipped meals in the preceding three months was as high as 70 per cent in Bihar, compared with only 17 per cent in Chhattisgarh – in spite of both states having much the same levels of rural poverty based on standard measures of per capita expenditure.

The decision to fix the PDS was not an act of charity on the part of the Chhattisgarh government, but – quite explicitly – an attempt to win votes (which need not be seen as a shameful act in a democracy, for that is part of how democracy operates). This decision was fol-lowed by a two-year battle (eventually settled in court) to transfer the management of ration shops from private dealers to community institutions such as Gram Panchayats and self-help groups. A wide range of other PDS reforms followed, aimed at restoring transpar-ency and accountability in the system. When the Raman Singh government (which initiated the reforms) was returned to office in

Table 7.2
The Public Distribution System: Old and New

	Bihar	Chhattisgarh
Proportion of BPL households who did not get any foodgrains from the PDS in the last 3 months (%)	35	0
Average foodgrain purchases of BPL households from the PDS in the last 3 months:		
In absolute terms (kg/month)	11	33
As a proportion of entitlements[a] (%)	45	95
Proportion of BPL respondents who said that they 'normally' get their full PDS entitlements (%)	18	97
Proportion of BPL respondents who agree with the entries in their ration cards (%)	25	94
Proportion of BPL households who skipped meals in the last three months (%)	70	17
Proportion of BPL households who would support the PDS being replaced with equivalent cash transfers (%)	54	2

[a] Entitlements: 25 kgs and 35 kgs per household per month in Bihar and Chhattisgarh, respectively (for rice and wheat combined).

Source: PDS Survey 2011 (see Khera, 2011c), based on a random sample of 264 households in 24 villages of Bihar and Chhattisgarh (six villages per district in two districts of each state).

Chhattisgarh in 2008, it was widely believed, rightly or wrongly, that the PDS turnaround played a major role in this electoral victory, which inspired some other states, later on, to reform their PDS too.

Along with this, popular demand for a functional PDS has grown enormously across the country because of steep increases in market prices of rice and wheat (PDS issue prices, meanwhile, remained the same and were even reduced in some states). Food price inflation greatly increased the value of PDS entitlements, giving people a much greater stake in the system. It also created a pressure to broaden the coverage of the PDS in many states, and this broader coverage, too, helped to restore accountability in the PDS. Like Chhattisgarh, many other states (Andhra Pradesh, Himachal Pradesh, Odisha and Rajasthan, among others) initiated wide-ranging PDS reforms to improve the system and prevent corruption.

Some early signs of broad-based PDS improvement emerged from the 66th Round of the National Sample Survey (NSS), dated 2009–10. Between 2004–5 (the previous 'thick round' of the NSS) and 2009–10, household purchases of wheat and rice from the PDS increased by 50 per cent in quantity terms. The proportion of households purchasing at least some rice or wheat from the PDS increased from 27 per cent in 2004–5 to 45 per cent in 2009–10. NSS data also suggest, for the first time, that the PDS is making a significant contribution to poverty reduction in rural India, especially – but not only – in states with a fully fledged 'new style PDS', like Tamil Nadu and Chhattisgarh.[48]

A survey conducted in nine states in May–June 2011 (based on a random sample of about 1,200 BPL households) also suggests that recent initiatives have led to significant results: the sample households had received 84 per cent of their full PDS entitlements during the preceding three months. Most of the shortfall was concentrated in Bihar, Jharkhand and Uttar Pradesh – in the other states (Andhra Pradesh, Chhattisgarh, Himachal Pradesh, Odisha, Rajasthan and Tamil Nadu), BPL households were routinely getting their full entitlements. Even in Bihar and Jharkhand there were clear signs of major improvement, considering that these are states where more than 80 per cent of central foodgrain allocations for the PDS were estimated to be 'diverted' to the black market as recently as 2004–5.[49]

None of this is to say that all is well with the PDS – far from it. Even a shortfall of 16 per cent in the delivery of PDS entitlements to BPL households is unacceptable, and adds up to huge losses at the national level. More importantly, it appears that there is still massive corruption in the APL quota, which lacks transparency.[50] And of course, even with small leakages this is an expensive system, with large transaction costs associated with the procurement, transportation and storage of grain. This is one reason why the case for replacing the PDS with a system of cash transfers continues to be made quite forcefully by many economists.

There are, however, grounds for some apprehension about the prospect of a wholesale replacement of the PDS with cash transfers. First, the PDS is – or at least can be – more than just income support. Several states have started delivering nutritious commodities such as pulses, edible oil and fortified salt under the PDS. This could act as an important nutrition supplement for poor households, more effectively than cash transfers (in so far as PDS entitlements work as a 'nudge' in the direction of nutritious food consumption).[51] A well-functioning PDS could have a useful nutritional role across the country.

Second, even the income support role of the PDS need not work in the same way as cash transfers, since income in kind is often used differently from income in cash. Food tends to be consumed sparingly, day after day, and everyone in the family gets a share (even if not exactly the same share). Cash, of course, can in principle be used with similar care, but there is also a risk of it being misused, frittered away, or inequitably shared. Cash is also more easily deflected towards the purchase of goods that are consumed mainly by adult members of the family, especially men, at the expense of undernourished girls and other children. While it is certainly true that even food given to a family can be sold to shopkeepers with the same opportunity of adult consumption, there tends to be some psychological barrier to such abuse of free or subsidized food.

Third, the adequacy of cash transfers as a substitute for food rations depends on the effectiveness of local food markets. The latter varies a great deal across India, with substantial problems of distance and exploitative pricing in the more remote areas (such as the tribal areas of Central India), where food insecurity also tends to be widespread.

Even in other areas, dismantling the PDS could have a destabilizing effect on local food markets.

Fourth, there is a question of preparedness. Almost every Indian village already has a functioning PDS outlet (or 'fair price shop'). Cash transfers require an infrastructure of their own, such as an effective banking system, which is still lacking in large parts of India. The prolonged disruption of NREGA that followed a hasty switch to banks (and post offices) as channels of payment of wages in mid-2008, without the required infrastructure being in place, has been a sobering experience in this regard.

Fifth, the real value of cash transfers may get eroded by inflation. In principle, of course, there is a simple remedy – indexing transfers to the price level. But the simplicity is deceptive. Cash transfers can be indexed to the general price level, but that would still leave the possibility of their value being eroded by local price increases. There is also an issue of political guarantee of the periodic price adjustments actually taking place, even when – say – the finance minister is under pressure to cut expenditure. The Central Government's repeated failure to index NREGA wages, even after promising to do so, is – again – an experience worth remembering in this context.

These and other concerns forcefully emerged in the field survey mentioned earlier, when the respondents were asked how they would feel about the PDS being replaced with cash transfers. While some of them had an open mind about cash transfers, or even favoured them over the PDS, the general pattern was a strong preference for the PDS wherever the system functioned relatively well.[52] It is only in Bihar, where the functioning of the PDS was very poor, that a majority (54 per cent) of respondents supported cash transfers as an alternative to the PDS (see Table 7.2).

These responses, of course, need to be interpreted with caution, and are not meant to settle the debate. However, people's concerns do call for acknowledgement and scrutiny. Indeed, one of the premises of the cash transfer argument is that people know best what is good for them (so that there is no need to 'patronize' them by giving them specific commodities instead of cash). But if people know best, then surely their views on these matters should carry some weight.

Last but not least, if the PDS were to be replaced with cash transfers, the government would have to devise good ways of using all the rice and wheat it procures every year. The procurement system has a momentum of its own, and is unlikely to be dismantled any time soon. Upbeat estimates of massive 'food subsidy' savings in the event of a transition to cash transfers effectively assume a discontinuation (or at least a sharp reduction) of foodgrain procurement, but this assumption is rarely discussed. Nor is the political feasibility or desirability of discontinuing food procurement given any room in these calculations.

In short, the case for replacing the PDS with cash transfers is not as compelling as it is often made out to be. In some circumstances, of course, cash transfers can be quite effective, as discussed earlier. But the hasty replacement of a functional PDS, which has become a very important source of support for millions of poor people, with a system of cash transfers that may or may not come up to expectations, could be a costly mistake. There is a case for consolidating what is already in place, rather than rushing at once for cash transfers, even though the role of such transfers may become more plausible in the long run.

The really important issue, however, is not 'cash versus kind' – it is to put in place an effective system of income support and economic security, whether it is based on cash transfers or on the Public Distribution System (or a combination of the two). Leaving poor people to their own devices is neither socially just nor smart public policy.

8

The Grip of Inequality

All countries in the world have inequalities of various kinds. India, however, has a unique cocktail of lethal divisions and disparities. Few countries have to contend with such extreme inequalities in so many dimensions, including large economic inequalities as well as major disparities of caste, class and gender. Caste has a peculiar role in India that separates it out from the rest of the world. Many countries, to be sure, have had in the past (and to some extent even right now) caste-like institutions that place people in confined boxes. But India seems to be quite unique both in terms of the centrality of caste hierarchies and in terms of their continuing hold in modern society (despite a great many pieces of legislation outlawing any practice of caste discrimination). And caste stratification often reinforces class inequality, giving it a resilience that is harder to conquer. Gender inequality, too, is exceptionally high in India, particularly in large parts of the northern and western regions, where the subjugation of women is fairly comprehensive. It is the mutual reinforcement of severe inequalities of different kinds that creates an extremely oppressive social system, where those at the bottom of these multiple layers of disadvantage live in conditions of extreme disempowerment.

India's heavy historical legacy of multiple inequalities is illustrated in Table 8.1, which compares literacy rates among Brahmins and Dalits (formerly called untouchables and now known as 'scheduled castes' with certain legally guaranteed opportunities) at the beginning of the twentieth century in different regions of British India. In most regions, a majority of Brahmin men (up to 73 per cent, in Baroda State) were already literate at that time. At the other extreme, the literacy rate among Dalit women was *zero* in most regions. This reflects a massive gender gap within each community (with men having a virtual

Table 8.1
Caste, Gender and Literacy in 1901

Region (Province or State)	Literacy Rates, 1901 (%) Brahmin[a]		Literacy Rates, 1901 (%) 'Scheduled Castes'[b]	
	Male	Female	Male	Female
Baroda State	73.0	5.6	1.2	0
Mysore State	68.1	6.4	0.9	0.1
Bombay Province	58.0	5.4	0.7	0
Madras Province	57.8	4.4	1.0	0
United Provinces	55.3	4.6	0.2	0
Central Provinces	36.5	0.9	0.4	0

[a] Kayashta, in United Provinces.
[b] Chamar in United Provinces and Central Provinces; Dhed and Mahar in Baroda State; Paraiyan in Madras Province; Holaya in Mysore; Dhed, Mahar and Vankar (combined) in Bombay. Because of changes in the classification of castes over time, it was not possible to estimate the overall literacy rates of all 'scheduled castes' (as they came to be known later) in 1901; an effort was made to identify the main scheduled castes in each region, among the castes listed in the 1901 Census.

Source: Census of India 1901, Subsidiary Tables, Table VI (see Risley and Gait, 1903).

monopoly of education within each group) as well as enormous caste-based disparities, with even Dalit men achieving literacy rates of at most 1 per cent at that time in each region – barely 1 per cent of the literacy rates of Brahmin men.

It is the mutual reinforcement of different inequalities (in this case, caste and gender) that creates such enormous disparities in Indian society. The disparities would look even worse if the class dimension were added in the picture. And just as inequalities of caste and gender tend to reinforce each other, so do those of, say, caste and class. For instance, caste divisions make it much harder for the economically underprivileged to organize and bargain for a better deal. As B. R. Ambedkar perceptively remarked, '. . . the Caste System is not merely a division of *labour*. It is a division of *labourers*.'*

---

* Ambedkar (1936), p. 47; emphasis added. He went further: 'The Caste System is not merely a division of labourers which is quite different from division of labour – it is a

The figures presented in Table 8.1 would look quite different today, especially in the younger age groups.[1] In fact, as the country approaches universal literacy in the younger age groups, the caste and gender gaps in literacy rates are bound to shrink. In historical perspective, this end of the virtual 'male upper-caste monopoly' of educational opportunities is an important breakthrough – and a useful reminder that, all said and done, some significant social change is taking place in India. However, it would be a big mistake to think that these historical inequalities have been overcome. For one thing, as we saw in Chapter 3, a large proportion of Indian children (mainly from underprivileged families) learn very little at school, and if one were to look at more advanced educational achievements than mere literacy, sharp disparities of class, caste and gender would re-emerge quite forcefully. For another, the social norms and value systems underlying these historical inequalities are still alive, even if their manifestations are moderated by modern laws, norms and institutions.

To this picture must be added the fact that educational inequalities are also important in their own right. Educational inequalities are partly, but only partly, a reflection of class, caste and gender inequalities. They also have an influence of their own, reflecting differences in access to schooling, learning abilities, parental education, and so on. For instance, there are often significant differences in educational achievements between siblings, even of the same sex, and of course (since they belong to the same family) of the same caste and class. And here again, India seems to fare very badly in international perspective, in terms of the extent of educational inequalities – both overall educational inequalities and inequalities among siblings.[2] For instance, the dispersion of years of schooling within a specific age group tends to be very high in India, especially among women.[3]

There are also other important social divisions in India, often reinforcing those already discussed. For instance, there is the division between those who know English and those who don't, emphasized

hierarchy in which the divisions of labourers are graded one above the other.' This feature of the caste hierarchy, as a system of 'graded inequality' (as Ambedkar called it), makes it even more pernicious as a division of labourers, and even more resistant to change.

for example by the socialist thinker Rammanohar Lohia, who even argued that 'high-caste, wealth, and knowledge of English are the three requisites, with anyone possessing two of these belonging to the ruling class'.[4] Indeed, knowing English opens all sorts of doors in India, even to someone who may not be particularly qualified otherwise. English is the language of the courts (from High Courts upwards), of higher education, of modern business, of high-level official documents, and to a large extent still, of the Internet. This division is increasingly reflected in the schooling system, split as it is between privileged 'English-medium' schools and the rest. It is a major barrier against the integration of all children in a common schooling system. Here again, one form of inequality stands in the way of tackling another.[5]

The mutual reinforcement of class, caste, gender and other inequalities has been particularly strong in the northern heartland, and is quite possibly an important clue to the tendency of that region to lag behind the rest of the country in many respects.[6] Elsewhere, recent experiences of rapid and broad-based social progress have involved dealing, in one way or another, with the historical burden of mutually reinforcing inequalities. We have discussed this in Chapter 3, with reference to recent experiences of rapid development in Kerala, Himachal Pradesh and Tamil Nadu. For India as a whole, this integrative task remains largely unaccomplished.

INCOME INEQUALITY AND ECONOMIC DIVISIONS

How unequal is India in terms of income distribution? The conventional economic reading in this respect has been that India is *not* particularly unequal, compared with other countries. This common impression is largely based on comparing the Gini coefficient of per capita *expenditure* in India with that of per capita *income* in other countries (because of the absence of reliable income data for India). This is a biased comparison, because the distribution of per capita expenditure, across the world, tends to be less unequal than that of per capita income. However, the India Human Development Survey, dated 2004–5, includes income data and makes it possible to estimate the Gini coefficient of per capita income for India, which turns out to be 0.54 (much higher than the values of 0.35 or so that typically emerge from per capita expenditure data). This suggests, as a World Bank study concludes, that 'inequality in India appears to be in the same league as that in Brazil and South Africa, both high-inequality countries'.[7] This conclusion is based on a single survey, and calls for further scrutiny, but what is clear is that the general belief that income distribution in India is less unequal than in many of the other developing countries in the world is very seriously open to question.

There is also much evidence of *growing* economic inequality in India in recent decades. For instance, per capita expenditure data suggest an increase in rural-urban disparities as well as growing inequality in urban areas. The comparatively affluent in urban areas have been the main beneficiaries of rapid economic growth in India in recent years. Similarly, per capita income data indicate a growing concentration of incomes at the top, and wealth data, patchy as they are, also point to growing disparities in the post-reform period.[8]

Had the distribution of incomes and expenditures remained unchanged (or improved) instead of becoming more unequal, poor people would have gained much more from India's rapid economic growth than they have. Instead, poverty decline has continued at a sluggish pace, more or less in line with earlier trends, even as growth has vastly accelerated.[9] Aside from this discouraging pattern, there are other reasons to be concerned with the growth of economic inequality in India, even if it goes hand in hand with continued poverty decline. Indeed, recent investigations across the world have brought out many adverse social consequences of inequality in itself, including economic inequality. For instance, economic inequality tends to be associated with lower health achievements – not just for the poor but also for the population as a whole.[10] There is also some evidence that high economic inequality makes a country more prone to crime. Economic disparities also tend to undermine social solidarity and civic cooperation. Further, a high concentration of wealth gives disproportionate political power to a privileged minority, often reinforcing the elitist biases of public policy and democratic politics.[11] And last but not the least, the continuation of caste and other inequalities depends greatly on their partial congruence with economic disparities, reinforcing each other. For these and other reasons, there is a case for doing more – much more – to prevent further growth of income inequality in India, and indeed, to reverse it. Recent experiences of economic redistribution in Latin America (where inequality has declined, not increased, in recent years), and even India's own recent experience with income support programmes (discussed in the preceding chapter), suggest that much can indeed be done in this respect.

Having said this, however, it can be argued that the main issue is not the recent intensification of economic inequality, but the extent and nature of the continuing inequalities from earlier on – not only class-based inequality but also other types of inequality (related for instance to caste and gender). As will be discussed presently, mutually reinforcing inequalities have created a resilient division between the privileged and the rest in Indian society.

As far as the economic dimension is concerned, the worst infringement of principles of equity in India is not so much the unseemly wealth of the rich or super-rich, but the fact that so many people still lack the basic requirements of dignified living – food, shelter, clothing, sanitation, health care, and schools for their children. It is against this background of mass deprivation that the opulence of the rich seems particularly grotesque. Indeed, China's economic inequality *per se* is no less than India's, and yet there is a real difference made by the fact that the poorer Chinese do not typically lack the basic amenities of life in the way that poor Indians do (we shall return to this issue in the last chapter). The first step towards more social justice in India is surely to guarantee the essentials to everyone, rather than leaving a vast number of people to face persistent deprivations in daily living.

THE CONTINUING HOLD OF CASTE

It is often argued that caste discrimination has subsided a great deal in the twentieth century.[12] Given the intensity of caste discrimination in India's past, this is true enough, without making the present situation particularly close to equality. In large parts of India, in the old days, Dalits were not allowed to wear sandals, ride bicycles, enter temples, or sit on a chair in the presence of higher castes – to give just a few examples of the vicious system of humiliation and subjugation that had developed around the caste system.[13] Many of these discriminatory practices have indeed declined or disappeared, thanks to the spread of education, movements of social reform, constitutional safeguards, as well as economic development, and also, of course, growing political resistance from the victims of discrimination.

This trend is far from uniform. Some caste prejudices, such as the disapproval of inter-caste marriages, remain rather strong today among many social groups. And while caste divisions are subsiding in large parts of the country and society, they have also been making inroads where they did not exist earlier, for instance among various Adivasi, Muslim, Sikh and Christian communities. More importantly, however, caste continues to be an important instrument of power in Indian society, even where the caste system has lost some of its earlier barbarity and brutality.

The continuing hold of the upper castes on public institutions is illustrated in Table 8.2, based on survey data collected in Allahabad – a sizeable city in northern India. The entries in the table indicate the share of the upper castes in positions of power and influence – the press club, the university faculty, the bar association, the top echelons of the police, and the commanding posts in trade unions, NGOs, media houses, among other public institutions. It turns out that this share is around 75 per cent, compared with a share of around 20 per cent for the upper castes in the population of Uttar Pradesh as a whole. Brahmins and Kayashtas alone (the two highest-ranked castes in Allahabad) have cornered about half of the posts – more than four times their share in the state's population.[14] These are approximate figures, partly based on guessing castes from surnames, but the pattern is clear enough: the upper castes continue to have overwhelming control over public institutions. It is not that other castes (or communities) are completely unrepresented, but with such a large majority, it is not surprising that members of the upper castes have remarkably unequal power. There was no evidence of any significant presence of Dalits in any of the sample institutions, with the partial exception of the university faculty, partly due to mandatory quotas.

It is worth noting that the dominance of the upper castes seems to

Table 8.2
Share of Upper Castes in Selected Groups, Allahabad (%)

Reference group[a]	Upper castes		Brahmin and Kayashta	
	In entire group	Among those 'identified'	In entire group	Among those 'identified'
Allahabad Press Club, office bearers (16)	100	100	75	75
Leaders of teachers' unions (17)	100	100	76	76
Proprietors of advertisement agencies (11)	91	91	55	55
Senior doctors (99)	89	94	37	39
Bar Association, executive committee (28)	86	96	68	76
Prominent publishers (12)	83	100	42	50
GB Pant Social Science Institute faculty (15)	80	80	60	67
Advocate Association executive committee (14)	79	100	57	73
NGO representatives (30)	77	88	47	54
Trade union leaders (clerical & manual workers) (49)	76	88	55	64
Allahabad University faculty* (112)	76	77	54	55
CDOs and BDOs (20)	75	88	40	53
Ashok Nagar residents (62)	74	82	32	36
Reporters of media houses (62)	74	85	53	61

(*Continued*)

Table 8.2: (*Continued*)

Reference group[a]	Upper castes		Brahmin and Kayashta	
	In entire group	Among those 'identified'	In entire group	Among those 'identified'
Former presidents, AU students' union (79)	73	89	44	54
Prominent artists (55)	71	89	47	59
Allahabad Press Club, members (104)	71	80	56	63
Police officers (district and block levels) (28)	68	100	39	58
IIIT faculty (47)	68	100	36	56
High Court judges (75)	68	81	32	38
High Court lawyers* (100)	67	88	44	58
Traders' association (6)	67	80	0	0
College principals (16)	56	69	19	23
Junior engineer, Allahabad municipality (20)	55	79	30	43
Total (1,077)	75	87	46	54

AU = Allahabad University.
BDO = Block Development Officer.
CDO = Chief Development Officer.
IIIT = Indian Institute of Information Technology.

[a] In brackets, size of the group (or of the sample, in cases – marked with an asterisk – where a sample was taken).

Note: The first column indicates the proportion of persons identified (with reasonable confidence) as upper-caste in the entire group. The second column indicates their proportion in the sub-set of all those (within the relevant group) whose caste could be identified. These figures can be interpreted as lower and upper bounds, respectively, on the actual proportion of upper-caste persons in the relevant group. Similarly with Brahmins and Kayashtas in the third and fourth columns.

Source: Survey data collected in August 2012 by Ankita Aggarwal, Jean Drèze and Aashish Gupta (see Aggarwal et al., 2013).

be, if anything, even stronger in institutions of 'civil society' than in state institutions. For instance, in Allahabad the share of the upper castes is around 80 per cent among NGO representatives and trade union leaders, close to 90 per cent in the executive committee of the Bar Association, and a full 100 per cent among office bearers of the Press Club (which is, in fact, made up almost entirely of Brahmins and Kayashtas). Even trade unions of workers who belong mainly to disadvantaged castes are often under the control of upper-caste leaders. There is some food for thought here about the tendency even of anti-establishment movements in India to reproduce, within their own political activities, images of the old divisions.

Perhaps Allahabad is particularly conservative in this respect. It is, of course, just one city, though it is worth mentioning that Allahabad is a centre of power in its own right. For instance, alumni of Allahabad University, one of India's oldest and largest universities, are found in large numbers in the civil services and other public institutions across India.[15] Still, there is no intention here of singling out Allahabad (merely because we happen to have more data on it). The point is to illustrate a general pattern that also applies to varying extents in many other parts of India, especially in the north of the country.

Indeed, a number of recent studies have brought out, in similar ways, the continued dominance of the upper castes (and virtual absence of Dalits, Adivasis and other disadvantaged communities) in media houses, corporate boards, judicial institutions, and even cricket or polo teams.[16] For instance, a recent survey of 315 editors and other leading members of the print and electronic media in Delhi, by the Centre for the Study of Developing Societies, found that *not one* of them belonged to a scheduled caste or scheduled tribe. In fact, about 85 per cent belonged to a small coterie of upper castes (accounting for only 16 per cent of India's population), and about half were Brahmins.[17] Obviously, this does not help to ensure that the concerns and views of Dalits and Adivasis are adequately represented in public debates (especially, but not only, public debates on issues like reservation policies). Very similar patterns emerged in a recent study of corporate boards in India: more than 90 per cent of their members were upper-caste, and almost half (45 per cent to be precise) were

Brahmins. Interestingly, in this case Brahmins were slightly outnumbered by Vaishyas (the traditional business and trading castes, also known as Baniyas), who accounted for 46 per cent of the seats on corporate boards.[18] Scheduled castes and scheduled tribes, for their part, get only 3.5 per cent of the seats, a small fraction of their share (about 24 per cent) in the population. In fact, in a *large majority* (70 per cent) of corporate boards, there was no 'diversity' at all, in the sense that *all* members belonged to the same caste group.

One of the barriers to rectifying caste-based discrimination is that caste has become virtually unmentionable in polite society in India, not just because any caste-based practice has to face legal challenge, but also because any kind of caste consciousness is taken to be socially retrograde and reactionary. This can be superficially justified as a contribution to the obliteration of caste consciousness, but it does not help to understand the world for what it is, let alone change it.

A similar problem exists for the poorer Muslims in India. Many Muslims are, of course, solidly part of the upper stratum of Indian society, including business tycoons, political leaders and professional classes, as we might expect from India's largely secular politics and the historical fact that the upper classes in pre-British India had a high proportion of Muslims, many of whom did not migrate to Pakistan when the country was divided in 1947. And yet at the other end, the poorer Muslims, often descendants of lower-caste Hindus who had converted to Islam (sometimes to escape caste-based discrimination), can have economic and social disadvantages comparable to those of lower-caste Hindus.[19] And in the affirmative legal provisions in post-independent India which give the scheduled castes and scheduled tribes preferential treatment in various spheres (including civil service appointments and entry into institutions of higher education), poorer Muslims as a category are not included. This gross injustice, resulting from treating caste discrimination as a unique problem that applies to the Hindus, is being rectified to some extent, but there is need for more speed there, and also a necessity to re-examine the structure of affirmative action, taking note of the fact that the continuation of caste inequality as well as inequality between poor Muslims and the less poor Indians (Muslims as well as others) is crucially dependent on the overlap of social stratification with economic inequality.

GENDER INEQUALITIES:
CONTINUITY AND CHANGE

Gender inequality is among the social disparities that keep large numbers of people on the margin of the 'new India' – not only women themselves, but also men and children who would benefit from a more active, informed and equal participation of women in social and public life. Like caste relations, gender relations too have changed in the recent past, and in some respects gender disparities have significantly diminished. For instance, as was noted earlier, girls (even among the higher castes) used to be virtually excluded from the education system a hundred years ago, but are now flocking to school across the country. As a result, the gender bias in school participation is now relatively small at the primary level, and is narrowing rapidly at other levels as well.

Seen from this angle, it might look as if India is well on its way towards removing traditional gender disparities. Furthermore, women occupy positions of importance in many walks of life in India, including academia and the professions as well as in politics, literature, arts and music. Given all this, the thesis of a hugely unequal deprivation of women in India often looks quite implausible to outside observers of the Indian society. And yet gender inequality is a very significant part of the Indian social reality.

One of the old problems of gender inequality in India is the larger incidence of mortality of female children over male. This is not because of female infanticide, or any form of deliberate killing, but largely due to the quiet – and not clearly perceived – neglect of the interests of female children in health care and nutrition. There are huge regional differences in the treatment of girls within India, but the average picture that emerges from the all-India figures is truly shocking.[20] The mortality rates of Indian girls are substantially higher, on average, than those of Indian boys – with a larger differential (in favour of boys) than in most other countries for which estimates are available.[21] Among the regional contrasts within India in this respect, there is more excess female mortality in the north-west, and less – or none – in many of the eastern and southern states. Given the regional differences, the average picture indicates how adverse the conditions of girls are compared with boys in the particularly gender-biased states – mainly in the north and the west of India. The states in the north and the west also show a dismally high incidence of 'natality discrimination' against girls – we shall turn to that subject presently.

There are many other ways in which gender inequality in India remains strong. For instance, women's workforce participation (conventionally defined, i.e. excluding household work within the family) remains extremely low by international standards, and shows little sign of increasing.[22] This is in sharp contrast to what has happened in many other Asian countries (including, as we saw in Chapter 3, Bangladesh) in their phase of rapid growth, which has usually been accompanied by a major increase in women's employment opportunities.* This contrast is partly a reflection of India's general problem of 'jobless growth', discussed in Chapter 2, but also a reflection of negative social attitudes towards women's work outside the household in large parts of the society. In fact, increases in income or education in India are often associated with a *decline* in women's workforce participation.

As was discussed in Chapter 3 (and also in Chapters 5 and 6), Bangladesh has not only progressed much more than India in many areas of human development, this progress has been led, to a great extent, by the role of women's agency – particularly in the provision and use of public services and in the social sector, from family planning and health care to teaching in schools. India has to be concerned not only with what can be done for women (important as it is), but also with what women can do for India, which remains, to a great extent, an untapped resource that can make India a very different country.

Another example of continuing gender disparity can be seen in women's political representation, even though the record here is

---

* Only 17 out of 184 countries for which data on women's workforce participation rates are given in *World Development Indicators* have a lower 'female labour force participation rate' (age 15 years and above) than India's abysmal 29 per cent. Most of these countries are in North Africa and West Asia.

rather mixed. On the one hand, women are now entitled to a minimum share of 33 per cent (even 50 per cent in some states) of elected posts in Panchayati Raj Institutions (PRIs) – a very positive development.[23] This has enabled millions of women to take active part in local politics, and there is some evidence of this having led to significant changes in the priorities, activities and perceptions of PRIs.[24] On the other hand, the Indian Parliament and state assemblies continue to be male bastions. Women's share of all seats in the Lok Sabha has never been higher than 10 per cent or so (the highest share so far was 10.9 per cent, in 2009); the share of women in state assemblies is also below 10 per cent in a majority of cases, and not higher than 14 per cent in any of the major states for which data are available.[25]

There are many other manifestations of India's patriarchal form of social and cultural relations: property inheritance is resolutely patrilineal, post-marital residence remains overwhelmingly patrilocal, women's freedom of movement continues to be quite restricted, and violence against women (including domestic violence) is still pervasive in large parts of the society. In fact, some of these patriarchal norms have had a tendency to spread rather than to vanish. For instance, the practice of dowry (which contributes to many gender-related social problems, including the well-known phenomenon of 'boy preference' and the harassment of married women on grounds of having brought an inadequate dowry) has steadily spread during the twentieth century to communities where it did not exist earlier. One possible reason for this is that many of these patriarchal norms, including dowry, which used to be confined only to parts of the upper-caste groups, are seen as markers of social status and upward mobility.[26] We surely have a long way to go in achieving anything like gender parity in vitally important aspects of economic, social and political life in India.

RAPE, VIOLENCE AND PROTEST

The aspect of gender inequality that has received most vocal attention in recent days is that of violence against women and in particular the high incidence of rape, and this issue has had a sudden and gigantic prominence which it did not have earlier. The transforming moment was the occurrence of an extremely brutal gang-rape in a closed bus in Delhi on 16th December 2012 (which ultimately also led to the death of the victim). Massive demonstrations against violence perpetrated on women continued for many days in Delhi as well as in some other cities, bringing out protesting crowds incomparably larger than any seen before involved in the rejection of gender inequity. There were large clashes with the police as well. Among the vocal complaints were those against the police for not providing adequate protection to women – and in this case also for not acting at all promptly even when the raped victim and her beaten male friend were found lying on the street. The lack of security and deep vulnerability of women to rape and harassment became overnight a national issue in a way it had never been earlier.

Whether this will prove to be a long-run turning point in bringing about greater security for women remains to be seen. Predictably, there was also some airing of male prejudice and sexism in blaming the victim, making such impertinent suggestions as that women should dress more modestly, should not offer temptation to vulnerable men, and must not go out at night. The fact that these apologia were immediately and loudly rebutted in public discussion indicates that at least for now the movement has not lost its reasoned basis. There were suggestions also that this kind of rape occurs only in modern India (what is sometimes called 'India, not Bharat') and does not happen so frequently – or at all – in rural areas, which is of course empirical nonsense given what we know both about violation and rape of Dalit women by upper-caste men (often landlords), and of marital rape of unwilling wives to do what their husbands may want. One of the positive consequences of this extremely tragic and barbaric incident is to draw attention both to the prevalence of sexual brutality and rape and to the fact that even known phenomena of the violation of women had tended to receive so little attention in the past. As the newspapers reinvented themselves as rape-reporting vehicles, many of them across the country have been devoting much space, often several pages every day, to reports of rape gathered together in a way they never had been before.

How frequent is rape in India? If there are pages and pages of rapes to report in the newspapers from across the country, the incidence cannot but be large. And yet it did not seem like that at all even a short while ago. One of the reasons for this subdued perception must be the underreporting of rapes, which is common because the police are often quite unfriendly to the victims, the courts are slow to act, and convictions are hard to secure. It has been frequently speculated that the majority of rapes go unreported, and the actual incidence of rape may be five or ten times what gets recorded by the police. This is very likely true, and it might be quite correct to conclude, as many observers have done, that India does indeed have a 'rape problem.'

However, whether or not India has a problem of extremely high incidence of rape, it surely has another problem in the form of victims getting little support from the police or the legal system. If we go by the rate of police-recorded rape, the United Nations Office on Drugs and Crime gives the incidence of rape in India for 2010 as 1.8 per 100,000 people – among the lowest in the world. India's figure of 1.8 can be compared with, for example, 27.3 in the USA, 28.8 in the United Kingdom, 63.5 in Sweden, or 120.0 in South Africa.[27] India's recorded number is certainly a huge underestimate, but even if we take 10 times that figure, the corrected number of rapes would still be lower in India than in the USA or UK or Sweden or South Africa (even with the assumption that there is no underreporting in these other countries). Of course the multiple required to correct for under-reporting in India could be, quite possibly (we do not really know), much higher than 10. We cannot be sure whether India has a special rape problem or not, but all the evidence suggests that India has a huge problem with making rape a seriously monitored and reported issue, with all that implies about the lack of preventive planning. India's main problem can well lie – consistently with what we do know – not so much in any exceptional frequency of rapes, but in having an uncaring police, bad security arrangements, an unfunctioning judicial system, and ultimately an uncaring society. India does not have to be 'the rape capital of the world' for it to be severely indicted.

What is also clear is that Delhi has a special problem that may not apply to the other megacities in India. The rate of recorded rapes per 100,000 people is 2.8 for Delhi in 2011, compared with 1.2 in

Mumbai, 1.1 in Bangalore, 0.9 in Chennai, and 0.3 in Kolkata. Since there is nothing to indicate that recording of rape is much more efficient in Delhi than in the other cities, it is indeed remarkable that Delhi has a record that is more than 9 times worse than Kolkata. Indeed, no matter how unfriendly to women the Indian society might or might not be, there is no reason why Delhi cannot even come close to making the city at least as safe as some of the other cities of India already are. The problems of administration, policing, trials and social indifference remain large for India as a whole, but there are parts of India that have bigger problems in the security of women than other parts. Huge heterogeneities within India can be seen in other areas of gender inequality as well, as will be presently discussed.

COOPERATIVE CONFLICT AND WOMEN'S AGENCY

The force and effectiveness of women's agency depend on a number of social influences of which the nature of the family is a significant component. A family is a system of cooperation that has elements of congruent interest as well as divergent priorities. The divisions within the family can be seen as a combination of cooperation (everyone may benefit from living together) and conflict (the benefits and chores generated by living together can be divided in many different ways, and in this respect men and women may have competitive, rather than congruent interests). Models of 'cooperative conflicts' can be fruitfully used in explaining intra-family divisions.[28]

In traditional arrangements, women tend to get a smaller share of benefits (for example, less favourable medical and educational attention) and a very much larger share of the chores (particularly in the frequently unshared burden of housework and the care of children and old people). There is, however, empirical evidence that the sharing of both the benefits and burdens can become more equitable when women – particularly young women – have a stronger voice, related, for example, to being literate and schooled, and to having recognizably gainful employment, rather than only unremunerated housework and unrecognized drudgery.[29]

The perception of who is doing how much 'productive' work, or who is 'contributing' how much to the family's prosperity, can be, in this context, very influential, even though the underlying 'theory' regarding how contributions or productivity are to be assessed may be rarely discussed explicitly.[30] Such interpretations of individual contributions and appropriate entitlements of women and men play a major role in the division of a family's joint benefits between them; and the circumstances that influence these perceptions of contributions and appropriate entitlements (such as women's ability to earn an independent income, to work outside the home, to be educated, to own property) often have a crucial bearing on these divisions. The impact of greater empowerment and agency of women, thus, includes the correction of the iniquities that blight the lives and well-being of women vis-à-vis men. For example, Bina Agarwal has shown, in her well argued book *A Field of One's Own*, how the asymmetry in land ownership – with women often owning very little land – can make a major difference to gender inequalities of various kinds.[31] Similarly, the positive impact of female education in resisting widespread gender inequality has also been shown to be quite large.[32]

The consequences of gender asymmetry can extend well beyond the domain of gender inequality itself, since the lives of other people are also involved. In this context, it is particularly important to see the role of women's agency in reducing child mortality, and restraining fertility. Both relate to concerns that are central to the process of development, and while they clearly do influence the well-being of women as well, their relevance is undoubtedly very much wider.

The adverse effects of very high birth rates include the denial of women's freedom to do other things – through persistent bearing and rearing of children – routinely imposed on many Asian and African women. It is, thus, not surprising that reductions in birth rates have often followed the enhancement of women's status and power. The lives that are most constrained by over-frequent bearing and rearing of children are those of young women, and any social change that increases their voice and influence on fertility decisions can be expected to have the effect of reducing the frequency of births.

Recent demographic work has also brought out the influence of women's agency and of women's empowerment in reducing child mortality.[33] The influence works through many channels, but perhaps most immediately it works through the importance that mothers typically attach to the welfare of the children, and the opportunity they have, when their agency is respected and empowered, to influence family decisions in that direction, away from being dominated by the lifestyles of adult males.

The positive impact of women's agency may extend well beyond the connection between women's empowerment and demographic change. As discussed in Chapter 3, women's agency seems to have played a crucial role in the recent progress of many aspects of living standards in Bangladesh, and also in recent experiences of relatively rapid social progress in India – notably in Himachal Pradesh, Kerala and Tamil Nadu. Many aspects of this far-reaching influence are becoming increasingly clear.

SELECTIVE ABORTION, SOCIETY AND ENLIGHTENMENT

Even though the impact of women's agency is remarkably extensive, there is a need to understand how the reach of that agency is also qualified – and sometimes restrained – by an inadequate understanding of social inequities and a reluctance to re-examine traditional values (for example, 'boy preference'). This lack of clarity and confidence may be influenced by a lack of awareness of the oddness of seeing girls as inferior to boys (including an inadequate knowledge of what happens in many countries or regions where these types of gender inequalities are not present). But even with increased knowledge, the reach of women's agency may be limited also by the need for courage and temerity to think differently – without which it may not be powerful enough to overturn iniquitous but entrenched practices and societal arrangements that are often accepted as part and parcel of an assumed 'natural order'.

The restrained reach of women's agency is illustrated, for example, in China or South Korea, where the standard routes to women's empowerment, such as female literacy and economic independence, have had major achievements. This progress has certainly contributed to many of the social advances in those countries and has done a great deal to remove some standard forms of gender inequality, such as survival asymmetry (the unnaturally high mortality rates of women relative to those of men have been largely eliminated in both South Korea and China). And yet women's agency alone has not been able to stem the tide of sex-specific abortions which specially target female foetuses (this can be called 'natality discrimination'). As the scientific techniques of determination of the sex of the foetus advanced in the 1980s, natality discrimination through sex-selective abortion became surprisingly common in Korea and China. This has led to initiatives in these countries consciously to cultivate the value of having daughters and not just sons. There is a complex issue of enlightened agency involved here, which takes the discussion beyond only seeking more power for women to exercise their agency.

In India too, the tendency to use new technology to abort female foetuses has grown in many parts of the country (particularly in the northern and western states), and women's education alone has not been able to serve as a strong barrier to this regressive movement.[34] Indeed, there is some evidence that decisions of sex-selective abortions are often taken by the mothers themselves. What is crucially important in this context is to overcome what Justice Leila Seth has aptly called the 'patriarchical mindset'.[35]

This raises questions as to how to interpret the agency of women and its social influence. It is important to see the concept of agency as stretching beyond immediate 'control' over decisions. The fuller sense of the crucial idea of 'agency' must, among other things, involve the freedom to question established values and traditional priorities.[36] Agency freedom must, in fact, include the freedom to think freely, without being severely restrained by pressured conformism, or by the ignorance of how the prevailing practices in the rest of the world differ from what can be observed locally. What is particularly critical in remedying the terrible biases involved in natality discrimination and sex-specific abortions is the role of women's informed and enlightened agency, including the power of women to overcome unquestioningly inherited values and attitudes. What may make a real difference in dealing with this new – and 'high tech' – face of gender disparity is the willingness, ability and courage to challenge the dominance of received and entrenched norms. When anti-female bias in action reflects the hold of traditional patriarchal values from which mothers themselves may not be immune, what is crucial is not just freedom of *action* but also freedom of *thought and its practice.* Informed critical agency is important in combating inequality of every kind, and gender inequality is no exception.

Regional patterns of sex-selective abortion in India are consistent with this understanding of the influence of patriarchal values (and of women's freedom – or the lack of it – to resist them). Looking first at the all-India picture, the situation looks most alarming. As is well known, the female-male ratio in the age group of 0–6 years (hereafter the 'child sex ratio') has been going down over time, and in the last decade it has fallen further, from 927 girls per 1,000 boys in 2001 to 914 girls per 1,000 boys in 2011. Further, there is evidence that this decline is largely driven by the spread of sex-selective abortion. The latest demographic analysis of census as well as National Family Health Survey data from 1990 onwards suggests that the number of selective abortions of girls between 1980 and 2010 was somewhere between 4 and 12 million, and that the *annual* number of sex-selective abortions is now around 0.3 to 0.6 million (or roughly 2 to 4 per cent of all pregnancies).[37] In the worst-affected districts (e.g. Jhajjar, Mahendragarh and Rewari in Haryana), the child sex ratio is now below 800 girls per 1,000 boys.[38]

There are no reliable birth statistics in India from which the female-male ratios at birth can be directly established. However, we can look instead at the female-male ratios in the age group of 0–6 years for which more reliable data exist, and which tend to be quite close to female-male ratios at birth, though they would of course be somewhat distorted by child mortality differentials.[39] Female-male ratios in the age group of 0–6 years are available from the Indian censuses, and estimates of female-male ratios at birth obtained by 'correcting' the census-based child sex ratios using sex-specific child mortality rates are also available from a recent demographic study (Kumar and Sathyanarayana, 2012).We shall use both sets of estimates – the female-male ratios of the 0–6 year age-group, and the estimated birth ratios after mortality rate corrections.

But how should an appropriate cut-off ratio of female to male children be identified? To make a reasoned identification, we can use the European demographic statistics. However, there are variations between different European countries as well. It is necessary to understand the demographic variations across the world of the number of girls born per 1,000 boys in order to be able to fix an appropriate cut-off point for diagnosing the likely presence of sex-selective abortion of female foetuses in an Indian state.

Everywhere in the world more boys are born than girls, and the female-male ratio at conception is even more sharply biased in the direction of males (the standard ratio is often taken to be 910 female foetuses to 1,000 male conceptions). But females do better than males in survival given symmetric care (which they tend to get in the uterus), and by the time births take place, the female-male ratio is around 940 to 950 females per 1,000 males in the European countries. During 2005–10, the average ratio of females to males at birth for Europe as a whole was 943 females per 1,000 males. There are, as noted, variations within the European countries, but these cannot be attributed to the effects of a presumed practice of sex-selective abortion. To be reasonably confident that the figure for a particular state in India indicates a significant prevalence of sex-selective abortion, we have to identify a cut-off ratio that would be consistent with the lower ranges *within* the European spectrum.

Among the larger European countries towards the lower end, the female-male ratio at birth is 941 in Italy, 940 in Spain, 939 in Greece and 935 in Ireland. There are some countries with even lower ratios than these figures, including Macedonia (926), Montenegro (926), and others, but in some of these cases the data and the causal influences behind them can perhaps be questioned. There is, however, a strong case for choosing the average of Italy, Spain and Greece, and taking the cut-off line to be 940.

Using this cut-off ratio and applying it to the 2011 census figures for female-male ratios among children of 0–6 years in age, it appears that all the states in the north and west of India show clear evidence of a strong hold of sex-selective abortion in a way that the states in the east and south do not, in general, show (see Table 8.3). The first thing to note is that we can draw a dividing line to cut India into two halves, with the states in the west and north of India (with clear

Table 8.3
Child Sex Ratios and Sex Ratio at Birth

State	Female-male ratio, age 0–6 years, 2001	Female-male ratio, age 0–6 years, 2011	Indirect estimates of female-male ratio at birth, 2011[a]
Haryana	819	830	842
Punjab	798	846	854
Jammu & Kashmir	941	859	870
Rajasthan	909	883	889
Maharashtra	913	883	902
Gujarat	883	886	891
Uttarakhand	908	886	890
Uttar Pradesh	916	899	911
Himachal Pradesh	896	906	916
Madhya Pradesh	932	912	917
Bihar	942	933	941
Odisha	953	934	936
Andhra Pradesh	961	943	942
Jharkhand	965	943	953
Karnataka	946	943	944
Tamil Nadu	942	946	946
West Bengal	960	950	947
Assam	965	957	952
Kerala	960	959	959
Chhattisgarh	975	964	963
India	927	914	919

[a] Estimated by combining Census data on female-male ratio data with Sample Registration System (SRS) estimates of age- and sex-specific mortality rates.

Sources: Government of India (2011b), Statement 13. The indirect estimates of sex ratio at birth are due to Kumar and Sathyanarayana (2012). States are ranked in increasing order of female-male ratio in the age group of 0–6 years in 2011 (second column).

evidence of sex-selective abortion) being separated from states in the east and south (without such evidence, except for Odisha).[40] The former group – with female-male ratios below 940 per 1,000 in 2011 – include Punjab, Haryana, Gujarat, Himachal Pradesh, Uttarkhand, Rajasthan, Uttar Pradesh, Maharashtra, Madhya Pradesh, Jammu & Kashmir and Bihar, whereas the ones with ratios above 940 per 1,000 are Assam, West Bengal, Kerala, Jharkhand, Chhattisgarh, Andhra Pradesh, Tamil Nadu and Karnataka. The state of Odisha fails to qualify in the latter list marginally, with a female-male ratio of 934 per 1,000, even though – like the other states in the east and the south – Odisha has a higher female-male ratio than every major state in the north and the west.

If we use instead the indirect estimates of birth ratios, we get a very similar picture (see Table 8.3, last column, and also the map opposite). A small exception, however, can be seen in Bihar, which was at the top of the list for the low female-male ratios in terms of statistics for children aged 0–6 years, and now, with a ratio of 941, crosses the cut-off line of 940 (and so places itself in the 'eastern and southern' league), whereas Odisha remains below the cut-off line with a ratio of 936. These minor exceptions to the overall picture do not significantly alter the basic contrast between the south and east on the one hand, and the north and west on the other, particularly since every major state in the east and south has a higher female-male ratio than each major state in the north and the west in terms of the solid count of children between the ages of 0 and 6.

This contrast was already apparent in 2001 census data as well.[41] Indeed, as Table 8.3 shows, it was already the case at that time that every major state in the north and west had a lower child sex ratio than every state in the south and east. Having said this, there have also been some important changes between the two census years as far as the absolute values of child sex ratios are concerned. Among other changes is a significant decline in the child sex ratio between 2001 and 2011 in many states, including some in the south and east. For instance, Odisha's child sex ratio fell from 953 in 2001 to 934 in 2011, with a particularly large fall (from 933 to 909) in urban areas, where sex-selective abortion is likely to be concentrated. In urban Jharkhand, too, the child sex ratio fell from 930 in 2001 to 904 in

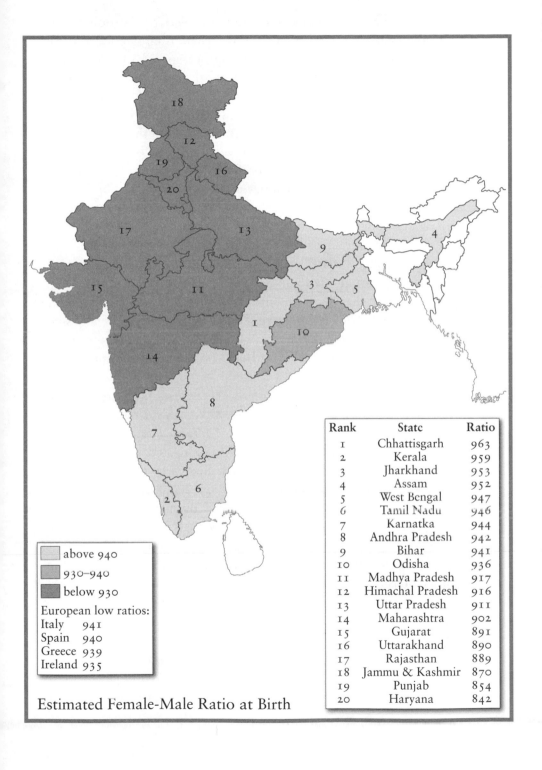

Rank	State	Ratio
1	Chhattisgarh	963
2	Kerala	959
3	Jharkhand	953
4	Assam	952
5	West Bengal	947
6	Tamil Nadu	946
7	Karnataka	944
8	Andhra Pradesh	942
9	Bihar	941
10	Odisha	936
11	Madhya Pradesh	917
12	Himachal Pradesh	916
13	Uttar Pradesh	911
14	Maharashtra	902
15	Gujarat	891
16	Uttarakhand	890
17	Rajasthan	889
18	Jammu & Kashmir	870
19	Punjab	854
20	Haryana	842

above 940

930–940

below 930

European low ratios:
Italy   941
Spain   940
Greece   939
Ireland 935

Estimated Female-Male Ratio at Birth

2011. These are some indications that sex-selective abortion may be spreading beyond the north and west.[42] There is an important warning here of the possible danger of further spread of sex-selective abortion in India. That warning must be taken seriously, even though the picture is far from uniform (for example, the child sex ratio went up, rather than down, in the southern state of Tamil Nadu).

It seems quite likely that in every state – even in the south and the east – there will be some takers of the opportunity of selective abortion in line with whatever 'boy preference' particular families have, using new and expanding facilities of sex determination of foetuses. While this may explain small changes of the child sex ratio in the unfavourable direction, the real question is whether this would remain mainly an aberration in the south and east, or whether the small beginning will translate itself into much more widespread use of selective abortion in the south and in the east (as seems to have happened in urban Jharkhand and urban Odisha). The explanation of the sharp regional divide is itself a very challenging issue, especially since even in the census of 2011, it remains true that every state in the south and east has a higher ratio of girls to boys than every state in the north and west.

Why is there such a regional difference – indeed such a striking contrast? This is only one of many such questions to which we do not have a ready-made answer, but the issue of cultural contrast is certainly worth investigating. There has been work on related aspects of gender relations in which similar contrasts, including variants of a broad contrast between the north and west on the one hand, and the south and east on the other, have received attention.[43] But what is emerging here is a particularly sharp contrast between two halves of the country, with no obvious explanation. Incidentally, the data from Bangladesh (the corresponding ratio there is 972, for the age group of 0–4 years) conforms robustly to the 'eastern' regional pattern within India – and more.

No matter how we slice the story, there is a general problem of the valuation of female children in India as a whole, and strong evidence of it in the north and west of India.* It is particularly discouraging

---

* A bit of a silver lining, if rather thin, is that the female-male ratio among children aged 0–6 years has improved in four of the most female-short states between 2001 and

that the traditional ally of gender justice – the education of girls – does not seem to do much to reduce the natality discrimination from which female foetuses suffer. This draws particular attention to the importance of enlightened public reasoning – free from prejudices of all kinds. And that, of course, is a central part of the general thesis of this book.

POWER IMBALANCES, OLD AND NEW

So far in this chapter, we have focused mainly on inequalities of the traditional kind, such as those of class, caste and gender. These old and deep-rooted inequalities continue to have a paramount influence on Indian society and politics. Some of them, as we saw, are subsiding in significant respects. However, new or rising inequalities are also reinforcing the vicious circle of disempowerment and deprivation. For instance, the last twenty years have seen a massive growth of corporate power in India, a force that is largely driven – with some honourable exceptions – by the unrestrained search for profits. The growing influence of corporate interests on public policy and democratic institutions does not particularly facilitate the reorientation of policy priorities towards the needs of the underprivileged.*

It is important to recognize the influence of elements of the corporate sector on the balance of public policies, but it would be wrong to take that to be something like an irresistible natural force. India's democratic system offers ways of resisting the new biases that may emanate from the pressure of business firms. One instructive example

---

2011 (Punjab, Haryana, Gujarat, and Jammu & Kashmir), even though the ratios for each of these states still show massive evidence of a continuing hold of selective abortion of female foetuses.

* As early as 1776, long before corporate power acquired anything like the influence it has today, Adam Smith had warned against the interference of commercial interests in public policy: 'The interest of the dealers, however, in any particular branch of trade or manufactures, is always in some respects different from, and even opposite to, that of the public . . . The proposal of any new law or regulation of commerce which comes from this order, ought always to be listened to with great precaution, and ought never to be adopted till after having been long and carefully examined, not only with the most scrupulous, but with the most suspicious attention.' (Adam Smith, 1776, p. 292).

both of a blatant attempt to denude an established public service and of the possibility of defeating such an attempt is the long saga of an attempted takeover of India's school meal programme by some biscuit-making firms.[44] India's midday meal programme, which provides hot cooked meals prepared by local women to some 120 million children with a substantial impact on both nutrition and school attendance, had been eyed for many years by packaged-food manufacturers, especially the biscuits industry. A few years ago, a 'Biscuit Manufacturers' Association' (BMA) launched a massive campaign for the replacement of cooked school meals with branded biscuit packets. The BMA wrote to all Members of Parliament, asking them to plead the case for biscuits with the concerned minister and assisting them in this task with a neat pseudo-scientific précis of the wonders of manufactured biscuits. Dozens of Members of Parliament, across most of the political spectrum (with the notable exception of Communist parties), promptly obliged and wrote to the minister, often just rehashing the BMA's bogus claims. According to one senior official, the Ministry was 'flooded' with such letters, 29 of which were obtained later under the Right to Information Act. Fortunately, the proposal was firmly shot down by the Ministry after being referred to state governments and nutrition experts, and public vigilance exposed what was going on. The minister, in fact, wrote to a state chief minister who sympathized with the biscuit lobby: 'We are, indeed, dismayed at the growing requests for introduction of pre-cooked foods, emanating largely from suppliers/marketers of packaged foods, and aimed essentially at penetrating and deepening the market for such foods.'

The bigger battle is still on. The BMA itself did not give up after being rebuked by the Minister for Human Resource Development, but proceeded to write to the Minister for Women and Child Development, with a similar proposal for supplying biscuits to children below the age of six years under the Integrated Child Development Services (ICDS). Other food manufacturers are also on the job, and despite much vigilance and resistance from activist quarters (and the Supreme Court), they have made significant inroads into child feeding programmes in several states.

Similar concerns apply in other fields of social policy. For instance, the prospects of building an effective public health care system in

India are unlikely to be helped by the growing influence of commercial insurance companies, very active in the field of health. As discussed in Chapter 6, India's health system is already one of the most privatized in the world, with predictable consequences – high expenditure, low achievements and massive inequalities. Yet there is much pressure to embrace the American model of health care provision, based on commercial insurance, despite the international recognition in the health community of its comparatively low achievement and significantly high cost.

However, recent events have also shown the possibility not just of winning isolated battles against inappropriate corporate influence, as happened with the biscuits lobby, but also of building institutional safeguards against abuses of corporate power. The Right to Information Act, for instance, though not directly applicable to information held by private corporations, is a powerful means of watching and containing the state-corporate nexus, as the biscuits story illustrates. Regulations and legislations pertaining to corporate funding of political parties, corporate lobbying, financial transparency, environmental standards and workers' rights also have an important role to play in bringing the Indian corporate sector into the discipline of the elementary norms of social justice.

THE PRIVILEGED AND THE REST

As we have discussed and extensively illustrated, India is full of inequalities of various kinds. Some Indians are comparatively rich; most are not. Some are fairly well educated; others are illiterate. Some lead easy lives; others toil hard for little reward. Some are politically powerful; others cannot influence anything outside their immediate sphere. Some have substantial opportunities for advancement in life; others lack them altogether. Some are treated with respect by the police no matter what they have done; others are treated like dirt at the slightest suspicion of transgression. These diverse contrasts reflect different kinds of inequality, and each of them individually requires serious attention.

But going beyond that – and this is a central issue in understanding the nature of inequality in India – it can be seen that the same people, often enough, are poor in income and wealth, suffer from illiteracy and bad schooling, work hard for little remuneration, have little influence on the administration of the country, lack social and economic opportunities that would allow them to move forward, and are treated with brutal callousness by the class-conscious police. The dividing line of 'haves' and 'have-nots' in India is not just a rhetorical cliché, but also an important part of diagnostic analysis, pointing us towards a pre-eminent division that is extremely important for an understanding of Indian society. The congruence of deprivations only increases the disparity between the privileged and the rest in distinct spheres, and places different people in altogether distinct compartments. There is a real challenge here for the pursuit of equity in India.

9

Democracy, Inequality and Public Reasoning

Democracy, as we know it today, has developed over a long period of time, drawing on different kinds of experiences and experiments. There were significant forms of democratic political practice in ancient Greece, from around the sixth century BC, even though they involved only a minority of adult male citizens (women and slaves, among others, were excluded). There were piecemeal attempts elsewhere as well at democratic local governance in a number of countries, including India, Persia and Bactria, more than two thousand years ago. The 'constitution of seventeen articles' promulgated in Japan in AD 604 by the Buddhist Prince Shotoku insisted on the need for wide consultation for decisions taken by the state. Various democratic methods, such as decision by consensus, have also been used in limited settings around the globe over the centuries.

However, democracy in its present form took a long time after that to emerge, bolstered by many developments – from the English Magna Carta in 1215, to the French and the American Revolutions in the eighteenth century, to the spread of adult franchise, initially male and eventually female as well, in Europe and North America in the nineteenth and early twentieth centuries. But it was in the latter half of the twentieth century that the idea of democracy was established as a form of government to which any nation is entitled – whether in Europe, America, Asia or Africa.[1] The flowering of democratic practice and its reach are, however, a continuing process.

The colonial masters from Europe were very sceptical of the possibility that India could flourish as a democracy were it to become independent. But independent India went straight for a firmly democratic system at a breathless speed as the British left in 1947. It is natural to ask: how well has democracy worked in India? Clearly, the basic norms of democracy have in general been followed with much success, and attempts at suspending democratic rights – as happened during the declared Emergency in the 1970s – have met with immediate rejection in electoral voting, with the rehabilitation of all the democratic rights that had been suspended. At an immediate level, it is difficult not to see a major achievement in this political history, given the fact that India was the first non-Western country – and also the first poor country in the world – to commit itself to a resolutely democratic way of governance, with systematic multi-party elections, subordination of the military to the civilian government, independence of the judiciary, protection of minority rights and freedom of speech. There is surely some accomplishment there.

To the extent that having a democratic system of governance is an end in itself, there is, then, much to celebrate. But it is as a social instrument for bettering the society, and in particular for removing injustices and social inequities, that the achievements of Indian democracy can be seriously disputed. The massive continuation – and sometimes even accentuation – of different kinds of inequalities in India, which were discussed in earlier chapters, provides strongly incriminating evidence against taking Indian democracy to be adequately successful in consequential terms.

That big failure is a major part of the focus of this book, and a central exercise in this work is to address the question: how can we get more out of democracy, particularly in reducing injustice and the huge disparities in the lives of citizens – more than Indian democracy has been able to achieve so far? But before we address that question, we should comment briefly on the flaws of Indian democracy even when it is judged only in terms of meeting the institutional rules of democratic practice.

BREACHES OF DEMOCRATIC PRACTICE

In his engaging book *India After Gandhi: The History of the World's Largest Democracy*, Ramachandra Guha divides that history into several distinct periods. He sees the first two decades after Indian independence as a period of constitutional democracy. This is followed by two decades of variations and a transition from constitutional democracy to the present period of 'populist' democracy – with political pressure impacting constantly on governance.[2]

There have certainly been varying strains on Indian democracy over time. The imperatives of the democratic constitution were followed rather more closely in the days of Nehru (and just after), but the violations – and the temptations to take short-cuts – became quite strong in the 1970s, particularly with the declaration of Emergency by the government led by Indira Gandhi. And it is also true that in the last two decades the government as well as the elected representatives in the Indian Parliament have been under pressure from strongly articulated demands of organized politics. An accentuation of the influence of political pressure is an important feature of contemporary India, though we can question whether yielding to such pressure can really be seen as 'populism', since the powerfully orchestrated demands are often fairly far removed from the interests and concerns of people at large, particularly of those at the bottom (we shall have more to say on this presently).

What may also need emphasis – going beyond Guha's basic periodization – is that the flaws in India's practice of constitutional democracy have, in fact, been present throughout the post-independence period, not excluding the time of Nehru. Even in those more 'regular' days of Nehru's prime ministership, Sheikh Abdullah, the principal leader of the Kashmiri people (and a staunch believer in a secular Kashmir), was incarcerated in 1953 for a decade or more. There was also a brutal suppression of the independence movement in Nagaland, based on a counter-insurgency strategy (called 'groupings', whereby people were herded into camps and those who did not join were hounded), apparently inspired by similar operations in Vietnam.[3] No less importantly, a popularly elected government of a state, Kerala, led by the Communist Party, which was bringing about many overdue social reforms without violating democratic norms, was suddenly removed from office, in the name of law and order, even though there is considerable evidence that in the creation of the tense law-and-order situation, the ruling party at the centre, in other words Congress, had an active – and arguably even an instigating – role.

Investigation of the practice – and violations – of democratic norms in India deserves a much fuller treatment than we can provide in this book. Nevertheless, we must briefly discuss some cases of lapses from democratic practice, if only to note that India's democratic achievements, significant as they are (especially in contrast with the prevalence of authoritarianism in many parts of the world, including in Asia, Africa and Latin America), are not unalloyed. One of the persistent problems has been a serious inadequacy in the acknowledgement and questioning of infringements of civil and political rights in Kashmir and in other areas where there are concerns – or alleged concerns – over national security, such as parts of the North-East.

There is a real problem here. The media may see it as 'self-discipline' not to interfere with national security, but its resulting silence on matters of civil rights and democracy in some critical areas is a huge departure from the general vigour of the democratic process in India. The subdued nature of media coverage arises from a variety of causes. In the specific case of Kashmir, the political situation there can be seen as a genuinely complex subject, especially since it is also connected with larger tensions between India and Pakistan. And yet the underlying issues call for open discussion and democratic engagement rather than silence.

The complexity of the issues does not detract from the critical importance of frankly reporting and firmly denouncing violations of personal and civil rights in Kashmir or anywhere else. Demanding more respect for human rights need not stand in the way of a peaceful political settlement in Kashmir, and may well facilitate it, since rough treatment generates further alienation of the population. The media's duties include subjecting these immensely important issues of democratic practice to a more critical examination, including reporting on the horrors that are committed not only by some extremist groups but also by the police and the Indian military. Even though New Delhi has made some efforts in recent years to reduce these violations and has given more autonomy to the elected government of the state, much bolder steps are required, and the Indian media can help greatly in this by bringing the issues of governance and human rights in Kashmir more into the public arena.

Even though Kashmir is the most prominent case of infringement of democratic norms in India, it is not unique. Other insurgencies and separatist movements (especially in the North-East of the country) have often been met also by the use of strong military force. The impediments to peace include not merely the political nature of these insurgencies, which deserves more serious investigation and causal scrutiny than it tends to get, but also the crude and often counterproductive nature of state-organized violence included in what are seen as preventive measures. The strategy of brutal suppression not only results in the violation of many basic human rights, but also it often ends up aggravating the situation.

A prime example is the widespread use, in Kashmir and in the troubled regions of the North-East, of draconian powers given to the armed forces under the Armed Forces (Special Powers) Act of 1958, known as AFSPA, which is something like a re-creation of the old British 'Armed Forces (Special Powers) Ordinance' of 1942 from the authoritarian days of colonial rule. These powers include wide discretion to shoot at sight and arrest without warrant as well as a virtual guarantee of immunity from prosecution for human rights abuses. These powers have frequently been used in a remarkably violent way, and have tended to aggravate rather than remove conflicts. As R. N. Ravi, former special director of the Intelligence Bureau, put it: 'With an intimate ringside view of the theatre for over two decades, one is increasingly convinced that among several reasons sustaining militancy in the North-East, the most crucial one is the unwarranted application of the Armed Forces (Special Powers) Act, 1958.'[4] Despite these and other criticisms (including calls for the repeal of AFSPA coming from the United Nations as well as from a government-appointed commission), the government's response has not gone beyond occasional promises of amendments in the Act. Similar comments apply to other undemocratic laws such as the sedition law, another relic of the colonial era described as 'highly objectionable and obnoxious' by Jawaharlal Nehru as early as 1951, but still in force and regularly utilized by the authorities.[5]

The problem is no less extensive in the centre of the country where there is a powerful Maoist movement, which builds on the seething discontent of the rural poor and sometimes uses very violent means, not sparing civilians when they are suspected to be on 'the wrong side'. The government, in turn, often retaliates with violence that is completely out of tune with the norms of democratic India, in these regions now officially called 'left-wing extremism affected districts'.

Maoist rebellion is the violent extreme of social discontent – a discontent with the social order but also with the ruling political classes, which is more extensive than the widespread civil disaffection with both the national and state governments. The concerns that all this raises about the future of Indian democracy have been well captured by Pankaj Mishra:

> China is shakily authoritarian while India is a stable democracy – indeed the world's largest. So goes the cliché, and it is true, up to a point . . . [But] public anger against India's political class appears more intense, and disaffection there assumes more militant forms, as in the civil war at the centre of the county, where indigenous, Maoist militants in commodities-rich forests are battling security forces. India, where political dynasties have been the rule for decades, also has many more 'princelings' than China – nearly 30 percent of the members of parliament come from political families. As the country intensifies its crackdown on intellectual dissent and falls behind on global health goals, it is mimicking China's authoritarian tendencies and corruption without making comparable strides in relieving the hardships faced by its citizens. The 'New India' risks becoming an ersatz China.[6]

These comments raise much broader issues than we are able to address in the book, and yet the questions that we do investigate cannot be adequately understood without taking note of reasoned anxiety about the future of Indian democracy which Mishra – among others – articulates.

India is, in general, a democratic success by contemporary standards, and Indians can justifiably relish the fact that their country is often described as 'the world's largest democracy', but the violations of democratic practice in specific contexts, on alleged grounds of national security and other concerns, are also a part of the picture. It is, ultimately, a particularly important subject for democratic engagement and scrutiny. Indeed, the future of Indian democracy depends a great deal on the spirited public defence of democratic rights whenever and wherever they are threatened.

DEMOCRATIC INSTITUTIONS
AND THEIR WORKING

Turning to another aspect of democratic norms, we should briefly discuss the working of institutions that make up Indian democracy. Dividing the institutional structure into the three components of legislature, executive and judiciary, we can begin with the legislatures at the centre (the Indian Parliament) and in the states (the state assemblies). Unlike in America where the chief executives – the President of the United States and the governors of the states – are elected, and so are many layers of judges, in India the elections involving the citizens (the electorate) relate mainly to the choice of the members of the parliament and the state legislatures.

Democracy is not just about elections, but the electoral process, obviously, is an important part of it. This could, in principle, be a powerful force for change, but the outcomes are far from automatic. As far as electoral institutions are concerned, India is doing reasonably well by historical and international comparisons. To illustrate, compared with the United States (an aspiring torch-bearer of democracy in the contemporary world), India fares better in many respects. For instance, India has much higher voter turnout rates (the United States is near the bottom of the international scale in that respect); it has more extensive provisions for the political representation of socially disadvantaged groups; and it is less vulnerable to the influence of 'big money' in electoral politics. There are fewer disputes on the outcome of elections in India than in the United States (the drama of 'hanging chads', as in the disputed US election of 2000, and other counting battles seem to separate the American elections from their Indian counterparts). There is also far greater pluralism in Indian than in US politics. Dozens of political parties, from extreme left to extreme right, are represented in the Indian Parliament, in contrast with just two parties (with very similar positions on many issues) in the United States Congress.* The comparison is not entirely to India's

---

* Between 1989 and 2009 the average number of political parties contesting Lok Sabha elections was as high as 199 (Kaushik and Pal 2012, p. 78).

advantage (for instance, there is more inner party democracy in US politics), but nevertheless India's electoral institutions appear in a reasonably good light by contemporary world standards.

There is, of course, plenty of scope for improvement. For instance, the work culture among elected representatives in India leaves something to be desired. To start with, they spend very little time 'in the house': in 2000–10 the average number of days of Legislative Assembly sittings per year ranged between 14 days (in Haryana) and 48 days (in West Bengal) among nine states for which relevant data are available from Parliamentary Research Services.[7] And of course, not everyone was present when the Assembly was in session. Even in the house, the behaviour of elected representatives is not always exemplary: 'Assembly adjourned amid pandemonium' is a common newspaper headline (in 2011 alone it was used in Andhra Pradesh, Jammu and Kashmir, Odisha, Rajasthan, Uttar Pradesh and Tripura), usually referring to such stunts as flinging or smashing chairs, fans, microphones and other items. The laxity was taken to new heights in the recent 'porngate' scandal, when some members of the Legislative Assembly in Karnataka were caught watching porn on their mobile phones in the front row of the Assembly while it was in session. It would, of course, be unfair to tar all elected representatives with this unflattering brush. Many of them are also public spirited, hard working and highly competent. But there is certainly some scope for improvement in general parliamentary norms.

More importantly, there are frequent expressions of frustration and cynicism about who the 'elected representatives' are and whose interests they represent – from entertaining cartoons to the odd shoe being hurled at them. The basic idea of electoral representation is that it gives people a chance to elect those who will do something for them and represent their interests. But in the competition for votes, what the candidates have done (or will do) for the public is just one consideration, and does not always count for much. The first step is to get a 'ticket', which means ingratiating oneself to the party leadership (not the party members, since inner party democracy is typically very limited in India). Accountability, therefore, is to the top rather than to the bottom. Another important step is to earn money. For an incumbent candidate, the easiest way to do this is to patronize local contractors and others in exchange for financial support. The contractors quietly do the dirty job of siphoning off public resources, and their political protectors take a share. From there, it can be argued, it is only a short step to criminal activity. In 2009, 30 per cent of all Lok Sabha members had criminal cases pending against them, rising to 45 per cent in Bihar and 57 per cent in Jharkhand, according to the Association for Democratic Reforms. Interestingly, the share of suspected criminals was much *higher* (30 per cent) among Members of Parliament than among all candidates in the 2009 Lok Sabha elections (15 per cent), indicating – rather oddly – that candidates who had been accused of criminality actually did better than others in winning elections, for whatever reason.[8]

None of this constitutes an indictment of democracy itself. Even among those who are otherwise cynical of elected representatives, respect for democratic principles is fairly high in India. For instance, in the recent National Election Study 2009 conducted by the Centre for the Study of Developing Societies, 70 per cent of the respondents felt that 'democracy is better than other forms of government', rising to 88 per cent if those without any opinion on this are ignored. Also interesting is that a large majority (about 60 per cent, rising to 78 per cent among those with a view) felt that their own vote had '[an] effect on how things are run in this country'. This view may or may not be objectively plausible, but it is certainly an interesting indication of the respondents' positive sense of participation in the electoral system.

It is also worth noting that the resonance of democratic principles, in some ways at least, seems to be particularly high among the underprivileged. For instance, voter turnout rates in Lok Sabha elections have been consistently higher among Dalits than among the upper castes.[9] As one Dalit intellectual put it (Chandra Bhan Prasad, 2011): 'Despite the political system being corrupt and inefficient, Dalits go with it – they generally make it a point to vote. Dalit youths know well that institutions outside the state are nothing but a collection of khap panchayats.' This statement is, strictly speaking, a little exaggerated (the voter turnout rates of Dalits are only a little higher than in the population as a whole, and the last sentence overlooks the diversity of 'institutions outside the state'), but similar sentiments have been expressed by many Dalit thinkers from Dr Ambedkar onwards.

The main lesson, perhaps, to draw from the limitations of electoral politics in India is that building democratic institutions – and a democratic culture – is a continuing process. Fortunately, electoral and democratic reforms are increasingly vibrant fields of public debate and action in India. There have already been major advances, such as the Right to Information Act (2005), which has opened vast possibilities for imparting transparency in public life and fostering informed participation in democratic processes. Many other momentous aspects of democratic reform have also become subjects of lively debate: women's political representation, the funding of elections, inner party democracy, judicial accountability, the right to recall, the need for 'pre-legislative consultation processes', to cite just a few examples. These initiatives are yet to translate into concrete change in many cases, but over time they could significantly extend the reach and effectiveness of democratic institutions in India.

Turning now to the executive arm of the government, the Indian ministries, whether at the centre or in the states, do not have the kind of independent status that the US presidents or governors or mayors have. The choice of executives comes through the legislatures, for example the Prime Minister (as the head of the Indian government) and the Cabinet get chosen and can survive only through the support that they have in the Indian Parliament. Any irregularities in the Parliament (for example electoral lapses) would also impact on the executive, which can get thrown out as and when it loses its hold over the Parliament. If a government loses its majority, another majority can be built up through new alliances (which may or may not involve shady deals), and shifting alliances have become particularly important in India's coalition politics. One result of this change is that vested interests can exercise greater influence on what may be called the 'politics of the executive'.

To achieve the kind of policy reorientation for which we have been arguing in this book would, thus, require going well beyond convincing the executive. The legislature would have to be persuaded of the need for a change not just because it may require new legislation, but also because the executive holds its office only through the support it has in the legislature. Convincing only the leadership of the executive – such as the Prime Minister – will not be adequate to put through and sustain a change in substantial policies. This point is important to grasp because the policy failures that are attributed to the government in office may or may not reflect its intent, since an executive in office may be willing but powerless to put through a policy change. For example, when agitations by powerful jewellers and others in early 2012 forced the government in office to give up a brief attempt to introduce a small import duty on gold and diamonds, which would have raised a good deal of useful public revenue (a case we will presently discuss), the main problem was not the lack of willingness of the executive to tax gold imports, but its inability to carry through and sustain the intended change. Thus, the policy changes we are arguing for need the support of more than just the ruling government. This makes public discussion even more important, going well beyond giving technical advice to the executive, even the Cabinet or the Prime Minister. This is one reason, among others, why this book is aimed much more as an attempted contribution to public reasoning, including discussion in the media, than at giving professional advice to the government in office.

The Indian judiciary is, unlike the executive, relatively independent. There is no contradiction here between this independence of the judiciary and the practice of democracy. Indeed, the direct election of judges in parts of the American system have tended to politicize judicial functions in a way that might be in some tension with the need for objectivity and impartial justice, which are also part of the goals of democracy. And the independence of the judiciary has also allowed the courts, particularly the Supreme Court of India, to take independent – and powerful – positions on many of the central issues of equity and justice in their judgement, including the protection of fundamental rights as well as of various economic and social rights defined in the Directive Principles of the constitution, such as the right to education and right to food.

We have had the occasion, earlier in the book, to comment on the interventions of the court in pursuit of the far-reaching objectives of the Constitution (including the Directive Principles), especially its general interest in economic justice as well as in political and social equity. Sometimes the initiatives of the courts have had to be followed up by fresh legislation in the Indian Parliament, but it would be a mistake not to give appropriate credit to the leadership role that the courts have been able to play. This is so even when the initiatives of the courts became more fully effective only through the support from Parliament following the lead of the courts, particularly the Supreme Court.* While many of these interventions have been justice-enhancing, the Indian courts have often played a regressive role through delays and inflexibility. We discussed in the last chapter how the difficulty in getting convictions in cases of rape within reasonable time, and without hassle or degrading obstacles, deters many victims of rape from taking their cases to the court, which adds to the administrative failure of which the limitations of policing is another part. In general, the slow working of the courts and their overcrowded agenda make the process of seeking legal redress rather difficult, and this is surely a huge limitation of democratic legality in India.

INEQUALITY AND DEMOCRATIC ENGAGEMENT

In the earlier parts of the book we have identified a number of significant failures in the reach and impact of India's economic and social development, and the persistence of inequality of various kinds is certainly a major contributor to them. The failure to remove the sharp division between the privileged and the rest is one large part of that story. In examining the practice of democracy, we have to ask: to what extent has Indian democracy been able to rise to the challenges these failures pose? India's democratic system has certainly given it huge opportunities to confront failures on the development front, but its

---

* It should be noted here that this role of the Indian Supreme Court is in very different spirit from the condemnation in the United States of what is called 'judicial activism.' The Indian approach involves quite a different reading by the Indian Supreme Court of the discipline of the constitution from the way the discipline of the US constitution has often – though not always – been read in the United States, particularly under the so-called 'originalist' interpretation. Some internal tensions of the US 'originalist' approach (advocated by Justice Scalia and several other US Supreme Court judges) are discussed in the Herbert Hart Lecture of one of us, published in the *Oxford Journal of Legal Studies* (Sen, 2011).

achievement in removing inequality and injustice has nevertheless been quite limited. While in some cases the opportunities have been well utilized to adapt the policies and practices in India in the appropriate direction (for example, in giving justiciable legal rights to people from disadvantaged castes, and setting up an extensive system of affirmative actions), many of the gaps (for example, the continuation of unequal opportunities for education and health care and of unequal treatment by the police and public servants) have not been adequately addressed through the means for rectification that democracy can provide.

The Constitution of the Republic of India, adopted more than six decades ago, provided firm legal guarantees for a series of 'fundamental rights' to every Indian citizen, including freedom of expression, the right of association, equality before the law and freedom from discrimination. These rights are enforceable in court, and indeed, the last fundamental right (under Article 32) is the right to seek redress from the Supreme Court in the event of any violation of fundamental rights: 'The right to move the Supreme Court by appropriate proceedings for the enforcement of the rights conferred by this Part is guaranteed.'

However, even though the makers of India's democratic constitution placed their hopes for the removal of unacceptable inequalities partly on the Indian legal system (including the operation of the courts), they did not end there. They also invoked the role of democratic means, including the electoral process, in pursuit of these objectives. Aside from fundamental rights, a series of economic and social rights were listed in the 'Directive Principles' of the constitution. These include, for instance, under Article 41, the 'right to work, to education and to public assistance'. These rights are not enforceable in court, and were not meant to be justiciable in the usual legal sense. Indeed, Article 37, which immediately precedes the Directive Principles, explicitly states that 'the provisions contained in this Part shall not be enforceable by any court'.

Immediately after that, however, the constitution proceeds to state (in Article 37 itself) that the Directive Principles 'are nevertheless fundamental in the governance of the country and it shall be the duty of the State to apply these principles in making laws'. But what if the government fails to do this? The principal architect of the constitution, B. R. Ambedkar, clarified during a debate on this in the Constituent Assembly that the hope was that the voting system of democratic India would provide the necessary remedy. He argued that even though the government 'may not have to answer for their breach in a Court of Law', nevertheless it 'will certainly have to answer for them before the electorate at election time'.[10]

The question that we have to examine is whether India's democratic system has actually provided the needed remedy to the continuation of glaring economic and social inequalities and inequities, in line with the trust that was placed in it by the constitution – and by those who fought for independence and for a democratic India. The answer seems to be partly yes, but – alas – mostly no. India has certainly avoided, as was discussed in the first chapter, sudden failures of governmental practice of the kind that generated the big Chinese famines at the time of the collapse of the Great Leap Forward (with a death toll that is estimated to be around 30 million people). The fact that the Indian government is under constant scrutiny by the media, and also has to answer questions from active opposition parties, has prevented the political leaders and the ruling parties from getting detached from the lives of the people in the way that occurred in China during the famines, linked with the Great Leap Forward, and also, later on, during the Cultural Revolution.

When it comes to catastrophic calamities – with the problems in the limelight for all to see – democracy tends to generate a basic accountability that has been important in the prevention of disasters like famines in India. It has also prevented the forced movement of people from one region to another with corresponding social terror, as also happened in China during the Cultural Revolution. That affirmative recognition leads to a more demanding enquiry: to what extent has the reach of accountability been extended to cover other kinds of problems of deprivation and disparity, which may not be as dramatic as famines, but which are still extremely important in the lives of ordinary Indians?

At an immediate level the answer seems to be clear and deeply disappointing. The kind of failures we have been discussing in the earlier chapters, for example, in the delivery of school education, or in providing elementary health care to all, or in running a responsible and efficacious system of public services, have not received ready solutions through the practice of democracy. And, in contrast, even though the understanding of the Chinese government of what is needed for the well-being of the people has varied greatly over time (as was also discussed in Chapter 1), the Chinese leadership has been able to demonstrate greater accomplishments in the recent decades in many of these fields, through its more focused and constructive handling of social needs and deprivations, than has been possible through the heat and noise of Indian politics.

As we have discussed in earlier chapters, it is hard to avoid the conclusion that Indian democratic practice has failed, in many ways, to rise to the challenges it faced in economic and social fields – particularly in terms of addressing the persistence of basic inequalities as well as the deficiency of accountability that the Indian people face on a regular basis. This calls for a closer examination of the reasons for this failure as well as of the means that can be used to extend the reach of Indian democracy.

PUBLIC REASONING AND DEMOCRACY

In examining these issues, we have to ask a rudimentary but crucially relevant question: what exactly is democracy? There is an old – and narrowly institutional – view of democracy that characterizes it mainly in terms of elections and ballots. That view has been championed by many authors, including Samuel Huntington: 'Elections, open, free and fair, are the essence of democracy, the inescapable sine qua non.'[11] However, in contemporary political philosophy the understanding of democracy has vastly broadened, so that democracy is no longer seen just in terms of the demands for public balloting (important as it may be in its limited context), but much more capaciously, in terms of what John Rawls calls 'the exercise of public reason'.[12] In his *Theory of Justice*, Rawls makes this his focus, and argues for seeing democracy as being centrally linked to public deliberation:

The definitive idea for deliberative democracy is the idea of deliberation itself. When citizens deliberate, they exchange views and debate their supporting reasons concerning public political questions.[13]

Jürgen Habermas, who has significantly enriched this way of looking at democracy, has drawn attention to the important fact that the reach of public reasoning has to include both 'moral questions of justice' and 'instrumental questions of power and coercion'.[14]

Interestingly enough, the importance of public discussion received early historical recognition in India in quite a prominent way, which remains relevant to thinking about democracy and justice in India today.* The so-called Buddhist Councils that took the form of organized discussion of different points of view, represented by participants drawn from different parts of India (and even outside it), were among the earliest social attempts at public reasoning – beginning in the sixth century BC. The championing of public discussion in India in the third century BC by Emperor Ashoka – who also hosted the largest Buddhist Council ever – is a good example.

Ashoka tried even to codify good rules of public discussion in one of his stone edicts that dealt both with individual conduct and public governance.[15] Emperor Akbar's initiative in the sixteenth century in arranging public discussion on religious differences in the multicultural country over which he ruled can also be counted as part of the rich history of organized public discussion in India. However, neither Ashoka nor Akbar proposed democratic governance as far as state institutions are concerned. And even though India has reason to remember with some pride the long tradition of public arguments, a modern democracy has to demand vastly more from public reasoning as a part of democratic practice than was championed either by Ashoka or by Akbar.

A closer entry into our questions comes from the approach of seeing democracy as 'government by discussion', a perspective that John Stuart Mill explored with great care and much insight (though the phrase – 'government by discussion' – was formulated later by Walter Bagehot). One limitation of seeing democracy exclusively – or even mainly – as a system of free elections and voting relates to the obvious

---

* The relation between democracy and justice is discussed in Amartya Sen, *The Idea of Justice* (2009), Chapters 15 and 16.

fact that how people vote depends on their understanding of the problems to be addressed and also their perception of what others – as well as they themselves – have reason to seek. Social and economic problems are not always easy to see and understand, and a vigorous exercise of public reasoning can play a major role both in expanding public understanding and in broadening enlightened politics.

This is not to say that 'government by discussion' (even broadly interpreted) is the beginning and the end of democracy. The demands of democracy can be further extended, for instance to include – at least as an ideal – the requirement of equal participation. This was, for instance, a central concern of Dr Ambedkar, who argued for a far-reaching view of democracy, ultimately seen not just as a method of government but as a 'mode of associated living'. But even Dr Ambedkar took positive note of the idea of democracy as government by discussion, and public reasoning was certainly central to his understanding of it. Most of his public life, indeed, was devoted to public reasoning in one way or another.

It is in this broad framework, involving both epistemology and social ethics, that we have to see the role of public reasoning and examine the ways in which Indian democratic politics has tended to leave critically important gaps in the social understanding of what is needed by Indian society and of what the voters – individually and collectively – have reason to seek.

REASONING, ARGUMENTS AND AGITATION

A clarification is needed here on the means that can be used in the pursuit of public reasoning. Reasoning with others involves presenting one's point of view and paying serious attention to the points of view of others. This can be done through the media or through public meetings, and through conversations with others on relevant subjects, but when it is hard to get a good hearing, more assertive means of communication may well be needed. Agitation, demonstration and campaigning can indeed be important parts of public reasoning, when people connect with each other through speech – even if noisy speech.

To illustrate, the publication of John Stuart Mill's *The Subjection of Women* in 1869 was an important contribution to public reasoning on the rights of women, but so were the animated suffragist movements that social conservatives found so distasteful in the early decades in twentieth-century England. India's own experience in influencing public opinion – not only through public debates but also through demonstrations, strikes, public-interest litigations and other means of democratic action – can be seen as part and parcel of public reasoning on very important subjects.

The role of public reasoning does not depend on any credulous assumption that what we tell each other must be invariably well reasoned and persuasive. Rather, it is public reasoning that helps to make us understand each other's problems and to see each other's perspectives – and this is absolutely central to the operation of an electoral democracy.

Consider, for example, the now widely accepted generalization that a functioning democracy tends to prevent the occurrence of famines.* How does it work? It is important to remember that the number of famine victims as a proportion of the population is typically quite small (usually no more than 5 per cent and hardly ever more than 10 per cent of the total population), and if the affected or threatened population were the only people to be moved by the importance and urgency of famine prevention (in line with their self-interest), then electoral outcomes would not typically be very sensitive to this priority. It is through public discussion that people in general – not just a famine-threatened minority – come to understand the urgency of preventing a famine, and also appreciate that famines can be stopped by prompt public intervention. And it is because of public reasoning, combined with regular and free elections, that the non-prevention of famines becomes an electoral nightmare for the ruling government in a functioning democracy, inducing it to take quick preventive action whenever a famine threatens.

---

* The role of a functioning democracy in famine prevention was discussed in Sen (1983) and Drèze and Sen (1989), and while there has been discussion on the veracity and reach of the connection, the proposition has stood up fairly well to empirical evidence from across the world. See the editorial 'Meanwhile, People Starve', *The New York Times*, 14 August 2005.

Famine prevention is just one example of what the combination of public reasoning and free elections can do. Democracy's contribution to social security can, of course, be far more extensive than famine prevention. South Korea or Indonesia might not have given much thought to democracy when the economic fortunes of all seemed to go up and up together in the economically balmy days of the 1980s and early 1990s. Even though governments as well as popular movements in the country were concerned with equitable growth when people's incomes were all going up together, there was rather little recognition that equitable growth does not guarantee social security in the absence of public safety nets, and that a non-democratic authoritarian system could fail to generate a sufficiently far-reaching public reasoning to protect citizens when things go down rather than up and up. However, when the economic crises came in 1997 (and divided they fell), democracy and political and civil rights were desperately missed by people at large, taking note of the deprivation of those whose economic means and lives were unusually battered by what was called the 'Asian economic crisis'. Democracy became, then, a central issue in these countries, and it was largely on a platform of democracy and social security that Kim Dae Jung fought – and won – the Korean election for the presidency of the country, immediately following the crisis.

This way of understanding democracy leads us to ask: what tends to limit adequate discussion of the critically important problems of deprivation and inequality that continue to be neglected in India? For this we have to look not merely at the nature of Indian politics, but also at the characteristics of Indian public communication, including the reach and biases of the media. As we have already argued, the limitation of public reasoning can restrain the reach of democracy both by impairing an adequate understanding of the nature and extent of the inequalities and deprivations in the country, and by confining public action to an unnecessarily narrow domain. Politics then tends to be dominated by an excessive focus on a relatively small part of the population whose lives and problems are much discussed and constantly aired in the public media.

It is, therefore, crucial to examine, among other factors, the role of the media, which is lively and powerful in India and adept at getting the attention of the people. The vigour of the Indian media is not in doubt, but its inadequacies are large when it comes to the reach, coverage and focus of news, opinions, perspectives – and entertainment.

STRENGTH AND LIMITS OF THE INDIAN MEDIA

India is estimated to have some 86,000 newspapers and periodicals, with a circulation of more than 370 million – significantly more than any other country in the world. It is also a country in which newspapers are growing in number and in circulation, in contrast with the worldwide trend of decreasing newspaper circulation and revenue.[16] And they reflect a huge variety of points of view that often differ sharply from each other.

The print media is supplemented by the huge presence of audio and video broadcasts in India. In addition to government channels (Door Darshan, Lok Sabha TV, Rajya Sabha TV and others), there are a large number of private satellite TV channels, offering information, analysis and entertainment. There were 831 such channels in the spring of 2012, and there are many others that have come into being since then, in this rapidly growing sector of the Indian economy. More than four hundred of these channels offer news on a regular basis.

The newspapers and TV channels do not have to toe the government line (and typically do not), and they reflect a good deal of diversity of approach and of pluralism in their evaluation of life in India as well as abroad. Freedom of expression is, by and large, well respected. It is doubtful that many governments in the world would accept quietly the publication, in a mainstream and widely read magazine, of a glowing account of armed insurgency aimed at overthrowing the Indian state, such as Arundhati Roy's highly sympathetic account of the underground Maoist movement.[17] It helps of course that the author, in this case, is one of the foremost literary figures in India, with a strong record of drawing attention to neglected problems in Indian society. Similarly, right-wing publications, varying from moderate to extremist, often calling for revolts of a different kind, are also extensively tolerated. It is not in governmental intervention that we can find the main clue to the systematically limited reach of the Indian media.

Further, freedom of expression is well accepted not only as a legal right, but also as a basic principle of public life. The general commitment to freedom of expression in India is well established and impressive, and stands up well in international comparisons

There are, to be sure, some lapses from this tolerant outlook. There has been a persistent blot in the record of freedom of speech in India in the form of prohibition and censorship related to two issues in particular. The first is an excessive tendency to see security threats – real or perceived – as an adequate reason to limit speech and expression in the country in general, and particularly in areas of tension, such as Kashmir, where the axe might fall far more frequently. We discussed earlier the limitations and penalties of this way of dealing with security problems, and its sad consequences on the practice of Indian democracy. Second, the multi-religious nature of Indian society has been frequently seen as a ground for banning anything that may anger – or appear to anger – any of the diverse religious groups in the country. It is, of course, extremely important to defend the interests and freedoms of minority groups or marginalized communities, but that pursuit requires public discussion of the real problems of these groups and communities, which in turn requires freedom of speech. If instead of focusing on real reasons for grievance (and their full discussion with no holds barred), governmental rules concentrate on keeping out anything that offends anyone, then the practice of democracy through public reasoning and governance by discussion would become very hard to achieve.

Speech and expression may sometimes have to be restrained for good social reasons, for example when they incite violence or create panic. But any perceived 'right of not being offended' cannot really be a protected right if democracy through free public discussion is to be pursued. However, it is some variation or other of that perceived entitlement which has served – explicitly or by implication – as the basis for a number of prohibitory orders on speech, writings and publications. The fact that India was the first country to ban Salman Rushdie's *The Satanic Verses* in 1988 is a prominent example of a serious departure from the right to publish freely. The government was clearly moved by the fear of protests from a section of the Muslim minority in India. There have also been, in some cases, inadequate protection by the government of the rights of targeted individuals under attack from the majority community: for example, it failed to prevent the relentless targeting of M. F. Husain, one of India's greatest contemporary painters, by political extremists of the Hindu right. The hounding forced Husain to emigrate from his own country, and indeed to die away from home. More recently, the Indian police arrested two young women over a Facebook post that disputed the authorities' decision to shut down Mumbai for mourning the death of Hindu extremist leader Bal Thackeray, rather than risk offending the activist followers of Thackeray. It would be hard to justify any of these prohibitions – in the cause of 'not offending' any religious or religio-political group – if free public reasoning is to be valued and protected. These are anomalies in the commitment of democratic India to protect basic civil liberties.

Having said this, the main explanation for the limitations in the coverage of the media has to be sought elsewhere. The weakness – and often failure – of the Indian media to rise to the challenge of India's problems, including the disparities and inequalities that characterize Indian society, arises mostly from the media's own bias and selective focus – playing up some issues and events while ignoring others, including some very important and neglected subjects. As we will presently argue, a major part of this bias ultimately relates to the unequal nature of Indian society, which influences what is easy to sell. Rather than confronting it, the media has tended to take the easy course of going along with it – and even humouring it.

INEQUALITIES AND THE MEDIA

Perhaps the biggest barrier to the free operation of the media in democratic India lies in its partiality in favour of the rich and the powerful, which is widespread in its coverage of news and analysis from across the country. There are many complex biases that can be detected, but what is remarkably obvious is a serious lack of interest in the lives of the Indian poor, judging from the balance of news selection and political analyses in the Indian media.[18] Even though this bias is rarely discussed and challenged (and its enormity tends to be seriously underestimated), it is plain to see for anyone who bothers to enquire into it.

Social commentators as diverse as Harsh Mander and Shobhaa Dé have pointed to the deep – and typically implicit – alienation of the Indian elite from the country's underprivileged. Mander, writing from the perspective of marginalized people, has drawn attention to the 'exile of the poor from our conscience and even consciousness', which has grown fast over the last twenty years. Shobhaa Dé, viewing the same phenomenon from the other end of the social spectrum, writes in her book *Superstar India*: 'The India we are lauding forms but a microcosm of this vast land. It is the India of the elite, the privileged, the affluent. The only India we want the rest of the world to see and acknowledge, because we are so damned ashamed of the other. Ashamed and ignorant.'[19]

Why this bias? There has been some public discussion of the fact that most of the media institutions in India are owned by the rich. While there is something there to watch out for, this is not really unusual in any country in the world. And there is enough diversity of editorial policies to make the ownership bias not a major explanation of the slanting of news coverage or editorial opinion.

There is probably more of an explanation in the fact that the media is an advertisement-driven business.[20] The economic dependence of the media on advertising creates a special focus on potential consumers – as a result of which the rich count more than the poor. The dependence on what is effectively corporate sponsorship also creates a general tendency to pander to corporate culture and values. There are also strong pressures on the journalists and editors in a corporate-sponsored world to be selective in what they say or write. For instance, according to one of India's leading magazine editors (who preferred not to be named), 'Mainstream media is reluctant to investigate corporates because of their advertising potential. The reluctance is the direct result of management pressure with which editors go along.'[21] The recent proliferation of 'paid news' – the phenomenon of paying newspapers or TV channels to report certain facts (rather than others) – has also brought out some deeply disturbing aspects of news coverage in India, including the chosen slants in the allegedly objective reporting of facts, and hiding the separation of advertisement from news.[22]

These pressures not only lead to misinformation, and give misleading clues to the reading of facts, but they also tend to reduce the space, time and resources available for public discussion of less dazzling matters of great importance to ordinary people, such as education, health, nutrition or sanitation. The bias is hardened also by the fact, discussed in the preceding chapter, that media professionals tend to come disproportionately from a privileged background in terms of caste and class.

THE DOMINANCE OF THE PRIVILEGED

Is there a sufficient explanation of the persistent pro-affluent bias in the coverage of the Indian media in these defective features of the media? Even though some part of the bias in media coverage can be linked, directly or indirectly, to its being influenced by advertising and sponsorship, and also by the class and caste background of media professionals and owners, there remains a huge residue to be explained by the deeply unequal character of Indian society, which tends to shape the nature of the media. This is a huge problem, for the media is not only moulded by the unequal society, its potentially corrective role in Indian social and political thinking is made more difficult by the society that has moulded it. Systematic illusions about the nature of the country and the sharpness of disparities within India tend to survive – and are sometimes hardened – by the limitations of the media.

Some of the biases are easy to detect and discuss. For example, there is very little coverage of rural issues in the mainstream media: a recent study found that rural issues get only 2 per cent of the total news coverage in national dailies (in spite of national dailies being widely read in rural areas).[23] The interests of what is described as the Indian 'middle class' (even though most members of this class are way above the middle of the spectrum of affluence of Indians as a whole) receive enormously more attention than the concerns of the under-privileged, with a bias that slants the papers and broadcast channels towards such subjects as fashion, gastronomy, Bollywood and cricket. As one leading editor put it to a group of children's rights advocates at a recent meeting in Delhi: 'Don't have any illusions, you will never be able to compete for attention with the wardrobe malfunction of a model on the ramp.'[24]

India is not unique in having biases of this type. Wardrobe malfunction and similar trivia get media coverage in many other countries. But what is special about India is that an overwhelming majority of the people of the country would have little idea of what a wardrobe is, and what a malfunction might mean in this context. If one reads only the newspapers, and watches the glitzy channels of broadcast, one would tend to have a largely misguided notion of how most Indians live and think. One would be only vaguely aware of the fact that India has the largest population of seriously undernourished people in the world – not just in absolute numbers, but, in terms of standard criteria, even relative to its population size. One would hardly know that half of all Indians live in accommodation that does not have any toilets – forcing people to return to nature to perform one of the most private activities of living. There are of course bits and pieces of coverage of the deprivations and struggles of the underprivileged in newspapers and TV outlets (more in some of the deliberately conscientious media channels than in others), but coverage of the lives of the deprived is astoundingly limited for the media as a whole.

The media itself certainly shares a big responsibility for the bias in the coverage of news and analyses, especially since it can play a large role in leading, and not merely following, public curiosity and concern. But the problem extends to a lack of interest and engagement from the relatively privileged parts of society on matters of social inequality and deprivation, since the media tends to be shaped substantially by the need to cater to them. The influential subscribers, readers, sponsors and champions of the media tend to come from this relatively small but, in absolute terms, large – and powerful – group.

THE BIG DIVIDE AND POLITICAL DIVERSION

What is particularly striking about this media bias is the way the deep imbalance has managed to become almost invisible to the classes whose voices count and whose concerns dominate public discussion.

What is really very special in India is the fact that the comparatively small group of the relatively privileged seem to have created a social universe of their own.

The privileged group in India includes not only businessmen and the professional classes, but also the bulk of the country's relatively affluent, including the educated classes. In an insightful essay, called 'Emergence of the Intelligentsia as a Ruling Class in India', Ashok Rudra argued more than two decades ago that the educated population of India, with a shared interest in the benefits to be derived from social inequality, has become part of the 'ruling coalition' which dominates policy discussions, and as a consequence, also governs what happens in the country.[25] There are, of course, many internal conflicts of interest within the broad group that Rudra called the Indian intelligentsia, but there are shared interests and concerns that tend to confine the concentration of public discussion on the lives of the relatively affluent.

Of course, among the relatively affluent, some are more so and some far less. And sometimes much is made of the internal divisions among the affluent – the 'common people' in political rhetoric are often the poorer among the generally privileged. But the entire group of the relatively privileged, including Rudra's 'intelligentsia', stand well above the lot of the underprivileged majority of Indians – among whom, again, some are much more underprivileged than others.

The 'relatively privileged' in this broad sense, who may be no more than a fourth or a fifth of the total population, comprise different strata – varying from tycoons, at one end, to educated ordinary people, at the other, who are not particularly rich but enjoy levels of living that separate them from the masses of the underdogs of society. As discussed in Chapter 4, many of the demands that are often called 'populist', such as higher pay scales for public sector employees or low fuel prices, are in fact primarily demands of the relatively affluent, with limited benefits – if any – for the underprivileged, especially in comparison with other entitlements or services that could be extended to them with the same resources. These demands are often championed by political parties from the right to the mainstream left, under the garb of 'demands of the common people', even when they actually deflect public resources that could be used to reduce the astonishing deprivation of the really deprived. The biggest gainers of these 'populist' demands come often from the most prosperous and affluent – the rich who drive around in luxury cars and SUVs that consume state-subsidized diesel, the large landowners who use free electricity to tap free groundwater, and the fertilizer companies that have been raking huge subsidies for many years in the name of food security for the common people.

Meanwhile, less influential but more committed groups of people who do stand in solidarity with the underprivileged tend to be comprehensively ignored or sidelined. It is quite common, for instance, for thousands of poor people to gather in New Delhi from all over the country to voice demands related to minimum wages, forced displacement, land rights, or caste discrimination without much notice being taken of them by the mainstream media or political parties.

If all this is not a failure of public reasoning, it would be hard to see what could count as a real failure. It is to that overarching division between the privileged and the rest that we have to look for an understanding of the contrast between the people whose lives get much attention in the media and public discussion, and the rest whose deprivations and despair are largely invisible or opaque in that communicational sphere. A great disparity between the privileged and the rest – notwithstanding their own internal divisions – fortifies the inequality of lives by an inequality of articulation and attention, which makes an overwhelming disparity in the lives of people both less discussed and correspondingly more resilient and stable.

PUBLIC POLICY AND SPENDING PRIORITIES

Among other serious consequences of this asymmetry of voice and influence of different groups are corresponding biases in the allocation of public revenue, which are, of course, influenced by group interests. One of the benefits of rapid economic growth is that it tends to generate larger public revenue which can be used for different purposes – varying from reducing the deprivations of the underdogs to serving the interests of the relatively privileged. Indeed, public revenue in India has tended to grow as fast as – sometimes more so than – the growth of GDP in the recent past. This has had the result that the gross tax revenue of the central government is about four times as large today, at constant prices, as it was just twenty years ago.[26]

In addition to drawing on the resources generated by the fast expansion of the GDP, it is possible to further expand the contribution of GDP growth to public revenue in many different ways, varying from preventing tax evasion, which is very large in India, to removing arbitrary exemptions and widening the tax base. Indeed, many constructive recommendations to raise India's tax-GDP ratio (which is quite low by international comparison), without choking off economic efficiency, have been made by successive expert committees.[27] But even as things stand today, with public revenue growing more or less at par with GDP, the resources available for public spending are expanding fast in India. This is a valuable opportunity to make good use of public revenue for enhancing living conditions, through public services and support. But it has also allowed the continuation – and sometimes expansion – of spending patterns that are not particularly easy to justify.

To illustrate, central government subsidies on petroleum and fertilizer alone are expected to cost more than Rs 165,000 crores in 2012–13 (nearly 1.7 per cent of India's GDP) at the time of writing.[28] This is about *four times* what the central government spends on health care.* There is a mind-boggling imbalance here, but it somehow goes virtually unchallenged and even unnoticed. There are similar imbalances at the state level. In many states, for instance, public expenditure on health and education consists overwhelmingly of salary payments (often based on fairly generous pay scales, as discussed in Chapter 5), with very little left for other essential items such as textbooks or medicines. In some states, the payment of public-sector salaries and

---

* Under the Indian Constitution, health is on the 'concurrent list' of joint social responsibilities of the central and state governments, so that a major part of public expenditure on health is borne by state governments. But even the combined expenditure of state and central governments on health is only around 1.2 per cent of GDP, as we saw in Chapter 6 – still less than the combined petroleum and fertilizer subsidies. Further, given that the bulk of state-government expenditure on health goes into salaries, central government health expenditure has to play an increasingly important role in the health sector.

pensions now absorbs the bulk of state government revenue, crowd-ing out other uses of public revenue and causing a serious threat of financial bankruptcy.

To give another example, consider the intense debate on the proposed National Food Security Bill tabled by the government in the Indian Parliament in December 2011, which was immediately described and very widely attacked by influential critics as being 'financially irresponsible'. The additional resources required to imple-ment the Bill were officially estimated, at that time, at Rs 27,000 crores per year (about 0.3 per cent of India's GDP). This is, of course, a large sum, and for that reason it may not be hard to understand why there was such a strong protest against it by vocally powerful commenta-tors, on grounds of its unaffordability, even for the otherwise laudable purpose of providing subsidized food to the poor.

As it happens, the National Food Security Bill has many problems other than its high cost, and is still being widely debated as we finish writing this book. But concentrating for the moment on the cost side only, we have to assess how unaffordable or 'irresponsible' is a com-mitment to spend an additional Rs 27,000 crores? The fact that India has the largest number of undernourished children in the world makes a programme of this kind – if well formulated and adequately scrutinized for effectiveness – well worth considering. The urgency of the nutrition situation does not obviate the need for critical assess-ment of the soundness of the Bill and of the measures it proposes to address this problem. But the summary dismissal of it as 'fiscally irresponsible' is hard to justify when much larger sums are spent on regressive subsidies, unbalanced salary hikes in the public sector, and other less exemplary purposes.

There are many other ways in which public revenue is sacrificed to cater to particular demands – often coming from influential groups. For example, as mentioned in Chapter 4, the exemption of diamond and gold imports from custom duties costs the exchequer more than Rs 57,000 crores a year, according to the Finance Ministry's official 'Revenue Forgone' statement. This is more than twice as much as the estimated additional cost of the National Food Security Bill. But there has been little clamour about its unaffordability in public discussions.

The estimated 'forgone revenue' from the custom duties exemption on gold and diamonds is likely to be an exaggeration, since those imports would probably decline somewhat if a duty were to be imposed, and also since some of the imports may be used for re-export after work on them for making jewellery. And yet, even after making allowances for this overestimation, it is hard to argue that the food security proposals were unaffordable in a way duty exemptions for diamond and gold imports are not.

When, in a meeting of the Indian Economic Association in December 2011, one of us explicitly raised this comparison between the alleged unaffordability of Rs 27,000 crores to feed the hungry and the acceptance – without a murmur – of the sacrifice of Rs 57,000 crores for keeping gold and diamond imports out of the tax net, most of the discussants indicated little awareness of the existence of such tax exemptions and of other ways in which public revenue is so substantially forgone. The Finance Ministry's statement does in fact provide a fairly comprehensive estimate of how much revenue is forgone through various channels, such as the Rs 57,000 crores of revenue lost by not having taxes on the import of gold and diamonds. Adding all such 'revenue forgone' together, the Ministry put the total public revenue lost at around Rs 480,000 crores for 2010–11 and Rs 530,000 crores for 2011–12 (more than 5 per cent of India's GDP).[29] There are exaggerations here, and the net loss may well be much smaller, and yet even after such adjustments, the net revenue forgone would be quite gigantic. The idea that India cannot afford to provide social assistance to the most food-deprived people in the world, because the country is too poor and public revenue is too small, is difficult to sustain on the basis of these – and other – available data.*

---

* As was mentioned in Chapter 4, some of the 'exemptions' that make up the figures of revenue forgone are not easy to capture in the form of fresh revenue (the total figure of 'revenue forgone' is a mixture of reality and unreality), but there are indeed many exemptions that can actually provide good sources of revenue. The gross anomalies are not, by any means, confined to gold and diamonds. For instance, a similar amount of revenue (close to Rs 60,000 crores) is forgone on account of custom duty exemptions for 'crude oil and mineral oils', adding to other regressive fuel subsidies discussed earlier. Even larger amounts of revenue are lost through custom duty exemptions for 'machinery' and allowances for 'accelerated depreciation', among other 'ridiculous tax incentives given to Indian companies to invest in capital equipment', as Jaithirth Rao

Interestingly, in his budget proposals made in February 2012, the Finance Minister proposed introducing a small excise duty on gold and precious metals used for jewellery. This immediately triggered massive protests from jewellers and other influential people whose interests were affected, and despite the very narrow base of this pressure group, the opposition was so vocal that the government had to withdraw the proposed levy within a month. This lenient policy towards goldsmiths and jewellers continued even as excessive gold imports became a major worry for the government later in 2012, with the Finance Ministry warning that 'the deluge of gold imports was straining the current account deficit' and whining that it is 'not easy to get housewives to give up [gold] purchases overnight'.[30] While the accusation of the profligacy of the government in having an expensive food security bill has remained quite alive in public memory, any significant public protest about the continued exemption of imports of gold and diamonds from the tax net has yet to gather momentum. The biases in public attention and protest clearly have serious consequences.

CHANGING THE REACH OF INDIAN DEMOCRACY

If India needs a new democratic politics, that requirement is closely connected with the necessity of paying much greater attention to the interests, demands and rights of the most deprived (as opposed to the 'relatively disadvantaged among the more advantaged'). The political parties will have a natural interest to change course if and only if the deprivations are more clearly recognized, more extensively brought

---

(2012), a business leader and a distinguished public commentator, has aptly described them. Many expert reports have called for the abolition of arbitrary exemptions, without being able to cure the 'cancer of concessions' (M. Govinda Rao, 2011). The point is not only that many extra sources of revenue exist, but that their existence is hardly acknowledged by the 'deficit hawks' who jump on to the bandwagon of 'fiscal responsibility' whenever the use of public expenditure for the benefit of well-being and freedom of the poorer Indians is proposed.

into focus, more widely talked about, and reflected in active agitations as well as critical discussions.

This is far from easy to accomplish given the prominence of other – quite different – issues that have a strong hold now over political parties. These other issues may vary from furtherance of Hindutva to sectarian caste politics, from the pursuit of pro-business advocacy to blind support for public-sector unions, and they can crowd out the possibility of the kind of political change that is badly needed. In one way or another, there is plenty of identity politics in the existing priorities, and this may not be easy to compete with. The underdogs of the society do, of course, have many shared interests and concerns, but to mould them into a defining political identity requires political organization of a kind the need for which is much easier to see than are the ways and means of actually achieving it.

And yet there is ground for hope, given the general vibrancy of democratic practice and social movements in India. Aside from familiar illustrations of popular movements before and just after independence, a wide range of more recent initiatives and agitations have contributed to bringing more justice and more critical reasoning into Indian politics. Some of these have also succeeded, often against considerable opposition, in bringing about constructive change. For instance, the last decade alone has seen the enactment of a series of social legislations that have been introduced in response to popular movements and demands: not only the well-known Right to Information Act and National Rural Employment Guarantee Act, but also laws concerned with the right to education, social security for unorganized workers, domestic violence, and the property rights of traditional forest dwellers, among other issues that matter a great deal to the underprivileged.[31] The effectiveness of these legislations has varied a great deal, from very impressive (e.g. the Right to Information Act) to solidly disappointing (e.g. the Unorganized Workers Social Security Act), but nevertheless there is a significant political development here and an important sign of the possibility of bringing democratic politics to bear on critical social issues. There have also been valuable efforts in recent years, based on public mobilization, media campaigns, judicial interventions, parliamentary lobbying and other democratic means, to achieve practical change in various domains such as environmental norms, public accountability, food security, children's rights, gender equality, among many others – with significant results in many cases. The notion that public policy in India is entirely unresponsive to well-organized democratic action would be hard to substantiate in the light of recent experience.

Another ground for hope is the possibility of much more active and leading participation by the underprivileged in these movements, and in democratic politics in general, in the relatively near future. For instance, the surge in school participation during the last twenty years or so (in spite of all the flaws of the schooling system, discussed in Chapter 5) is likely to facilitate the involvement of women, disadvantaged castes and other underprivileged groups in public life and democratic action – not just as followers but, increasingly, as leading defenders of their own rights and interests. As we saw in Chapter 3, the growing political participation of the underprivileged has played a very important role in some of India's more progressive states, including Kerala and Tamil Nadu, and contributed in a major way to their social achievements. Similar developments in other states, particularly in northern India, could generate a great deal of political energy and social change, and also positively alter – over time – the outlook and priorities of political parties.

It is also important to recognize that the kind of changes in public discussion and public action we are arguing for are not 'all or nothing' actions. Given the nature of democratic practice in India, change is likely to occur as sequential progress, rather than as an inclusive avalanche. What is of the greatest urgency now is to acknowledge the need for steps to overcome systemic deprivations which doom the bulk of the Indian people to diminished lives, and which militate against the well-being of the people, particularly the less advantaged, as well as against good functioning of the Indian economy.

What the Constitution of the Indian Republic saw as 'fundamental in the governance of the country' can come to have democratic force behind it when empirical misconceptions and delusional political priorities, some of which we have discussed in the earlier chapters, give way to better-informed and more assertive public reasoning. Subjecting these biases and misapprehensions to critical and reasoned scrutiny will have vast implications for the nature and practice of democracy in India.

10

The Need for Impatience

The Indian media is much occupied these days with the predicament of the country. This is as it should be, and there is much to rejoice in the fact that the neglected issues of widespread corruption and inefficient delivery of public services are receiving intense – if somewhat haphazard – attention. And yet the balance of focus in the media reflects a serious bias that needs critical scrutiny.

There is certainly a lot of discussion, not just in the business media, of the need to raise the rate of growth of the Indian economy, which has fallen from its peak of 9 per cent per year not long ago to around 6 per cent at the beginning of 2013 and may well fall to 5 per cent as we complete this book. Though Europe and the USA would feel lucky to be assured of even half of the reduced rate of growth that India currently has, the deep concern about increasing economic growth is perfectly understandable. Growth does raise household incomes and helps to remove poverty, especially if health, education and other basic capabilities that enable people to participate in the growth process are widely shared. It also generates public revenue that can be used to expand the social and physical infrastructure as well as for other constructive purposes. However, enhancing overall economic growth is only one of many different concerns that need attention in reversing the deprivations of the vast majority of Indians, and in reducing the astounding inequalities that characterize India today.

As we have discussed, these challenges call for wide-ranging changes in public policy and a reorientation of the democratic dialogue in India. There is a strong case for forceful public demand for much larger allocations to basic public services (such as school education, health care, nutritional support and environmental protection), and for much more comprehensive programmes of economic equity and social security, as well as the development of the physical and social infrastructure. There is a need also for radical reform of the organization of public services to make them more accountable and efficient.

The contrasting picture of rapid economic growth and slow progress in living standards (which we discussed particularly in Chapters 2 and 3) points to the necessity for an intelligent understanding of the importance of economic growth. To rectify this huge imbalance, it is essential that calls for higher growth be accompanied by demanding more participatory growth, and also by a commitment to make productive use of resources generated by growth to remedy the deplorable lack of public services and basic amenities that is holding India back so greatly today.

There is a large part of the Indian population – a relatively small minority but still quite large in absolute numbers – for whom growth alone does just fine, since they are already comparatively privileged and need no special social assistance to benefit from economic growth. They are in a good position to obtain substantial benefits from GDP expansion, as indeed they have been doing – sometimes intensified by governmental intervention in their direction (through, for example, fuel subsidies, from which they disproportionately benefit), as was discussed in the earlier chapters. This adds to their already privileged economic and social opportunities.

Some improvements in the lives of even the disadvantaged do, of course, tend to occur with economic growth, as employment and entrepreneurial opportunities expand, particularly for those who are not prevented from seizing these opportunities by ill health, lack of schooling, social barriers, or other disadvantages. But public support to the underprivileged is extremely important, in general, in helping them to overcome these disadvantages and in ensuring that the fruits of economic growth are shared widely. Without it, a great many lives will continue to be tormented by hunger, poverty, illness and other deprivations, despite spurts in aggregate economic growth (as indeed has been happening over the recent past).

The constructive use of public resources generated by economic growth to enhance human capabilities contributes not only to the quality of life but also to higher productivity and further growth. In fact, the so-called 'Asian experience', beginning with Japan in the late nineteenth century, then South Korea, Taiwan, Singapore, and eventually all of China, has been based on a skilful use of the complementarity of economic expansion and human advancement through education, health care, better nutrition, and other determinants of human capability. This is a two-way relationship, of which relatively little use has been made by India, thereby not only making the country fall behind in terms of quality of life and social indicators of living standards, but also making its long-run growth process more fragile and less participatory than it would have been otherwise.

There is some tragic irony here. Deep insights about the intimate connections between health, education and productivity were not at all absent from the visions of the pioneers of the economic and industrial development in India, such as Jamshetji Tata. As F. R. Harris describes the conception of Jamshedpur in his biography of Jamshetji, 'from the time of driving in the first stake the Iron and Steel Company assumes the function of a municipality', focusing on free health care, decent schooling, provision of safe water and basic sanitation, among other industrial and social initiatives.[1] A broad understanding of the complementarity between production and productivity, on the one hand, and human well-being and capability formation, on the other, was also powerfully articulated in the famous report of the Bhore Committee on health policy in 1946: 'If it were possible to evaluate the loss, which this country annually suffers through the avoidable waste of valuable human material and the lowering of human efficiency through malnutrition and preventable morbidity, we feel that the result would be so startling that the whole country would be aroused and would not rest until a radical change had been brought about.'[2] Alas, the country has not been 'aroused' by the neglect of health and education and other public services; on the contrary, this neglect and its far-reaching consequences have received little attention in public discussions over six decades and more of the functioning of independent and democratic India.

India has missed out fairly comprehensively on a large part of the lessons of Asian economic development, which has rapidly enhanced human well-being and capability along with – indeed as a part of – pursuing fast economic growth. A critical part of the 'East Asian strategy' has been the use of public revenue, itself expanded by economic growth, to remove huge deficiencies in social, educational and health services, and to meet the growing demands of social and physical infrastructure, while making public services more accountable and efficiently organized. China's experience also shows that devoting much more public revenue than India does to the education, health care and nutrition of the people is compatible with – and can be very helpful for – high and sustained economic growth. Comparing India's miserable allocation of 1.2 per cent of GDP to public expenditure on health with China's much higher figure of 2.7 per cent, what is striking is not only the lack of understanding of the demands of public health in India (one of the main factors behind India's deficient health achievements, as we discussed in Chapter 6), but also how limited the understanding of many champions of economic growth are of the actual requirements for fast and sustained economic growth. We are bombarded by deafening rhetoric on 'the priority of economic growth,' with little thought given to health, education and other aspects of the formation of human capabilities – reflecting a disarmingly foggy understanding of how long-run growth and participatory development can actually be achieved and sustained.

THE NATURE OF INDIAN INEQUALITY

In assessing the nature of contemporary India, it is essential to take note not only of the pervasive reach of inequality, but also of its rather special nature. Even though income inequalities are large in India, this is not the only – or perhaps even the primary – element in the disparities that characterize the country. In fact, judged by the standard measures of economic inequality (such as the Gini coefficient of the income distribution), India does not look significantly different from, say, China or Brazil. However, this comparison misses out two major issues.

First, when the income levels of the poor are so low that they cannot afford even very basic necessities, the gulf between their lives and those of the more prosperous has an intensity – indeed an outrageousness – that aggregate inequality indicators cannot capture.[3] Second, measures of private incomes miss the role of public services, in such fields as education, health care, social facilities and environmental support, which can make a big difference in protecting people from deprivation and expanding their freedoms. For both these reasons, inequality in India takes the terrible form of a massive disparity between the privileged and the rest, with a huge deficiency of the basic requirements for a minimally acceptable life for the underdogs of society. The basic facilities of a usable school, an accessible hospital, a toilet at home, or two square meals a day, are missing for a huge proportion of the Indian population in a way they are not in, say, China. This makes comparisons of inequality in terms of the aggregate inequality indicators (such as Gini coefficients) of income distributions less relevant and telling.

The division between the rich and the poor is very large in China as well, and China exceeds India in terms of numbers of billionaires. The ratio of top incomes to bottom incomes is no less in China than in India, but the extraordinary feature of the lack of basic amenities for large sections of the people is a characteristic of Indian inequality that contrasts sharply with the nature of Chinese inequality (large as it is). The lack of health care, tolerably good schools and other basic facilities important for human well-being and elementary freedoms, keeps a majority of Indians shackled to their deprived lives in a way quite rarely seen in other self-respecting countries that are trying to move ahead in the world.

To illustrate with an extraordinary lacuna that may not be easily discussable in polite society, it is not clear how many readers of Indian newspapers are aware of the fact that the involuntary practice of open defecation is more widespread in India than in almost any other country for which data are available. In 2011 half of all Indian households did not have any access to toilets, forcing them to resort to open defecation on a daily basis, compared with less than 10 per cent of households lacking this facility in Bangladesh and only 1 per cent or so in China. When the Indian figures emerged from the decennial census, in 2011, there was a brief spark of media interest and public discussion, lasting one or two days, but little more, and with hardly any practical impact on public policy, or even any long-run change in the concentration of public discussion. The possibility of space missions seems to capture the imagination of the privileged far more than flush toilets, which could liberate half the citizens of modern India from this peculiarly nasty form of inequality.

The entrenched division of India between the privileged and the rest reflects, in part, the mutual reinforcement of different types of disparities – of class, caste, community and gender (as was discussed in Chapter 8). This is another aspect of the special nature of inequality in India, which is of great importance in understanding the country's predicament and the prospects for change. It is, for instance, an important clue to the country's limited progress in the field of elementary education (especially quality education), hampered as it has been by the socially compartmentalized nature of educational opportunities, aspirations and expectations. A Dalit girl from a poor family who dreams of becoming a doctor or engineer may have to struggle not only with a lack of adequate schooling facilities in the neighbourhood and economic penury at home, but also, quite possibly, with indifferent social attitudes towards her education as well as with gender discrimination in the family and society. Given the wide-ranging personal and social roles of basic education (especially female education) in development, these multiple social barriers and divisions have exacted a heavy price.

The special nature of Indian inequality has an important bearing on the priorities of struggles for social justice. Resisting the concentration of wealth and power is, of course, an important part of these struggles in India – as it is elsewhere. However, given that one of the worst features of social injustice in India is the continued exclusion of a large part of the population from essential facilities and opportunities that ought to be available to everyone, the struggle against injustice has to be clearly connected with constructive demands for essential public services and basic entitlements.

As we saw in Chapter 3, this connection played an important role in the social history of some of India's more progressive states, including Kerala and Tamil Nadu. These demands for access to education, health care, social security and other entitlements were an integral part of the struggles of disadvantaged groups (particularly Dalits) for the removal of caste-related indignities and inequalities. Yet the intimate connection between greater social justice and better public services for the most disadvantaged, which successfully motivated many past agitations, tends to get relatively little attention in mainstream democratic politics in India today.

PUBLIC SERVICES AND SOCIAL DIVISION

In perpetuating the lopsidedness of development priorities in India, a big role is played by the lack of clarity – and deficient public discussion – about how the people of India are actually doing. An exaggerated concentration on the lives of the privileged, which is an endemic feature of Indian public discussion (typically amplified by the media), gives an unreal picture of the lives of Indians in general.

We have already commented, earlier in this book, on many examples of blind spots – social failures that are of enormous importance for development and yet have received astonishingly little attention in public debates. The lack of public awareness about open defecation (its extent, the health hazards involved, or how India compares with other countries in this respect), mentioned earlier, is one striking example. More generally, as we saw in Chapter 6, the state of India's health care system is rarely discussed in the mainstream media, let alone recognized for what it is – an antiquated 'out of pocket system' where most patients buy health care for cash from private providers, in stark contrast with the worldwide trends towards universal health coverage based on public funding and planning (typically supplemented, rather than being driven, by private insurance). Many other blind spots have also been discussed earlier in this book: the near-stagnation of real wages in the last 20 years or so, which is particularly striking in contrast with China's real-wage boom (Chapter 2); India's declining position within South Asia, in terms of standard social indicators (Chapter 3); the abysmal levels of pupil achievements in Indian schools (Chapter 5); India's pathetic record with child immunization (Chapter 6); and the extraordinary imbalances of public spending, involving lavish concessions to powerful lobbies along with a crucial neglect of investments that could enhance the living standards and human capabilities of the underprivileged (Chapter 9).

None of these issues have been widely debated in public in recent years.

This incomplete and distorted understanding of the country's predicament is associated with an exceptionally narrow view of economic development on the part of the new Indian elite. Rammanohar Reddy, the editor of the distinguished publication *Economic and Political Weekly*, has succinctly outlined one of the problems faced in India's choice of agenda:

> Today's elite is more involved with itself. It is impatient with anything that holds back the expansion of its economic muscle. Hence the talk now of 'policy paralysis' and the political investment in something as trivial as foreign direct investment in retail. The 'self-confidence' about India that is part of the dominant narrative is simultaneously intolerant of any questioning from within or without.[4]

That intolerance of a broader agenda would not have been so costly but for the fact that the 'self-confidence' that Reddy identifies is often thoroughly misplaced: it misses not only important causal connections in generating and sustaining economic growth (supported by a more healthy, better educated and less deprived population), but also the basic demands of a humane democratic society.

And yet Indian democracy offers much scope for removing blind spots and turning them into lively social issues, which is the first step towards remedying them. In fact, where these opportunities have been seized, the reach of public discussion has often expanded radically at some speed, and we have noted such developments earlier in the book. One recent example is the impact of the wave of media coverage of violence towards women that occurred in India in December 2012, following – and sustaining – the general public outrage about the terrible gang-rape of a young medical student in Delhi (discussed in Chapter 8). The terms of public discourse on issues such as corruption, undernutrition, involuntary displacement, the right to education, and public sector accountability have also significantly changed in India, in a way that would have been hard to predict just a few years ago. There are some signs of change, but the large need for a transformation of agenda still gets far less attention than it deserves.

The need for a fuller and clearer understanding of how India is doing also applies to the *positive achievements* of constructive initiatives to improve people's lives, which are often underestimated or relatively unsung. For example, the tremendous progress of elementary education in Himachal Pradesh from the early 1970s onwards – itself the result of a political process that broadened the outlook of the state government – went more or less unnoticed for a long time in the country at large, even though the results achieved were quite remarkable. Similarly, Tamil Nadu's impressive advances in health and early child care were not widely acknowledged until very recently. As discussed in Chapters 3 and 6, these achievements fit in a larger pattern of relatively active and effective social policies in some states – including Himachal Pradesh and Tamil Nadu, and of course in Kerala (from much earlier). Other states, as we discussed in Chapter 3, have much to learn from these successful experiences – both about the value of broadening public discourse and about the results achieved through more, and more efficiently delivered, public services.

Even in other states, and in India as a whole, there are significant examples of constructive initiatives that have done a great deal to improve people's lives, without always receiving the recognition they deserve. If one were to go by many of the media reports, one would get the impression that programmes like the National Rural Employment Guarantee Act (NREGA), the Public Distribution System (PDS) and the Integrated Child Development Services (ICDS) are little more than hotbeds of corruption and waste. It is, of course, a good thing that the media is active in exposing failures of governance, since this can contribute to their improvement. But there is considerable evidence that these programmes are, in fact, making a significant difference to people's lives in many states, and that there is enormous scope for extending these achievements to other states as well.

There is certainly no reason for complacency here, but recent trends do affirm earlier evidence of the real possibility of change through constructive action. This is an important insight to draw from recent experiences – both in India and abroad (for example from the introduction of universal health coverage in Mexico and a huge extension of public services in Brazil). Indeed, an appreciation of constructive possibilities is as important as a fuller realization of how serious and severe India's deprivations really are.

IMPATIENCE AND DEMOCRACY

'Patience,' wrote Ambrose Bierce in *The Devil's Dictionary* (1906), is 'a minor form of despair, disguised as a virtue.' Over the centuries, India has seen a lot of this alleged virtue. There has been extraordinary tolerance of inequalities, stratification and caste divisions – accepted as allegedly necessary parts of social order. There has been tolerance also of the gross inequities of the colonial Raj, assumed to be what backward India needed to put its house in order. There has been debilitating patience with economic stagnation, accepted as the only available option for slow-rhythm India. There has been the silent resignation of Indian women to the lack of freedom imposed on them on the alleged grounds of biological or social necessity. There has been patient endurance of the lack of accountability and the proliferation of corruption – taken to be unavoidable consequences of the cupidity of human nature. And – of course – there has been adaptive submission by the underdogs of society to continuing misery, exploitation and indignity, seen as inescapable accompaniments of a stable economic order.

Patience has not helped to remedy any of these inequities and injustices; nor has it proved to be rewarding in any other readily detectable way. In contrast, positive changes have often occurred and yielded some liberation when the remedying of ailments has been sought actively and pursued with vigour. Even the oppression of British colonialism ended only when Indian political impatience generated popular movements that made the Raj ungovernable.

Contemporary India does not suffer from lack of complaints and protests. What is, however, important to assess is whether the vocally strong and politically powerful protests adequately reflect the deprivations and injustices from which underprivileged Indians persistently suffer. The political importance and power of the relatively privileged Indians, even those who are not really rich but whose income and living standards place them well above the median Indian, tend to serve as a barrier to the attention that the voices of the really poor can actually get. The result, frequently enough, is a near-exclusion on many political issues of the majority of intensely deprived people in India.

This exclusion, in turn, leads to a pervasive disregard for the interests of the underprivileged in public policy. The neglect of school education, health care, social security and related matters in Indian planning is one aspect of this general pattern. But the biases of public policy towards privileged interests also take many other forms, including the neglect of agriculture and rural development, the tolerance of environmental plunder for private gain, and the showering of public subsidies (implicit or explicit) on privileged groups.

Multidimensional inequality tends to generate, as we have discussed, the means for its own perpetuation, particularly through the distortion of public debates and media coverage. The big social division carries with it large inequalities in the voice and power of different groups, and in addition, it helps to obscure the intense nature of the deprivation of the underdogs of society through biases in media coverage and in public discussion, which primarily seem to cater to the interests and engagements of a large – and lively – population of not so deprived people. In this and other ways, the enormity of the social division between the relatively privileged and the rest makes it much harder to use the normal tools of democracy, including the use of vocal discontent, to confront the inequalities involved.

The fog of obscurity has been so strong about the incidence and intensity of extreme suffering that the very idea of common people – the object of immediate support from vocal political leaders – has undergone a vast redefinition. The relatively affluent who are yet less affluent than the really rich very often tend to see themselves as 'ordinary people' – 'aam aadmi' in Hindi – whose self-vision places them as underdogs of society, which can be a fitting description only if we compare them with the top layer of the really prosperous.

In an insightful remark, George Lindsay Johnstone, one of the early East India Company officials, said in the London Parliament in 1801 that Britain's Indian empire was 'an empire of opinion,' and it was founded on the disinclination of 'the natives to reflect upon their own strength'.[5] The reluctance of Indians in general to reflect upon their own strength was a big factor in the continuing submission of India to Britain in Johnstone's time, but that particular failure disappeared from India a long time ago. What remains true, partly because of the circumstances of Indian politics, is that underprivileged Indians are reluctant to rise and demand a rapid and definitive removal of their extraordinary deprivation. The complaints of 'the comparatively privileged but not most privileged', which constitutes the category of the so-called 'ordinary people', are powerfully aired, and the perspectives of this easily mobilizable group get the lion's share of the championing by the major political parties. This is in sharp contrast with the relative lack of attention paid to the massive – and long-standing – deprivations of the underdogs of Indian society.

And yet the democratic politics of India do offer opportunities for the most deprived Indians 'to reflect on their own strength', and to demand that the critically important inequalities that ruin the lives of so many people in the country be rapidly remedied. This is, of course, partly a matter of political organization, but there is also an important role for a clear-headed understanding of the extensive reach and peculiar nature of deprivation and inequality in India. This is surely one of the principal challenges facing India today.

Statistical Appendix

EXPLANATORY NOTE

The economic and social statistics presented in this book draw principally on *World Development Indicators* for purposes of international comparisons, and on authoritative national sources for India-specific information – particularly the decennial censuses, the Central Statistical Organization, the Finance Ministry's annual *Economic Survey*, the Reserve Bank of India, the National Sample Survey, the National Family Health Surveys, the Sample Registration System and the India Human Development Survey. We have tried to stay clear of unreliable or possibly unreliable sources.

For *World Development Indicators* (WDI), we have used online figures (from data.worldbank.org), accessed on 1 January 2013 – most of these figures are also available in the printed edition of these indicators (World Bank, 2012). For purposes of international comparisons, we have excluded countries with a population of less than 2 million.

Sometimes there are minor discrepancies between WDI figures for India and the corresponding figures from national sources (e.g. because the latter are more up to date). For instance, India's infant mortality rate in 2011 is 47 per 1,000 live births according to WDI, but more recent data from the Sample Registration System suggest that it is actually 44 per 1,000.* When making international comparisons, we have used the WDI figures for India, without attempting to 'update' them based on national sources, since there are likely to be

---

* WDI figures are regularly updated as new data emerge; this and other discrepancies may diminish or disappear in due course.

similar lags in other countries. In any case, the discrepancies tend to be quite small.

Some aspects of Indian statistics, particularly social statistics, are a little out of date at the time of writing. The findings of the 2011 Census have been partially released, but many critical indicators (e.g. age-specific literacy rates and female labour force participation) are yet to be placed in the public domain. More importantly, the last national survey with comprehensive health and nutrition data is the third National Family Health Survey, conducted in 2005–6. Reliable child nutrition data, in particular, are not available for more recent years. We hope this gap will be partly remedied very soon, with the release of the second India Human Development Survey as well as the fourth National Family Health Survey. Meanwhile, we have used the most recent figures available from authoritative sources.

This Appendix presents further statistical information on aspects of Indian economic and social development. Table A.1 focuses on international comparisons of development indicators for selected Asian countries. Table A.2 attempts to integrate some of these comparisons with similar evidence of internal contrasts within India. Six Indian states are included in that table: three (Himachal Pradesh, Kerala and Tamil Nadu) with relatively favourable social indicators, and three (Bihar, Madhya Pradesh and Uttar Pradesh) from the comparatively deprived 'northern heartland'. Table A.3 presents a broad range of indicators for India's major states (those with a population of at least 5 million in 2011), and Table A.4 focuses on the smaller states of the north-eastern region. Finally, Table A.5 provides some information on trends over time at the all-India level. The sources used in Table A.3, on which many other tables in this book also draw, are listed at the end of this Appendix along with brief explanatory remarks.

Throughout Table A.3, except for 2004–5 data based on the India Human Development Survey (IHDS), figures for 'North-East' are indicative population-weighted averages of state-specific figures for Arunachal Pradesh, Manipur, Meghalaya, Mizoram, Nagaland, Sikkim and Tripura. In cases of missing data for specific north-eastern states (e.g. District Level Household Survey 2007–8 for Nagaland), the average was taken over the north-eastern states for which data are available. Also in Table A.3, all IHDS-based figures for 'Maharashtra' in 2004–5 apply to Maharashtra and Goa combined (see Desai et al., 2010).

Finally, Table A.5 presents two series of estimates of real agricultural wages: a series ending in 1999–2000, based on *Agricultural Wages in India* (see Drèze and Sen, 2002), and a new series starting from 1998–9, based on the Labour Bureau's *Wage Rates in Rural India* database, ably analysed by Yoshifumi Usami (2011, 2012). Both series use the Consumer Price Index for Agricultural Labourers to convert money wages into real wages. The figures in Table A.5 are based on the category 'unskilled labour' (adult male) for both series. In Tables 2.2 and 7.1 (Chapters 2 and 7 respectively), the post-2000 wage figures are also based on Usami's series. There, the wage rates for 'agricultural labour', 'non-agricultural labour' and 'rural labour' refer to unweighted averages of activity-specific wage rates for the relevant activities (e.g. ploughing, sowing, transplanting and harvesting, in the case of male agricultural labour). Since the trends in real wage rates are much the same for different activities, the exact method used to weigh different activities does not matter much for our purposes. We also constructed our own series of activity-specific real wage rates from the Labour Bureau's database and obtained results similar to those of Yoshifumi Usami.

Table A.1: Economic and Social Indicators in India and Selected Asian Countries, 2011

	India	Bangladesh	Nepal	Pakistan	Sri Lanka	China	South Korea	Indonesia	Thailand
Population (millions)	1,241	150	30	177	21	1,344	50	242	70
Per-capita Income and Related Indicators									
GDP per capita (Constant 2000 US$)	838	588	275	672	1,402	2,640	16,684	1,207	2,699
PPP estimates of GDP per capita (2005 international dollars)	3,203	1,569	1,106	2,424	4,929	7,418	27,541	4,094	7,635
Average annual growth rate of per capita GDP, 1961–2011 (%)	3.1	1.7	1.4	2.6	3.3	6.8	5.4	3.7	4.3
Average annual growth rate of per capita GDP[h] (%)									
1961–70	1.8	1.1	0.5	4.5	2.2	2.4	5.7	1.6	5.0
1970–80	0.9	−0.5	−0.2	2.2	2.6	5.4	5.5	5.3	4.6
1980–90	3.3	0.7	1.7	3.2	2.8	7.6	6.5	4.5	5.7
1990–2000	3.6	2.7	2.4	1.3	4.1	8.6	5.5	3.3	4.1
2000–11	5.5	4.4	2.0	2.5	4.7	9.6	3.9	4.1	3.1

Estimated proportion of the population below international poverty line of PPP $2/day, 2010 (%)	68.7	76.5	57.3	60.2[b]	29.1[c]	29.8[b]	n/a	46.1	4.6[a]
Longevity, Mortality and Fertility									
Life expectancy at birth (years)									
Female	67	70	70	65[f]	78[f]	75[f]	84[f]	71	77
Male	64	68	68	64[f]	72[f]	72[f]	77[f]	67	71
Persons	65	69	68	65[f]	75[f]	73[f]	81[f]	69	74
Infant mortality rate (per 1,000 live births)	47	37	39	59[f]	11[f]	13[f]	4[f]	25	11
Proportion of low-birth weight babies, 2010 (%)	28[d]	22[d]	21[d]	32[c]	17[c]	3[b]	–	11	7[a]
Maternal mortality ratio, 2010 (per 100,000 live births)	200	240	170	26[c]	35	37	16	220	48
Total fertility rate	2.6	2.2	2.7	3.4[i]	2.3[f]	1.6[f]	1.2[f]	2.1	1.6
Literacy and Education									
Adult literacy rate (age 15+), 2010 (%)									
Female	51[d]	52	48	40	90	91	–	90[a]	92[e]
Male	75[d]	61	73	69	93	97	–	96[a]	96[e]

(Continued)

Table A.1: (*Continued*)

	India	Bangladesh	Nepal	Pakistan	Sri Lanka	China	South Korea	Indonesia	Thailand
Youth literacy rate (age 15–24), 2010 (%)									
Female	74[d]	78	78	61	99	99	–	99[a]	98[e]
Male	88[d]	75	88	79	98	99	–	100[a]	98[e]
Proportion of children reaching grade 5, 2009 (%)	69[d]	66	62[c]	62	99[d]	–	99	92	–
Estimated mean years of schooling (age 25+)	4.4	4.8	3.2	4.9	9.3	7.5	11.6	5.8	6.6
Pupil-teacher ratio at primary level (pupils per teacher), 2010	40[g]	43	32	41	24	17	21	16	16[b]
Other Gender-related Indicators									
Female-male ratio in the population (females per 1,000 males)	937	976	1,016	968	1,027	926	1,006	1,006	1,035
Female labour participation rate, age 15+ (%)	29	57	80	22	35	68	49	51	64
Savings, Investment and Trade									
Gross domestic savings as a proportion of GDP (%)	31	16	9	8	15	53	31	34	31

Gross fixed capital formation as a proportion of GDP (%)	30	25	21	11	27	46	27	32	26
Foreign direct investment, net inflows as a proportion of GDP (%)	1.7	0.7	0.5	0.6	1.6	3.0	0.4	2.1	2.3
Exports of goods and services as a proportion of GDP (%)	25	23	9	14	23	31	56	26	77
Average annual growth rate of value of exports[h] (%)									
1961–90	6.1	6.3	n/a	6.8	3.2	n/a	20.6	5.1	11.5
1990–2011	13.6	12.0	n/a	6.0	5.7	16.5	12.0	7.4	8.4

[a] 2009
[b] 2008
[c] 2007
[d] 2006
[e] 2005
[f] 2010
[g] 2004
[h] Unweighted averages of annual growth rates.

Sources: *Human Development Report 2013* for mean years of schooling; all other indicators are from *World Development Indicators* (online, as on 1 January 2013). Unless stated otherwise, all figures related to 2011.

Table A.2: India in Comparative Perspective, 2011

Country or state	Population (millions)	Growth rate of per capita GDP or SDP[a] (% per year)			Youth literacy rate, aged 15–24, 2010[b] (%)		Estimated life expectancy at birth[c] (years)		Under-5 mortality rate (per 1,000 live births)	Total fertility rate[d]	Prevalence of undernutrition, children aged under 5 years[e] (%)	
		1980–1 to 1990–1	1990–1 to 2000–1	2000–1 to 2010–11	Female	Male	Female	Male			Height-for-age	Weight-for-age
Bangladesh	150	0.9	2.6	4.4	78	75	70	68	46	2.2	43	41
Nepal	30	2.1	2.3	1.7	78	88	70	68	48	2.7	49	39
Sri Lanka	21	2.4	3.9	4.5	99	98	78	72	12	2.3	17	21
Kerala	33	1.7	4.6	7.0	99	99	77	72	13	1.8	25	23
Himachal Pradesh	7	2.9	4.5	5.4	95	99	72	68	46	1.8	39	37
Tamil Nadu	72	3.7	5.1	7.5	93	97	71	67	25	1.7	31	30
Bihar	104	2.5	0.4	5.0	52	81	66	66	59	3.6	56	56
Madhya Pradesh	73	1.7	2.9	4.5	68	88	64	61	77	3.1	50	60
Uttar Pradesh	200	2.5	1.3	3.9	65	85	64	62	73	3.4	57	42
INDIA	1,241	3.1	3.9	5.9	74	88	67	64	61	2.6	48	43

China	1,344	83	9.0	9.7	99	99	75	72	15	1.6	10	4
South Korea	50	7.5	4.7	3.5	–	84	77	5	1.2	–	–
Thailand	70	5.4	3.1	3.5	98	98	78	71	12	1.6	16	7

[a] Gross domestic product (GDP) for countries; state domestic product (SDP) for Indian states; estimates are based on semi-log regression.

[b] 2005 for Thailand; 2005–6 for India and Indian states.

[c] 2010 for China, South Korea and Sri Lanka; 2006–10 for Indian states.

[d] 2010 for China and South Korea.

[e] 2006–10 (latest year for which data are available within that period) for countries; 2005–6 for India and Indian states.

Note: Figures pertain to 2011 or nearest year for which data are available (as indicated). The six Indian states listed here include three each with relatively good (Kerala, Himachal Pradesh, Tamil Nadu) and relatively poor (Bihar, Madhya Pradesh, Uttar Pradesh) development indicators, respectively.

Sources: Country-specific figures (including India) from *World Development Indicators* (online, as on 1 January 2013) and UNICEF (2012), Table 2. On state-specific figures for Indian states, see Table A.3 (the youth literacy rates are based on the National Family Health Survey 2005–6). There are minor discrepancies between the India figures from the World Development Indicators used here and the corresponding figures from national sources (e.g. due to differences in reference periods); for further details of the statistics for Indian states, see Table A.3.

Table A.3: Selected Indicators for Major Indian States

Part 1: Income-related Indicators

	Population, 2011 (millions)	Average household expenditure per capita, 2009–10 (Rs/month)		Growth rate of per capita state domestic product, 2000–1 to 2010–11 (% per year)	Poverty estimates, 2009–10 (head-count ratio)			Proportion (%) of population falling in India's lowest wealth quintile, 2005–6	Proportion (%) of population 'multi-dimensionally poor', 2005–6
		Rural	Urban		Rural	Urban	Total		
Andhra Pradesh	84.7	1,234	2,238	6.9	22.8	17.7	21.1	10.8	44.5
Assam	31.2	1,003	1,755	3.4	39.9	26.1	37.9	19.8	60.1
Bihar	103.8	780	1,238	5.0	55.3	39.4	53.5	28.2	79.3
Chhattisgarh	25.5	784	1,647	6.3	56.1	23.8	48.7	39.6	69.7
Gujarat	60.4	1,110	1,909	8.2	26.7	17.9	23.0	7.2	41.0
Haryana	25.4	1,510	2,321	6.8	18.6	23.0	20.1	4.1	39.3
Himachal Pradesh	6.9	1,536	2,654	5.4	9.1	12.6	9.5	1.2	29.9
Jammu & Kashmir	12.5	1,344	1,759	3.7	8.1	12.8	9.4	2.8	41.0
Jharkhand	33.0	825	1,584	4.6	41.6	31.1	39.1	49.6	74.8
Karnataka	61.1	1,020	2,053	5.8	26.1	19.6	23.6	10.8	43.2
Kerala	33.4	1,835	2,413	7.0	12.0	12.1	12.0	1.0	12.7
Madhya Pradesh	72.6	903	1,666	4.5	42.0	22.9	36.7	36.9	68.1

Maharashtra	112.4	1,153	2,437	7.5	29.5	18.3	24.5	10.9	37.9
'North-East'[a]	14.4	1,224	1,700	5.5	25.3	23.2	24.3	8.9	48.4
Odisha	41.9	818	1,548	6.9	39.2	25.9	37.0	39.5	63.2
Punjab	27.7	1,649	2,109	4.2	14.6	18.1	15.9	1.4	24.6
Rajasthan	68.6	1,179	1,663	5.0	26.4	19.9	24.8	24.2	62.8
Tamil Nadu	72.1	1,160	1,948	7.5	21.2	12.8	17.1	10.6	30.5
Uttar Pradesh	199.6	899	1,574	3.9	39.4	31.7	37.7	25.3	68.1
Uttarakhand	10.1	1,747	1,745	10.0	14.9	25.2	18.0	6.0	39.5
West Bengal	91.3	952	1,965	5.1	28.8	22.0	26.7	25.2	57.4
India	1,210.2	1,054	1,984	6.0[b]	33.8	20.9	29.8	20.0	53.7

[a] Throughout Table A.3, figures for 'North-East' are indicative population-weighted averages of state-specific figures (see Explanatory Note).
[b] Growth rate of 'per capita net national product'.

	Life expectancy at birth, 2006–10[a] (years)		Infant mortality rate, 2011 (per 1,000 live births)	Under-5 mortality rate, 2011 (per 1,000 live births)	Maternal mortality ratio, 2007–9[a] (per 100,000 live births)	Death rate, 2011 (per 1,000)	Birth rate, 2011 (per 1,000)	Total fertility rate, 2011 (births per woman)
	Female	Male						
Andhra Pradesh	68.2	63.5	43	45	134	7.5	17.5	1.8
Assam	63.2	61.0	55	78	390	8.0	22.8	2.4
Bihar	66.2	65.5	44	59	261	6.7	27.7	3.6
Chhattisgarh	n/a	n/a	48	57	n/a	7.9	24.9	2.7
Gujarat	69.0	64.9	41	52	148	6.7	21.3	2.4
Haryana	69.5	67.0	44	51	153	6.5	21.8	2.3
Himachal Pradesh	72.4	67.7	38	46	n/a	6.7	16.5	1.8
Jammu & Kashmir	71.1	69.2	41	45	n/a	5.5	17.8	1.9
Jharkhand	n/a	n/a	39	54	n/a	6.9	25.0	2.9
Karnataka	69.7	64.9	35	40	178	7.1	18.8	1.9
Kerala	76.9	71.5	12	13	81	7.0	15.2	1.8
Madhya Pradesh	63.8	61.1	59	77	269	8.2	26.9	3.1
Maharashtra	71.9	67.9	25	28	104	6.3	16.7	1.8
'North-East'	n/a	n/a	30	n/a	n/a	5.2	17.4	2.1[b]

Odisha	63.9	62.2	57	72	258	8.5	20.1	2.2
Punjab	71.6	67.4	30	38	172	6.8	16.2	1.8
Rajasthan	68.3	64.7	52	64	318	6.7	26.2	3.0
Tamil Nadu	70.9	67.1	22	25	97	7.4	15.9	1.7
Uttar Pradesh	63.7	61.8	57	73	359	7.9	27.8	3.4
Uttarakhand	n/a	n/a	36	n/a	n/a	6.2	18.9	2.6[b]
West Bengal	71.0	67.4	32	38	145	6.2	16.3	1.7
India	**67.7**	**64.6**	**44**	**55**	**212**	**7.1**	**21.8**	**2.4**

[a] Life expectancy and maternal mortality figures for Bihar, Madhya Pradesh and Uttar Pradesh apply to 'undivided' states (including Jharkhand, Chhattisgarh and Uttarakhand, respectively).

[b] 2010

Part 3: Literacy and Education

| | Literacy rate, age 7 years and above, 2011 (%) | | Proportion (%) of non-literate persons in the age group 15–19 years, 2007–8 | | Proportion (%) of population aged 15–19 years, 2007–8, who have completed: | | | |
| | | | | | 5 years of schooling | | 8 years of schooling | |
	Female	Male	Female	Male	Female	Male	Female	Male
Andhra Pradesh	59.7	75.6	19.0	8.7	87.8	90.9	69.6	72.8
Assam	67.3	78.8	10.8	6.9	85.3	83.4	56.5	52.6
Bihar	53.3	73.4	37.3	15.0	69.7	75.5	39.6	45.2
Chhattisgarh	60.6	81.5	16.7	6.7	72.3	80.3	34.0	41.2
Gujarat	70.7	87.2	16.3	7.4	85.9	88.5	52.6	61.2
Haryana	66.8	85.4	11.9	5.1	87.8	90.7	61.4	64.8
Himachal Pradesh	76.6	90.8	1.6	1.2	94.3	96.0	76.9	76.7
Jammu & Kashmir	58.0	78.3	12.4	2.9	92.2	94.4	68.1	68.2
Jharkhand	56.2	78.5	29.6	12.7	76.0	78.7	46.2	46.8
Karnataka	68.1	82.9	10.5	7.2	85.2	90.3	64.9	70.1
Kerala	92.0	96.0	0.9	0.8	99.2	98.8	93.6	87.1
Madhya Pradesh	60.0	80.5	22.9	11.1	78.9	83.9	37.4	43.0
Maharashtra	75.5	89.8	8.8	4.7	92.2	92.9	71.2	72.2
'North-East'	76.4	84.9	6.6	5.2	77.9	76.1	40.5	39.7

Odisha	64.4	82.4	20.9	3.9	79.8	83.7	56.4	58.3
Punjab	71.3	81.5	6.8	5.7	89.3	89.8	63.5	59.0
Rajasthan	52.7	80.5	27.2	3.4	72.5	86.0	36.6	49.2
Tamil Nadu	73.9	86.8	2.5	1.3	93.8	94.4	74.4	73.6
Uttar Pradesh	59.3	79.2	25.1	10.5	77.7	82.9	47.7	52.4
Uttarakhand	70.7	83.3	4.9	2.3	90.6	93.9	65.4	71.6
West Bengal	71.2	82.7	15.5	9.0	71.0	71.7	31.6	36.8
India	65.5	82.1	15.8	7.4	83.7	86.2	55.9	57.5

Part 4: School Attendance

	Proportion (%) of children aged 6–14 years who are currently in school, 2005–6		Proportion (%) of never-enrolled children in the 6–14 age group, 2004–5		Proportion of children aged 6–14 enrolled in a private school, 2004–5[a]	Annual private schooling costs for children aged 6–14 years, 2004–5 (Rs per child)	
	Female	Male	Female	Male		Government schools	Private schools
Andhra Pradesh	78.1	84.6	6	4	31	574	3,260
Assam	83.6	85.1	12	13	6	371	1,636
Bihar	56.2	71.5	31	19	18	704	2,466
Chhattisgarh	77.6	84.6	10	8	15	317	2,039
Gujarat	78.5	87.0	8	4	22	766	4,221
Haryana	81.2	86.5	9	8	47	1,043	4,372
Himachal Pradesh	95.2	97.1	2	1	19	1,709	6,273
Jammu & Kashmir	85.7	89.7	7	4	47	1,045	3,719
Jharkhand	66.1	77.2	22	19	32	502	2,932
Karnataka	82.0	85.9	7	6	28	638	3,848
Kerala	97.7	97.6	2	4	31	1,537	3,259
Madhya Pradesh	76.9	80.1	15	11	27	333	1,935
Maharashtra	85.5	88.7	5	3	20	599	2,370
'North-East'	80.1	79.4	4	4	34	1,441	4,237

Odisha	74.7	80.3	8	5	8	612	2,851
Punjab	84.7	85.8	5	6	52	1,444	5,160
Rajasthan	65.9	84.2	23	11	32	676	2,612
Tamil Nadu	92.7	95.1	2	1	23	606	3,811
Uttar Pradesh	73.8	80.2	13	9	43	427	1,733
Uttarakhand	88.1	92.4	6	7	27	972	3,422
West Bengal	80.1	79.4	10	10	10	1,136	5,045
India	**76.4**	**82.6**	**12**	**8**	**28**	**688**	**2,920**

[a] Among children enrolled in any school.

| | Proportion (%) of government schools with the following facilities, 2009–10: | | | | | Proportion (%) of government schools, 2009–10, providing: | | Average pupil-teacher ratio in government schools, 2009–10 | Average pupil-classroom ratio (all schools), 2009–10 |
| | Drinking water | Toilet | | Electricity | Computer | Midday meal | Health check-up | | |
		Common	Separate for girls						
Andhra Pradesh	89.8	71.3	60.7	32.4	13.2	92.0	46.9	20	24
Assam	83.9	42.2	39.4	11.5	4.8	80.5	8.6	25	30
Bihar	92.6	48.3	37.7	3.9	0.9	72.3	19.4	57	89
Chhattisgarh	94.2	36.9	33.9	19.1	5.2	88.6	85.0	27	28
Gujarat	96.2	38.9	54.6	94.0	36.4	92.5	91.2	31	34
Haryana	99.4	53.9	85.1	93.5	16.4	92.3	79.5	29	32
Himachal Pradesh	97.3	36.7	54.2	54.5	6.3	99.0	73.0	16	15
Jammu & Kashmir	83.7	29.3	16.0	7.9	4.4	97.7	16.5	16	17
Jharkhand	85.2	31.3	50.0	5.7	5.0	95.0	17.7	43	47
Karnataka	65.5	87.9	64.9	87.6	12.1	98.9[a]	93.5	25	25
Kerala	99.0	54.1	83.3	88.5	87.4	96.4	68.3	23	27
Madhya Pradesh	93.1	56.1	32.8	8.7	5.1	93.7	75.1	37	30
Maharashtra	91.6	34.7	62.3	65.6	25.1	94.7	93.1	26	31

'North-East'	79.9	54.1	40.2	14.8	9.4	90.6	19.2	18	21
Odisha	89.3	83.5	37.3	14.2	6.4	87.7	18.7	34	30
Punjab	98.6	92.9	98.5	87.5	32.3	93.5	62.7	26	23
Rajasthan	95.5	50.9	88.8	21.7	9.5	96.6	85.2	27	24
Tamil Nadu	100.0	48.4	61.4	91.7	29.5	97.7	94.2	30	27
Uttar Pradesh	97.7	44.5	70.5	16.7	2.4	82.2	35.4	42	36
Uttarakhand	88.2	59.6	55.7	26.8	16.9	95.1	53.1	22	19
West Bengal	96.3	80.8	48.0	22.4	5.6	85.7	45.2	43	42
India	**91.9**	**54.5**	**55.0**	**31.4**	**10.6**	**87.5**	**55.3**	**33**	**32**

[a] 2010–11 figure, for government and government-aided schools together.

Note: 'Schools' refers to primary and upper-primary schools. Private schools are excluded, except in the case of midday meals (where 'government-aided' private schools are included) and pupil-classroom ratios (where private schools – aided or unaided – are included).

Part 6: Gender-related Indicators

| | Sex ratio, 2011 (females per 1,000 males) | | Estimated ratio of female to male death rate in the age group of 1–4 years, 2007–9[a] | Proportion (%) of women aged 20–24 married by age 18, 2005–6 | Female labour force participation rate, age 15–59 years, 2009–10 (%) | Proportion (%) of women among organized sector employees, 2009 |
	All ages	Age 0–6 years				
Andhra Pradesh	992	943	1.42	54.8	48.9	21.8
Assam	954	957	1.39	38.6	21.1	33.3
Bihar	916	933	1.51	69.0	9.0	5.2
Chhattisgarh	991	964	(1.59)	55.0	45.4	13.9
Gujarat	918	886	1.44	38.7	35.3	14.7
Haryana	877	830	(1.83)	41.2	28.9	17.1
Himachal Pradesh	974	906	(1.80)	12.3	58.3	15.6
Jammu & Kashmir	883	859	(0.58)	14.4	31.1	10.7
Jharkhand	947	943	1.49	63.2	21.1	7.5
Karnataka	968	943	0.94	41.8	40.2	32.7
Kerala	1,084	959	1.04	15.4	33.6	40.1
Madhya Pradesh	930	912	1.23	57.3	35.2	13.8
Maharashtra	925	883	1.24	39.4	38.6	16.8
'North-East'	961	953	n/a	27.9	35.8	25.2

Odisha	978	934	1.08	37.2	27.2	15.3
Punjab	893	846	1.72	19.7	28.6	21.3
Rajasthan	926	883	2.13	65.2	36.4	17.4
Tamil Nadu	995	946	0.84	22.3	42.3	33.7
Uttar Pradesh	908	899	1.83	58.6	18.2	11.6
Uttarakhand	963	886	n/a	23.0	43.7	14.3
West Bengal	947	950	0.83	54.0	20.5	12.5
India	**940**	**914**	**1.47**	**47.4**	**30.7**	**19.9**

NSS = National Sample Survey.

[a] Figures for some of the smaller states (in parentheses) may not be reliable due to the small sample size. For related information on the estimated sex ratio at birth, see Table 8.3 in Chapter 8.

Part 7: Reproductive Health and Related Matters

	Contraceptive prevalence, 2005–6 (%)			Proportion (%) of births assisted by skilled health personnel, 2005–6	Proportion (%) of women who gave birth with specific types of maternal care, 2005–6			
	Any method	Modern permanent methods	Modern temporary methods		At least one ANC visit/ antenatal care	Tetanus vaccine (at least 2 doses)	IFA for 90 days	Post-natal check-up
Andhra Pradesh	67.6	65.8	1.4	74.9	94.3	85.3	41.2	73.3
Assam	56.5	13.2	13.9	31.0	70.7	65.4	16.2	15.9
Bihar	34.1	24.4	4.5	29.3	34.1	73.2	9.7	17.8
Chhattisgarh	53.2	44.0	5.1	41.6	88.5	74.6	20.7	36.5
Gujarat	66.6	43.5	13.0	63.0	86.7	80.4	37.0	61.4
Haryana	63.4	38.9	19.4	48.9	88.3	83.4	26.7	57.6
Himachal Pradesh	72.6	55.3	15.7	47.8	86.4	72.1	37.9	50.6
Jammu & Kashmir	52.6	28.9	15.9	56.5	84.6	81.0	27.6	51.6
Jharkhand	35.7	23.8	7.3	27.8	58.9	67.6	14.2	19.6
Karnataka	63.6	57.6	5.0	69.7	89.3	78.6	39.3	66.9
Kerala	68.6	49.7	8.2	99.4	94.4	88.7	75.1	87.4
Madhya Pradesh	55.9	45.6	7.2	32.7	79.5	70.6	12.4	33.8
Maharashtra	66.9	53.2	11.7	68.7	90.8	85.1	31.4	64.0

'North-East'	46.1	32.9	16.1	43.5	72.5	62.8	15.5	35.0
Odisha	50.7	34.1	10.6	44.0	86.9	83.3	33.8	40.9
Punjab	63.3	32.0	24.1	68.2	88.9	83.8	27.9	63.7
Rajasthan	47.2	35.0	9.4	41.0	74.9	65.2	13.1	31.8
Tamil Nadu	61.4	55.4	4.6	90.6	98.6	95.9	41.6	91.3
Uttar Pradesh	43.6	17.5	11.9	27.2	66.0	64.5	8.8	14.9
Uttarakhand	59.3	33.9	21.6	38.5	69.4	68.5	26.4	35.8
West Bengal	71.2	32.9	17.0	47.6	91.9	90.9	25.7	44.3
India	**56.3**	**38.3**	**10.1**	**46.6**	**76.4**	**76.3**	**23.1**	**41.2**

ANC = Ante-natal care.
IFA = Iron and folic acid.

	Proportion (%) of women aged 15-49 years, 2005-6, with:		Proportion (%) of persons with moderate or severe anaemia, 2005-6		Proportion (%) of children below age 5 who are undernourished, 2005-6			Proportion (%) of households using adequately iodized salt, 2005-6
	Low BMI	Any anaemia	Women aged 15-49 years	Children aged 6-59 months	Weight-for-age	Height-for-age	Weight-for-height	
Andhra Pradesh	33.5	62.9	23.9	47.1	32.5	42.7	12.2	31.0
Assam	36.5	69.5	24.6	40.9	36.4	46.5	13.7	71.8
Bihar	45.1	67.4	16.9	48.4	55.9	55.6	27.1	66.1
Chhattisgarh	43.4	57.5	17.6	47.2	47.1	52.9	19.5	54.9
Gujarat	36.3	55.3	19.1	44.7	44.6	51.7	18.7	55.7
Haryana	31.3	56.1	18.4	46.5	39.6	45.7	19.1	55.3
Himachal Pradesh	29.9	43.3	11.7	29.0	36.5	38.6	19.3	82.5
Jammu & Kashmir	24.6	52.1	14.7	32.8	25.6	35.0	14.8	75.8
Jharkhand	43.0	69.5	19.9	41.0	56.5	49.8	32.3	53.6
Karnataka	35.5	51.5	17.1	41.8	37.6	43.7	17.6	43.3
Kerala	18.0	32.8	7.0	21.0	22.9	24.5	15.9	73.9
Madhya Pradesh	41.7	56.0	15.1	47.0	60.0	50.0	35.0	36.3
Maharashtra	36.2	48.4	15.6	41.4	37.0	46.3	16.5	61.0

'North-East'	20.7	50.2	12.7	28.2	33.2	41.2	18.7	83.0
Odisha	41.4	61.2	16.4	36.1	40.7	45.0	19.5	39.6
Punjab	18.9	38.0	11.8	44.7	24.9	36.7	9.2	74.6
Rajasthan	36.7	53.1	17.9	46.9	39.9	43.7	20.4	40.8
Tamil Nadu	28.4	53.2	15.8	37.2	29.8	30.9	22.2	41.3
Uttar Pradesh	36.0	49.9	14.8	48.6	42.4	56.8	14.8	36.4
Uttarakhand	30.0	55.2	18.8	32.9	38.0	44.4	18.8	45.9
West Bengal	39.1	63.2	17.4	30.9	38.7	44.6	16.9	69.1
India	**35.6**	**55.3**	**16.8**	**43.1**	**42.5**	**48.0**	**19.8**	**51.1**

BMI = Body Mass Index.

	Proportion (%) of children aged 12–23 months, 2005–6, with:		Proportion (%) of children aged 12–35 months who had at least one dose of Vitamin A in last 6 months, 2005–6	Proportion (%) of children under three years, 2007–8, who started breastfeeding:		Proportion (%) of children aged 0–3 years who suffer from diarrhoea, 2007–8	Proportion (%) of diarrhoea-affected children treated with oral rehydration therapy, 2005–6
	Full immunization	No immunization		Within 1 hour of birth	Later than 24 hours after birth		
Andhra Pradesh	46.0	3.8	29.0	47.5	24.4	6.7	43.1
Assam	31.4	15.2	18.7	64.9	7.1	4.1	24.6
Bihar	32.8	7.0	32.6	16.0	43.4	12.1	39.7
Chhattisgarh	48.7	2.5	14.4	49.6	19.4	6.3	46.4
Gujarat	45.2	4.5	20.6	48.0	22.2	11.8	38.8
Haryana	65.3	7.8	15.9	16.5	44.6	16.5	32.3
Himachal Pradesh	74.2	1.9	33.1	56.5	10.2	9.0	69.9
Jammu & Kashmir	66.7	4.5	17.2	54.1	10.5	12.3	44.0
Jharkhand	34.2	4.4	27.5	34.5	18.9	8.2	31.3
Karnataka	55.0	6.9	22.8	46.5	26.8	9.0	46.5
Kerala	75.3	1.8	46.5	64.6	3.2	5.9	80.9
Madhya Pradesh	40.3	5.0	20.1	42.7	27.7	15.0	44.2

Maharashtra	58.8	2.8	37.6	52.5	19.7	19.9	52.1
'North-East'	40.3	13.9	25.2	56.2	10.2	8.2	56.5
Odisha	51.8	11.6	29.5	63.2	11.0	13.4	48.6
Punjab	60.1	6.6	20.8	44.1	19.4	13.5	39.3
Rajasthan	26.5	5.5	16.4	41.4	20.0	8.4	21.4
Tamil Nadu	80.9	0.0	44.8	76.1	6.6	5.6	54.5
Uttar Pradesh	23.0	2.7	8.7	15.1	66.4	16.2	22.3
Uttarakhand	60.0	9.1	20.4	63.5	13.9	12.7	49.1
West Bengal	64.3	5.9	46.8	38.5	19.5	6.0	52.3
India	43.5	5.1	24.8	40.5	29.1	11.7	38.5

	Average population per PHC, 2007–8 (000)	Proportion (%) of PHCs with the following facilities, 2007–8						
		Medical officer	Pharmacist	Regular power supply	Newborn care equipment	Functional OT	Cold chain equipment	Essential drugs
Andhra Pradesh	48.1	79.3	74.1	45.5	48.9	89.0	92.0	94.7
Assam	111.4	91.3	97.4	57.4	43.1	72.3	78.0	71.3
Bihar	158.3	87.6	32.6	9.5	9.9	43.9	59.2	57.3
Chhattisgarh	25.7	53.0	48.2	67.7	31.1	46.6	25.9	62.6
Gujarat	38.2	62.2	62.7	72.3	30.4	74.2	90.6	87.5
Haryana	41.5	76.8	93.5	41.8	24.7	60.5	66.2	84.8
Himachal Pradesh	13.2	75.7	72.9	61.8	14.6	34.7	67.4	75.0
Jammu & Kashmir	25.8	51.8	95.1	6.3	14.0	25.2	39.2	29.3
Jharkhand	127.3	93.5	72.8	44.0	31.5	65.8	89.1	79.4
Karnataka	25.7	61.2	69.1	13.4	37.0	75.5	82.0	96.1
Kerala	29.7	85.0	98.3	96.9	1.1	1.4	97.2	74.0
Madhya Pradesh	43.4	66.0	32.1	20.4	30.0	78.4	49.4	52.7
Maharashtra	45.3	90.8	88.9	13.6	42.2	81.5	88.8	85.7
'North-East'	21.7	88.6	82.5	38.6	23.0	64.5	68.0	38.1

Odisha	38.0	80.4	95.1	41.5	14.5	29.2	34.9	30.6
Punjab	29.2	59.0	96.3	7.5	20.9	50.0	53.0	40.3
Rajasthan	28.3	62.0	0.7	12.1	20.7	75.1	81.1	65.2
Tamil Nadu	32.1	85.3	93.9	86.5	63.8	90.1	94.8	97.9
Uttar Pradesh	69.0	79.6	79.0	11.6	15.0	44.6	21.4	54.6
Uttarakhand	24.4	67.9	95.2	52.4	17.9	50.0	46.4	73.8
West Bengal	37.9	80.3	76.9	37.2	7.6	25.2	32.4	43.1
India	**49.2**	**75.8**	**69.2**	**35.7**	**27.9**	**61.3**	**67.2**	**69.6**

PHC = Primary Health Centre.
OT = Operating theatre.

	Proportion (%) of villages, 2007–8, with:			Proportion (%) of households, 2005–6, with:			Proportion (%) of children under 6 who received any service from an Anganwadi in the past year, 2005–6	Proportion (%) of rural households employed under NREGA, 2009–10
	Primary or middle school	Any government health facility	Anganwadi worker	Electricity	Improved water source	Toilet facility		
Andhra Pradesh	98.7	46.7	80.9	88.4	94.0	68.3	27.5	35.4
Assam	94.3	57.1	92.3	38.1	72.4	69.9	26.8	18.2
Bihar	91.7	36.0	91.7	27.7	96.1	17.0	8.8	9.9
Chhattisgarh	99.1	32.1	95.2	71.4	77.9	17.9	55.2	47.9
Gujarat	98.3	46.9	96.5	89.3	89.8	43.5	40.5	21.5
Haryana	99.2	49.1	98.2	91.5	95.6	56.3	21.2	5.1
Himachal Pradesh	99.1	49.1	97.1	98.4	88.4	55.9	34.7	33.4
Jammu & Kashmir	97.7	62.2	93.7	93.2	80.8	60.2	16.6	9.7
Jharkhand	89.1	30.0	94.2	40.2	57.0	14.5	38.6	19.2
Karnataka	96.3	42.1	95.7	89.3	86.2	37.2	33.5	8.0
Kerala	100.0	99.8	100.0	91.0	69.1	96.7	28.7	11.2
Madhya Pradesh	97.7	28.9	92.3	71.4	74.2	22.9	43.8	40.6

Maharashtra	98.0	42.6	96.5	83.5	92.7	47.4	38.0	4.4
'North-East'	92.8	57.5	92.1	78.0	68.7	89.0	28.2	n/a
Odisha	94.6	66.3	70.6	45.4	78.4	16.9	60.5	22.0
Punjab	95.8	43.8	97.6	96.3	95.5	75.9	10.5	5.2
Rajasthan	98.6	48.9	94.9	66.1	81.8	25.1	15.9	61.8
Tamil Nadu	95.0	61.8	96.9	88.6	93.5	39.3	41.6	33.5
Uttar Pradesh	92.4	39.7	91.5	42.8	93.7	26.4	18.6	16.2
Uttarakhand	97.9	29.5	83.6	80.0	87.4	53.2	24.5	29.2
West Bengal	90.2	40.0	95.4	52.5	95.7	56.3	38.0	43.2
India	95.1	46.2	91.8	67.9	87.9	49.3	28.4	24.9

NREGA = National Rural Employment Guarantee Act (see Chapter 7).

Part 12: Household Amenities

Proportion (%) of households having various amenities, 2011

	Drinking water source:		Electricity as source of lighting	Sanitation facility:			Phone (landline or mobile)	Possession of durables goods:	
	Within premises	Far away		Latrine within premises	Public latrine	Open defecation		Two-wheeler	Television
Andhra Pradesh	43.2	19.5	92.2	49.5	2.5	48.0	63.1	18.6	58.8
Assam	54.8	18.5	37.1	64.9	1.9	33.2	47.9	10.2	27.5
Bihar	50.1	12.0	16.4	23.1	1.1	75.8	55.5	8.1	14.5
Chhattisgarh	19.0	26.5	75.3	24.6	1.4	74.0	30.7	15.6	31.3
Gujarat	64.0	12.4	90.4	57.4	2.3	40.4	69.0	34.1	53.8
Haryana	66.5	12.1	90.5	68.6	1.5	29.8	79.3	33.3	67.9
Himachal Pradesh	55.5	9.5	96.8	69.1	1.2	29.7	82.3	15.5	74.4
Jammu & Kashmir	48.2	23.1	85.1	51.2	2.7	46.1	69.5	12.9	51.0
Jharkhand	23.2	31.9	45.8	22.0	1.0	77.0	48.0	16.1	26.8
Karnataka	44.5	18.2	90.6	51.2	3.8	45.0	71.6	25.6	60.0
Kerala	77.7	8.2	94.4	95.1	1.1	3.8	89.7	24.1	76.8
Madhya Pradesh	23.9	30.5	67.1	28.8	1.2	70.0	46.0	18.8	32.1
Maharashtra	59.4	13.1	83.9	53.1	12.9	34.0	69.1	24.9	56.8

'North-East'	30.0	30.5	70.6	78.8	3.0	18.2	52.4	10.3	42.9
Odisha	22.4	35.4	43.0	22.0	1.4	76.6	39.8	14.5	26.7
Punjab	85.9	4.1	96.6	79.3	1.2	19.5	82.1	47.5	82.6
Rajasthan	35.0	25.9	67.0	35.0	0.7	64.3	70.6	24.1	37.6
Tamil Nadu	34.9	7.0	93.4	48.3	6.0	45.7	74.9	32.3	87.0
Uttar Pradesh	51.9	12.1	36.8	35.7	1.3	63.0	66.9	19.6	33.2
Uttarakhand	58.3	15.2	87.0	65.8	1.1	33.1	74.6	22.9	62.0
West Bengal	38.6	26.6	54.5	58.9	2.5	38.6	49.2	8.5	35.3
India	**46.6**	**17.6**	**67.3**	**46.9**	**3.2**	**49.8**	**63.2**	**21.0**	**47.2**

Part 13: Exposure to Mass Media

	Periodicals circulated per 100 persons, 2010	Proportion (%) of adults aged 15–49 years, 2005–6, who:									
		Read a newspaper or magazine at least once a week		Watch television at least once a week		Listen to radio at least once a week		Go to the cinema at least once a month		Are not exposed to any media	
		Female	Male	Female	Male	Female	Male	Female	Male	Female	Male
Andhra Pradesh	6.3	21.6	51.6	74.3	78.4	19.8	21.3	17.7	54.2	18.1	8.4
Assam	3.2	19.8	39.1	44.4	56.6	35.4	44.8	2.2	10.2	38.6	22.1
Bihar	1.2	10.8	40.4	23.1	33.4	27.7	50.7	2.5	19.4	58.2	27.3
Chhattisgarh	3.2	11.7	44.2	44.8	55.6	18.4	30.7	2.2	8.0	47.4	30.2
Gujarat	2.7	31.2	59.0	62.0	69.5	23.4	45.6	6.4	17.6	28.4	15.3
Haryana	5.4	25.0	50.6	62.1	63.1	19.0	30.6	3.0	5.9	32.3	21.8
Himachal Pradesh	5.4	32.5	64.6	72.4	79.9	34.5	48.9	2.4	7.2	21.3	7.0
Jammu & Kashmir	1.1	24.4	45.2	64.5	62.6	58.5	64.3	2.2	3.9	17.6	12.8
Jharkhand	2.5	9.9	33.3	31.8	36.8	12.6	25.7	3.5	16.9	60.0	40.2
Karnataka	7.2	27.2	59.1	69.5	80.4	32.4	57.4	10.4	38.3	22.1	7.8
Kerala	18.5	59.6	87.6	73.0	80.7	41.5	49.1	8.1	35.6	9.5	1.7
Madhya Pradesh	2.8	17.7	40.9	43.0	49.8	24.5	38.2	2.8	10.0	46.9	30.8
Maharashtra	14.2	39.2	68.0	69.4	76.3	33.7	48.8	7.0	23.3	23.6	10.5

'North-East'	n/a	29.8	46.7	62.1	67.1	33.7	43.3	5.5	8.7	27.1	19.7
Odisha	7.3	11.5	43.6	52.1	60.8	22.3	38.8	2.8	14.1	38.8	24.8
Punjab	5.8	31.9	55.7	80.4	84.8	19.0	30.5	4.8	7.4	15.7	9.5
Rajasthan	3.9	18.2	57.3	40.4	55.0	13.9	32.6	2.2	10.7	53.1	26.4
Tamil Nadu	6.9	27.5	67.8	81.4	83.9	46.8	63.1	7.9	31.1	11.2	5.1
Uttar Pradesh	2.1	14.3	49.7	40.1	50.1	29.7	52.0	1.6	8.3	47.5	23.1
Uttarakhand	4.9	26.1	56.6	66.3	70.4	20.8	29.1	3.7	7.1	26.8	16.6
West Bengal	5.0	18.5	43.9	51.6	56.9	33.7	43.2	5.7	15.4	36.0	22.3
India	5.6	22.9	53.0	55.0	63.2	28.8	44.3	5.6	19.5	34.6	18.3

Part 14: Electoral Participation and Outcomes

	Voter turnout, Lok Sabha elections, 2009 (%)		Share (%) of women in:				Proportion (%) of candidates/MPs with pending criminal cases, Lok Sabha 2009		Proportion (%) of 'hereditary' MPs' among Lok Sabha MPs, 2010	Average number of days of Assembly/ Parliament sittings in a year, 2000–2010[a]
	Female	Male	Lok Sabha seats, 2009	Rajya Sabha seats, 2012	Assembly seats, 2011 All women	SC/ST women	Candidates	MPs		
Andhra Pradesh	71.4	73.4	11.9	16.7	n/a	n/a	11	26	38	n/a
Assam	66.7	72.1	14.3	14.3	11.9	2.4	8	14	14	26
Bihar	42.6	46.1	10.0	0	14.8	2.1	28	45	23	32
Chhattisgarh	52.2	58.2	18.2	20.0	13.2	5.5	5	18	17	n/a
Gujarat	43.4	52.1	15.4	18.2	8.8	3.3	19	42	19	31
Haryana	65.8	68.8	20.0	0	11.1	2.2	10	20	70	14
Himachal Pradesh	59.1	57.6	0	33.3	4.4	0.0	3	0	25	31
Jammu & Kashmir	33.8	45.0	0	0	3.4	n/a	5	17	33	26
Jharkhand	47.7	53.9	0	0	n/a	n/a	31	57	0	n/a
Karnataka	56.6	60.9	3.6	0	1.5	0.0	11	32	25	42
Kerala	72.6	73.8	0	11.1	5.0	1.4	22	35	19	n/a
Madhya Pradesh	43.9	57.6	20.7	27.3	10.9	6.1	10	14	24	n/a

Maharashtra	47.4	53.7	6.3	10.5	n/a	n/a	18	54	29	42
'North-East'	74.9	76.6	n/a	n/a	n/a	n/a	n/a	n/a	15	n/a
Odisha	64.4	66.1	0	10.0	4.7	3.4	21	24	38	n/a
Punjab	69.4	70.1	30.8	14.3	6.0	1.7	9	15	77	n/a
Rajasthan	44.8	51.5	12.0	10.0	14.5	7.0	10	8	20	n/a
Tamil Nadu	71.9	74.0	5.1	16.7	3.8	n/a	8	26	23	n/a
Uttar Pradesh	44.2	50.7	15.0	9.7	5.7	2.0	16	39	39	n/a
Uttarakhand	50.6	55.5	0	0	7.1	1.4	14	20	20	n/a
West Bengal	80.3	82.3	16.7	0	11.2	4.7	13	17	19	48
India	**55.8**	**60.2**	**10.9**	**11.0**	**–**	**–**	**15**	**30**	**29**	**72**

MP = Member of Parliament.

[a] 'Hereditary MPs' refers to MPs who are sons or daughters of former MPs, or have other strong family connections to politics.

	Average daily wages/earnings of casual labourers aged 15–59 years, 2009–10ᵃ (Rs/day)				Proportion of persons aged 60+ getting old-age or widow pension, 2004–5	Murder rate, 2010 (per 100,000)	Suicide rate, 2010 (per 100,000)
	Rural		Urban				
	Male	Female	Male	Female			
Andhra Pradesh	115	76	155	93	16.3	3.0	18.9
Assam	94	75	116	82	1.7	3.9	9.7
Bihar	81	66	94	60	10.2	3.2	1.3
Chhattisgarh	71	65	127	72	10.0	4.2	26.6
Gujarat	87	71	119	66	1.9	1.7	10.7
Haryana	146	99	154	71	60.6	4.0	11.8
Himachal Pradesh	141	110	149	158	19.0	1.9	8.1
Jammu & Kashmir	157	207	152	137	2.2	1.7	1.9
Jharkhand	104	82	109	74	4.7	5.1	4.0
Karnataka	97	63	123	68	8.6	3.0	21.5
Kerala	227	119	237	121	6.9	1.1	24.6
Madhya Pradesh	74	58	89	75	7.9	3.3	12.5
Maharashtra	86	58	122	58	4.2	2.4	14.5
'North-East'	127	98	140	100	15.3	3.9	9.8
Odisha	81	59	100	73	24.8	3.1	10.4
Punjab	133	92	143	86	11.8	3.3	3.4

Rajasthan	132	94	146	100	8.5	2.1	7.3
Tamil Nadu	132	73	155	76	3.4	2.6	24.5
Uttar Pradesh	97	69	109	72	5.9	2.2	1.8
Uttarakhand	122	96	141	99	5.6	1.7	2.9
West Bengal	88	66	99	78	3.1	2.6	17.8
India	**102**	**69**	**132**	**77**	**9.0**	**2.8**	**11.4**

a Excluding public works

Sources: **Population, 2011:** Government of India (2011b), Statement 3, p. 47, based on Census data. **Average household expenditure per capita, 2009–10:** National Sample Survey Office (2011b), Tables T5C-R and T5C-U, pp. 26–7. **Growth rate of per capita state domestic product:** Calculated (by semi-log regression) from SDP data presented in Reserve Bank of India (2012). The all-India figure applies to per capita net national product at 2004–5 prices. **Poverty estimates, 2009–10:** Planning Commission estimates based on National Sample Survey data, presented in Government of India (2012c), p. 29. **Proportion of population falling in India's lowest wealth quintile, 2005–6:** International Institute for Population Sciences (2007a), Table 2.7, p. 44, based on the third National Family Health Survey (NFHS-3). **Multi-dimensional poverty, 2005–6:** Alkire, Roche and Seth (2011). **Life expectancy at birth, 2006–10:** Government of India (2012j), based on Sample Registration System (SRS) data. **Infant mortality rate, 2011:** Government of India (2012g), Table 1, based on SRS data. **Under-5 mortality rate, 2011:** Government of India (2012i), based on SRS data. **Maternal mortality ratio, 2007–9:** Government of India (2011), based on SRS data. **Death rate, 2011:** Government of India (2012g), Table 1, based on SRS data. **Total fertility rate, 2010:** Government of India (2012i), based on SRS data. **Birth rate, 2011:** Government of India (2012g), Table 1, based on SRS data. **Literacy rate, age 7+, 2011+:** Government of India (2011b), Statement 22(d)2, p. 106, based on Census data. **Literacy and schooling achievements, in the 15–19 age group, 2007–8:** Compiled from Table 2.4 of the state reports of the District Level Household and Facility Survey 2007–8 (International Institute for Population Sciences, 2010b). **Proportion of children aged 6–14 who are currently in school, 2005–6:** Compiled from Table 6 of the NFHS-3 state reports (International Institute for Population Sciences, 2008). **Proportion of never-enrolled children in the 6–14 age group, 2004–5:** Calculated from India Human Development Survey (IHDS) data available at icpsr.umich.edu/icpsrweb/DSDR/studies/22626; see also Desai et al. (2010). **Proportion of children aged 6–14 enrolled in a private school, 2004–5:** Desai et al. (2010), p. 92, based on IHDS data. **Schooling costs:** Desai et al. (2010), p. 84, based on IHDS data. **Drinking water and other facilities in government schools, 2009–10:** National

University of Educational Planning and Administration (2011b), Table 2.1, p. 10. **Proportion of government and government-aided schools providing midday meals:** National University of Educational Planning and Administration (2011a), Table 2.12, p. 69. **Proportion of government schools providing health check-ups,** 2009–10: National University of Educational Planning and Administration (2011b), Table 2.1, p. 10. **Pupil-teacher and pupil-classroom ratios,** 2009–10: National University of Educational Planning and Administration (2011c), pp. 5 and 14. **Female-male ratios,** 2011: Government of India (2011b), Statement 13, p. 88, based on Census data. **Estimated ratio of female to male death rate in the age group of** 1–4, 2007–9: Three-year average calculated from SRS data (Government of India, various years). **Proportion of women aged 25–49 married by age 18,** 2005–6: Compiled from Table 29 of the NFHS-3 state reports (International Institute for Population Sciences, 2008). **Female labour force participation rate,** 2009–10: National Sample Survey Office (2011a), Table S5, p. 33, based on 'current weekly status'. **Proportion of women among organized sector employees, 2009:** Government of India (2011f), Table 2.8, p. 57. **Contraceptive prevalence,** 2005–6: International Institute for Population Sciences (2007a), Table 5.7, p. 127, based on NFHS-3 data. **Proportion of births attended by skilled health personnel,** 2005–6: International Institute for Population Sciences (2007a), Table 8.22, p. 210, based on NFHS-3 data. 'Skilled provider' includes doctor, ANM/nurse/midwife/Lady Health Visitor, and other health personnel. **Coverage of ante-natal care,** 2005–6: International Institute for Population Sciences (2007a), Table 8.10, p. 204, based on NFHS-3 data. **Coverage of post-natal care,** 2005–6: International Institute for Population Sciences (2007a), Table 8.22, p. 220, based on NFHS-3 data. Figures are based on the last live birth in the five years preceding the survey; post-natal check-ups are checks on the woman's health within 42 days of the birth. **Proportion of women aged 15–49 with low BMI,** 2005–6: International Institute for Population Sciences (2007a), Table 10.23.1, p. 308, based on NFHS-3 data; low BMI means a Body Mass Index below 18.5 kg/m^2. **Proportion of women aged 15–49 with any anaemia,** 2005–6: International Institute for Population Sciences (2007a), Table 10.25, p. 313, based on NFHS-3 data. Women are classified as anaemic if their haemoglobin count is below 12.0 g/dll (11.0 g/dl for pregnant women), with adjustments for altitude and smoking status, if known. **Proportion of adult women with moderate or severe anaemia,** 2005–6: International Institute for Population Sciences (2007a), Table 10.25, p. 313, based on NFHS-3 data. Women are classified as moderately or severely anaemic if their haemoglobin count is below 9.9 g/dl, with adjustments for altitude and smoking status, if known. **Proportion of children aged 6–59 months with moderate or severe anaemia,** 2005–6: Calculated from NFHS-3 data presented in the International Institute for Population Sciences (2007a), Table 10.13, p. 290. **Proportion of children below 5 who are undernourished,** 2005–6: International Institute for Population Sciences (2007a), Table 10.2, p. 273, based on NFHS-3 data (using the WHO Child Growth Standards released in 2006). **Proportion of households using adequately iodized salt,** 2005–6: International Institute for Population Sciences (2007a), Table 10.18, p. 298, based on NFHS-3 data. Adequately iodized salt means salt containing more than 15 ppm of iodine. **Immunization** of children aged 12–23 months, 2005–6: International Institute for Population Sciences (2007a), Table 9.5, p. 231, based on NFHS-3 data. Full immunization means all BCG, measles, and three does each of DPT and polio vaccines (excluding polio vaccine given at birth). **Coverage of Vitamin A supplementation among children aged 12–35 months, 2005–6:** International Institute for Population Sciences (2007a), Table 10.16, p. 295, based on NFHS-3 data. **Breastfeeding practices, 2007–8:** International Institute for Population Sciences (2010a), Table 5.5, p. 88, based on the District Level Household and Facility Survey 2007–8 (DLHS-3). **Proportion of children aged c–3 years who suffer from diarrhoea, 2007–8:** International Institute for Population Sciences (2010a), Table 5.13, p. 102, based on DLHS-3 data. **Proportion of children with diarrhoea who were treated with ORS therapy, 2005–6:** International Institute for Population Sciences (2007a), Table 9.13, p. 245, based on NFHS-3 data. ORS therapy means giving oral rehydration solution or 'gruel' to children with diarrhoea. **Average population per PHC, 2007–8:** International Institute for Population Sciences (2010a), Table 9.1, p. 213, based on DLHS-3 data. **Other indicators (Part 10), 2007–8:** International Institute for Population Sciences (2010a), Tables 9.6, 9.7 and 9.8, pp. 219–21, based on DLHS-3 data. **Proportion of villages with school, health or anganwadi facilities, 2007–8:** International Institute for Population Sciences (2010a), Table 2.13, p. 29, based on DLHS-3 data. **Proportion of households with various amenities, 2007–8:** International Institute for Population Sciences (2007a), Table 2.9, p. 22, based on DLHS-3 data. **Effective coverage of anganwadi services, 2005–6:** International Institute for Population Sciences (2007a), Table 9.19, p. 254, based on NFHS-3 data. **Proportion of rural households employed under NREGA, 2009–10:** Dutta et al. (2012), Table 1, p. 57, based on National Sample Survey data. **Proportion of households having various amenities, 2011:** Government of India (2012h), based on Census data. **Periodicals circulated per 100 persons, 2010:** Calculated from Audit Bureau of Circulation (2010). **Proportion of adults exposed to various media, 2005–6:** International Institute for Population Sciences (2007a), Table 3.6.1 and 3.6.2, pp. 68–9, based on NFHS-3 data. **Voter turnout, Lok Sabha elections, 2009:** Election Commission of India (2009), Chapter 3, Figure 3.1. **Share of women in Lok Sabha seats, 2009:** Election Commission of India (2009), Chapter 3, Figure 3.1. **Share of women in Rajya Sabha seats, 2012:** Secretariat of the Rajya Sabha (2012). **Share of women in Legislative Assembly seats, 2013:** Compiled from websites of state governments and legislative assemblies. **Proportion of Lok Sabha candidates/MPs with pending criminal cases, 2009:** Association for Democratic Reforms (2010), p. 11. **Proportion of 'hereditary MPs' among Lok Sabha MPs, 2010:** The India Site (2011). **Average number of days of Assembly sittings in a year, 2000–10:** PRS Legislative Research (2011). **Average daily wages/ earnings of casual labourers, 2009–10:** National Sample Survey Office (2011a), Table S-39, pp. 95–6. **Proportion of persons aged 60 or above getting old-age or widow pension, 2004–5:** Desai et al. (2010), p. 206, based on IHDS data. **Murder rate, 2010:** Calculated from National Crime Records Bureau (2011b), Table 3.1, and population figures from Census of India 2011. **Suicide rate, 2010:** National Crime Records Bureau (2011a), p. viii.

Table A.4: Selected Indicators for the North-Eastern States (Part 1)

	Population, 2011 (millions)	Female-male ratio, 2011 (females per 1,000 males)		Average household expenditure per capita, 2009–10 (Rs/month)		Proportion (%) of population falling in India's lowest wealth quintile, 2005–6	Proportion (%) of non-literate persons in the age group 15–19 years, 2007–8		Literacy rate, age 7+, 2011 (%)		Female labour force participation rate, age 15–59 years, 2009–10 (%)
		0–6	All ages	Rural	Urban		Female	Male	Female	Male	
Arunachal Pradesh	1.4	960	920	1,546	1,947	21.1	2.5	2.9	59.6	73.7	39.3
Manipur	2.7	934	987	1,027	1,106	2.4	2.4	3.1	73.2	86.5	27.4
Meghalaya	3.0	970	986	1,110	1,629	11.3	9.6	10.5	73.8	77.2	48.7
Mizoram	1.1	971	975	1,262	1,947	2.5	2.7	2.2	89.4	93.7	49.0
Nagaland	2.0	944	931	1,476	1,862	7.8	n/a	n/a	76.7	83.3	37.0
Sikkim	0.6	944	889	1,321	2,150	1.9	4.8	3.8	76.4	87.3	42.4
Tripura	3.7	953	961	1,176	1,871	11.0	10.3	4.3	83.2	92.2	24.7
'North-East'[a]	14.4	953	961	1,224	1,700	8.9	6.6	5.2	76.4	84.9	35.8
India	1,210.2	914	940	1,054	1,984	20.0	15.8	7.4	65.5	82.1	30.7

[a] Population-weighted average of the state-specific figures (except for the population figure itself, in the first column).

Table A.4: Selected Indicators for the North-Eastern States (Part 2)

| | Proportion (%) of women aged 20–24 married by age 18, 2005–6 | Infant mortality rate, 2011 (per 1,000 live births) | Proportion of children aged below 5 years who are underweight (%) | Proportion of children aged 6–14 who are currently in school, 2005–6 | | Proportion (%) of children aged 12–23 months, with 2005–6 | | Proportion of births assisted by skilled health personnel, 2005–6 (%) |
				Female	Male	Full immunization	No immunization	
Arunachal Pradesh	42.0	32	32.5	69.0	75.8	28.4	24.1	30.2
Manipur	12.9	11	22.1	84.2	85.9	46.8	6.5	59.0
Meghalaya	24.6	52	48.8	68.5	64.3	32.9	16.5	31.1
Mizoram	20.6	34	19.9	88.2	91.5	46.5	7.0	65.4
Nagaland	21.4	21	25.2	78.1	74.9	21.0	18.4	24.7
Sikkim	30.1	26	19.7	82.7	81.8	69.6	3.2	53.7
Tripura	41.6	29	39.6	88.7	86.5	49.7	14.7	48.8
'North-East'[a]	27.9	30	33.2	80.1	79.4	40.3	13.9	43.5
India	**47.4**	**44**	**42.5**	**76.4**	**82.6**	**43.5**	**5.1**	**46.6**

[a] Population-weighted average of the state-specific figures.

Sources: See Table A.3.

Table A.5: Time Trends

	1950–51	1960–61	1970–71	1980–81	1990–91	1993–4	2000–2001	2004–5	2010–11
Population (millions)	361	439	548	683	846	–	1,029	–	1,210
Gross Domestic Product at constant prices (1950–51=100)	100	147	211	286	482	544	838	1,063	1,766
GDP at constant prices (1950–51 = 100)									
Primary sector	100	136	172	204	296	319	394	433	545
Secondary sector	100	183	315	458	811	890	1,421	1,855	3,113
Tertiary sector	100	150	238	364	694	825	1,429	1,909	3,426
Per capita net national product at constant prices (1950–51 = 100)	100	125	141	151	201	213	286	339	511
Index of agricultural production (triennium ending 1981–2 =100)	46.2	68.8	85.9	102.1	148.4	–	165.7	–	215.3
Index of industrial production (1993–4 = 100)	7.9	15.6	28.1	43.1	91.6	100	162.6	204.8	–
Per capita net availability of cereals and pulses[b] (grams/day, three-year average)	397	460	463	440	485	477	455	443	447
Gross domestic capital formation (as % of GDP)	9.3	14.3	15.1	19.2	26.0	22.2	24.4	32.8	36.8

Volume index of foreign trade (1978–9 = 100)									
Exports	–	–	59	108	194	258	576	825	1,401
Imports	–	–	67	138	238	329	698	1,058	2,193
Employment in the organized private sector (million persons)	–	5.0	6.7	7.4	7.7	7.9	8.6	8.5	11.4
Employment in the public sector (million persons)	–	7.1	10.7	15.5	19.1	19.4	19.3	18.0	17.5
Per capita emoluments of central public-sector enterprises (Rs/month at 2010–11 prices)	–	–	10,542	12,141	17,681	19,365	34,296	38,190	61,000
Real wages of male agricultural labourers									
Rs/day at 1960 prices	–	–	1.52	1.65	2.48	2.59	2.95[a]	–	–
Rs/day at 1986–7 prices	–	–	–	–	–	–	17.8	17.6	20.3
Proportion of population below the poverty line (%) Datt and Ravallion estimates based on official poverty line[d]									
Rural	46.5	48.1	56.6	50.7	35.9	37.0	–	28.9	–
Urban	36.8	46.7	46.2	37.8	32.1	30.2	–	25.1	–

(Continued)

Table A.5: (*Continued*)

	1950–51	1960–61	1970–71	1980–81	1990–91	1993–4	2000–2001	2004–5	2010–11
Tendulkar Committee methodology									
Rural	–	–	–	–	–	50.1	–	41.8	33.8[b]
Urban	–	–	–	–	–	31.8	–	25.7	20.9[b]
Gini coefficient of per capita consumer expenditure									
Rural	33.7	32.5	28.8	–	27.7	28.6	26.3[a]	30.5	29.9[b]
Urban	40.0	35.6	34.7	–	34.0	34.3	34.7[a]	37.6	39.3[b]
Literacy rate, age 7 years and above[c] (%)									
Female	9	15	22	30	39	–	54	–	65
Male	27	40	46	56	64	–	76	–	82
Total fertility rate	5.9	5.8	5.2	4.5	3.6	3.5	3.1	2.9	2.4
Infant mortality rate (per 1,000 live births)	≈ 180	n/a	129	110	80	74	66	58	44
Life expectancy at birth (years)	32.1	41.3	45.6	53.9	59.0	60.5	–	63.5	66.1

[a] 1999–2000.
[b] 2009–10.
[c] 2010.

d Unweighted average of the two nearest years for which estimates are available, except in years of NSS 'thick round' (1993–4 and 2004–5).

e Age 5 years and above for 1951, 1961 and 1971.

Sources: **Population:** Government of India (2011b), p. 41, based on decennial censuses. **GDP at constant prices:** Calculated from Government of India (2013). **Per capita net national product at constant prices:** Government of India (2012a), p. A-1. **Index of agricultural production:** Government of India (2012a), p. A-1. **Per capita availability of cereals and pulses:** Government of India (2012a), p. A-1. **Index of industrial production:** Government of India (2012a), p. A-22 (three-year average centred on the reference year, except for 1950–51 and 2010–11 where the three-year averages pertain to 1951–3 and 2009–11 respectively). **Gross domestic capital formation:** Government of India (2013), p. A-11. **Volume index of foreign trade:** Reserve Bank of India (2012), using 1999–2000 as the 'link year' between two different series. **Employment in organized private sector and in the public sector:** Government of India (2013), p. A-56, and Drèze and Sen (2002), Table A.6 ('2000–2001' figure applies to 2000). **Per capita emoluments of employees of central public-sector enterprises:** Calculated from Government of India (2013), p. A-57 (using the Consumer Price Index for Industrial Workers as deflator). **Real wages of male agricultural labourers:** Drèze and Sen (2002), Table A.6; the second series was calculated from Usami (2012), based on the Labour Bureau's 'Wage Rates in Rural India' database, partly published in Wage Rates in Rural India (the figures in this series pertain to 'unskilled labour' and are three-year averages centred on the reference year, except for the last figure which is a two-year average). **Head-count index of poverty:** Datt and Ravallion (2010), Government of India (2009c), and Government of India (2012c), based on National Sample Survey data. **Gini coefficients:** Jayaraj and Subramanian (2012), Table 1, for 1993–2000, 2004–5 and 2009–10; Drèze and Sen (2002), Table A.6, for earlier years. **Literacy rates:** Decennial censuses (see Government of India 2011b). The 1981 literacy rates exclude Assam, and the 1991 literacy rates exclude Jammu and Kashmir. **Total fertility rate:** United Nations Population Division (2011), for 1951 and 1961; Sample Registration System data (Government of India, 2011f, 2012i) from 1971 onwards. **Infant mortality rate:** Government of India (1999, 2011f, 2012g), Table 1, and Government of India (2011f), p. 3. The 1951 estimate is from Dyson (1997), pp. 111–17. **Life expectancy at birth:** Up to 1970–71: Census-based estimates presented in Government of India (2001b), p. S-1; 1980–81, 1990–91 and 1993–4: SRS-based estimates presented in Government of India (1999); 2004–5: Government of India (2008), estimate for 2002–6; 2010–11: Government of India (2012i), estimate for 2006–10. See also Drèze and Sen (2002), Statistical Appendix, Table A.6.

Note: In cases where the original source gives figures for calendar years, we have placed the figure for a particular year in the column corresponding to the pair of years *ending* in that year (e.g. the 1991 literacy rate appears in the 1990–91 column).

Notes

I A NEW INDIA?

1. Among these gaps are important breaches of democratic norms associated with the role of the military in specific parts of the country, particularly Kashmir and parts of the North-East, with draconian laws that give sweeping powers to the armed forces. The fact that these powers of the military are determined by the civilian and democratically elected government at the centre does not eliminate the violation of human rights as well as of local democratic norms involved in the existence of such authoritarian power in the locations involved. We shall return to this issue in Chapter 9.

2. 'India's Novartis Decision', *The New York Times*, 5 April 2013. *The Times*, commenting on the Indian Supreme Court's decision to prevent 'evergreening' of old drugs through new patents by making small variations, pointed to the fact that the Indian produced drug Gleevec ('a highly effective treatment of leukemia') costs 'less than one-20th of the roughly $70,000 a year it costs in the United States'.

3. For more detailed information on long-term trends in India since independence, see Statistical Appendix, Table A.5.

4. This was part of Dr Ambedkar's 'final words of advice' at the All-India Depressed Classes Conference held in Nagpur in 1942; quoted in Keer (1971), p. 351.

5. *World Development Indicators* (online, 1 January 2013). See also Statistical Appendix, Table A.3.

6. This is one important insight from the periodic surveys conducted by the Centre for the Study of Developing Societies (CSDS, New Delhi); see Chapter 9.

7. There have been some mild Internet restrictions (or attempted restrictions) in the recent past, for instance on allegedly inflammatory material, and in some cases also in the form of clumsy (and mostly unsuccessful)

337

attempts to defuse certain kinds of government criticism. More importantly, there are significant restrictions on Internet access in Kashmir and parts of the North-East.

8. This is another insight that emerges from the CSDS surveys (see Chapter 9); see also Sanjay Kumar (2009) and Ahuja and Chhibber (2012).

9. Death-penalty figures are a state secret in China, but there are empirically researched estimates based on such sources as reports of actual executions in local newspapers. According to Amnesty International (2012), 'thousands of people . . . were believed to have been executed in China in 2011' (p. 7), compared with none in India in the same year. However, the handing down of death sentences, with rare or no execution, continues in a distressing way in India (110 persons had been sentenced to death in India in 2011 alone), and given the absence of actual execution, there is an accumulation of people in jails who are meant to be awaiting execution (though in fact they may not be actually executed). There is a strong movement in India for a major reform of capital punishment laws, both in favour of abolishing the death penalty altogether (which has been abolished in a great many countries in the world – a position with which we agree) and against the psychological tormenting involved in 'death penalty but possibly no death'.

10. We have discussed the distinctions involved in *Hunger and Public Action* (Drèze and Sen, 1989) and *India: Development and Participation* (Drèze and Sen, 2002); see also N. Ram (1990).

11. On both episodes (the dismantling of the cooperative medical system in the late 1970s, and reinstatement of social health insurance in 2004), see e.g. Shaoguang Wang (2008). See also Chapter 3.

2 INTEGRATING GROWTH AND DEVELOPMENT

1. These figures are based on data from the International Monetary Fund and the World Bank; see Alan Wheatley (2012).

2. The underlying reasoning behind the Indian position was well presented by Montek Singh Ahluwalia (2010).

3. See Adam Smith (1776), Book I, Chapter XI; Pliny the Elder, *Natural History*, Book 6; McCrindle (1885). Poverty and famines, of course, were also common features of India's pre-colonial history. But that applies to other regions of the globe as well, including Europe.

4. Adam Smith (1776), Book IV, Chapter IX, p. 683.

5. Prasannan Parthasarathi (2011), Chapter 2, especially pp. 38–39.

6. Adam Smith (1776), Book IV, Chapter V, p. 527.

7. See Sivasubramonian (2000), Table 7.4; also Amiya Bagchi (2010).

8. See e.g. the poverty estimates presented in Datt and Ravallion (2010).

9. Pulapre Balakrishnan's recent work (Balakrishnan, 2007, 2010) has been of much value in clarifying the nature of economic policies in the early post-independence period. See also Ashok Rudra (1975), P. B. Desai (1979), I. G. Patel (1987), Sukhamoy Chakravarty (1987), Little and Joshi (1994) and Bhagwati and Panagariya (2013), among others.

10. Planning Commission (1951), Chapter 33.

11. Even an economist like Raj Krishna, who was very critical of the 'licence Raj' and an early advocate of liberalization, considered that many of the early planning initiatives (such as 'the building up of a strong and diversified capital goods base') were 'a historical necessity' (Raj Krishna, 1982, quoted in Balakrishnan, 2007, p. 56).

12. Calculated from Government of India (2012a), Statistical Appendix, Table 1.4, p. A7.

13. Lal Bahadur Shastri, Prime Minister for one and a half years from June 1964, made a brief attempt to liberalize the economy, initially sustained by Indira Gandhi (who was under pressure from international donors, including the IMF and the World Bank, when war and crop failures led to a balance of payments crisis in 1966). Indira Gandhi's rapprochement with Washington and the devaluation of the rupee in 1966 did not go down well with the public and she soon made a U-turn. On this and other aspects of Indira Gandhi's economic policies, see Hankla (2006) and earlier work cited there.

14. Hankla (2006), p. 11. On the nationalization of banks, see also I. G. Patel (2002).

15. See Drèze and Sen (1995), Table 9.3; also Himanshu (2005) and Table A.5 in the Statistical Appendix of this book. There is also some evidence that per capita expenditure rose faster for the poor than for the rich in the 1980s, at least in rural areas (see Deaton and Drèze, 2009, Table 4).

16. See e.g. Datt and Ravallion (2010). See also Statistical Appendix, Table A.5.

17. Arunabha Ghosh (2006: 419). The initial round of economic reforms is not usually described in India as an IMF-imposed stabilization programme, but that is more or less what it was, even though the Finance Minister 'insisted [in Parliament] that India was bound only by the conditionalities it had proposed' (Ghosh, 2006: 418).

18. Calculated from data on per capita expenditure at constant prices from the National Sample Survey Office (2011b); see also Shalini Gupta (2012), Table 1. These figures should be read in the light of a growing gap, over time, between NSSO data on per capita expenditure and indirect estimates

of average consumer expenditure from the 'national accounts' (which tend to be higher). The most obvious explanation is that there is growing underestimation, in the National Sample Surveys, of consumer expenditure at the top (for instance because rich people often do not cooperate with the survey, or understate their expenditure). As one recent study puts it, 'it seems likely that the surveys are missing the growth in top-end incomes' (World Bank, 2011a, p. xvii). In any case, as the same study also mentions, there is no obvious reason why the NSSO surveys would seriously misrepresent the growth of per capita expenditure *among the poor*, which is our main concern here.

19. See e.g. Deaton and Drèze (2009), Table 4.

20. This development, incidentally, appears to have been greeted with consternation in particular business and policy circles, and there have been some attempts to restrain this so-called 'wage boom' (Aiyar, 2011a, 2011b), notably by de-linking NREGA from minimum wage laws. For further discussion, see Chapter 7.

21. See UNCTAD (2011), Table 1.4.

22. See e.g. Tao Yang et al. (2010), who 'document dramatic rising wages in China for the period 1978–2007 based on multiple sources of aggregate statistics' (p. 482). The authors estimate that real wages increased about sevenfold over this period.

23. On this see also Rajakumar (2011) and Asian Development Bank (2012). While the share of labour income in industrial value added has declined in many countries over the same period, this is one of the steepest declines on record, and the Indian ratio today is one of the lowest in the world.

24. See Government of India (2009c), p. 14, and Government of India (2012c), Table 2. Both figures are based on the 'Tendulkar poverty line', using the same methodology.

25. See particularly Figure 13, p. 1, 186, and the authors' discussion of it. For further evidence, from different perspectives, of the sluggish pace of poverty decline in India during the last twenty years, see also Jayaraj and Subramanian (2010), Lenagala and Ram (2010), Alkire and Seth (2013), Kotwal and Roy Chaudhuri (2013), among others.

26. The poverty line was later revised upwards, based on the recommendations of the Tendulkar Committee report (Government of India, 2009c).

27. There is a considerable literature on this (especially jobless growth in organized manufacturing, which is particularly conspicuous) and related issues. See Alessandrini (2009), Nagaraj (2004, 2011), Kannan and Raveendran (2009), Kotwal et al. (2011), Rajakumar (2011) and Thomas (2012), among others.

28. To quote Kotwal et al. (2011) again: '. . . there are two Indias: one of educated managers and engineers who have been able to take advantage of the opportunities made available through globalization and the other – a huge mass of undereducated people who are making a living in low productivity jobs in the informal sector – the largest of which is still agriculture' (p. 1,196).

29. For further discussion, see Deaton and Drèze (2009). As the authors note, it is possible that the decline of nutrient intakes is partly driven by a reduction in calorie and other nutritional requirements, e.g. due to lower activity levels or an improved epidemiological environment. But they also emphasize that, had per capita incomes increased more rapidly among the poor, this decline in requirements (such as it may be) would have been more than compensated by the positive effects of higher incomes on nutrient intake. Thus, the (unconfirmed) hypothesis of changing requirements does not obviate the need for concern about the decline of average nutrient intakes.

30. The literature on this is vast, but see, among other contributions, Douglass North (1990), Ha–Joon Chang (2002, 2010), Elhanan Helpman (2004), Pranab Bardhan (2005), Eric Beinhocker (2006), and Trebilcock and Daniels (2008).

31. Acemoglu and Robinson (2012), p. 118.

32. Acemoglu and Robinson (2012), p. 119.

33. Mokyr (2002); Helpman (2004).

34. Glaeser et al. (2004).

35. Trebilcock and Prado (2011), p. 36.

36. See Drèze and Sen (2002), and the literature cited there.

37. See Yale Center for Environmental Law and Policy and Columbia Center for International Earth Science Information Network (2012). In terms of overall 'environmental performance', India ranks 125th among these 132 countries, and last within the 'Asia and Pacific' region (21 countries including Bangladesh, China, Pakistan and Nepal).

38. UNU-IHDP and UNEP (2012), pp. 310–11. However, these are rough estimates, based on a somewhat exploratory method.

39. Brijesh Pandey (2012), based on information obtained from the government under the Right to Information Act, suggesting that more than 600 dams (including 155 'medium and large dams') are being planned in this river basin.

40. Ramachandra Guha (2012). On India's environmental irresponsibility, see also Praful Bidwai (2012), Shrivastava and Kothari (2012), and the periodic reports of the Centre for Science and Environment on 'the state of India's environment' (e.g. Centre for Science and Environment, 2012).

41. On this see Drèze and Sen (2002), Chapter 6. See also Sen (2009).
42. Nicholas Stern (2009, 2012).

3 INDIA IN COMPARATIVE PERSPECTIVE

1. Anand Giridharadas (2011), p. 1.
2. See Drèze and Sen (2002), Chapter 3.
3. *World Development Indicators*, online. Age-specific literacy rates from the Census of India 2011 are not available at the time of writing, and it is quite possible that India's (and therefore South Asia's) literacy figures will improve somewhat after they are released.
4. See Chapter 6, Table 6.3.
5. Recent work on multidimensional poverty indexes, partly presented in *Human Development Report 2013*, suggests astonishingly rapid progress in Nepal between 2006 and 2011 (Sabina Alkire, personal communication). This new development is yet to be fully investigated.
6. OXFAM International (2006), p. 9.
7. See e.g. Chaudhury and Hammer (2004), with reference to health facilities.
8. For useful contributions to a better understanding of these achievements, see S. R. Osmani (1991, 2010), Simeen Mahmud (2003), B. Sen et al. (2007), World Bank (2007), Wahiduddin Mahmud (2008), Begum and Sen (2009), Naila Kabeer (2011), Koehlmoos et al. (2011), David Lewis (2011), Rehman Sobhan (2011), Chowdhury et al. (2012), among others.
9. On this connection see Drèze and Sen (1989, 2002) and Sen (1999). According to World Bank data, 'women's participation in economic activity [in Bangladesh] increased from 9% in 1983 to 57% in 2011' (Chowdhury et al., 2012). Even allowing for a substantial margin of error in the earlier estimates, this points to an astonishing increase in the participation of women in the economy, which has absolutely no parallel in India.
10. The last point should be read in light of the fact that there is some reservation of parliamentary seats for women in Bangladesh; see e.g. P. K. Panday (2008). In India, a constitutional amendment proposed for this purpose (the 'Women's Reservation Bill') has been held up in the Indian Parliament for many years.
11. See Drèze and Sen (2002), and the literature cited there; also Chapter 8 of this book.
12. See e.g. Chowdhury et al. (2012).
13. For further discussion, see Chapter 8.
14. There is also a possibility that lack of sanitation facilities is playing a major role in the persistence of exceptionally high levels of child under-

nutrition in India; on this, see Dean Spears (2012a, 2012b, 2013). In a few countries such as Chad and Eritrea, the incidence of open defecation is as high as (or even a little higher than) in India. But no country seems to come close to India in terms of the intensity of open defecation per square mile, which – it has been argued – is what really matters from the point of view of health hazards, including child undernutrition (Dean Spears, personal communication).

15. In some Indian states, the use of toilets is difficult to promote because of inadequate water supply facilities. Bangladesh, where there is abundant groundwater, may have a 'comparative advantage' in this respect. But even Indian states that are well endowed with groundwater (West Bengal, Uttar Pradesh, Bihar, among others) have much higher rates of open defecation than Bangladesh, e.g. 39 per cent in West Bengal and 63 per cent in Uttar Pradesh; see Statistical Appendix, Table A.3.

16. See e.g. Zafrullah Chowdhury (1995).

17. See Mahmud (2008), Chowdhury et al. (2012), El Arifeen et al. (2012), among others.

18. The proportion of the rural population covered by the cooperative medical system crashed from 90 per cent to 10 per cent between 1976 and 1983 (the period when market-oriented reforms were initiated), and stayed around 10 per cent for a full 20 years. From 2004, when the 'new cooperative medical scheme' was launched, it rose again to more than 90 per cent within a few years; see Shaoguang Wang (2008), Figure 6. On China's new cooperative medical scheme, see also Yip and Mahal (2008), Lin Chen et al. (2012), Qun Meng et al. (2012), Yip et al. (2012), among others.

19. On this, see e.g. Joseph Stiglitz (2002), Chapter 5.

20. See e.g. Alfio Cerami (2009). On 'postcommunist welfare states' in the former Soviet Union and Eastern Europe, see Mitchell Orenstein (2008) and the literature cited there.

21. See e.g. Barr and Harbison (1994). As the authors observe (p. 17), based on 1991 data: 'What is noteworthy about social spending in Central and Eastern Europe is that it does not differ greatly as a proportion of GDP from spending in the highly industrialized economies, whose per capita incomes are much higher.'

22. See Drèze and Sen (1989), particularly Chapter 10; also Drèze and Sen (1995).

23. Drèze and Sen (1995), p. 183.

24. See Cataife and Courtemanche (2011), da Silva and Terrazas (2011), Comim (2012), Comim and Amaral (2012), among other critiques.

25. Jurberg and Humphreys (2010), p. 646. Another recent study (Cataife and Courtemanche 2011) suggests that access to public health care in

Brazil is now more or less independent of income within localities, even though regional disparities persist. On Brazil's health system, see also the collection of papers published in *The Lancet* on 21 May 2011, particularly Paim et al. (2011), and the literature cited there.

26. Sonia Fleury (2011), p. 1724.

27. See Martin Ravallion (2011), Tables 1 and 2. For further discussion of economic inequality in India, see Chapter 8.

28. See e.g. Ferreira de Souza (2012), and the literature cited there.

29. For a helpful introduction to *Bolsa Família*, see Fabio Soares (2011); see also Francesca Bastagli (2008, 2011), Soares et al. (2010), Ferreira de Souza (2012) and the literature cited there. Bolsa Família is, however, only one programme (though it has received enormous attention abroad), and Brazil's social security system extends much beyond this particular scheme.

30. Partly due to social assistance programmes, the incomes of the poor in Brazil grew quite rapidly during this period, in spite of the near-stagnation of per capita GDP (Ferreira et al., 2010). This is in sharp contrast with the situation in India, where, as we noted in Chapter 2, the growth of per capita expenditure among the poor was just a fraction of the growth of per capita GDP during the last twenty years or so.

31. On this see e.g. Bruns et al. (2012), and earlier work cited there.

32. Bruns et al. (2012), Figure 1, p. 5, showing that the proportion of Brazilian children enrolled in private schools at the primary level hovered around 10 per cent between 1991 and 2009. In India, the proportion of children studying in private schools at the elementary level (roughly corresponding to Brazil's primary level) was already as high as 28 per cent in 2004–5 (see Statistical Appendix, Table A.3), and is growing rapidly. For further discussion of India's schooling system, see Chapter 5.

33. Bruns et al. (2012).

34. Ferreira de Souza (2012), Table 3, p. 9.

35. Ferreira de Souza (2012), Figure 5, p. 10.

36. Bruns et al. (2012). On the PISA study, see also Chapter 5.

37. Based on data reported in Bruns et al. (2012), p. xxii. This statement applies not only to years of schooling (about eight on average, for a 20-year-old in the poorest income group in 2009), but also, to a large extent, to pupil achievements as measured by PISA test scores, at least in mathematics.

38. See Gastón Pierri (2012), Graphic 2, p. 11 (the reference year is 2008); see also Ferreira and Robalino (2010), Table 2, p. 37. Brazil and Cuba have similar levels of public expenditure on health and social security, as a proportion of GDP (close to 20 per cent in both cases). However, Cuba

spends much more on education, and therefore, on the social sectors (health, education and social security) as a whole.

39. On this point, see Lloyd-Sherlock (2009).

40. This section draws on more detailed analyses of the development experiences of Kerala, Himachal Pradesh and Tamil Nadu in our earlier work (Drèze and Sen, 2002), as well as on more recent studies of these experiences. On Tamil Nadu, see also Chapter 6.

41. The idea of multi-dimensional poverty is that poverty manifests itself in multiple deprivations, such as poor health, lack of education, absence of sanitation facilities, and various kinds of material deprivations. A person is counted as 'multi-dimensionally poor' if he or she experiences at least a certain proportion (say one third) of these deprivations. This approach can help to make detailed comparisons of living standards across countries, regions or communities, going beyond income-based criteria such as the World Bank's universal benchmark of 'two dollars a day' (adjusted for purchasing power parity). For further examination and use of this approach, see Alkire and Foster (2011).

42. These states – minus Odisha – used to be known by the unflattering acronym of BIMARU (*bimar* means 'ill' in Hindi), which referred to undivided Bihar (including Jharkhand), undivided Madhya Pradesh (including Chhattisgarh), Rajasthan and Uttar Pradesh. The acronym was sometimes modified to BIMAROU, to include Odisha.

43. See Alkire and Santos (2012) and Alkire and Seth (2012). The 'multi-dimensional poverty index' (MPI) is the percentage of multi-dimensionally poor persons in the population multiplied by the average number of deprivations they have.

44. These 27 countries are (in descending order of MPI): Niger, Ethiopia, Mali, Burkina Faso, Burundi, Somalia, Central African Republic, Mozambique, Guinea, Liberia, Angola, Sierra Leone, Rwanda, Benin, Comoros, DR Congo, Senegal, Malawi, Tanzania, Uganda, Madagascar, Côte d'Ivoire, Mauritania, Chad, Zambia, Gambia and Nigeria. Their combined population is around 600 million, of which 71 per cent are estimated to live in multi-dimensional poverty. In the seven Indian states mentioned in the text, 70 per cent of the population are estimated to live in multi-dimensional poverty. For further details of the basis of these calculations, see Alkire and Santos (2012).

45. According to Gaurav Datt and Martin Ravallion's time series of state-specific poverty estimates (analysed in Datt et al., 2003), Kerala was the poorest Indian state in the 1950s and 1960s, in terms of the proportion of the population below the poverty line. Tamil Nadu was also

among the poorest states (more or less on a par with Bihar), while Punjab and Haryana already had much lower poverty levels than any other major state at that time. We are grateful to Gaurav Datt for sharing these unpublished poverty estimates.

46. See Drèze and Sen (1989, 1995, 2002), V. K. Ramachandran (1996), and the literature cited there; also Patrick Heller (1999, 2000, 2009), M. A. Oommen (1999, 2009), Achin Chakraborty (2005), Prerna Singh (2010a, 2010b), among others. The term 'Kerala model' has often been used in this literature, and more distressingly has occasionally been attributed – entirely erroneously – to our analysis. We have never used this particular rhetoric. There is much to learn from scrutinizing the experience of Kerala – and of the other high-performing states – but there is little evidence for seeing Kerala as a model to be mechanically emulated.

47. See e.g. Isaac and Tharakan (1995) and Tharamangalam (1998). While some of these warnings were simple prophecies of gloom, others proved to be useful enough in that they drew attention to some deficiencies in Kerala's approach, including the need for more constructive economic policies with attention paid to the role of markets, and may have contributed to the policy revisions that happened later, contributing to the rapid economic growth complementing and sustaining the state's active social policies.

48. On the 'schooling revolution' in Himachal Pradesh, see PROBE Team (1999) and De et al. (2011). On Himachal Pradesh's development experience, see Kiran Bhatty (2011) and the literature cited there.

49. See e.g. Government of India (1993) and World Bank (2011a).

50. On this see particularly Vivek Srinivasan (2010).

51. See M. A. Oommen (2009), Harriss et al. (2010), Prerna Singh (2010a, 2010b), Vivek Srinivasan (2010), among others.

52. See e.g. M. A. Oommen (2009), with reference to Kerala, aptly described by the author as 'a movement society par excellence; not only political, but also social, cultural and environmental movements' (p. 31).

4 ACCOUNTABILITY AND CORRUPTION

1. See Pranab Bardhan (2010), particularly Chapter 4. For a more detailed account of the development of the power sector in China, see Center for Environmental Science and Policy (2006).

2. Bardhan (2010), pp. 56–7. The losses of state electricity distribution companies are estimated to cost as much as 2 percent of India's GDP (Chitnis et al. 2012).

3. Gurcharan Das (2012) points to an important analysis by the Santhanam Committee in 1966, offering an insight into the process of public decision-making that still remains sadly relevant (p. 224): 'To avoid direct responsibility for any major policy decision, efforts are made to get as many departments and officials associated with such decisions as is considered desirable. Again, such consultation must be in writing; otherwise there would be nothing on record. Therefore a file must move – which itself requires some time – from one table to another and from one Ministry to another for comments and it is months before the decision is conveyed to the party concerned.'

4. On this 'structural disincentive' in the power sector, see particularly Prayas Energy Group (2012).

5. See e.g. Integrated Research and Action for Development (2012). According to this report, telecom towers alone consume 2.75 billion litres of subsidized diesel per year, at a cost of Rs 2,500 crores to the exchequer. Were they to run on solar power instead, this would also avert 5.2 million tonnes of carbon dioxide emissions per year.

6. There is a view that reducing fuel subsidies hurts poor families because of the 'cascading effects' of higher fuel prices on other prices. However, subsidizing fuel (mainly for the benefit of the rich) is a roundabout and wasteful way of protecting the purchasing power of the poor – directly supporting them (through food subsidies, guaranteed employment, cash transfers, public health care, and so on) is much more effective. It is also far from clear that reducing fuel subsidies actually helps to contain price increases, since fiscal deficits tend to have an inflationary effect (IRADe, 2012). The environmental damage caused by indiscriminate fuel subsidies, including air pollution, enhanced carbon emissions and the depletion of groundwater resources, reinforces the case for a different approach.

7. See e.g. Gulati and Narayanan (2003) and Shenggen Fan et al. (2008).

8. Some studies and writings do shed useful light on these matters; see e.g. Srivastava et al. (2003), Howes and Murgai (2006), Kirit Parikh (2010), Surya Sethi (2010), Mukesh Anand (2012), IRADe (2012), Lahoti et al. (2012).

9. Calculated from Government of India (2012e), p. 36. A series of expert reports, including the second 'Kelkar Committee' report (Government of India, 2004a), have made a strong case for dropping many exemptions as well as for widening the tax base and enforcing better compliance with the tax rules. However, there has been relatively little progress on this front, and this is one reason for India's low and stagnant tax/GDP

ratio. Here again, there are interesting contrasts between India and China, including the very much wider base of personal income taxes in China (about 20 per cent of the population in 2008) compared with India (about 2 per cent); on this, see Piketty and Qian (2009).

10. The handing over of valuable natural resources (such as land, coal, gas, minerals and spectrum) at highly concessional prices to private companies is yet another example of ill-aimed public largesse, recently highlighted by a wave of resource-related scandals (of which 'Coalgate' and the allocation of '2G' spectrum received understandable public criticism).

11. See e.g. Arundhati Roy (1999), Padel and Das (2010) and Shrivastava and Kothari (2012). The number of people involuntarily displaced by development projects since independence (not counting displacement due to violent conflict) is estimated to be around 60 million, mostly consisting of Adivasis, Dalits and other vulnerable groups. According to a recent submission of India's National Human Rights Council to the United Nations Human Rights Council, 'usually those displaced are given neither adequate relief nor the means of rehabilitation'. See Planning Commission (2011b), p. 50, and Working Group on Human Rights in India and the UN (2012), p. 4 and Annex E.

12. What James Martin calls the 'Russian roulette with civilization' in his wonderfully interesting – and chilling – forthcoming book, *The War and Peace of the Nuclear Age*, applies not merely to the presence of nuclear weapons in the world, but in many ways also to the widespread use of civilian nuclear energy, with inadequate protection against accidents and subversion and theft.

13. For instance, in a 1994 assessment by the IAEA, *all* of India's nuclear reactors (there were nine at that time) were found to be among the 50 least reliable in the world (out of a total of 399), and four were among the worst six; see Peter Arnett (1998). These assessments can be – and have been – challenged, but it would be very hard to deny that the risk evaluation of Indian nuclear power plants is severely incomplete and this is indeed a cause for justified anxiety. On these and related issues, see also M. V. Ramana (2012).

14. For enlightening examples of the use of social audits to restore transparency and accountability in various contexts, see e.g. Aakella and Kidambi (2007), Dipa Sinha (2008) and Kidambi (2011).

15. That is indeed one lesson from the relative success of the Right to Information Act: penalties on recalcitrant officials are actually imposed only in a small number of cases, but the fear of penalty does keep most of them on their toes.

16. See Basu (2011). For a critical comment, see Drèze (2011).

17. Section 12 states that 'abetting' an offence punishable under the Act (such as taking a bribe) is itself a punishable offence. Section 24 exempts from prosecution under Section 12 anyone who testifies to having 'offered or agreed to offer' a bribe to a public servant.

18. In China, apparently, the Amended Criminal Law of 1997 already states that giving a bribe is a crime only when it is paid 'for the purpose of obtaining unjust benefits'; see Xingxing Li (2012), who also argues that this initiative actually had a limited impact on the incidence of corruption in China.

19. Noorani (2012). The author argues that 'no other democracy' has the sort of immunity provisions that are available to public servants and elected representatives in India.

20. See Central Information Commission (2012), Table 2.1, p. 10. Insightful evaluations of India's Right to Information Act include Society for Participatory Research in Asia (2008, 2009), Price Waterhouse Coopers (2009), Public Cause Research Foundation (2009), RTI Assessment and Analysis Group (2009); for a useful review, see Alasdair Roberts (2010).

21. For further discussion of the Public Distribution System, see Chapter 7.

22. These and related issues (technical reliability, potential misuse, privacy concerns, among others) have emerged sharply in the recent debate about India's 'unique identity' (UID) project; see e.g. Usha Ramanathan (2010), R. S. Sharma (2010), Reetika Khera (2011a), Bharat Bhatti (2012).

23. Chattopadhyay and Duflo (2004). Also of interest, in the context of the National Rural Employment Guarantee Act, is the fact that corruption seems to be easier to control when NREGA works are implemented by Gram Panchayats than when they are implemented by centralized government departments (such as the Forest Department or Irrigation Department); see Reetika Khera (2011d).

24. Gabrielle Kruks-Wisner (2012). See also Kruks-Wisner (2011), where the author observes that disadvantaged groups in Tamil Nadu, including women and Dalits, seem to have more voice in Gram Panchayats than in traditional institutions.

25. Organizations and collectives such as the Association for Democratic Rights, the National Campaign for People's Right to Information, India Against Corruption, the Aam Aadmi Party, and hundreds of smaller initiatives at local or state levels have played a crucial role in this revival of public interest in (and involvement with) issues of accountability, transparency and participatory democracy.

26. Centre for Media Studies (2011), pp. 3–5.
27. Adam Smith, *The Theory of Moral Sentiments* (1759, 1790), Part Three, Chapter Two.

5 THE CENTRALITY OF EDUCATION

1. Interview with *Izvestia*, 1930, quoted in Dutta and Robinson (1995), p. 297.
2. On this see Sen (2009), Chapter 17, and also Katharine Young (2012).
3. Salma Sobhan (1978).
4. See Chapter 8, and the literature cited there.
5. See PROBE Team (1999) and Pratichi Trust (2002, 2009a).
6. Sometimes, though rather rarely, a reluctance on the part of children to attend school has been observed, particularly connected with the austere methods of teaching and the use of corporal punishment (see Pratichi Trust, 2012a, 2012b). But this has to be distinguished from any general reluctance of children to go to school, which was emphatically not observed in the same studies.
7. Adam Smith (1776), I.ii (p. 27), and V.i.f (p. 785).
8. On the education transition in nineteenth-century Japan, see Ronald Dore (1965), Carol Gluck (1985), Marius Jansen (1989, 2002), among others.
9. See Gluck (1985), p. 166; see also the literature cited there.
10. We have discussed these contrasts in our previous works, particularly in Drèze and Sen (1989, 2002).
11. For further details, including state-specific figures, see Statistical Appendix, Table A.3.
12. On the need for a radical departure in improving the quality of education in non-Western universities, see the Report of the Task Force on Higher Education and Society, set up by UNESCO and the World Bank, and chaired by Mamphela Ramphele and Henry Rosovsky, *Peril and Promise* (2000).
13. See De et al. (2011) and PROBE Team (1999). Himachal Pradesh was also included in these surveys, but the findings for this state were reported separately, as Himachal Pradesh is in a somewhat different category as far as elementary education is concerned (see Chapter 3). For a wealth of further insights on the state of India's schooling system, see also Bhattacharjea et al. (2011).
14. These 'enrolment rates' in the age group of 6–12 years are much higher than the 'school attendance rates' in the 6–14 age group reported earlier in this chapter for the same year (2006), based on the third National

Family Health Survey (NFHS-3). Aside from the difference in age groups, the contrast may be due to the fact that the NFHS definition of school attendance requires more than mere enrolment. As discussed further on, pupil absenteeism rates in India are very high. (There is also a possibility of some underestimation in the NFHS-3 school attendance figures; indeed, it is not clear why some of them are *lower* than the corresponding figures for 1998-9 from NFHS-2.)

15. See De et al. (2011), p. 2. The schools without midday meals were mainly in Bihar, where the programme was still in the process of being put in place in 2006 (despite Supreme Court orders that had made it mandatory to provide midday meals in government primary schools as early as 2002).

16. Reported by R. Venkataramanam (2011); see also Educational Initiatives (2011).

17. See Maurice Walker (2011). About half of the countries or economies included in the survey were OECD countries, but a number of developing countries were also included – Albania, Brazil, Colombia, Kazakhstan, Kyrgystan, Mexico, Thailand, Tunisia, Uruguay, among others.

18. See Pritchett and Pande (2006), Bhattacharjea et al. (2011), Kartik Muralidharan (2012b), Mukerji and Walton (2012), and the literature cited there. See also Pratham Education Foundation (2012, 2013).

19. Pritchett and Beatty (2012), Table 1.

20. On this see also Goyal and Pandey (2012) and Mukerji and Wadhwa (2012).

21. See the latest 'Annual Status of Education Report' (Pratham Education Foundation, 2013), based on a country-wide survey of pupil achievements.

22. This section draws on Sen (2005).

23. This is one insight from the work of the MV Foundation in Andhra Pradesh. The Foundation has rescued thousands of child labourers and helped them to re-enter the schooling system by taking the Class 7 Board Exam. Most of them are able to pass the exam after just one year of intensive coaching.

24. For other perspectives on teacher salaries, leading to similar conclusions, see Geeta Kingdon (2010).

25. See OECD (2011), Chart D3.3 and Table D3.4. Estimates for China (or India) are not available in this publication.

26. See Kartik Muralidharan (2012b). Things might be different, of course, in a system where salaries are related, in one way or another, to teaching standards or teacher competence, but this is not the case in India.

27. For further discussion of this process see Drèze and Sen (2002), Chapter 5, and De et al. (2011); also Kingdon and Sipahimalani-Rao (2010) and the literature cited there.

28. For reviews of the evidence, see e.g. Muralidharan (2012b) and Mukerji and Walton (2012).

29. See e.g. Pritchett and Murgai (2007) and Muralidharan (2012b).

30. On this point, see Jain and Dholakia (2010).

31. A system of school vouchers is often advocated in India as a recipe for curing the defects of the schooling system and restoring accountability. It is indeed tempting to think that a voucher system can transform the schooling system into a thriving market, where schools compete for state subsidies and parents choose intelligently on the basis of the established records of different schools. This advice is, however, typically based on taking little account of the international experience with this approach, which brings out the many complexities and limitations of voucher systems. There are many examples of failures, and the only firm experience of a successful nationwide school voucher system seems to be in Chile, which, however, builds on administrative capacities that are badly lacking in India. The Chilean voucher system also draws on the existence, which has continued, of relatively well-functioning municipal schools that set minimum standards for private schools to match (such public schools still cater to about half of the country's children). The rather theoretical enthusiasm for school vouchers, in India and elsewhere, also benefits from the relatively unexamined belief that private enterprise which works so well in some other fields can help to transform Indian school education as well, if the relatively poorer students can be included in the intake – a belief that draws some strength from political ideology in the face of empirical findings to the contrary (see Belfield and Levin, 2005). On these issues, see also Helen Ladd (2002), Gauri and Vawda (2004), Hsieh and Urquiola (2006), Rouse and Barrow (2009), among others.

32. For an early and enlightening discussion of this 'exit' problem, see Albert Hirschman (1970). As Hirschman observes, the informational problems discussed earlier (specifically, the fact that education is a bit of a 'connoisseur good', as he called it) reinforce the problem.

33. *Economic Times*, 7 June 2012, based on a recent meeting of the Central Advisory Board on Education involving education ministers from several states. Some ministers complained that 'children in government schools are not evaluated at all', with the result that 'parents are no longer being strict with the children to study'. On a more positive note, some states

have made efforts to develop effective tools of comprehensive and continuous evaluation (such as imaginative 'child report cards'). The deployment of these tools on the ground, however, is still at a very early stage, and is likely to require an extended phase of 'learning by doing'.

34. For a summary critique, see PROBE Team (1999), Chapter 6.

35. According to the manual on continuous and comprehensive evaluation at the upper-primary level prepared by the Central Board of Secondary Education (CBSE), children are supposed to be graded based on indicators such as 'takes interest in the national freedom struggle', 'remains cool and calm under adverse conditions', 'finds it natural and easy to share and discuss the feelings with others', 'uses gestures, facial expressions and voice intonations to emphasize points', 'confronts anyone who criticises school and school-based programmes', 'generates computer animation', and 'writes literary criticism'. The teacher is even supposed to grade children based on daily observations of the following sort: 'Sarbari differed with my viewpoint; she argued but never got irritated; but Shanti got angry because Sarbari was arguing with me.' There may well be merit in such comparative 'grading', but it can hardly play the role that more standard grading of educational achievements (including the ability to do well in reading, writing, composing, doing mathematics and gathering useful knowledge) has tended to play across the world. For further discussion of the CBSE manual, see Disha Nawani (2013).

36. This issue is well discussed by Majumdar and Rana (2012).

37. The Right to Information Act does require all teachers to spend a specified number of hours in teaching ('including preparation hours') every month, but this obligation is largely symbolic since there is no way of monitoring preparation time. Similarly, the Act is supposed to make teachers accountable to the 'school management committee' (including parents), but under the Model Rules of the Act, the head teacher of a school is also the convener of this committee. In any case, the committee has no powers of disciplinary action under the Act.

38. See e.g. PROBE Team (1999) and Kartik Muralidharan (2012b).

39. See Government of India (1992).

6 INDIA'S HEALTH CARE CRISIS

1. See Citizens' Initiative for the Rights of Children Under Six (2006), Chapter 1; also HAQ: Centre for Child Rights (2005).

2. Even these countries, however, have higher immunization rates than, say, Uttar Pradesh, which is more than twice as large (in terms of population)

as these four countries combined; see UNICEF and Government of India (2010), Table 4.8, p. 33, and UNICEF (2012), Table 3, pp. 96–99. In fact, even in sub-Saharan Africa, it is only in the most deprived countries (say Chad or Somalia) that child immunization rates are as low as in Uttar Pradesh.

3. This pattern of very slow progress of immunization rates in India in the 1990s and early 2000s emerged quite clearly from the third National Family Health Survey, conducted in 2005-6 (see e.g. International Institute for Population Sciences, 2007a, p. 232), but passed largely unnoticed. As discussed further in this chapter, there are some signs of faster progress in recent years; however, the accumulated deficit of prolonged neglect earlier on is such that India's immunization rates are still very low in international perspective, even today.

4. The eradication of polio in India is an important achievement, but it has come at the price of an unfortunate displacement of many other essential health activities (including routine child immunization) by the 'vertical' polio eradication programme during the last twenty years or so. On this 'paralysis by polio', see e.g. Paul et al. (2011). The entire immunization programme of India demands more public resources, as well as better delivery.

5. Chaudhury et al. (2006). See also Kaveri Gill (2009), who concludes, based on inspections of public health facilities in four states in 2008-9, that absenteeism is 'rife at all levels and across all categories of staff' (p. 32).

6. See Banerjee, Deaton and Duflo (2004).

7. Sreevidya and Sathyasekaran (2003). On related irregularities in the private health sector in India, see also Sunil Nandraj (1997, 2012) and Nandraj et al. (2001).

8. See Das et al. (2012). See also Das and Hammer (2004) and Hammer, Aiyar and Samji (2007).

9. For some early appraisals of RSBY, see e.g. D. Narayana (2010), Rajasekhar et al. (2011), Gita Sen (2012), Selvaraj and Karan (2012), Varshney et al. (2012).

10. A recent USAID report, generally favourable to private health insurance, acknowledges the problem clearly: '... hospitalization coverage is the basis for almost all health insurance ... Generally, health insurance coverage does not correspond well to the primary sources of the burden of disease in India' (USAID, 2008, p. 1).

11. Many of the problematic aspects of RSBY (including moral hazard, bias towards hospital care, and lack of regulation) are well illustrated by the recent issue of unnecessary hysterectomies in Bihar, Chhattisgarh and other states where thousands of women were persuaded to have their

uterus removed by private health care providers who were making handsome profits from this operation – whether or not it was medically advisable – using the insurance scheme; see e.g. Majumdar (2013). While this particular instance of abuse did come to light, there are likely to be others too.

12. See Government of India (1946) and Government of India (2011a), respectively. The government is yet to take a view on the recommendations of the second report.

13. For a far-reaching examination of the demands of fairness and justice in health care and the role of public responsibility in meeting these demands, see Ruger (2009).

14. Peter Svedberg's book *Poverty and Undernutrition* (Svedberg, 2000) showed convincingly how extreme the levels of undernutrition are in India, particularly for children, in terms of international comparisons.

15. See UNICEF (2012), Table 2; this statement ignores Timor-Leste, with even worse nutrition indicators than India but a population of barely 1 million.

16. On this see also Micronutrient Initiative and UNICEF (2004, 2009). The NNMB figures cited in this paragraph are from Gopaldas (2006), Table 1.

17. Short height and low weight in childhood are often a sign of a real deficiency and tend to accompany serious health issues, in childhood or later in life. In fact, these deficiencies seem to have, statistically, an association with lower performance in many fields of actual living. Short height, for example, tends to be associated with lower wages, lower earnings and lower educational achievements. A recent study based on Indian data also found a strong correlation between child height and learning scores (after controlling for a wide range of other variables). In fact, the gradient of learning scores with respect to height was found to be much steeper in the Indian data than in earlier studies based on US data (Dean Spears, 2011).

18 For further discussion, see Deaton and Drèze (2009), Jayachandran and Pande (2013), and Deaton (forthcoming).

19. Ramalingaswami et al. (1996). The original title was actually 'the Asian enigma', which is a little misleading; but the term 'South Asian enigma' was used in the text, and widely adopted later on.

20. See e.g. Osmani and Sen (2003), Santosh Mehrotra (2006), Nira Ramachandran (2007).

21. Calculated from DHS data available at www.measuredhs.com; see also Deaton and Drèze (2009), Table 13. The Demographic and Health Surveys (DHS) are comparable household surveys conducted in many countries

(including India, where they are known as National Family Health Surveys). The estimate for sub-Saharan Africa mentioned here is a population-weighted average for 32 countries for which DHS data are available.

22. Parts of this section draw on Jean Drèze's contribution to the *Focus on Children Under Six* report, also known as 'FOCUS Report' (Citizens' Initiative for the Rights of Children Under Six, 2006); see also Drèze (2006a) and Working Group on Children Under Six (2007, 2012).

23. More detailed, state-specific indicators of childcare are presented in the Statistical Appendix, Table A.3.

24. This is the main point of a Supreme Court order dated 13 December 2006 (see Citizens' Initiative for the Rights of Children Under Six, 2006, pp. 143–4).

25. This initiative, like that of midday meals for all schoolchildren, must count among the rather few areas in which India launched its initiative for helping children before China took similar action. These have been subjects of intensive research at the China Development Research Foundation (CDRF), led by Lu Mai. Recently, China has made rapid advance in both these fields.

26. Similar findings are reported by Eeshani Kandpal (2011), who concludes that 'even in its current form, ICDS generates substantial [economic] returns' (p. 1,420), aside from leading to significant improvements in children's heights. See also Hazarika and Viren (2013).

27. On this see e.g. Sudha Narayanan (2006), and literature cited there. See also Harold Alderman (2010), Alderman and Behrman (2006), Alderman and Horton (2007), Nores and Barnett (2010).

28. For instance, Maharashtra has made significant efforts to improve ICDS services for children under two in recent years. A recent survey of children under two in Maharashtra suggests major improvements in child health and nutrition indicators since 2005-6 (when the last comparable survey, NFHS-3, was conducted), including a major decline in the prevalence of stunting; see International Institute for Population Sciences (2012).

29. Planning Commission (2011a), Table 5.2.

30. There is also some evidence of significant improvement in the functioning of ICDS in many other states in recent years. See, for instance, International Institute for Population Sciences (2012) on Maharashtra, Voice for Child Rights Odisha (2012) on Odisha, Vikas Samvad et al. (2013) on Madhya Pradesh, Samir Garg (2006) and Sheila Vir (2012) on Chhattisgarh.

31. Drèze and Sen (2002), Chapter 6; see also Muraleedharan et al. (2011). Private medical services are also flourishing in Tamil Nadu, but there is

at least a reasonably well-guaranteed possibility of free treatment in public facilities for many health contingencies.

32. See Drèze and Sen (2002), pp. 213–18.

33. See e.g. Leela Visaria (2000), Jean Drèze (2006b), Vivek Srinivasan (2010), Reetika Khera (2012), Dipa Sinha (2013).

34. See Dipa Sinha (2013), Table 3.11, and National Sample Survey Organization (2006).

35. See also Statistical Appendix, Table A.3.

36. On public health in Tamil Nadu, see particularly Das Gupta et al. (2010). Among other achievements of public health in Tamil Nadu is good disaster preparedness. The 'complete avoidance of any epidemic' after a tsunami hit Tamil Nadu in 2004 was described as a 'truly remarkable achievement' by the World Health Organization, and teams from Tamil Nadu were sent to Gujarat in 1994 and Odisha in 1999 to help deal with outbreaks of cholera and plague, respectively.

37. See Statistical Appendix, Table A.3.

38. For an enlightening case study of a model anganwadi in Tamil Nadu, see Vivek (2006).

39. In north India, the front-line workers of ICDS (anganwadi workers and helpers) are also women, but trainers, administrators and planners are usually men, sometimes on deputation from other departments such as the veterinary department; see FOCUS Report, Chapter 6.

40. Another aspect of social policy where Tamil Nadu has taken the lead (along with Kerala) is that of social security schemes in the unorganized sector as well as for vulnerable groups such as widows, disabled persons and the elderly. See Drèze and Sen (2002), and earlier studies cited there.

41. See Khera (2011c) and Drèze and Khera (2012b); for further discussion of the Public Distribution System in India and Tamil Nadu, see also Chapter 7.

42. See Khera and Muthiah (2010) and Khera (2011d); also Srinivasan (2010).

43. See Paul et al. (2006). This study is based on a detailed evaluation of five basic services: supply of drinking water, primary health care, primary education, the public distribution system and public transport.

44. See Srinivasan (2010), p. 6. The pros and cons of targeting in the PDS are discussed in Chapter 6.

45. In China, the state is also the main employer of health workers, in contrast with India where a large proportion of health workers are private entrepreneurs (often with limited educational or medical qualifications). China has a much higher ratio of health workers to population than

India, and this applies even more to government health workers. The distribution of health workers is also far more equal in China than India (with, for instance, less rural-urban inequality). On these and other aspects of the health workforce in China and India, see Sudhir Anand (2010) and Anand and Fan (2010).

46. Government of India (1946), Vol. 1, p. 11.

47. This is again an issue in which the idea of 'cost of inaction' can be very important (Anand et al 2012).

48. Another area of major neglect of public health is tobacco policy. The inability to develop an appropriate public policy about smoking has been a major failure of public action in India, in common, in this case, with China. As Dr. Prabhat Jha and his colleagues show in a recent article in the *New England Journal of Medicine*, 'smokers lose at least one decade of life expectancy, as compared with those who have never smoked,' and yet 'cessation before the age of 40 years reduces the risk associated with continued smoking by about 90%' (Jha et al, 2013, p. 231). The discouragement induced by the government through warning messages and higher taxes has been quite inadequate to negate the impact of vigorous advertising and hidden but powerful advocacy by tobacco companies – domestic and international. On related issues, including the ravage and ruin caused by chewing tobacco in India, see also Sawalkar et al. (2013).

49. See e.g. UNICEF and Government of India (2010), and also the more recent findings of 'annual health surveys' conducted in nine states by the Office of the Registrar General.

50. Between 2005–6 and 2009 institutional deliveries increased from 41 to 74 per cent of all births, and the proportion of births attended by a 'skilled birth attendant' increased from 49 to 76 per cent; see UNICEF and Government of India (2010) and International Institute for Population Sciences (2007a).

51. See Amarjeet Sinha (2012), who argues that the NRHM has already had a remarkable impact in many states and 'contributed to the public [health] system becoming functional again in many parts of the country' (p. 17). These states include not only progressive states like Tamil Nadu but also others like Bihar, where, according to the author, the number of patients examined at Primary Health Centres (PHCs) shot up from negligible in 2005 to 3,500 per month per PHC four years later. On related matters, see also Amarjeet Sinha (2013).

52. See Balabanova et al. (2011) and the literature cited there, including Halstead et al. (1985), where the possibility of 'good health at low cost'

was first highlighted based on specific international experiences – from China, Costa Rica, Kerala and Sri Lanka. Other recent experiences of interest discussed in Balabanova et al. (2011) include Bangladesh, Tamil Nadu and Thailand, among others.

53. Compared with India's measly 1.2 per cent, public expenditure on health as a proportion of GDP is 2.7 per cent in China, 2.9 per cent in Thailand, 3.1 per cent in Mexico, and 4.2 per cent in Brazil (*World Development Indicators*, online). These countries, or course, are significantly richer than India in terms of per-capita GDP, but that does not apply to Vietnam (see Chapter 3), which also spends 2.6 per cent of its GDP on public health expenditure, and is much closer to universal health coverage than India is.

7 POVERTY AND SOCIAL SUPPORT

1. See Drèze and Sen (1989, 1995, 2002) and the literature cited there.
2. See Drèze and Sen (1989), Chapter 7.
3. See Kenneth Arrow (1963), George Akerlof (1970), Michael Spence (1973), Joseph Stiglitz (1975), Rothschild and Stiglitz (1976), Stiglitz and Weiss (1981), among other pioneering contributions to this literature.
4. Robert Aumann (1987), pp. 35–6. On this issue, see also Thaler and Sunstein (2008), Banerjee and Duflo (2011), Chakravarty et al. (2011), among many others, and the vast literature cited there.
5. On India's midday meal programme and its wide-ranging social benefits, see Drèze and Goyal (2003), Khera (2006), Drèze and Khera (2009a), Afridi (2010, 2011), Afridi, Barooah and Somanathan (2013), Jayaraman and Simroth (2011), Singh et al. (2013). Restrictions on 'inter-dining' (sharing of food among people of different castes) play an important role in the enforcement and perpetuation of the caste system. While school meals can help to break these socially regressive norms, there have also been instances where caste prejudices have actually invaded the midday meal scheme itself, e.g. in the form of upper-caste parents refusing to allow their children to eat food cooked by 'low caste' women. See e.g. Drèze and Goyal (2003), Thorat and Lee (2005) and Gatade (2013).
6. The next 'BPL Census', due in 2007, was repeatedly postponed, largely due to persistent confusion about the BPL identification methodology. A new method for identifying BPL households was introduced with the Socio-Economic and Caste Census (SECC) initiated in 2011, but this method came under heavy fire even before the Census was completed. On 3 October 2011 a joint statement of the Planning Commission and

Ministry of Rural Development retracted some aspects of this method (such as the use of state-wise official poverty estimates to 'cap' the BPL list). At the time of writing, it is not clear how BPL households are supposed to be identified from the SECC data.

7. Similar comments apply to the Integrated Child Development Services (ICDS), introduced in the preceding chapter. Plans were afoot, about ten years ago, to restrict ICDS to children from BPL households. This, again, would have been a case of misplaced targeting, since nutritional deficiencies and other deprivations of Indian children are not confined to BPL households – far from it. As discussed in the preceding chapter, other considerations (such as the role of social norms in childcare, and the influence of 'externalities', including those associated with communicable diseases) also argue against targeting in this context. As with midday meals, the recent universalization of ICDS (reversing the initial move towards targeting) has helped to impart new life to the programme.

8. This happened (under pressure from the Finance Ministry) just before the 'National Rural Employment Guarantee Bill' was tabled in Parliament, in December 2004. For further details, see Ian MacAuslan (2008) and Deepta Chopra (2010, 2011).

9. For further discussion, see Khera (2011b, 2011c), Drèze (2012), Drèze and Khera (2010b, 2012b). There are some indications that this more inclusive approach tends to give better results not only in terms of the general functioning of the PDS, but also in terms of its impact on *poverty reduction* (Drèze and Khera 2012b). This pattern, if verified, would be somewhat contrary to the tenets of the targeting school, which holds that focusing public resources on the poor is essential to maximize the 'poverty reduction' impact of public policies.

10. See e.g. Dutta et al. (2010), Aashish Gupta (2013), Sandesh Lokhande (2013), and Marulasiddappa et al. (2013).

11. T. V. Sekher (2012), p. 58. On the complementarity between conditional cash transfers and the public provision of essential services, see Francesca Bastagli (2011) and Sudha Narayanan (2011).

12. The powerful attraction of free food has been observed in many circumstances. For another example, see Banerjee and Duflo (2011), who report how distributing small quantities of free pulses at vaccination camps greatly helps to attract mothers and children to the camps.

13. Tamil Nadu was the first state to initiate this scheme, which has been emulated in many other states. For evidence of its positive impact on school enrolment, with reference to Bihar, see Muralidharan and Prakash (2012).

14. See J-PAL (2011) and Bates, Glennerster, Gumede and Duflo (2012), and studies cited there.

15. This is another important insight of behavioural and experimental economics, especially the recent literature on (so-called) 'social preferences' – see e.g. Fehr and Fischbacher (2000), Bowles and Hwang (2008), Bowles and Reyes (2009).

16. See Titmuss (1970). See also Mellström and Johannesson (2008) and Sandel (2012).

17. Bowles (2007). A related phenomenon is that when specific duties of civil servants and government functionaries are 'incentivized', *other* duties tend to be neglected if not ignored. This pattern has been observed, for instance, among India's 'accredited social health activists' (ASHA), the front-line workers of the National Rural Health Mission.

18. For an informative review, see Sekher (2012). The issue of sex-selective abortion in India is taken up again in Chapter 8.

19. For further discussion of the process that led to the enactment of NREGA, see Drèze (2010); also MacAuslan (2008), Chopra (2010). For a useful introduction to the economic literature on NREGA, see Khera (2011d) and Government of India (2012b). The Act was renamed 'Mahatma Gandhi National Rural Employment Guarantee Act' in October 2009.

20. Under the Act, any adult residing in rural areas is entitled to being employed on local public works within 15 days of applying, subject to a maximum of 100 days per household per year. If employment is not provided, an unemployment allowance is supposed to be paid, though this rarely happens in practice. For further details of workers' entitlements under NREGA, and other aspects of the Act, see e.g. Dey, Drèze and Khera (2006).

21. On Maharashtra's employment guarantee scheme (EGS), see e.g. Mahendra Dev and Ranade (2001), Aruna Bagchee (2005), and earlier work cited there. About half a million workers were employed on an average day on Maharashtra's EGS in the 1970s and 1980s, albeit at a very low wage. In the 1990s, however, the scheme somewhat fizzled out, for reasons that have not been fully elucidated; on this see Moore and Jadhav (2006). The first draft of the National Rural Employment Guarantee Act was largely adapted from Maharashtra's Employment Guarantee Act.

22. On this aspect of Maharashtra's employment guarantee scheme, see e.g. Shaji Joseph (2006) and Anuradha Joshi (2010).

23. This is just one – the most basic – of the numerous 'transparency safeguards' that were built into the Act (and later in the NREGA Guidelines). Others include regular updating of workers' 'job cards', mandatory social audits, strict modalities for wage payments, end-to-end computerization, and more. For further details, see e.g. Khera (2011d).

24. The NREGA came into force in February 2006 in 200 districts – the most deprived districts, according to an index of 'backwardness' devised by the Planning Commission. It was extended to another 130 districts on 1 April 2007, and to the whole country on 1 April 2008.

25. See Government of India (2012b), p. 4. The NREGA employment figures emerging from National Sample Survey data for 2009–10 are lower, e.g. about 42 million households employed as opposed to 52 million according to the Ministry of Rural Development for the same year. The NSS estimates, however, may be on the low side (e.g. due to recall problems), and the truth is likely to be somewhere in between.

26. On the positive effects of NREGA on agricultural wages, see Azam (2011), Imbert and Papp (2011), Berg et al. (2012). The first of these changes (actual payment of statutory minimum wages on public works) was partially undone in January 2009, when the central government attempted to 'delink' NREGA from the Minimum Wages Act. This move, however, has been challenged in court, and is – as we write this book – in the process of being reconsidered by the central government.

27. On this point, see particularly Imbert and Papp (2011). This study suggests that the indirect benefits of NREGA for rural households, in the form of higher earnings in private employment, are roughly of the same order of magnitude as the direct benefits, in the form of NREGA wages. On related benefits of NREGA, see also Liu and Deininger (2010), Afridi et al. (2012), Papp (2012), Klonner and Oldiges (2013), among others.

28. See e.g. Drèze and Khera (2009b), Liu and Deininger (2010), Imbert and Papp (2011), Silvia Mangatter (2011), Dutta et al. (2012), Government of India (2012b), Liu and Barrett (2013).

29. Government of India (2012b), p. 4.

30. See Government of India (2012b), p. 19. The main exception to this pattern is Uttar Pradesh, where women's share of NREGA employment is yet to cross 20 per cent on a sustained basis.

31. See Drèze and Khera (2009b). The programme provides valuable employment opportunities to women not only as NREGA workers but also as worksite supervisors ('mates'), data entry operators, project officers, and so on. The payment of equal wages to women and men at all levels is another significant contribution of NREGA to gender equality in rural areas.

32. See e.g. Sudha Narayanan (2008), National Federation of Indian Women (2008), Khera and Nayak (2009), Pankaj and Tankha (2010), Hirway and Batabyal (2011), Afridi et al. (2012), Dheeraja and Rao (forthcoming).

33. This is one of the messages emerging from social audits of NREGA works around the country; see e.g. Drèze, Khera and Siddhartha (2008).

Another relevant indication is the growing consistency over time between official employment generation figures published by the Ministry of Rural Development and independent National Sample Survey estimates of NREGA employment. Even in Bihar, a recent study found reasonable consistency between official records and survey-based estimates of employment generation under NREGA; see Dutta et al. (forthcoming).

34. See e.g. Centre for Science and Environment (2008), Drèze and Khera (2009b), SAMARTHAN (2010), Shah et al. (2010), Shah and Makwana (2011), Verma (2011). In the survey reported by Drèze and Khera (2009b), the positive perception of NREGA works was not just that of NREGA workers (92 per cent of whom considered the work they were doing as 'useful' or 'very useful'), but also that of field investigators (81 per cent).

35. See Government of India (2012b), Chapter 3, and studies cited there; also Aggarwal et al. (2012).

36. On the numerous operational problems and other hurdles that have affected NREGA (including the unenthusiastic if not hostile attitude of the bureaucracy towards NREGA in many states), see various contributions in Khera (2011d). See also Ambasta et al. (2008) and National Consortium of Civil Society Organisations (2009, 2011).

37. Going to court is not an effective option for most NREGA workers, given their poverty and lack of social power. In fact, despite NREGA being a law and its provisions being routinely violated, not a single NREGA worker has gone to court to enforce his or her entitlements so far, and even public interest litigations have been extremely rare (we are aware of only three so far). One reason for this is that a court case involves enormous trouble and expense, and also delay, and typically rather little chance of redress. This aspect of the legal system is a major liability for NREGA, and for social legislations in general.

38. There have been interesting initiatives on this in some of the leading states. For instance, Andhra Pradesh has put in place a system of automatic compensation of NREGA workers for delays in wage payments – every step of the payment process is computerized, including compensation for delays when wages are paid beyond the statutory limit of 15 days. This also makes it possible to fix responsibility for the delays, and fine the responsible functionaries if need be. This is a good example of the possibility, discussed in Chapter 4, of bringing technology to bear on accountability problems – provided that there is a political willingness to foster accountability. For further details, see Chopra and Khera (2012).

39. Much of this section draws on collaborative work between Jean Drèze and Reetika Khera; see Drèze and Khera (2010a, 2010b, 2011, 2012b, 2013), Khera (2011c), Drèze (2012).

40. This description of India's PDS is inevitably sketchy. For further details, see e.g. Jha and Ramaswami (2010) and Khera (2011c).

41. Strictly speaking, the use of poverty estimates to determine state-wise allocations applies to the 'BPL quota' only. The APL quota is effectively at the discretion of the central government and tends to act as a dumping ground for excess food stocks. It was largely phased out in the early 2000s, but revived later as food procurement kept going up.

42. Throughout the country, 'Antyodaya' (poorest of the poor) households are entitled to 35 kgs of subsidized foodgrains per month under the PDS. To keep things simple, we are subsuming this group under the 'BPL' category in this section. In fact, Antyodaya was initially a sub-category of the BPL group.

43. See e.g. Jha and Ramaswami (2010), Kotwal et al. (2012).

44. See particularly Khera (2011c); for case studies of specific states, see also Anindita Adhikari (2011), Ankita Aggarwal (2011), Jijo Jose (2011), Swathi Meenakshi (2011), Ria Sawhney (2011), Raghav Puri (2012).

45. In some districts of Chhattisgarh, pulses are also distributed through the PDS at Rs 5 per kg (again, a symbolic price, considering that the market price is at least ten times as high).

46. See e.g. Khera (2011c), Drèze and Khera (2010b), Puri (2012), Parker (2012), Vir (2012). This statement, however, may not apply in parts of South Chhattisgarh (the old 'Bastar' region), where armed conflict has disrupted the normal functioning of the administrative machinery and Panchayati Raj Institutions.

47. See e.g. Drèze (2001), on which the anecdote mentioned at the beginning of this chapter is based.

48. See Drèze and Khera (2012b, 2013). The 'poverty gap index' of rural poverty in 2009-10 was about 18 per cent lower than it would have been without PDS transfers at the all-India level, and 40 to 50 per cent lower in Chhattisgarh and Tamil Nadu. For similar findings, see also Himanshu (2012).

49. See Khera (2011).

50. See Drèze and Khera (2011c).

51. On the idea of 'nudge' of private behaviour on public grounds, see Thaler and Sunstein (2008). Even when it is restricted to rice and wheat, the PDS seems to enhance calorie consumption more than an equivalent cash transfer; see Himanshu and Sen (2013).

52. See Khera (2011c), Table 8.

8 THE GRIP OF INEQUALITY

1. See e.g. Drèze and Sen (2002), Table 5.1, pp. 147–8.

2. See e.g. Wail et al. (2011), Crespo-Cuaresma et al. (2012), Emran and Shilpi (2012).

3. Even in the younger age groups, the Gini coefficient of years of schooling is still very high in India: around 0.5 in the age group of 25–29 years in 2000, compared with less than 0.1 in a more educationally egalitarian country like South Korea, where education among the youth is 'almost perfectly equally distributed'; see Crespo-Cuaresma et al. (2012), p. 10. The authors present a striking case study of educational inequality in India and South Korea and how it has changed over time – declining radically in South Korea, but not in India. Note that the Gini coefficient of years of schooling is likely to grossly *underestimate* educational inequalities in India, because of the fact – discussed in Chapter 5 – that there are also major disparities in the quality of schooling, which tend to magnify inequalities in the 'quantity' of schooling – much more so than in many other countries.

4. Quoted in Lion Agrawal (2008), p. 214. On Lohia's life and thought, see Yogendra Yadav (2010a, 2010b).

5. Another resilient social division is that between Adivasis ('scheduled tribes') and the rest. Adivasis account for about 8 per cent of India's population, and many of them face the same sort of disadvantages and discrimination as the Dalits or 'scheduled castes', as well as other vulnerabilities such as frequent exposure to forced displacement. Further, while Dalits are a significant political force, there has been little organized political pressure for Adivasi interests, perpetuating their disadvantaged position in Indian society.

6. See Drèze and Gazdar (1996), with reference to Uttar Pradesh.

7. World Bank (2011a), p. 23. On income inequality in India, see also Vanneman and Dubey (forthcoming).

8. See Deaton and Drèze (2002), Banerjee and Piketty (2005), Jayadev et al. (2007), Sarkar and Mehta (2010), World Bank (2011a), Weisskopf (2011), Asian Development Bank (2012), among others.

9. See Deaton and Drèze (2002), Himanshu (2007), World Bank (2011a), Datt and Ravallion (2010), Kapoor (2013), Kotwal and Roy Chaudhuri (2013).

10. See e.g. Wilkinson and Marmot (2003) and Wilkinson and Pickett (2009).

11. For further discussion of these and other social consequences of economic inequality, see Thomas Weisskopf (2011) and the literature cited there.

12. There is a large sociological and anthropological literature on this; for a review, see André Béteille (2012). On the caste system (and how it is

changing) in contemporary India, see also M. N. Srinivas (1995), Kancha
Ilaiah (1996), C. J. Fuller (1997), Ghanshyam Shah et al. (2006), Gail
Omvedt (2008, 2010), Thorat and Newman (2010), K. Balagopal (2011),
among many others.

13. Powerful first-hand accounts of this oppression have been written by
Laxman Gaikwad (1998), Omprakash Valmiki (2003), B. R. Ambedkar
(2011), among many others. See also Sharmila Rege (2006) and Shah et
al. (2006).

14. The position of Kayashtas in the traditional fourfold *varna* system
(Brahmin, Kshatriya, Vaishya, Shudra) is not entirely clear and varies
between different regions of India. They are often regarded as Kshatri-
yas. What is not in doubt is that they are in that sort of league – near
the top.

15. As it happens, at least 7 of India's 14 prime ministers (Jawaharlal Nehru,
Lal Bahadur Shastri, Indira Gandhi, Rajiv Gandhi, Gulzarilal Nanda, V. P.
Singh and Chandra Shekhar) were also born, brought up, educated or
elected in Allahabad.

16. See e.g. B. N. Uniyal (1996), J. Balasubramaniam (2011) and Robin Jeffrey
(2012) on media houses; Harish Damodaran (2008) and Ajit et al. (2012)
on corporate boards and industry leadership; Karan Tejpal (2012) on polo
teams; Richard Cashman (1980), S. Anand (2003), Andrew Stevenson (2008) on cricket teams. At the time of Stevenson's count, in 2008,
7 out of 11 players in the Indian cricket team were Brahmins (about
4 per cent of Indians belong to the Brahmin caste); the chairman of the
national cricket academy – also a Brahmin – apparently dismissed this as a
'coincidence'.

17. See Chamaria, Kumar and Yadav (2006).

18. See Ajit, Donker and Saxena (2012), Table 1, p. 41, based on an analysis
of the board membership of India's top 1,000 companies (in terms of
total assets). See also Gandhi and Walton (2012) on the caste composition of India's billionaires.

19. Useful evidence of these disadvantages is presented in the 'Sachar
Committee Report' (Government of India, 2006).

20. For state-specific estimates of sex differentials in child mortality in India,
see Statistical Appendix, Table A.3.

21. See United Nations (2011), Table III.1, where estimates of sex-specific
child mortality rates are presented for 122 countries. According to these
estimates, the ratio of female to male 'child mortality' (probability of
dying at ages 1–4 years) is higher in India then in any other country in
the world.

22. See e.g. Chandrasekhar and Ghosh (2011), Mazumdar and N (2011), and

Thomas (2012). Both census data and National Sample Survey data suggest that women's workforce participation in India has remained fairly stable (and has certainly not increased) during the last few decades.

23. The 33 per cent norm is a national minimum guaranteed by the Constitution (73rd Amendment) Act 1992. A further amendment, raising this minimum from 33 per cent to 50 per cent, has been approved by the Union Cabinet, but is yet to become law. Meanwhile, several states (including Bihar, Himachal Pradesh and Madhya Pradesh) have already started implementing 50 per cent reservation for women in Panchayati Raj Institutions.

24. See e.g. Chattopadhyay and Duflo (2004); also Beaman et al. (2006), Duflo (2011), Sathe et al. (2013), and the literature cited there. While there is growing evidence that women's political representation in institutions of local governance does make a difference (at least in India), the precise connections involved are far from simple – this is still a lively field of investigation.

25. See Statistical Appendix, Table A.3.

26. This is another example of the mutual reinforcement of different inequalities (in this case of caste and gender inequalities). Many of India's radical thinkers and reformers, from the 18th century onwards if not earlier, clearly perceived the complementarity between gender and caste hierarchies as well as the difficulty of destroying one without the other. The fiercest critics of the caste system were often far ahead of their times in defending women's rights. Tarabai Shinde, Jotirao Phule, B. R. Ambedkar and Periyar are some examples, among others (see e.g. Ambedkar 1917, Veeramani 1992, O'Hanlon 1994, Geetha 1998, Sinha 2012, Rege 2013).

27. United Nations Office on Drugs and Crime (2013).

28. See Sen (1990) and Drèze and Sen (2002) .

29. See Drèze and Sen (2002) and the literature cited there.

30. On this see Sen (1984), Chapters 5 and 16, and Sen (1990); also Folbre (1986), Brannen and Wilson (1987), and Ferber and Nelson (1993), among other contributions.

31. Agarwal (1994).

32. This subject was extensively discussed in our earlier books, Drèze and Sen (1995, 2002), citing empirical studies on which this reading is based.

33. On various aspects of the role of women's agency in mortality as well as fertility decline, see Murthi, Guio and Drèze (1995) and Drèze and Murthi (2001), and the literature cited there; also John Cleland (2002), Kishor and Gupta (2004), Øystein Kravdal (2004), Baker et al. (2011), LeVine et al. (2012), United Nations Population Fund (2012a), among others.

34. In fact, the propensity to resort to sex-selective abortion seems to be higher among more educated women (Jha et al., 2011). However, this is a

bivariate correlation, and it is not clear whether it holds after controlling, say, for economic status (per capita income is positively correlated with female education as well as with the incidence of sex-selective abortion).

35. See Leila Seth (2012). For valuable evidence on the nature of this patriarchal mindset and its influence on family planning, see John et al. (2009) and Arokiasamy and Goli (2012).

36. On this see Sen (1985, 2002a, 2002b).

37. See Jha et al. (2011). Independent estimates by Bhalotra and Cochrane (2010) are in the same range – about 0.5 million sex-selective abortions per year during the 1995–2005 period.

38. Kumar and Sathyanarayana (2012), p. 71, and Appendix Table A.1. Judging from available data, it is unlikely that any country in the world has a lower child sex ratio than these Indian districts (nor for that matter than Haryana as a whole), though some Chinese provinces do; see United Nations Population Fund (2012b).

39. For evidence that the extent of this distortion is likely to be quite small, see Kumar and Sathyanarayana (2012).

40. If we look at smaller states, there is some exception to this clear division in the statistics from the north-eastern edge of the country.

41. For further discussion, see Drèze and Sen (2002), Chapter 7. The 2001 child sex ratios discussed there are slightly different from those presented here (in Table 8.3), because the earlier figures were based on 'provisional population totals' from the 2001 census.

42. On this, see also Jha et al. (2011).

43. See e.g. David Sopher (1980), Dyson and Moore (1983), and Barbara Miller (1981, 1989). Miller (1989), looking at 'juvenile sex ratios' (at a time when sex-selective abortion was rare, so that imbalances in these sex ratios were driven mainly by differences in mortality rates between boys and girls), identified a broad 'north-west vs south-east' pattern, with a different boundary. This pattern, like that identified here, differs from the more discussed 'north-south' dichotomy that is often invoked in analyses of regional contrasts in gender relations in India. There is, of course, no claim here that the regional contrast applying to child sex ratios applies to other features of gender relations in India as well. The details of regional contrasts in gender relations, kinship systems and related matters in India are ultimately quite complex, as Irawati Karve (1968) pointed out many years ago.

44. See Drèze and Khera (2008), on which the remainder of this section is based. The distorting effects of unequal power of the corporate sector in India, including the 'growing private expropriation of public wealth', have been well discussed by Raghuram Rajan (2008); see also Gandhi and Walton (2012) and Atul Kohli (2012), among others.

9 DEMOCRACY, INEQUALITY
AND PUBLIC REASONING

1. On the history and the changing ideas of democracy, see Alan Ryan (2012), and also Ian Shapiro (1999) and John Dunn (2005).
2. Ramachandra Guha (2007).
3. See e.g. Bela Bhatia (2011).
4. Ravi (2012). On this issue, see also Jeevan Reddy Committee (2005) and Sanjoy Hazarika (2013a, 2013b).
5. Dr Binayak Sen is one well-known victim of this abuse, but there are many others. Just to give one example, thousands of persons (as many as 8,000, according to one report) protesting against the setting up of a nuclear plant in Koodankulam were recently booked for sedition; see Soumik Mukherjee (2012).
6. Pankaj Mishra (2012).
7. See Statistical Appendix, Table A.3.
8. See Statistical Appendix, Table A.3.
9. See e.g. Sanjay Kumar (2009).
10. B. R. Ambedkar (1950), 'Basic Features of the Indian Constitution', reprinted in Rodrigues (2002), p. 490.
11. Samuel Huntington (1991), p. 9.
12. On this issue, see Amartya Sen (2009), especially Chapters 15–17.
13. John Rawls, *Collected Papers* (1999), pp. 579–80. See also his *A Theory of Justice* (1971), *Political Liberalism* (1993) and *Justice as Fairness: A Restatement* (2001).
14. Jürgen Habermas (1996).
15. As Upinder Singh has observed, 'excavating the world of ideas embodied in [the inscriptions] is an important part of the analysis of these material remains of the past' (Singh, 2012, p. 131). See also Singh (2009), and the earlier classic contributions of Romila Thapar (1963, 1984). Among recent interpretations of Ashokan edicts, see also Rajeev Bhargava (forthcoming).
16. Latest figures (for 2011–12) from the Registrar of Newspapers.
17. See Arundhati Roy (2010).
18. For insightful analyses of the successes and limitations of the Indian newspapers industry, see N. Ram (1990, 2011, 2012). See also Robin Jeffrey (2000), Prabhat Patnaik (2002), P. Sainath (2009), Ken Auletta (2012).
19. Shobhaa Dé (2008), p. 41.
20. As the managing editor of one of India's leading dailies (*The Times of India*) put it in a recent interview, 'we are not in the newspaper business, we are in the advertising business' (see Auletta, 2012).

21. A few years ago, Pepsi and Coca Cola were exposed by the Centre for Science and Environment for using contaminated water in their products. Yet, according to the same commentator, 'the electronic media jumped to the defence of the soft drink manufacturers – both are big advertisers on TV'.

22. On this (and also the related issue of so-called 'private treaties' between media houses and business groups), see Reddy and Thakurta's (2010) report to the Press Council of India; also P. Sainath (2009, 2010) and Guha Thakurta (2011).

23. Vipul Mudgal (2011). For similar findings on regional dailies, see The Hoot (2011).

24. Paranjoy Guha Thakurta, comment made at an informal dialogue between media editors and the right to food campaign, Indian Social Institute, 29 November 2011.

25. Ashok Rudra (1989). Rudra's analysis builds on a very broad interpretation of the term 'intelligentsia', more or less synonymous with 'persons who earn their living by the sale of mental labour' (p. 144).

26. See e.g. Government of India (2011h), Table 2.18, pp. A-1 and A-51.

27. See e.g. Government of India (2002a, 2002b, 2004a); see also Amaresh Bagchi et al. (2005) and earlier expert reports cited there.

28. Government of India (2012d), Annex 2, p. 19.

29. See Government of India (2012e). For a helpful analysis of this statement, see Kavita Rao (2013).

30. Quoted in *The Times of India*, 6 December 2012, and *The Economic Times*, 3 January 2013. India is the largest gold importer in the world, with gold imports estimated at nearly 1,000 tonnes in 2011–12, worth US $60 billion or about 3 per cent of India's GDP (C. Rangarajan, Chairman of the Prime Minister's Economic Advisory Council, quoted in *The Financial Express*, 2 December 2012). The recent binge of gold imports was such that, in the Finance Ministry's latest Revenue Forgone Statement (just released as this book goes to press), the estimate of revenue forgone in 2011–12 on account of custom duty exemptions on gold and diamonds had to be revised upward, from Rs 57,000 crores to an astounding Rs 66,000 crores.

31. Further legislations or draft legislations of the same variety are pending in Parliament, notably the National Food Security Bill 2011, the Lok Pal and Lokayuktas Bill 2011, the Right of Citizens for Time Bound Delivery of Goods and Services and Redressal of their Grievances Bill 2011, the Land Acquisition, Rehabilitation and Resettlement Bill 2011, and a constitutional amendment (the 'women's reservation bill') that provides for one third of all seats in the Parliament and Legislative Assemblies to be reserved for women.

10 THE NEED FOR IMPATIENCE

1. See Harris (1958), Chapter X; see also Fraser (1919), Appendix D.
2. Government of India (1946), *Report of the Health Survey and Development Committee*, vol 2, p. 1 (typos corrected).
3. See Sen (1973, 1997), Atkinson (1975, 1983), and Foster and Sen (1997).
4. Rammanohar Reddy (2012).
5. Cited in Emma Rothschild (2011), p. 127.

References*

Aakella, K. V. and Kidambi, S. (2007), 'Challenging Corruption with Social Audits', *Economic and Political Weekly*, 3 February.

Acemoglu, D. and Robinson, J. (2012), *Why Nations Fail: The Origins of Power, Prosperity and Poverty* (London: Profile Books).

Adhikari, Anindita (2011), 'Strong Revival', *Frontline*, 31 December.

Afridi, Farzana (2010), 'Child Welfare Programs and Child Nutrition: Evidence from a Mandated School Meal Program in India', *Journal of Development Economics*, 92.

Afridi, Farzana (2011), 'The Impact of School Meals on Student Participation in Rural India', *Journal of Development Studies*, 47.

Afridi, F., Barooah, B. and Somanathan, R. (2013), 'School Meals and Classroom Effort: Evidence from India', Working Paper, International Growth Centre, London School of Economics.

Afridi, F., Mukhopadhyay, A. and Sahoo, S. (2012), 'Female Labour Force Participation and Child Education in India: The Effect of the National Rural Employment Guarantee Scheme', Discussion Paper 6593, Institute for the Study of Labor, Bonn.

Agarwal, Bina (1994), *A Field of One's Own* (Cambridge: Cambridge University Press).

Agarwal, Manmohan (1991), 'Sukhamoy Chakravarty as a Development Economist', *Economic and Political Weekly*, 31 August.

Aggarwal, Ankita (2011), 'The PDS in Rural Orissa: Against the Grain?', *Economic and Political Weekly*, 3 September.

Aggarwal, A., Drèze, J. P. and Gupta, A. (2013), 'Notes on the Caste Composition of Public Institutions in Allahabad', mimeo, Department of Economics, Allahabad University.

* A substantial proportion of the publications listed here are available online. Hyperlinks are given in cases of publications that appear to be available only on the Internet.

Aggarwal, A., Gupta, A. and Kumar, A. (2012), 'Evaluation of NREGA Wells in Jharkhand', *Economic and Political Weekly*, 1 September.

Agrawal, Lion (2008), *Freedom Fighters of India*, vol. II (Delhi: Isha).

Ahluwalia, Montek Singh (2010), 'Message from Delhi: Don't Cut Too Soon', *Financial Times*, 23 July.

Ahuja, A. and Chhibber, P. (2012), 'Why the Poor Vote in India', *Studies in Comparative International Development*, 47.

Aiyar, Swaminathan A. (2011a), 'Agricultural Wages have Skyrocketed: Poor have Benefited from GDP Growth', *Economic Times*, 7 June.

Aiyar, Swaminathan A. (2011b), 'Wage Boom Proves Inclusive Growth', *Economic Times*, 7 July.

Ajit, D., Donker, H. and Saxena, R. (2012), 'Corporate Boards in India: Blocked by Caste?', *Economic and Political Weekly*, 11 August.

Akerlof, George A. (1970), 'The Market for "Lemons": Quality Uncertainty and the Market Mechanism', *Quarterly Journal of Economics*, 84.

Alderman, Harold (2010), 'The Economic Cost of a Poor Start in Life', *Journal of Developmental Origins of Health and Disease*, 1.

Alderman, H. and Behrman, J. (2006), 'Reducing the Incidence of Low Birth Weight in Low-Income Countries has Substantial Economic Benefits', *World Bank Research Observer*, 21.

Alderman, H. and Horton, S. (2007), 'The Economics of Addressing Nutritional Anemia', in K. Kraemer and M. B. Zimmermann (eds.) (2007), *Nutritional Anemia* (Basel: Sight and Life Press).

Alessandrini, Michelle (2009), 'Jobless Growth in Indian Manufacturing: A Kaldorian Approach', Discussion Paper 99, Centre for Financial and Management Studies, University of London.

Alkire, S. and Foster, J. (2011), 'Counting and Multidimensional Poverty Measurement', *Journal of Public Economics*, 95.

Alkire, S., Roche, J. M. and Seth, S. (December 2011), 'Table 3.3: Contribution of Deprivations to the MPI, by Sub-National Regions', Oxford Poverty and Human Development Initiative; available at http://www.ophi.org.uk (accessed November 2012).

Alkire, S. and Santos, M. E. (2012), 'Acute Multidimensional Poverty: A New Index for Developing Countries', mimeo, Oxford Poverty and Human Development Initiative, University of Oxford.

Alkire, S. and Seth, S. (2012), 'Multidimensional Poverty Index (MPI) Rates in Rural and Urban Indian States', mimeo, Oxford Poverty and Human Development Initiative, University of Oxford; available at http://ophi.qeh.ox.ac.uk.

Alkire, S. and Seth, S. (2013), 'Multidimensional Poverty Reduction in India between 1999 and 2006: Where and How?', OPHI Working Paper 60, Oxford Poverty and Human Development Initiative, University of Oxford.

Ambasta, P., Vijay Shankar, P. S. and Shah, M. (2008), 'Two Years of NREGA: The Road Ahead', *Economic and Political Weekly*, 23 February.

Ambedkar, B. R. (1917), 'Castes in India: Their Mechanism, Genesis and Development', *Indian Antiquary*, 41; reprinted in Government of Maharashtra (1979–98), vol. 1; also reprinted in Manoranjan Mohanty (ed.) (2004), *Class, Caste and Gender* (New Delhi: Sage).

Ambedkar, B. R. (1936), *The Annihilation of Caste*, reprinted 1990 with an introduction by Mulk Raj Anand (New Delhi: Arnold).

Ambedkar, B. R. (1952), 'Conditions Precedent for the Successful Working of Democracy', speech delivered at the Poona District Law Library; reprinted in Bhagwan Das (2010).

Ambedkar, B. R. (2011), *Reminiscences of Untouchability*, reprinted from Government of Maharashtra (1979–98), vol. 12 (New Delhi: Critical Quest).

Amnesty International (2012), *Death Sentences and Executions 2011* (London: Amnesty International Publications).

Anand, Mukesh K. (2012), 'Diesel Pricing in India', Working Paper 2012-108, National Institute of Public Finance and Policy, New Delhi.

Anand, S. (2003), 'The Retreat of the Brahmin', *Outlook*, 10 February.

Anand, Sudhir (2010), 'Measuring Health Workforce Inequalities: Methods and Application to China and India', *Human Resources for Health Observer*, 5, World Health Organization, Geneva.

Anand, S., Desmond, C., Fuje, H. and Marques, N. (2012), *Cost of Inaction: Case Studies from Rwanda and Angola* (Cambridge, MA: Harvard University Press).

Anand, S. and Fan, V. (2010), 'The Health Workforce in India, 2001', report submitted to the Planning Commission, New Delhi.

Arnett, Peter (1998), 'Big Science, Small Results', *Bulletin of the Atomic Scientists*, July/August.

Arokiasamy, P. and Goli, S. (2012), 'Explaining the Skewed Child Sex Ratio in Rural India', *Economic and Political Weekly*, 20 October.

Arrow, Kenneth (1963), 'Uncertainty and the Welfare Economics of Medical Care', *American Economic Review*, 53.

Asian Development Bank (2012), *Asian Development Outlook 2012: Confronting Rising Inequality in Asia* (Manila: ADB).

Association for Democratic Reforms (2010), *Lok Sabha National Election Watch 2009* (New Delhi: ADR).

Atkinson, A. B. (1975), *The Economics of Inequality* (Oxford: Oxford University Press).

Atkinson, A. B. (1983), *Social Justice and Public Policy* (Brighton: Wheatsheaf).

Audit Bureau of Circulation (2010), 'National and Statewise Trends', available online, accessed December 2011.

Auletta, Ken (2012), 'Citizens Jain: Why India's Newspaper Industry is Thriving', *The New Yorker*, 8 October.

Aumann, Robert J. (1987), 'What is Game Theory Trying to Accomplish?', in K. Arrow and S. Honkapohja (eds.) (1987), *Frontiers of Economics* (Oxford: Basil Blackwell).

Azam, Mehtabul (2011), 'The Impact of Indian Job Guarantee Scheme on Labor Market Outcomes: Evidence from a Natural Experiment', Discussion Paper 6548, Institute for the Study of Labour, Bonn.

Bagchee, Aruna (2005), 'Political and Administrative Realities of Employment Guarantee Scheme', *Economic and Political Weekly*, 15 October.

Bagchi, A., Rao, R. K. and Sen, B. (2005), 'Raising the Tax-Ratio by Reining in the "Tax Breaks": An Agenda for Action', Working Paper, Tax Research Unit, National Institute of Public Finance and Policy, New Delhi.

Bagchi, Amiya K. (2010), *Colonialism and Indian Economy* (New Delhi: Oxford University Press).

Baker, D. P., Leon, J., Smith Greenaway, E. G., Collins, J. and Movit, M. (2011), 'The Education Effect on Population Health: A Reassessment', *Population and Development Review*, 37.

Balabanova, D., McKee, M. and Mills, A. (eds.) (2011), *'Good Health at Low Cost' 25 Years On* (London: London School of Hygiene and Tropical Medicine).

Balagopal, K. (2011), *Ear to the Ground: Selected Writings on Class and Caste* (New Delhi: Navayana).

Balakrishnan, Pulapre (2007), 'The Recovery of India: Economic Growth in the Nehru Era', *Economic and Political Weekly*, 17 November.

Balakrishnan, Pulapre (2010), *Economic Growth in India: History and Prospect* (New Delhi: Oxford University Press).

Balasubramaniam, J. (2011), 'Dalits and a Lack of Diversity in the Newsroom', *Economic and Political Weekly*, 12 March.

Banerjee, A., Deaton, A. and Duflo, E. (2004) 'Health Care Delivery in Rural Rajasthan', *Economic and Political Weekly*, 28 February.

Banerjee, A. and Duflo, E. (2011), *Poor Economics* (London: Random House).

Banerjee, A. and Piketty, T. (2005), 'Top Indian Incomes, 1922–2000,' *World Bank Economic Review*, 19.

Bangladesh Bureau of Statistics (2011), *Population and Housing Census: Preliminary Results July 2011* (Dhaka: Ministry of Planning, Government of the People's Republic of Bangladesh).

Bardhan, Pranab (2005), *Security, Conflict, and Cooperation: Essays in the Political and Institutional Economics of Development* (Cambridge, MA: MIT Press).

Bardhan, Pranab (2010), *Awakening Giants, Feet of Clay: Assessing the Economic Rise of China and India* (Princeton, NJ: Princeton University Press).

Barr, N. and Harbison, R. W. (1994), 'Overview: Hopes, Tears, and Transformation', in Barr (1994).

Barr, Nicholas (ed.) (1994), *Labor Markets and Social Policy in Central and Eastern Europe* (Oxford: Oxford University Press).

Bastagli, Francesca (2008), 'The Design, Implementation and Impact of Conditional Cash Transfers Targeted on the Poor: An Evaluation of Brazil's *Bolsa Família*', PhD thesis, London School of Economics.

Bastagli, Francesca (2011), 'Conditional Cash Transfers as a Tool of Social Policy', *Economic and Political Weekly*, 21 May.

Basu, Kaushik (2011), 'Why, for a Class of Bribes, the Act of *Giving* a Bribe Should be Treated as Legal', mimeo, Ministry of Finance, New Delhi; available at finmin.nic.in/workingpaper/act_giving_bribe_legal.pdf

Basu, K. and Maertens, A. (eds.) (2012), *The New Oxford Companion to Economics in India* (New Delhi: Oxford University Press).

Bates, M. A., Glennerster, R., Gumede, K. and Duflo, E. (2012), 'The Price is Wrong', *FACTS Reports*, Special Issue 4.

Beaman, L., Duflo, E., Pande, R. and Topalova, P. (2006), 'Women Politicians, Gender Bias, and Policy-Making in Rural India', background paper for *The State of the World's Children 2007*, UNICEF.

Begum, S. and Sen, B. (2009), 'Maternal Health, Child Well-Being and Chronic Poverty: Does Women's Agency Matter?', *Bangladesh Development Studies*, 32.

Behrman, J., Alderman, H. and Hoddinott, J. (2004), 'Hunger and Malnutrition', in B. Lomborg (ed.) (2004), *Gobal Crises, Global Solutions* (Cambridge: Cambridge University Press).

Beinhocker, E. D. (2006), *The Origin of Wealth: Evolution, Complexity and the Radical Remaking of Economics* (Cambridge, MA: Harvard Business School Press).

Belfield, C. and Levin, H. M. (2005), 'Vouchers and Public Policy: When Ideology Trumps Evidence', *American Journal of Education*, 111.

Berg, E., Bhattacharya, S., Durgam, R. and Ramachandra, M. (2012), 'Can Rural Public Works Affect Agricultural Wages? Evidence from India', Working Paper 2012–05, Centre for the Study of African Economies, University of Oxford.

Béteille, André (2012), 'The Peculiar Tenacity of Caste', *Economic and Political Weekly*, 31 March.

Bhagwati, J. and Panagariya, A. (2013), *Why Growth Matters: How Economic Growth in India Reduced Poverty and the Lessons for Other Developing Countries* (Public Affairs).

Bhalotra, S. and Cochrane, T. (2010), 'Where Have All the Young Girls Gone? Identifying Sex Selection in India', Working Paper 10/254, Centre for Market and Public Organisation, University of Bristol.

Bhargava, Rajeev (forthcoming), 'Beyond Toleration: Civility and Principled Coexistence in Asokan Edicts', to be published in A. Stepan and C. Taylor (eds.) (forthcoming), *The Boundaries of Toleration* (New York: Columbia University Press).

Bhatia, Bela (2011), 'Awaiting Nachiso: Naga Elders Remember 1957', *Himal*, August.

Bhattacharjea, S., Wadhwa, W. and Banerji, R. (2011), *Inside Primary Schools* (Mumbai: ASER).

Bhatti, Bharat (2012), 'Aadhaar-enabled Payments for NREGA Workers', *Economic and Political Weekly*, 8 December.

Bhatty, Kiran (2011), 'Social Equality and Development: Himachal Pradesh and its Wider Significance', M.Phil. thesis, London School of Economics.

Bidwai, Praful (2012), *The Politics of Climate Change and the Global Crisis: Mortgaging our Future* (New Delhi: Orient Blackswan).

Bowles, Samuel (2007), 'Social Preferences and Public Economics: Are Good Laws a Substitute for Good Citizens?', Working Paper, Santa Fe Institute, New Mexico.

Bowles, S. and Reyes, S. P. (2009), 'Economic Incentives and Social Preferences: A Preference-based Lucas Critique of Public Policy', Working Paper 2009–11, Department of Economics, University of Massachusetts.

Bowles, S. and Hwang, Sung-Ha (2008), 'Social Preferences and Public Economics', *Journal of Public Economics*, 92.

Brannen, J. and Wilson, G. (eds.) (1987), *Give and Take in Families* (London: Allen & Unwin).

Bruns, B., Evans, D. and Luque, J. (2012), *Achieving World-Class Education in Brazil* (Washington, DC: World Bank).

Cashman, R. (1980), *Players, Patrons and the Crowd* (Delhi: Orient Longman).

Cataife, G. and Courtemanche, C. (2011), 'Is Universal Health Care in Brazil Really Universal?', Working Paper 17069, National Bureau of Economic Research, Cambridge, MA.

Center for Environmental Science and Policy (2006), 'Rural Electrification in China 1950–2004: Historical Processes and Key Driving Forces', Working Paper 60, Program on Energy and Sustainable Development, Stanford University, CA.

REFERENCES

Central Information Commission (2012), *Annual Report 2011–12* (New Delhi: CIC).

Centre for Media Studies (2011), *India Corruption Study: 2010* (New Delhi: Centre for Media Studies).

Centre for Science and Environment (2008), 'An Assessment of the Performance of the National Rural Employment Guarantee Programme in Terms of its Potential for Creation of Natural Wealth in India's Villages', available at knowledge.nrega.net.

Centre for Science and Environment (2012), *Excreta Matters* (New Delhi: Centre for Society and Environment).

Cerami, Alfio (2009), 'Welfare State Developments in the Russian Federation: Oil-Led Social Policy and "The Russian Miracle"', *Social Policy and Administration*, 43.

Chakraborty, Achin (2005), 'Kerala's Changing Development Narratives', *Economic and Political Weekly*, 5 February.

Chakravarty, S., Friedman, D., Gupta, G., Hatekar, N., Mitra, S. and Sunder, S. (2011), 'Experimental Economics: A Survey', *Economic and Political Weekly*, 27 August.

Chakravarty, Sukhamoy (1987), *Development Planning: The Indian Experience* (New Delhi: Oxford University Press).

Chamaria, A., Kumar, J. and Yadav, Y. (2006), 'Survey of the Social Profile of the Key Decision Makers in the National Media', unpublished report, Centre for the Study of Developing Societies, New Delhi.

Chandrasekhar, C. P. and Ghosh, J. (2011), 'Women's Work in India: Has Anything Changed', *Macroscan*, August; available at www.macroscan.org.

Chang, Ha-Joon (2002), *Kicking Away the Ladder: Development Strategy in Historical Perspective* (London: Anthem).

Chang, Ha-Joon (2010), 23 *Things They Didn't Tell You About Capitalism* (New York: Allen Lane).

Chattopadhyay, R. and Duflo, E. (2004), 'Impact of Reservation in Panchayati Raj', *Economic and Political Weekly*, 28 February.

Chaudhury, N. and Hammer, J. (2004), 'Ghost Doctors: Absenteeism in Rural Bangladeshi Health Facilities', *World Bank Economic Review*, 18.

Chaudhury, N., Hammer, J., Kremer, M., Muralidharan, K. and Rogers, F. H. (2006), 'Missing in Action: Teacher and Health Worker Absence in Developing Countries', *Journal of Economic Perspectives*, 20.

Chavan, P. and Bedamatta, R. (2006), 'Trends in Agricultural Wages in India', *Economic and Political Weekly*, 23 September.

Chitnis, A., Dixit, S. and Josey, A. (2012), 'Bailing out Unaccountability', *Economic and Political Weekly*, 22 December.

Chomsky, Noam (1999), *Powers and Prospects* (London: Pluto).

Chopra, Deepta (2010), 'National Rural Employment Guarantee Act (NREGA) in India: Towards an Understanding of Policy Spaces', PhD thesis, Department of Geography, University of Cambridge.

Chopra, Deepta (2011), 'Policy Making in India: A Porous and Relational Process of "State Craft"', *Pacific Affairs*, 84.

Chopra, S. and Khera, R. (2012), 'Cutting Delays in NREGA Wages', available at www.ideasforindia.in.

Chowdhury, M., Bhuiya, A., Chowdhury, M. E., Rasheed, S., Hussain, A. M. Z. and Chen, L. C. (2012), 'The Bangladesh Paradox: Exceptional Health Achievement despite Economic Poverty', mimeo, International Centre for Diarrhoeal Disease Research, Bangladesh; to be published in *The Lancet*.

Chowdhury, Zafrullah (1995), *The Politics of Essential Drugs: The Makings of a Successful Health Strategy: Lessons from Bangladesh* (London: Zed).

Ciniscalco, Maria Teresa (2004), 'Teachers' Salaries', Background paper for the *Education for All: Global Monitoring Report 2005*, UNESCO.

Citizens' Initiative for the Rights of Children Under Six (2006), *Focus on Children Under Six*; available at www.righttofoodindia.org/data/rtfo6focusreportabridged.pdf.

Cleland, John (2002), 'Education and Future Fertility Trends, with Special Reference to Mid-Transitional Countries', *Population Bulletin of the United Nations*, Special Issue, 48/49.

Comim, Flavio (2012), 'Poverty and Inequality Reduction in Brazil throughout the Economic Crisis', ISPI Analysis, no. 106, Instituto per gli Studi di Politica Internazionale, Milan.

Comim, F. and Amaral, P. (2012), 'The Human Values Index: Conceptual Foundations and Evidence from Brazil', background paper for Brazil's Human Development Report; to be published in *Cambridge Journal of Economics*.

Conti, G. and Heckman, J. J. (2012), 'The Developmental Approach to Child and Adult Health', NBER Working Paper 18664, National Bureau of Economic Research, Cambridge, MA.

Corbridge, S., Harriss, J. and Jeffrey, C. (2012), *India Today: Economy, Politics and Society* (Cambridge: Polity Press).

Crespo-Cuaresma, J., Samir, K. C. and Sauer, P. (2012), 'Gini Coefficients of Educational Attainment, Age Group Specific Trends in Educational (In) Equality', paper presented at the annual meeting of the Population Association of America, San Francisco, 3–5 May 2012; available at paa2012.princeton.edu.

da Silva, V. A. and Terrazas, F. V. (2011), 'Claiming the Right to Health in

Brazilian Courts: The Exclusion of the Already Excluded?', *Law and Social Enquiry*, 36.

Damodaran, Harish (2008), *India's New Capitalists: Caste, Business, and Industry in a Modern Nation* (Ranikhet: Permanent Black).

Das Gupta, Monica (2005), 'Public Health in India: Dangerous Neglect', *Economic and Political Weekly*, 3 December.

Das Gupta, M., Desikachari, B. R., Shukla, R., Somanathan, T. V., Padmanaban, P. and Datta, K. K. (2010), 'How Might India's Public Health Systems be Strengthtened? Lessons from Tamil Nadu', *Economic and Political Weekly*, 6 March.

Das, Bhagwan (ed.) (2010), *Thus Spoke Ambedkar* (New Delhi: Navayana).

Das, Gurcharan (2012), *India Grows at Night: A Liberal Case for a Strong State* (New Delhi: Penguin).

Das, J. and Hammer, J. (2004), 'Strained Mercy: Quality of Medical Care in Delhi', *Economic and Political Weekly*, 28 February.

Das, J., Holla, A., Das, V., Mohanan, M., Tabak, D. and Chan, B. (2012), 'In Urban and Rural India, a Standardized Patient Study Showed Low Levels of Provider Training and Huge Quality Gaps', *Health Affairs*, 31.

Datt, Gaurav (1998), 'Poverty in India and Indian States: An Update', *Indian Journal of Labour Economics*, 41.

Datt, G., Kozel, V. and Ravallion, M. (2003), 'A Model-Based Assessment of India's Progress in Reducing Poverty in the 1990s', *Economic and Political Weekly*, 25 January.

Datt, G. and Ravallion, M. (1998), 'Why Have Some States Done Better than Others at Reducing Rural Poverty?', *Economica*, 65.

Datt, G. and Ravallion, M. (2010), 'Shining for the Poor Too?', *Economic and Political Weekly*, 13 February.

De, A., Khera, R., Samson, M. and Shiva Kumar, A. K. (2011), PROBE *Revisited: A Report on Elementary Education in India* (New Delhi: Oxford University Press).

De, A., Samson, M., Chakravarty, A. and Das, S. (2010), 'Schooling for Children in Interstate Border Areas', study commissioned by NEG-FIRE; available at www.cordindia.com.

Dé, Shobhaa (2008), *Superstar India* (New Delhi: Penguin).

Deaton, Angus (forthcoming), *The Great Escape: Health, Wealth and the Origins of Inequality* (Princeton, NJ: Princeton University Press).

Deaton, A. and Drèze, J. P. (2002), 'Poverty and Inequality in India: A Reexamination', *Economic and Political Weekly*, 7 September.

Deaton, A. and Drèze, J. P. (2009), 'Food and Nutrition in India: Facts and Interpretations', *Economic and Political Weekly*, 14 February.

Desai, P. B. (1979), *Planning in India, 1951–78* (New Delhi: Vikas).

Desai, S. B., Dubey, A., Joshi, B. L., Sen, M., Shariff, A. and Vanneman, R. (2010), *Human Development in India: Challenges for a Society in Transition* (New Delhi: Oxford University Press).

Dey, N., Drèze, J. and Khera, R. (2006), *Employment Guarantee Act: A Primer* (New Delhi: National Book Trust).

Dheeraja, C. and Rao, K. H. (forthcoming), *Changing Gender Relations: A Study of MGNREGS Across Different States* (Hyderabad: NIRD).

Dore, Ronald (1965), *Education in Tokugawa Japan* (London: Routledge and Kegan Paul).

Drèze, Jean (2001), 'Right to Food and Public Accountability', *The Hindu*, 5 December.

Drèze, Jean (2004), 'Democracy and the Right to Food', *Economic and Political Weekly*, 24 April.

Drèze, Jean (2005), 'Dr. Ambedkar and the Future of Indian Democracy', *Indian Journal of Human Rights*, 9.

Drèze, Jean (2006a), 'Universalization with Quality: ICDS in a Rights Perspective', *Economic and Political Weekly*, 26 August.

Drèze, Jean (2006b), 'Tamil Nadu Viewed from the North', in Citizen's Initiative for the Rights of Children Under Six (2006).

Drèze, Jean (2010), 'Employment Guarantee and the Right to Work', in N. G. Jayal and P. B. Mehta (eds.) (2010), *The Oxford Companion to Politics in India* (New Delhi: Oxford University Press); reprinted in Khera (2011d).

Drèze, Jean (2011), 'The Bribing Game', *Indian Express*, 23 April.

Drèze, Jean (2012), 'Poverty, Targeting and Food Security', *Seminar*, 634.

Drèze, J. P. and Gazdar, H. (1996), 'Uttar Pradesh: The Burden of Inertia', in Drèze and Sen (1996).

Drèze, J. P. and Goyal, A. (2003), 'The Future of Midday Meals', *Economic and Political Weekly*, 1 November.

Drèze, J. P. and Khera, R. (2008), 'Glucose for Lok Sabha?', *Hindustan Times*, 14 April.

Drèze, J. P. and Khera, R. (2009a), 'Mid-Day Meals in Primary Schools', in A. Kumar and A. P. Singh (eds.) (2009), *Elementary Education in India: Issues and Challenges* (New Delhi: Uppal).

Drèze, J. P. and Khera, R. (2009b), 'The Battle for Employment Guarantee', *Frontline*, 3 January; reprinted in Khera (2011d).

Drèze, J. P. and Khera, R. (2010a), 'The BPL Census and a Possible Alternative', *Economic and Political Weekly*, 27 February.

Drèze, J. P. and Khera, R. (2010b), 'Chhattisgarh Shows the Way', *The Hindu*, 13 November.

Drèze, J. P. and Khera, R. (2011), 'PDS Leakages: The Plot Thickens', *The Hindu*, 13 August.

Drèze, J. P. and Khera, R. (2012a), 'Regional Patterns of Human and Child Development', *Economic and Political Weekly*, 29 September.

Drèze, J. P. and Khera, R. (2012b), 'A Bill that Asks too Much of the Poor', *The Hindu*, 5 September.

Drèze, J. P. and Khera, R. (2013), 'Poverty and the Public Distribution System', mimeo, Institute of Economic Growth, Delhi University.

Drèze, J. P., Khera, R. and Siddhartha (2008), 'Corruption in NREGA: Myths and Reality', *The Hindu*, 22 January.

Drèze, J. P. and Murthi, M. (2001), 'Fertility, Education and Development: Evidence from India', *Population and Development Review*, 27.

Drèze, J. P. and Sen, A. K. (1989), *Hunger and Public Action* (Oxford: Oxford University Press).

Drèze, J. P. and Sen, A. K. (1995), *India: Economic Development and Social Opportunity* (Oxford: Oxford University Press).

Drèze, J. P. and Sen, A. K. (2002), *India: Development and Participation* (Oxford: Oxford University Press).

Drèze, J. P. and Sen, A. K. (eds.) (1990), *The Political Economy of Hunger*, 3 vols. (Oxford: Oxford University Press).

Drèze, J. P. and Sen, A. K. (eds.) (1996), *Indian Development: Selected Regional Perspectives* (Oxford: Oxford University Press).

Duclos, P., Okwo-Bele, J. M., Gacic-Dobo, M. and Cherian, T. (2009), 'Global Immunization: Status, Progress, and Future', *BMC International Health and Human Rights*, 9.

Duflo, Esther (2011), 'Women's Empowerment and Economic Development', Working Paper 17702, National Bureau of Economic Research, Cambridge, MA.

Dunn, John (2005), *Democracy: A History* (New York: Atlantic Monthly Press).

Dutta, K. and Robinson, A. (1995), *Rabindranath Tagore: The Myriad-Minded Man* (New York: St Martin's Press).

Dutta, P., Howes, S. and Murgai, R. (2010), 'Small but Effective: India's Targeted Unconditional Cash Transfers', *Economic and Political Weekly*, 25 December.

Dutta, P., Murgai, R., Ravallion, M. and Van de Walle, D. (2012), 'Does India's Employment Guarantee Scheme Guarantee Employment?', *Economic and Political Weekly*, 21 April.

Dutta, P., Murgai, R., Ravallion, M. and Van de Walle, D. (forthcoming), *Rozgar Guarantee? Assessing India's Biggest Anti-Poverty Program in India's Poorest State* (Washington, DC: World Bank).

Dyson, Tim (1997), 'Infant and Child Mortality in the Indian Subcontinent, 1881–1947', in A. Bideau, B. Desjardins and H. P. Brignoli (eds.) (1997), *Infant and Child Mortality in the Past* (Oxford: Clarendon Press).

Dyson, T. and Moore, M. (1983), 'On Kinship Structure, Female Autonomy, and Demographic Behavior in India', *Population and Development Review*, 9.

Educational Initiatives (2011), *Quality Education Study* (Bangalore: Educational Initiatives).

El Arifeen, S. et al. (2012), 'Community-based Approaches and Partnerships: Innovations in Health Service Delivery in Bangladesh', mimeo, International Centre for Diarrhoeal Diseases Research, Dhaka.

Election Commission of India (2009), *Statistical Report of General Elections 2009* (New Delhi: Election Commission of India).

Emran, M. S. and Shilpi, F. (2012), 'Gender, Geography and Generations: Intergenerational Educational Mobility in Post-Reform India', paper presented at IGC-ISI conference, Indian Statistical Institute, New Delhi, July 2012.

Fan, S., Gulati, A. and Thorat, S. (2008), 'Investment, Subsidies, and Pro-Poor Growth in Rural India', *Agricultural Economics*, 39.

Fehr, E. and Fischbacher, U. (2000), 'Why Social Preferences Matter: The Impact of Non-selfish Motives on Competition, Cooperation and Incentives', *Economic Journal*, 112.

Ferber, M. A. and Nelson, J. A. (eds.) (1993), *Beyond Economic Man* (Chicago, IL: Chicago University Press).

Ferreira de Souza, Pedro H. G. (2012), 'Poverty, Inequality and Social Policies in Brazil, 1995–2009', Working Paper 87, International Policy Centre for Inclusive Growth, Brasilia.

Ferreira, F. and Robalino, D. (2010), 'Social Protection in Latin America: Achievements and Limitations', Policy Research Working Paper 5305, World Bank, Washington, DC.

Ferreira, F., Leite, P. and Ravallion, M. (2010), 'Poverty Reduction without Economic Growth? Explaining Brazil's Poverty Dynamics 1985–2004', *Journal of Development Economics*, 93.

Fleury, Sonia (2011), 'Brazil's Health-Care Reform: Social Movements and Civil Society', *The Lancet*, 377.

Folbre, Nancy (1986), 'Hearts and Spades: Paradigms of Household Economics', *World Development*, 14.

Foster, J. and Sen, A. K. (1997), 'On Economic Inequality after a Quarter Century', in Sen (1973, 1997).

Fraser, Lovat (1919), *Iron and Steel in India: A Chapter from the Life of Jamsetji N. Tata* (Bombay: The Times Press).

Friedman, Milton (1955), 'A Memorandum to the Government of India', *New Delhi*, 5 November; available at http://www.indiapolicy.org/debate/Notes/friedman.htm.

Fuller, C. J. (ed.) (1997), *Caste Today* (New Delhi: Oxford University Press).

Gaikwad, Laxman (1998), *The Branded: Uchalya* (New Delhi: Sahitya Akademi).

Gaitonde, R. and Shukla, A. (2012), 'Setting Up Universal Health Care Pvt. Ltd.', *The Hindu*, 13 September.

Gandhi, A. and Walton, M. (2012), 'Where Do India's Billionaires Get Their Wealth?', *Economic and Political Weekly*, 6 October.

Gandhi, M. K. (1937a), editorial published in Harijan, 11 September; partly reprinted in Narayan (1968).

Gandhi, M. K. (1937b), editorial published in Harijan, 5 June; partly reprinted in Narayan (1968).

Garg, Samir (2006), 'Grassroot Mobilisation for Children's Nutrition Rights', *Economic and Political Weekly*, 26 August.

Gatade, Subhash (2013), 'Schools of Discrimination', *Infochange*, January.

Gauri, V. and Vawda, A. (2004), 'Vouchers for Education in Developing Economies: An Accountability Perspective', *World Bank Research Observer*, 19.

Geetha, V. (1998), 'Periyar, Women and an Ethic of Citizenship', *Economic and Political Weekly*, 25 April.

Ghosh, Arunabha (2006), 'Pathways through Financial Crisis: India', *Global Governance*, 12.

Gill, Kaveri (2009), 'A Primary Evaluation of Delivery under the National Rural Health Mission', Working Paper 1/2009, Programme Evaluation Organisation, Planning Commission, New Delhi.

Giridharadas, Anand (2011), *India Calling: An Intimate Portrait of a Nation's Remaking* (New Delhi: Fourth Estate).

Glaeser, E., La Porta, R., Lopez-de-Silanes, F. and Shleifer, A. (2004), 'Do Institutions Cause Growth?', *Journal of Economic Growth*, 9.

Gluck, Carol (1985), *Japan's Modern Myths: Ideology in the Late Meiji Period* (Princeton, NJ: Princeton University Press).

Gopaldas, Tara (2006), 'Hidden Hunger', *Economic and Political Weekly*, 26 August.

Government of India (1946), *Report of the Health Survey and Development Committee*, 2 vols. (Calcutta: India Press).

Government of India (1992), *National Policy on Education 1986 (With Modifications Undertaken in 1992)* (New Delhi: Ministry of Human Resource Development).

Government of India (1993), *Report of the Expert Group on Estimation of Proportion and Number of Poor* (New Delhi: Planning Commission).

Government of India (1999), *Compendium of India's Fertility and Mortality Indicators 1971–1997* (New Delhi: Office of the Registrar General).

Government of India (2001a), *Handbook of Industrial Policy and Statistics* (New Delhi: Ministry of Commerce and Industry).

Government of India (2001b), *Economic Survey 2000–2001* (New Delhi: Ministry of Finance).

Government of India (2002a), *Report of the Task Force on Direct Taxes* (New Delhi: Ministry of Finance).

Government of India (2002b), *Report of the Task Force on Indirect Taxes* (New Delhi: Ministry of Finance).

Government of India (2004a), *Report of the Task Force on Implementation of the Fiscal Responsibility and Budget Management Act, 2003* (New Delhi: Ministry of Finance).

Government of India (2004b), *Central Government Subsidies in India: A Report* (New Delhi: Ministry of Finance).

Government of India (2006), *Social, Economic and Educational Status of the Muslim Minority of India: A Report* (New Delhi: Cabinet Secretariat).

Government of India (2008), *Sample Registration System Abridged Life Tables 2002–06* (New Delhi: Office of the Registrar General).

Government of India (2009a), *State of Environment Report: India 2009* (New Delhi: Ministry of Environment and Forests).

Government of India (2009b), *Sample Registration System: Statistical Report 2008* (New Delhi: Office of the Registrar General).

Government of India (2009c), *Report of the Expert Group to Review the Methodology for Estimation of Poverty* (New Delhi: Planning Commission).

Government of India (2009d), *Sample Registration System, Statistical Report 2008, Report No. 1 of 2008* (New Delhi: Office of the Registrar General, Ministry of Home Affairs).

Government of India (2010a), *Handbook of Labour Statistics* (Chandigarh: Labour Bureau).

Government of India (2010b), *Report on Employment and Unemployment Survey (2009–10)* (Chandigarh: Labour Bureau).

Government of India (2010c), *Wage Rates in Rural India* (Chandigarh: Labour Bureau).

Government of India (2011a), *High-Level Expert Group Report on Universal Health Coverage for India* (New Delhi: Planning Commission).

Government of India (2011b), 'Provisional Population Tables', Census of India 2011, Series 1 (India), Paper 1 of 2011 (New Delhi: Office of the Registrar General).

Government of India (2011c), 'Sample Registration Bulletin' (New Delhi: Office of the Registrar General).

Government of India (2011d), *Evaluation Report on Integrated Child Development Services* (New Delhi: Planning Commission).

Government of India (2011e), *Annual Report 2011–12 on the Working of State Power Utilities and Electricity Departments* (New Delhi: Planning Commission).

Government of India (2011f), *Selected Socio-Economic Statistics: India, 2011* (New Delhi: Ministry of Statistics and Programme Implementation).

Government of India (2011g), *Elementary Education in India under Government Managements 2009–10, Selected Tables Based on DISE 2009–10* (New Delhi: National University of Educational Planning and Administration).

Government of India (2011h), *Economic Survey 2010–11* (New Delhi: Ministry of Finance).

Government of India (2011i), *Special Bulletin on Maternal Mortality in India 2007–9* (New Delhi: Office of the Registrar General).

Government of India (2012a), *Economic Survey 2011–12* (New Delhi: Ministry of Finance).

Government of India (2012b), *MGNREGA Sameeksha: An Anthology of Research Studies on the Mahatma Gandhi National Rural Employment Guarantee Act, 2005* (New Delhi: Orient Blackswan).

Government of India (2012c), 'Press Note on Poverty Estimates, 2009–10' (New Delhi: Planning Commission).

Government of India (2012d), *Report of the Committee on Roadmap for Fiscal Consolidation* (New Delhi: Ministry of Finance).

Government of India (2012e), 'Revenue Forgone Under the Central Tax System: Financial Years 2010–11 and 2011–12' (New Delhi: Ministry of Finance).

Government of India (2012f), *Agricultural Statistics at a Glance* (New Delhi: Ministry of Agriculture).

Government of India (2012g), *Sample Registration Bulletin October 2012* (New Delhi: Office of the Registrar General).

Government of India (2012h), 'Houses, Household Amenities and Assets, 2011', available at www.censusofindia.gov.in/2011census/hlo/hlo_highlights.htm.

Government of India (2012i), *Sample Registration System Statistical Report 2011* (New Delhi: Office of the Registrar General).

Government of india (2012j), *SRS-based Abridged Life Tables 2003–7 to 2006–10* (New Delhi: Office of the Registrar General); available at www.censusindia.gov.in.

Government of India (2013), *Economic Survey 2012–13* (New Delhi: Ministry of Finance).

Government of India (various years), *Sample Registration System Statistical Report* (New Delhi: Office of the Registrar General).

Government of Maharashtra (1979–98), *Dr Babasaheb Ambedkar: Writings and Speeches*, 16 vols., ed. V. Moon (Mumbai: Department of Education).

Govinda Rao, M. (2011), 'Curing the Cancer of Concessions', *Financial Express*, 5 December.

Goyal, S. and Pandey, P. (2012), 'How Do Government and Private Schools Differ?', *Economic and Political Weekly*, 2 June.

Guha, Ramachandra (2007), *India After Gandhi: The History of the World's Largest Democracy* (London: Macmillan).

Guha, Ramachandra (2012), 'Terminal Damage', *Hindustan Times*, 24 July.

Guha Thakurta, P. (2011), 'Manufacturing "News"', *Economic and Political Weekly*, 2 April.

Gulati, A. and Narayanan, S. (2003), *The Subsidy Syndrome in Indian Agriculture* (New Delhi: Oxford University Press).

Gupta, Aashish (2013), 'The Old-age Pension Scheme in Jharkhand and Chhattisgarh', Working Paper, Department of Economics, Allahabad University; forthcoming in *Economic and Political Weekly*.

Gupta, Shalini (2012), 'Food Expenditure and Intake in the NSS 66th Round', *Economic and Political Weekly*, 14 January.

Habermas, Jürgen (1996), 'Three Normative Models of Democracy', in Seyla Benhabib (ed.) (1996), *Democracy and Difference: Contesting the Boundaries of the Political* (Princeton, NJ: Princeton University Press).

Halstead, S. B. et al. (eds.) (1985), *Good Health at Low Cost* (New York: Rockefeller Foundation).

Hammer, J., Aiyar, Y. and Samji, S. (2007), 'Understanding Government Failure in Public Health Services', *Economic and Political Weekly*, 6 October.

Hankla, C. R. (2006), 'Party Linkages and Economic Policy: An Examination of Indira Gandhi's India', *Business and Politics*, 8.

Hanushek, E. A. and Woessmann, L. (2008), 'The Role of Cognitive Skills in Economic Development', *Journal of Economic Literature*, 46.

HAQ: Centre for Child Rights (2005), *Says a Child . . . Who Speaks for my Rights? Parliament in Budget Session 2005* (New Delhi: HAQ).

Harris, F. R. (1958), *Jamsetji Nusserwanji Tata: A Chronicle of His Life*, 2nd edn. (Bombay: Blackie).

Harriss, J., Jeyarajan, J. and Nagaraj, K. (2010), 'Land, Labour and Caste Politics in Rural Tamil Nadu in the 20th Century', *Economic and Political Weekly*, 31 July.

Hart, Caroline Sarojini (2012), *Aspirations, Education and Social Justice: Applying Sen and Bourdieu* (London: Bloomsbury).

Hazarika, G. and Viren, V. (2013), 'The Effect of Early Child Developmental

Program Attendance on Future School Enrollment in Rural North India', *Economics of Education Review*, 34.

Hazarika, Sanjoy (2013a), 'An Abomination Called AFSPA', *The Hindu*, 12 February.

Hazarika, Sanjoy (2013b), 'It is Just not Just', *Hindustan Times*, 11 March.

Heckman, James J. (2008), 'Capability Formation, Early Intervention, and Long-Term Health', presentation at Outcomes Research Workshop, University of Chicago, 1 October.

Heller, Patrick (1999), *The Labor of Development: Workers and the Transformation of Capitalism in Kerala, India* (Ithaca, NY: Cornell University Press).

Heller, Patrick (2000), 'Degrees of Democracy: Some Comparative Lessons from India', *World Politics*, 52.

Heller, Patrick (2009), 'Democratic Deepening in India and South Africa', *Journal of Asian and African Studies*, 44.

Helpman, Elhanan (2004), *The Mystery of Economic Growth* (Cambridge, MA: Harvard University Press).

Himanshu (2005), 'Wages in Rural India: Sources, Trends and Comparability', *Indian Journal of Labour Economics*, 48.

Himanshu (2007), 'Recent Trends in Poverty and Inequality: Some Preliminary Results', *Economic and Political Weekly*, 10 February.

Himanshu (2012), 'Poverty and Food Security in India', paper presented at a symposium on 'Food Security in Asia and the Pacific', University of British Columbia, 17–18 September.

Himanshu (2013), 'The Dubious Promise of Cash Transfers', *Livemint*, 14 March.

Himanshu, Lanjouw, P., Mukhopadhyay, A. and Murgai, R. (2011), 'Non-Farm Diversification and Rural Poverty Decline: A Perspective from Indian Sample Survey and Village Study Data', Working Paper 44, Asia Research Centre, London School of Economics.

Himanshu and Sen, A. (2013), 'In-kind Food Transfers: Impact on Poverty Reduction and Nutrition', mimeo, Jawaharlal Nehru University, New Delhi.

Hirschman, Albert O. (1970), *Exit, Voice, and Loyalty: Responses to Decline in Firms, Organizations, and States* (Cambridge, MA: Harvard University Press).

Hirway, I. and Batabyal, S. (2011), *MGNREGA and Women's Empowerment* (New Delhi: UN Women South Asia).

Horton, Richard (2012), 'Offline: Universal Coverage, Universally', *The Lancet*, 20 October.

Howes, S. and Murgai, R. (2006), 'Subsidies and Salaries: Issues in the Restructuring of Government Expenditure in India', in P. Heller and Govinda M. Rao (eds.) (2006), *A Sustainable Fiscal Policy for India: An International Perspective* (New Delhi: Oxford University Press).

Hsieh, C. T. and Urquiola, M. (2006), 'The Effects of Generalized School Choice on Achievements and Stratification: Evidence from Chile's Voucher Program', *Journal of Public Economics*, 90.

Huntington, Samuel (1991), *The Third Wave: Democratization in the Late Twentieth Century* (Norman, OK, and London: University of Oklahoma Press).

Ilaiah, K. (1996), *Why I am not a Hindu* (Kolkata: Samya).

Imbert, C. and Papp, J. (2011), 'Equilibrium Distributional Impacts of Government Employment Programs: Evidence from India's Employment Guarantee', mimeo, Princeton University, NJ.

Integrated Research and Action for Development (2012), *Taming Diesel Subsidy to Curtail Inflation and Foster Economic Growth* (New Delhi: IRADe).

International Institute for Population Sciences (2000), *National Family Health Survey (NFHS-2): India* (Mumbai: IIPS).

International Institute for Population Sciences (2007a), *National Family Health Survey (NFHS-3), 2005–06: India* (Mumbai: IIPS).

International Institute for Population Sciences (2007b), *2005–06 National Family Health Survey (NFHS-3): National Fact Sheet* (Mumbai: IIPS).

International Institute for Population Sciences (2008), *National Family Health Survey (NFHS-3), 2005–06: State Reports* (Mumbai: IIPS).

International Institute for Population Sciences (2010a), *District Level Household and Facility Survey (DLHS-3), 2007–08: India* (Mumbai: IIPS).

International Institute for Population Sciences (2010b), *District Level Household and Facility Survey (DLHS-3), 2007–08: State Reports* (Mumbai: IIPS).

International Institute for Population Sciences (2012), *Comprehensive Nutrition Survey in Maharashtra 2012: Fact Sheet (Provisional Data)* (Mumbai: IIPS).

International Labour Organization (2012), *Global Wage Report 2012–13* (Geneva: ILO).

Isaac, T. and Tharakan, M. (1995), 'Kerala: Towards a New Agenda', *Economic and Political Weekly*, 5 August.

Jain, Monica (2012), 'India's Struggle against Malnutrition: Is the ICDS Program the Answer?', mimeo, Department of Economics, University of California, Riverside; available at http://monica-jain.com/wp-content/uploads/2011/10/Job-Market-Paper_Monica-Jain1.pdf

Jain, P. S. and Dholakia, R. H. (2010), 'Feasibility of Implementation of Right to Education Act', *Economic and Political Weekly*, 20 June.

Jalan, Bimal (2012), 'Indira Gandhi', in Basu and Maertens (2012).

Jansen, Marius B. (2002), *The Making of Modern Japan* (Cambridge, MA: Harvard University Press).

Jansen, Marius B. (ed.) (1989), *The Cambridge History of Japan. Vol 5: The Nineteenth Century* (Cambridge: Cambridge University Press).

Jansen, M. B. and Rozman, G. (eds.) (1986), *Japan in Transition: From Tokugawa to Meiji* (Princeton, NJ: Princeton University Press).

Jayachandran, S. and Pande, R. (2013), 'Parental Preferences as a Cause of India's High Rate of Child Stunting', mimeo, Harvard University.

Jayadev, A., Motiram, S. and Vakulabharanam, V. (2007), 'Patterns of Wealth Disparities in India during the Liberalisation Era', *Economic and Political Weekly*, 22 September.

Jayaraj, D. and Subramanian, S. (2010), 'A Chakravarty-D'Ambrosio View of Multidimensional Deprivation: Some Estimates for India', *Economic and Political Weekly*, 6 February.

Jayaraj, D. and Subramanian, S. (2012), 'On the Interpersonal Inclusiveness of India's Consumption Expenditure Growth', *Economic and Political Weekly*, 10 November.

Jayaraman, R. and Simroth, D. (2011), 'The Impact of School Lunches on Primary School Enrolment: Evidence from India's Midday Meal Scheme', Working Paper 11-11, European School of Management and Technology, Berlin.

Jeevan Reddy Committee (2005), 'Report of the Committee to Review the Armed Forces (Special Powers) Act, 1958', report submitted to the Government of India; available at www.hindu.com/nic/afa/.

Jeffrey, Robin (2000), *India's Newspaper Revolution* (New Delhi: Oxford University Press).

Jeffrey, Robin (2012), 'Missing from the Indian Newsroom', *The Hindu*, 9 April.

Jha, P., Kesler, M. A., Kumar, R., Ram, F., Ram, U., Aleksandrowicz, L., Bassani, D. G., Chandra, S. and Banthia, J. K. (2011), 'Trends in Selective Abortions of Girls in India: Analysis of Nationally Representative Birth Histories from 1990 to 2005 and Census Data from 1991 to 2011', *The Lancet*, 377.

Jha, Prabhat et al. (2013), '21st-Century Hazards of Smoking and Benefits of Cessation in the United States', *The New England Journal of Medicine*, 368.

Jha, S. and Ramaswami, B. (2010), 'How Can Food Subsidies Work Better? Answers from India and the Philippines', ADB Economics Working Paper 221, Asian Development Bank, Manila.

John, M., Kaur, R., Palriwala, R. and Raju, S. (2009), 'Dispensing with Daughters: Technology, Society, Economy in North India', *Economic and Political Weekly*, 11 April.

John, T. J. and Choudhury, P. (2009), 'Accelerating Measles Control in India', *Indian Pediatrics*, 46.

Jose, Jijo (2011), 'The PDS Learning Curve', *Down to Earth*, 18 August.

Joseph, Shaji (2006), 'Power of the People: Political Mobilisation and Guaranteed Employment', *Economic and Political Weekly*, 16 December.

Joshi, Anuradha (2010), 'Do Rights Work? Law, Activism, and the Employment Guarantee Scheme', *World Development*, 38.

Joshi, V. and Little, I. M. D. (1994), *India: Macroeconomics and Political Economy 1964–1991* (Washington, DC: World Bank).

J-PAL (2011), 'The Price is Wrong: Charging Small Fees Dramatically Reduces Access to Important Products for the Poor', J-PAL Bulletin, Abdul Latif Jameel Poverty Action Lab, Massachusetts Institute of Technology, April 2011; available at www.povertyactionlab.org/publication/the-price-is-wrong

Judt, Tony (2010), *Ill Fares the Land* (New York: Penguin).

Jurberg, C. and Humphreys, G. (2010), 'Brazil's March Towards Universal Coverage', WHO *Bulletin*, 88.

Kabeer, Naila (2011), 'Between Affiliation and Autonomy: Navigating Pathways of Women's Empowerment and Gender Justice in Rural Bangladesh', *Development and Change*, 42.

Kandpal, Eeshani (2011), 'Beyond Average Treatment Effects: Distribution of Child Nutrition Outcomes and Program Placement in India's ICDS', *World Development*, 39.

Kannan, K. P. and Raveendran, G. (2009), 'Growth Sans Employment: A Quarter Century of Jobless Growth in Indian Manufacturing', *Economic and Political Weekly*, 7 March.

Kapoor, Radhicka (2013), 'Inequality Matters', *Economic and Political Weekly*, 12 January.

Kapur, D. and Mehta, P. B. (eds.) (2005), *Public Institutions in India: Performance and Design* (New Delhi: Oxford University Press).

Karve, Irawati (1968), *Kinship Organization in India* (Bombay: Asia Publishing House).

Kaushik, A. and Pal, R. (2012), 'How Representative Has the Lok Sabha Been?', *Economic and Political Weekly*, 12 May.

Kavita Rao, R. (2013), 'Revenue Foregone Estimates: Some Analytical Issues', *Economic and Political Weekly*, 30 March.

Keer, Dhananjay (1971), *Dr Ambedkar: Life and Mission*, 3rd edn. (Mumbai: Popular Prakashan).

Khera, Reetika (2006), 'Mid-day Meals in Primary Schools: Achievements and Challenges', *Economic and Political Weekly*, 18 November.

Khera, Reetika (2011a), 'The UID Project and Welfare Schemes', *Economic and Political Weekly*, 26 February.

Khera, Reetika (2011b), 'Trends in Diversion of Grain from the Public Distribution System', *Economic and Political Weekly*, 21 May.

Khera, Reetika (2011c), 'Revival of the Public Distribution System: Evidence and Explanations', *Economic and Political Weekly*, 5 November.

Khera, Reetika (ed.) (2011d), *The Battle for Employment Guarantee* (New Delhi: Oxford University Press).

Khera, Reetika (2012), 'Tamil Nadu's Striking Progress in Welfare', available at www.indiatogether.org/2012/sep/gov-tnwelfare.htm

Khera, R. and Muthiah, K. (2010), 'Slow but Steady Success', *The Hindu*, 25 April.

Khera, R. and Nayak, N. (2009), 'Women Workers and Perceptions of the National Rural Employment Guarantee Act', *Economic and Political Weekly*, 24 October; reprinted in Khera (2011d).

Kidambi, Sowmya (2011), 'Termites, Earthworms, and Other Organic Gardeners', *Seminar*, 625.

Kingdon, Geeta (2010) 'The Implications of the Sixth Pay Commission on Teacher Salaries in India', RECOUP Working Paper 29, Faculty of Education, University of Cambridge.

Kingdon, G. and Sipahimalani-Rao, V. (2010), 'Para Teachers in India: Status and Impact', *Economic and Political Weekly*, 20 March.

Kishor, K. and Gupta, K. (2009), *Gender Equality and Women's Empowerment in India* (Mumbai: International Institute for Population Sciences).

Kishor, S. and Gupta, K. (2004), 'Women's Empowerment in India and its States: Evidence from the NFHS', *Economic and Political Weekly*, 14 February.

Klonner, S. and Oldiges, C. (2013), 'Can an Employment Guarantee Alleviate Poverty? Evidence from India's National Rural Employment Guarantee Act', draft paper, University of Heidelberg.

Knaul, F. M. et al. (2012), 'The Quest for Universal Health Coverage: Achieving Social Protection for All in Mexico', *The Lancet*, 380.

Koehlmoos T. P., Islam, Z., Anwar, S., Hossain, S. A. S., Gazi, R., Streatfield, P. K. and Bhuiya, A. U. (2011), 'Health Transcends Poverty: The Bangladesh Experience', in Balabanova et al. (2011).

Kohli, Atul (2012), *Poverty amid Plenty in the New India* (Cambridge: Cambridge University Press).

Kohli, Vanita (2006), *The Indian Media Business* (New Delhi: Sage).

Kotwal, A., Murugkar, M. and Ramaswami, B. (2012), 'PDS Forever?', *Economic and Political Weekly*, 21 May.

Kotwal, A. and Roy Chaudhuri, A. (2013), 'Why is Poverty Declining so

Slowly in India?', paper presented at the Silver Jubilee Conference of the Indira Gandhi Institute of Development Research, Mumbai.

Kotwal, A., Ramaswami, B. and Wadhwa, W. (2011), 'Economic Liberalization and Indian Economic Growth: What's the Evidence?', *Journal of Economic Literature*, 49.

Kravdal, Øystein (2004), 'Child Mortality in India: The Community-level Effect of Education', *Population Studies*, 58.

Kremer, M., Muralidharan, K. Chaudhury, N., Hammer, J. and Rogers, F. H. (2005), 'Teacher Absence in India: A Snapshot', *Journal of the European Economic Association*, 3.

Krishna, Raj (1982), 'Assessing India's Economic Development', *Mainstream*, 25 October.

Kruks-Wisner, Gabrielle (2011), 'Seeking the Local State: Gender, Caste and the Pursuit of Public Services in post-Tsunami India', *World Development*, 39.

Kruks-Wisner, Gabrielle (2012), 'How Rural India Negotiates with the State', *Business Line*, 3 July.

Kruks-Wisner, Gabrielle (2013), 'Claiming the State: Citizen-State Relations and Public Service Delivery in Rural India', PhD thesis, Department of Political Science, Massachusetts Institute of Technology.

Kumar, S. and Sathyanarayana, K. M. (2012), 'District-level Estimates of Fertility and Implied Sex Ratio at Birth in India', *Economic and Political Weekly*, 18 August.

Kumar, Sanjay (2009), 'Patterns of Political Participation: Trends and Perspective', *Economic and Political Weekly*, 26 September.

Ladd, Helen F. (2002), 'School Vouchers: A Critical Review', *Journal of Economic Perspectives*, 16.

Lahoti, R., Suchitra, J. Y. and Goutam, P. (2012), 'Subsidies for Whom? The Case of LPG in India', *Economic and Political Weekly*, 3 November.

Lenagala, C. and Ram, R. (2010), 'Growth Elasticity of Poverty: Estimates from New Data', *International Journal of Social Economics*, 37.

LeVine, R. A., LeVine, S., Schnell-Anzola, B., Rowe, M. E. and Dexter, E. (2012), *Literacy and Mothering: How Women's Schooling Changes the Lives of the World's Children* (Oxford: Oxford University Press).

Lewis, David (2011), *Bangladesh: Politics, Economics and Civil Society* (Cambridge: Cambridge University Press).

Li, Xingxing (2012), 'Bribery and the Limits of Game Theory – the Lessons from China', Guest post, Financial Times blog (http:/blogs.ft.com).

Lin Chen, de Haan, A., Zhang, X. and Warmerdam, W. (2012), 'Addressing Vulnerability in an Emerging Economy: China's New Cooperative Medical Scheme (NCMS)', *Canadian Journal of Development Studies*, 32.

Liu, Y. and Barrett, C. (2013), 'Heterogeneous Pro-Poor Targeting in the National Rural Employment Guarantee Scheme', *Economic and Political Weekly*, 9 March.

Liu, Y. and Deininger, K. (2010), 'Poverty Impacts of India's National Rural Employment Guarantee Scheme: Evidence from Andhra Pradesh', paper prepared for presentation at a meeting of the Agricultural and Applied Economics Association, Denver, Colorado, 25–27 July 2010.

Lloyd-Sherlock, P. (2009), 'Social Policy and Inequality in Latin America', *Social Policy and Administration*, 43.

Lokhande, Sandesh (2013), 'Social Security Pensions in Maharashtra: A Case Study', mimeo, Indian Institute of Technology, Delhi.

MacAuslan, Ian (2008), 'India's National Rural Employment Guarantee Act: A Case Study of How Change Happens', in D. Green (ed.) (2008), *From Poverty to Power: How Active Citizens and Effective States Can Change the World* (Oxford: OXFAM International).

Mahendra Dev, S. and Ranade, A. (2001), 'Employment Guarantee Scheme and Employment Security', in Mahendra Dev et al. (2001).

Mahendra Dev, S., Antony, P., Gayathri, V. and Mamgain, R. P. (eds.) (2001), *Social and Economic Security in India* (New Delhi: Institute of Human Development).

Mahmud, Simeen (2003), 'Is Bangladesh Experiencing a Feminization of the Labor Force?', *Bangladesh Development Studies*, 29.

Mahmud, Wahiduddin (2008), 'Social Development in Bangladesh: Pathways, Surprises and Challenges', *Indian Journal of Human Development*, 2.

Majumdar, M. and Rana, K. (2012), 'In Defence of Public Education: Voices from West Bengal', *Economic and Political Weekly*, 6 October.

Majumdar, Swapna (2013), 'Forced Hysterectomies, Unscrupulous Doctors', available at southasia.oneworld.net.

Mangatter, Silvia (2011), 'Does the Mahatma Gandhi National Rural Employment Guarantee Act (MGNREGA) Strengthen Rural Self-Employment in Bolpur Subdivision (West Bengal, India)?', Master's thesis, Faculty of Economics, Philipps-Universität Marburg.

Marulasiddappa, M., Raonka, P. and Sabhikhi, I. (2013), 'Social Security Pensions for the Elderly: A Case Study', mimeo, Planning and Development Unit, Allahabad University.

Mazumdar, I. and N, Neetha (2011), 'Gender Dimensions: Employment Trends in India, 1993–94 to 2009–10', *Economic and Political Weekly*, 22 October.

McCrindle, J. W. (1885), *Ancient India as Described by Ptolemy* (London: Trübner & Co.).

Meenakshi, Swathi (2011), 'Universalism for Real: The PDS in Tamil Nadu and Himachal Pradesh', partly published in *The Tribune*, 7 September.

Mehrotra, Santosh (2006), 'Child Malnutrition and Gender Discrimination in South Asia', *Economic and Political Weekly*, 11 March.

Mehta, Pratap Bhanu (2012), 'Breaking the Silence: Why We Don't Talk about Inequality – And How to Start Again', *Caravan*, 1 October.

Mellström, C. and Johannesson, M. (2008), 'Crowding Out in Blood Donation: Was Titmuss Right?', *Journal of the European Economic Association*, 6.

Micronutrient Initiative and UNICEF (2004), *Vitamin and Mineral Deficiency: A Global Progress Report* (Ottawa: Micronutrient Initiative).

Micronutrient Initiative and UNICEF (2009), *Investing in the Future: A United Call to Action on Vitamin and Mineral Deficiencies* (Ottawa: Micronutrient Initiative).

Mill, J. S. (1859), *On Liberty*, republished 1974 (Harmondsworth: Penguin).

Miller, Barbara D. (1981), *The Endangered Sex: Neglect of Female Children in Rural North India* (Ithaca, NY: Cornell University Press).

Miller, Barbara D. (1989), 'Changing Patterns of Juvenile Sex Ratios in Rural India, 1961 to 1971', *Economic and Political Weekly*, 3 June.

Mishra, Pankaj (2012), 'How India is Turning into China: And Not in a Good Way', *New Republic*, 31 December.

Mokyr, J. (2002), *The Gifts of Athena* (Princeton, NJ: Princeton University Press).

Moore, M. and Jadhav, V. (2006), 'The Politics and Bureaucratics of Rural Public Works: Maharashtra's Employment Guaranteed Scheme', *Journal of Development Studies*, 42.

Mudgal, Vipul (2011), 'Rural Coverage in the Hindi and English Dailies', *Economic and Political Weekly*, 27 August.

Mukerji, S. and Wadhwa, W. (2012), 'Do Private Schools Perform Better than Public Schools? Evidence from Rural India', paper presented at the 55th Annual Conference of the Comparative and International Education Society, Montreal, Quebec.

Mukerji, S. and Walton, M. (2012), 'Learning the Right Lessons: Measurement, Experimentation and the Need to Turn India's Right to Education Act Upside-Down', in IDFC Foundation (2012), *India Infrastructure Report 2012: Private Sector in Education* (New Delhi: Routledge India).

Mukherjee, Soumik (2012), '1 Democratic Protest. 8,000 Sedition Cases. Is this a Free Country?', *Tehelka*, 8 September.

Muraleedharan, V. R., Dash, U. and Gilson, L. (2011), 'Tamil Nadu 1980s–2005: A Success Story in India', in Balabanova et al. (eds.) (2011).

Muralidharan, Karthik (2012a), 'Teacher and Medical Worker Incentives', in Basu and Maertens (2012).

Muralidharan, Karthik (2012b), 'Priorities for Primary Education Policy in India's 12th Five Year Plan', mimeo, Department of Economics, University of California San Diego; to be published in NCAER-Brookings (forthcoming), *India Policy Forum 2013* (New Delhi: NCAER).

Muralidharan, K. and Prakash, N. (2012), 'Cycling to School: Increasing Secondary School Enrollment for Girls in India', paper presented at the annual Growth and Development Conference, Indian Statistical Institute, New Delhi, December 2012.

Murthi, M., Guio, A. M. and Drèze, J. P. (1995), 'Mortality, Fertility and Gender Bias in India: A District Level Analysis', *Population and Development Review*, 21.

Nagaraj, R. (2004), 'Fall in Manufacturing Employment: A Brief Note', *Economic and Political Weekly*, 24 July.

Nagaraj, R. (2006), 'Public Sector Performance since 1950: A Fresh Look', *Economic and Political Weekly*, 24 June.

Nagaraj, R. (2011), 'Growth in Organised Manufacturing Employment: A Comment', *Economic and Political Weekly*, 19 March.

Nandraj, Sunil (1997), 'Unhealthy Prescriptions: The Need for Health Sector Reform in India', in *Informing and Reforming*, Newsletter of the International Clearinghouse of Health System Reform Initiatives, no. 2.

Nandraj, Sunil (2012), 'Unregulated and Unaccountable: Private Health Providers', *Economic and Political Weekly*, 4 January.

Nandraj, S., Muraleedharan, V. R., Baru, R. V., Qadeer, I. and Priya, R. (2001), *The Private Health Sector in India* (Bombay: CEHAT).

Narayan, Shriman (ed.) (1968), *Selected Works of Mahatma Gandhi. Volume 6: The Voice of Truth* (Ahmedabad: Navajivan Publishing House).

Narayana, D. (2010), 'Review of the Rashtriya Swasthya Bhima Yojana', *Economic and Political Weekly*, 17 July.

Narayanan, Sudha (2006), 'Child Development as an "Investment"', in Citizens' Initiative for the Rights of Children Under Six (2006).

Narayanan, Sudha (2008), 'Employment Guarantee, Women's Work and Child Care', *Economic and Political Weekly*, 1 March.

Narayanan, Sudha (2011), 'A Case for Reframing the Cash Transfer Debate in India', *Economic and Political Weekly*, 21 May.

National Consortium of Civil Society Organisations (2009), *NREGA Reforms: Building Rural India*, first NCCSO report on NREGA; available at www.nregaconsortium.in.

National Consortium of Civil Society Organisations (2011), *MGNREGA:*

Opportunities, Challenges and the Road Ahead, second NCCSO report on MGNREGA; available at www.nregaconsortium.in.

National Crime Records Bureau (2011a), *Accidental Deaths and Suicides in India 2010* (New Delhi: NCRB).

National Crime Records Bureau (2011b), *Crime in India 2010* (New Delhi: NCRB).

National Federation of Indian Women (2008), 'Socio-economic Empowerment of Women under NREGA', report to the Ministry of Rural Development.

National Institute of Population Research and Training (2009), *Bangladesh Demographic and Health Survey 2007* (Dhaka, Bangladesh, and Calverton, MD, USA: National Institute of Population Research and Training, Mitra and Associates, and Macro International).

National Sample Survey Office (2011a), *Key Indicators of Employment and Unemployment in India: NSS 66th Round (July 2009–June 2010)* (New Delhi: NSSO).

National Sample Survey Office (2011b), *Key Indicators of Household Consumer Expenditure in India 2009–2010* (New Delhi: NSSO).

National Sample Survey Organisation (2006), 'Morbidity, Health Care and the Condition of the Aged: NSS 60th Round (January–June 2004)', Report 507, NSSO, New Delhi.

National University of Educational Planning and Administration (2011a), *Elementary Education in India: Progress towards UEE, Analytical Tables 2009–10* (New Delhi: NUEPA).

National University of Educational Planning and Administration (2011b), *Elementary Education in India under Government Managements 2009–10, Selected Tables Based on DISE 2009–10* (New Delhi: NUEPA).

National University of Educational Planning and Administration (2011c), *Elementary Education in India: Progress towards UEE, Flash Statistics 2009–10, Selected Tables Based on DISE 2009–10* (New Delhi: NUEPA).

Nawani, Disha (2013), 'Continuously and Comprehensively Evaluating Children', *Economic and Political Weekly*, 12 January.

Noorani, A. G. (2012), 'How the Political Class has Looted India', *The Hindu*, 30 July.

Nores, M. and Barnett, W. S. (2010), 'Benefits of Early Childhood Interventions Across the World: (Under) Investing in the Very Young', *Economics of Education Review*, 29.

North, Douglass (1990), *Institutions, Institutional Change and Economic Perfomance* (Cambridge: Cambridge University Press).

OECD (2011), *Education at a Glance 2011: OECD Indicators* (Paris: OECD Publishing).

O'Hanlon, Rosalind (1994), *A Comparison between Women and Men: Tara-bai Shinde and the Critique of Gender Relations in Colonial India* (Madras: Oxford University Press).

Ohkawa, K. and Rosovsky, H. (1973), *Japanese Economic Growth: Trend Acceleration in the Twentieth Century* (Stanford, CA: Stanford University Press).

Omvedt, Gail (2004), *Ambedkar: Towards an Enlightened India* (New Delhi: Penguin).

Omvedt, Gail (2008), *Seeking Begumpura: The Social Vision of Anticaste Intellectuals* (New Delhi: Navayana).

Omvedt, Gail (2010), *Understanding Caste: From Buddha to Ambedkar and Beyond* (New Delhi: Orient Blackswan).

Oommen, M. A. (2009), 'Development Policy and the Nature of Society: Understanding the Kerala Model', *Economic and Political Weekly*, 28 March.

Oommen, M. A. (ed.) (1999), *Rethinking Development: Kerala's Development Experience* (New Delhi: Concept).

Orenstein, Mitchell A. (2008), 'Postcommunist Welfare States', *Journal of Democracy*, 19.

Osmani, Siddiq R. (1991), 'Social Security in South Asia', in S. E. Ahmad, J. P. Drèze, J. Hills and A. K. Sen (eds.) (1991), *Social Security in Developing Countries* (Oxford: Oxford University Press).

Osmani, Siddiq R. (2010), 'Towards Achieving the Right to Health', *Bangladesh Development Studies*, 33.

Osmani, Siddiq R. (ed.) (1992), *Nutrition and Poverty* (Oxford: Oxford University Press).

Osmani, S. R. and Sen, A. K. (2003), 'The Hidden Penalties of Gender Inequality: Fetal Origins of Ill-Health', *Economics and Human Biology*, 1.

OXFAM International (2006), *Serve the Essentials: What Governments and Donors Must Do to Improve South Asia's Essential Services* (New Delhi: OXFAM India Trust).

Padel, F. and Das, S. (2010), *Out of this Earth: East India Adivasis and the Aluminium Cartel* (New Delhi: Orient Blackswan).

Paim, J., Travassos, C., Almeida, C., Bahia, L. and Macinko, J. (2011), 'The Brazilian Health System: History, Advances, and Challenges', *The Lancet*, 377.

Panday, Pranab Kumar (2008), 'Representation without Participation: Quotas for Women in Bangladesh', *International Political Science Review*, 29.

Pandey, Brijesh (2012), 'Ganga Dammed', *Tehelka*, 2 June.

Pankaj, A. and Tankha, R. (2010), 'Empowerment Effects of the NREGS on Women Workers: A Study in Four States', *Economic and Political Weekly*, 24 July.

Papp, John (2012), 'Essays on India's Employment Guarantee', PhD thesis, Princeton University, NJ.

Parikh, Kirit (2010), 'The Logic of the Expert Group Report on Petroleum Prices', *Economic and Political Weekly*, 15 May.

Parker, John (2012), 'Development in India: A Tale of Two Villages', *The Economist*, 17 November.

Parthasarathi, Prasannan (2011), *Why Europe Grew Rich and Asia Did Not: Global Economic Divergence 1600–1850* (Cambridge: Cambridge University Press).

Patel, I. G. (1987), 'Free Enterprise in the Nehru Era', in D. Tripathi (ed.) (1987), *State and Business in India: A Historical Perspective* (Delhi: Manohar).

Patel, I. G. (2002), *Glimpses of Economic Policy: An Insider's View* (New Delhi: Oxford University Press).

Patnaik, Prabhat (2002), 'Markets, Morals and the Media', Convocation Address, Asian College of Journalism, Chennai.

Paul, S., Balakrishnan, S., Thampi, G. K., Sekhar, S. and Vivekananda, M. (2006), *Who Benefits from India's Public Services?* (New Delhi: Academic Foundation).

Paul, V. K., Sachdev, H. S., Mavalankar, D., Ramachandran, P., Sankar, M. J., Bhandari, N., Sreenivas, V., Sundararaman, T., Govin, D., Orsin, D. and Kirkwood, B. (2011), 'Reproductive Health, and Child Health and Nutrition in India: Meeting the Challenge', *The Lancet*, 377.

Periyar, E. V. R. (1965), *Social Reform or Social Revolution?*, English translation by A. M. Dharmalingam (Chennai: Dravidar Kazhagam Publications).

Pierri, Gastón (2012), 'Development Strategies and Law in Latin America: Argentine, Brazilian and Chilean Conditional Cash Transfer Programs in Comparative Perspective', Documentos de Trabajo 05/2012, Instituto Universitario de Análisis Económico y Social, Universidad de Alcala.

Piketty, T. and Qian, N. (2009), 'Income Inequality and Progressive Income Taxation in China and India, 1986–2015', *American Economic Journal: Applied Economics*, 1.

Planning Commission (1951), *The First Five-Year Plan* (New Delhi: Planning Commission).

Planning Commission (1956), *The Second Five-Year Plan* (New Delhi: Planning Commission).

Planning Commission (2011a), 'Evaluation Study on Integrated Child Development Scheme', PEO Report no. 218 (New Delhi: Programme Evaluation Organisation, Planning Commission).

Planning Commission (2011b), *Faster, Sustainable and More Inclusive*

Growth: An Approach to the Twelfth Five-Year Plan (New Delhi: Planning Commission).

Pliny the Elder, *Natural History*, English translation by John Bostock and H. T. Riley; available online at http://www.perseus.tufts.edu.

Prasad, Chandra Bhan (2011), 'Shades of Mobility', *Outlook*, 31 October.

Pratham Education Foundation (2012), *Annual Status of Education Report (Rural) 2011, Provisional Report* (Mumbai: Pratham Education Foundation).

Pratham Education Foundation (2013), *Annual Status of Education Report (Rural) 2012, Provisional Report* (Mumbai: Pratham Education Foundation).

Pratichi Trust (2002), *The Pratichi Education Report I* (Delhi: Pratichi Trust in association with TLM Books).

Pratichi Trust (2005), *The Pratichi Health Report* (Delhi: Pratichi Trust in association with TLM Books).

Pratichi Trust (2009a), *The Pratichi Education Report II – Primary Education in West Bengal: Changes and Challenges* (Delhi and Kolkata: Pratichi Trust).

Pratichi Trust (2009b), *The Pratichi Child Report* (Delhi and Kolkata: Pratichi Trust).

Pratichi Trust (2010), *The Pratichi Report on Mid-Day Meal: The Mid-Day Programme in Urban Primary and Rural Upper Primary Schools in West Bengal* (Delhi and Kolkata: Pratichi Trust).

Pratichi Trust (2012a), *A Child's View of the World* (Kolkata: Pratichi Trust in collaboration with Child Rights and You).

Pratichi Trust (2012b), *The Joy of Reading*, Report of a series of children's reading festivals (Kolkata: Pratichi Trust in collaboration with Child Rights and You).

Prayas Energy Group (2012), 'Ensuring Electricity for All: Overcoming Structural Disincentive', paper presented at a Round Table on 'Electricity for All: Approaches and Challenges' at the Giri Institute of Development Studies, Lucknow, 28 September.

PricewaterhouseCoopers (2009), *Understanding the 'Key Issues and Constraints' in Implementing the RTI Act* (New Delhi: PwC).

Pritchett, L. and Beatty, A. (2012), 'The Negative Consequences of Overambitious Curricula in Developing Countries', Working Paper RWP12-035, Kennedy School of Government, Harvard University, MA.

Pritchett, L. and Murgai, R. (2007), 'Teacher Compensation', in National Council of Applied Economic Research (2007), *India Policy Forum 2006/07* (New Delhi: Sage).

Pritchett, L. and Pande, V. (2006), 'Making Primary Education Work for India's Rural Poor', Social Development Papers, South Asia Series, no. 95, World Bank, Washington, DC.

PROBE Team (1999), *Public Report on Basic Education* (New Delhi: Oxford University Press).

PRS Legislative Research (2011), 'Data from State Assemblies: Some Trends', available at www.prsindia.org (accessed 1 January 2013).

Public Cause Research Foundation (2009), 'State of Information Commissions in India: A Performance Evaluation', Public Cause Research Foundation, New Delhi; available at www.rtiawards.org.

Puri, Raghav (2012), 'Reforming the Public Distribution System: Lessons from Chhattisgarh', *Economic and Political Weekly*, 4 February.

Qun Meng et al. (2012), 'Trends in Access to Health Services and Financial Protection in China between 2003 and 2011: A Cross-Sectional Study', *The Lancet*, 379.

Rajakumar, J. Dennis (2011), 'Size and Growth of Private Corporate Sector in Indian Manufacturing', *Economic and Political Weekly*, 20 April.

Rajan, Raghuram (2008), 'Is There a Threat of Oligarchy in India?', Speech to the Bombay Chamber of Commerce on its Founders Day celebration, 10 September; available at http://faculty.chicagobooth.edu/raghuram.rajan.

Rajasekhar, D., Berg, E., Ghatak, M., Manjula, R. and Roy, S. (2011), 'Implementing Health Insurance: The Rollout of Rashtriya Swasthya Bhima Yojana in Karnataka', *Economic and Political Weekly*, 14 May.

Ram, N. (1990), 'An Independent Press and Anti-Hunger Strategies', in Drèze and Sen (1990).

Ram, N. (2011), 'The Changing Role of the News Media in Contemporary India', address as president of the Contemporary India section of the Indian History Congress, 72nd Session, Patiala, 10 December.

Ram, N. (2012), 'Sharing the Best and the Worst: The Indian News Media in a Global Context', James Cameron Memorial Lecture delivered at City University London, 3 October 2012.

Ramachandran, Nira (2007), 'Women and Food Security in South Asia', in B. Guha-Khasnobis et al. (eds.) (2007), *Food Insecurity, Vulnerability and Human Rights Failure* (New York: Palgrave).

Ramachandran, V. K. (1996), 'Kerala's Development Achievements', in Drèze and Sen (1996).

Ramalingaswami, V., Jonsson, U. and Rohde, J. (1996), 'The Asian Enigma', in *UNICEF: The Progress of Nations 1996*, available at www.unicef.org/pon96/nuenigma.htm

Ramana, M. V. (2012), *The Power of Promise: Examining Nuclear Energy in India* (New Delhi: Penguin).

Ramanathan, Usha (2010), 'A Unique Identity Bill', *Economic and Political Weekly*, 24 July.

Rana, Kumar (ed.) (2012), *Kalamchari* (Kolkata: Pratichi Institute and UNICEF).

Rao, Jaithirth (2012), 'No Law for Worker Rights', *Tehelka*, 8 September.

Ravallion, Martin (2011), 'A Comparative Perspective on Poverty Reduction in Brazil, China and India', *World Bank Research Observer*, 26.

Ravi, R. N. (2012), 'The Biggest Impediment to Peace', *The Statesman*, 8 July.

Rawls, John (1971), *A Theory of Justice* (Cambridge, MA: Harvard University Press).

Rawls, John (1993), *Political Liberalism* (New York: Columbia University Press).

Rawls, John (1999), *Collected Papers* (Cambridge, MA: Harvard University Press).

Rawls, John (2001), *Justice as Fairness: A Restatement* (Cambridge, MA: Harvard University Press).

Reddy, K. S. and Guha Thakurta, P. (2010), '"Paid News": How Corruption in the Indian Media Undermines Democracy', Draft report prepared for the Press Council of India; available at ocw.iimb.ernet.in.

Reddy, Rammanohar (2012), 'How is India Doing (2012)?', S. Guhan Memorial Lecture, Chennai, 5 December; partly published in *The Hindu*, 29 December.

Rege, Sharmila (ed.) (2006), *Writing Caste/Writing Gender: Narrating Dalit Women's Testimonios* (New Delhi: Zubaan).

Rege, Sharmila (ed.) (2013), *Against the Madness of Manu: B. R. Ambedkar's Writings on Brahmanical Patriarchy* (New Delhi: Navayana).

Reserve Bank of India (2012), 'Database on the Indian Economy 2010–11', available at http://dbie.rbi.org.in.

Risley, H. H. and Gait, E. A. (1903), *Report on the Census of India, 1901* (Calcutta: Superintendent of Government Printing); also available at http://www.chaf.lib.latrobe.edu.au/dcd/census1901.htm.

Roberts, Alasdair (2010), 'A Great and Revolutionary Law? The First Four Years of India's Right to Information Act', *Public Administration Review*, 70.

Rodrigues, Valerian (ed.) (2002), *The Essential Writings of B. R. Ambedkar* (Oxford: Oxford University Press).

Rothschild, Emma (2011), *The Inner Life of Empires: An Eighteenth-Century History* (Princeton, NJ: Princeton University Press).

Rothschild, M. and Stiglitz, J. E. (1976), 'Equilibrium in Competitive Insurance Markets: An Essay on the Economics of Imperfect Information', *Quarterly Journal of Economics*, 90.

Rouse, C. E. and Barrow, L. (2009), 'School Vouchers and Student Achievement', *Annual Review of Economics*, 1.

Roy, Arundhati (1999), *The Cost of Living* (London: Flamingo).

Roy, Arundhati (2010), 'Walking with the Comrades', *Outlook*, 29 March.

RTI Assessment and Analysis Group (2009), 'Safeguarding the Right to Information', available at www.rti-assessment.org.

Rudra, Ashok (1975), *Indian Plan Models* (New Delhi: Allied Publishers).

Rudra, Ashok (1988), 'Emerging Class Structure in Rural India', in Srinivasan and Bardhan (1988).

Rudra, Ashok (1989), 'Emergence of the Intelligentsia as a Ruling Class in India', *Economic and Political Weekly*, 21 January.

Ruger, Jennifer Prah (2009), *Health and Social Justice* (Oxford: Oxford University Press).

Ryan, Alan (2012), *On Politics: A History of Political Thought from Herodotus to the Present* (London: Allen Lane).

Sachdev, H. P. S. (2012), 'Overcoming Challenges to Accelerating Linear Growth in Indian Children', *Indian Pediatrics*, 49.

Sainath, P. (2009), 'The Medium, Message and the Money', *The Hindu*, 26 October.

Sainath, P. (2010), 'Paid News Undermining Democracy: Press Council Report', *The Hindu*, 21 April.

SAMARTHAN (2010), 'Impact Assessment of MGNREGA in Madhya Pradesh', Report to the Poverty Monitoring and Policy Support Unit, State Planning Commission, Madhya Pradesh.

Samson, M. and Gupta, N. (2012), 'Schooling for Children on the Bihar Jharkhand Border', study commissioned by NEG-FIRE; available at www.cordindia.com.

Samuelson, Paul (1954), 'The Pure Theory of Public Expenditure', *Review of Economics and Statistics*, 36.

Sandel, Michael J. (2012), *What Money Can't Buy: The Moral Limits of Markets* (London: Allen Lane).

Sarkar, M. and Rana, K. (2010), 'Roles and Responsibilities of the Teachers' Unions in the Delivery of Primary Education: A Case of West Bengal', Pratichi Occasional Paper no. 3, Pratichi Trust, Kolkata.

Sarkar, S. and Mehta, B. S. (2010), 'Income Inequality in India: Pre- and Post-Reform Periods', *Economic and Political Weekly*, 11 September.

Sathe, D., Klasen, S., Prieve, J. and Biniwale, M. (2013), 'Can the Female

Sarpanch Deliver? Evidence from Maharashtra', *Economic and Political Weekly*, 16 March.

Sawalkar, S., Deshmukh, M., Kalkonde, Y., Shah, D. and Bang, A. (2013), 'Tobacco vs Development: Private Spending on Tobacco in Gadchiroli District', *Economic and Political Weekly*, 2 February.

Sawhney, Ria Singh (2011), 'The PDS in Rajasthan: A New Start', partly published in *The Tribune*, 7 September.

Secretariat of the Rajya Sabha (2012), 'List of Women Members', available online on Rajya Sabha website (http://164.100.47.5/Newmembers/women.aspx), accessed 14 November 2012.

Sekher, T. V. (2012), 'Ladlis and Lakshmis: Financial Incentive Schemes for the Girl Child', *Economic and Political Weekly*, 28 April.

Selvaraj, S. and Karan, A. K. (2012), 'Why Publicly Financed Health Insurance Schemes are Ineffective in Providing Financial Risk Protection', *Economic and Political Weekly*, 17 March.

Sen, Amartya (1973), *On Economic Inequality*, expanded edn. 1997 with a substantial annexe by James E. Foster and Amartya Sen (Oxford: Oxford University Press).

Sen, Amartya (1983), 'Development: Which Way Now?', *Economic Journal*, 93.

Sen, Amartya (1984), *Resources, Values and Development* (Cambridge, MA: Harvard University Press).

Sen, Amartya (1985), 'Well-being, Agency and Freedom: The Dewey Lectures 1984', *Journal of Philosophy*, 82.

Sen, Amartya (1990), 'Gender and Cooperative Conflict', in I. Tinker (ed.) (1990), *Persistent Inequalities* (New York: Oxford University Press).

Sen, Amartya (1999), *Development as Freedom* (New York: Knopf, and Oxford: Oxford University Press).

Sen, Amartya (2002a), *Rationality and Freedom* (Cambridge, MA: Harvard University Press).

Sen, Amartya (2002b), 'Open and Closed Impartiality', *Journal of Philosophy*, 99.

Sen, Amartya (2003), '"Missing Women" Revisited', *British Medical Journal*, 327.

Sen, Amartya (2005), 'The Country of First Boys', *The Little Magazine*, 6 (1 and 2).

Sen, Amartya (2009), *The Idea of Justice* (Harmondsworth and Delhi: Penguin, and Cambridge, MA: Harvard University Press).

Sen, Amartya (2011), 'Rights, Laws and Language', *Oxford Journal of Legal Studies*, 31.

Sen, B., Mujeri, M. K. and Shahabuddin, Q. (2007), 'Explaining Pro-Poor Growth in Bangladesh: Puzzles, Evidence, and Implications', in T. Besley and L. J. Cord (eds.) (2007), *Delivering on the Promise of Pro-Poor Growth* (New York: Palgrave Macmillan).

Sen, Gita (2012), 'Universal Health Coverage in India: A long and Winding Road', *Economic and Political Weekly*, 25 February.

Seth, Leila (2012), 'The Girl Child and Governance', lecture delivered at the India International Centre, New Delhi, 19 July.

Sethi, Surya P. (2010), 'Analysing the Parikh Committee Report on Pricing of Petroleum Products', *Economic and Political Weekly*, 27 March.

Shah, G., Mander, H., Thorat, S., Deshpande, S. and Baviskar, A. (2006), *Untouchability in Rural India* (New Delhi: Sage).

Shah, T. et al. (2010), 'Asset Creation through Employment Guarantee?: Synthesis of Student Case Studies in Nine States of India', International Water Management Institute.

Shah, V. C. and Makwana, M. (2011), 'Impact of NREGA on Wage Rates, Food Security and Rural Urban Migration in Gujarat', Agro-economic Research Centre, Sardar Patel University, Vallabh Vidyanagar.

Shapiro, Ian (1999), *Democratic Justice* (New Haven, CT: Yale University Press).

Sharma, R. S. (2010), 'Identity and the UIDAI: A Response', *Economic and Political Weekly*, 28 August.

Shrivastava, A. and Kothari, A. (2012), *Churning the Earth: The Making of Global India* (New Delhi: Penguin).

Simons, E., Ferrari, M., Fricks, J., Wannemuehler, K., Anand, A., Burton, A. and Strebel, P. (2012), 'Assessment of the 2010 Global Measles Mortality Reduction Goal: Results from a Model of Surveillance Data', *The Lancet*, 379.

Singh, A., Park, A. and Dercon, S. (2012), 'School Meals as a Safety Net: An Evaluation of the Midday Meal Scheme in India', Discussion Paper 9031, Centre for Economic Policy Research, London; forthcoming in *Economic Development and Cultural Change*.

Singh, Prerna (2010a), 'We-ness and Welfare: A Longitudinal Analysis of Social Development in Kerala, India', *World Development*, 39.

Singh, Prerna (2010b), 'Subnationalism and Social Development: A Comparative Analysis of Indian States', PhD thesis, Princeton University; to be published as a monograph.

Singh, Upinder (2009), *A History of Ancient and Early Medieval India* (New Delhi: Pearson Longman).

Singh, Upinder (2012), 'Governing the State and the Self: Political Philosophy and Practice in the Edicts of Asoka', *South Asian Studies*, 28.

Sinha, Amarjeet (2012), 'Health Evidence from the States', *Economic and Political Weekly*, 11 February.

Sinha, Amarjeet (2013), *An India for Everyone: A Path to Inclusive Development* (New Delhi: Harper Collins).

Sinha, Chitra (2012), *Debating Patriarchy: The Hindu Code Bill Controversy in India (1941–1956)* (New Delhi: Oxford University Press).

Sinha, Dipa (2008), 'Social Audit of Midday Meal Scheme in AP', *Economic and Political Weekly*, 1 November.

Sinha, Dipa (2013), 'Health and Human Development: Comparative Experiences of Tamil Nadu and Uttar Pradesh', PhD thesis, Jawaharlal Nehru University.

Sivasubramonian, S. (2000), *The National Income of India in the Twentieth Century* (New Delhi: Oxford University Press).

Skidelsky, R. and Skidelsky, E. (2012), *How Much is Enough? The Love of Money, and the Case for the Good Life* (London: Allen Lane).

Smith, Adam (1759, 1790), *The Theory of Moral Sentiments*, anniversary edn. (New York and London: Penguin, 2009).

Smith, Adam (1776), *An Inquiry into the Natures and Causes of the Wealth of Nations*, republished in R. H. Campbell and A. S. Skinner (eds.) (1976), *Adam Smith: An Inquiry into the Natures and Causes of the Wealth of Nations* (Oxford: Clarendon Press).

Soares, Fabio V. (2011), 'Brazil's Bolsa Família: A Review', *Economic and Political Weekly*, 21 May.

Soares, F. V., Ribas, R. P. and Osório, R. G. (2010), 'Evaluating the Impact of Brazil's Bolsa Família: Conditional Cash Transfers in Perspective', *Latin American Research Review*, 45.

Sobhan, Rehman (2011), 'Bangladesh at 40: Looking Back and Moving Forward', mimeo, Centre for Policy Dialogue, Dhaka.

Sobhan, Salma (1978), *Legal Status of Women in Bangladesh* (Dhaka: Bangladesh Institute of Legal and International Affairs).

Society for Participatory Research in Asia (2008), *Demanding Accountability from the State: An Assessment of Right to Information* (New Delhi: PRIA).

Society for Participatory Research in Asia (2009), *Accessing Information under RTI: Citizens' Experiences in Ten States* (New Delhi: PRIA).

Sopher, David (ed.) (1980), *An Exploration of India: Geographical Perspectives on Society and Culture* (Ithaca, NY: Cornell University Press).

Spears, Dean (2011), 'Height and Cognitive Achievement among Indian Children', *Economics and Human Biology*, 10.

Spears, Dean (2012a), 'Effects of Rural Sanitation on Child Mortality and Human Capital: Evidence from India's Total Sanitation Campaign', Working Paper, Research Institute for Compassionate Economics.

Spears, Dean (2012b), 'How Much International Variation in Child Height

Can Sanitation Explain?', Working Paper, Research Institute for Compassionate Economics.

Spears, Dean (2013), 'The Long and Short of Open Defecation', *The Hindu*, 14 March.

Spence, Michael A. (1973), 'Job Market Signalling', *Quarterly Journal of Economics*, 83.

Sreevidya, S. and Sathyasekaran, B. W. C. (2003), 'High Caesarean Rates in Madras (India): A Population-based Cross-sectional Study', *BJOG: An International Journal of Obstretics and Gynaecology*, 110.

Srinivas, M. N. (1995), *Social Change in Modern India* (Delhi: Orient Longman).

Srinivasan, T. N. and Bardhan, P. K. (eds.) (1988), *Rural Poverty in South Asia* (New York: Columbia University Press).

Srinivasan, Vivek (2010), 'Understanding Public Services in Tamil Nadu: An Institutional Perspective', PhD dissertation, University of Syracuse, NY; to be published as a monograph.

Srivastava, D. K., Rao, C. B., Chakraborty, P. and Rangamannar, T. S. (2003), *Budgetary Subsidies in India: Subsidising Social and Economic Services* (New Delhi: National Institute of Public Finance and Policy).

Stern, Nicholas (2009), *A Blueprint for a Safer Planet* (London: Bodley Head).

Stern, Nicholas (2012), 'Ethics, Equity and the Economics of Climate Change', Working Paper 97, Centre for Climate Change Economics and Policy, London School of Economics.

Stevenson, Andrew (2008), 'A Class Act? Opinions Differ', *Sydney Morning Herald*, 5 January.

Stiglitz, Joseph E. (1975), 'The Theory of "Screening", Education, and the Distribution of Income', *American Economic Review*, 65.

Stiglitz, Joseph E. (2002), *Globalization and its Discontents* (New York: Norton & Co.).

Stiglitz, J. E. and Weiss, A. (1981), 'Credit Rationing in Markets with Imperfect Information', *American Economic Review*, 71.

Svedberg, Peter (2000), *Poverty and Undernutrition: Theory, Measurement, and Policy* (Oxford: Oxford University Press).

Tagore, Rabindranath (1931), *Russiar Chitthi*, trans. Sasadhar Sinha (1960), *Letters from Russia* (Calcutta: Visva-Bharati).

Tao Yang, D., Weijia Chen, V. and Monarch, R. (2010), 'Rising Wages: Has China Lost its Global Labor Advantage?', *Pacific Economic Review*, 15.

Tarozzi, Alessandro (2008), 'Growth Reference Charts and the Status of Indian Children', *Economic and Human Biology*, 6.

Tejpal, Karan (2012), 'My Rajput Friends Believed that Polo was Reserved for Them', *Tehelka*, 14 April.

Thaler, R. and Sunstein, C. (2008) *Nudge: Improving Decisions about Health, Wealth and Happiness* (New Haven, CT: Yale University Press).

Thapar, Romila (1963), *Asoka and the Decline of the Mauryas* (Delhi: Oxford University Press).

Thapar, Romila (1984), *The Mauryas Revisited* (Calcutta: K. P. Bagchi).

Tharamangalam, Joseph (1998), 'The Perils of Social Development without Economic Growth: The Development Debacle of Kerala, India', *Bulletin of Concerned Asian Scholars*, 30.

The Commonwealth Fund (2010), *International Profiles of Health Care Systems* (Washington, DC: The Commonwealth Fund).

The Hoot (2011), 'What Makes News: A Content Study of Regional Media', available at www.thehoot.org.

The India Site (2011), 'More Family Politics', available at http://www.theindiasite.com/dynastic-politics-by-state/ (accessed January 2012).

Thomas, Jayan Jose (2012), 'India's Labour Market during the 2000s', *Economic and Political Weekly*, 22 December.

Thorat, S. and Lee, J. (2005), 'Caste Discrimination and Food Security Programmes', *Economic and Political Weekly*, 24 September.

Thorat, S. and Newman, K. S. (eds.) (2010), *Blocked by Caste: Economic Discrimination and Social Exclusion in Modern India* (New Delhi: Oxford University Press).

Titmuss, Richard M. (1970), *The Gift Relationship* (London: Allen & Unwin).

Trebilcock, M. J. and Daniels, R. J. (2008), *Rule of Law and Development: Charting the Fragile Path of Progress* (Cheltenham: Edward Elgar).

Trebilcock, M. J. and Prado, M. M. (2011), *What Makes Poor Countries Poor? Institutional Determinants of Development* (Cheltenham: Edward Elgar).

UNCTAD (2011), *Trade and Development Report 2011* (New York: United Nations).

UNICEF (2012), *The State of the World's Children 2012* (New York: UNICEF).

UNICEF and Government of India (2010), *Coverage Evaluation Survey 2009* (New Delhi: UNICEF).

United Nations (2011), *Sex Differentials in Childhood Mortality* (New York: Population Division, United Nations).

United Nations Development Programme (2011), *Human Development Report 2010* (New York: UNDP).

United Nations Office on Drugs and Crime (2013), 'Rape at the National

Level: Number of Police-Reported Offences', Spreadsheet, available at www.unodc.org, accessed 21 January 2013.

United Nations Population Division (2011), *World Population Prospects: The 2010 Revision*, CD-ROM edn. (New York: United Nations).

United Nations Population Fund (2011), *Trends in Sex Ratio at Birth and Estimates of Girls Missing at Birth in India (2001–2008)* (New Delhi: UNFPA).

United Nations Population Fund (2012a), *State of World Population 2012: By Choice, not Chance: Family Planning, Human Rights and Development* (New York: UNFPA).

United Nations Population Fund (2012b), *Sex Imbalances at Birth: Current Trends, Consequences and Policy Implications* (Bangkok: UNFPA).

Uniyal, B. N. (1996), 'In Search of a Dalit Journalist', *The Pioneer*, 16 November.

UNU-IHDP and UNEP (2012), *Inclusive Wealth Report 2012: Measuring Progress Toward Sustainability* (Cambridge: Cambridge University Press).

USAID (2008), *Private Health Insurance in India: Promise and Reality* (New Delhi: USAID/India).

Usami, Yoshifumi (2011), 'A Note on Recent Trends in Wage Rates in Rural India', *Review of Agrarian Studies*, 1.

Usami, Yoshifumi (2012), 'Recent Trends in Wage Rates in Rural India: An Update', *Review of Agrarian Studies*, 2.

Vaidyanathan, A. (1983), 'The Indian Economy since Independence (1947–70)', in D. Kumar and M. Desai (eds.) (1983), *The Cambridge Economic History of India. Vol. 2: c. 1757–c. 1970* (Cambridge: Cambridge University Press).

Valmiki, Omprakash (2003), *Joothan: A Dalit's Life* (New York: Columbia University Press).

Vanneman, R. and Dubey, A. (forthcoming), 'Horizontal and Vertical Inequalities in India', in J. Gornick and M. Jantti (eds.) (forthcoming), *Income Inequality: Economic Disparities and the Middle Classes in Affluent Countries* (Stanford: Stanford University Press).

Varshney, Vibha (2012), 'Planning Commission Push to Health Care Privatization', *Down to Earth*, 9 August.

Varshney, V., Gupta, A. and Pallavi, A. (2012), 'Universal Health Scare', *Down to Earth*, 30 September.

Vashishtha, Vipin M. (2009), 'Routine Immunization in India', *Indian Pediatrics*, 46.

Veeramani, K. (1996), *Is There a God? Selections from Periyar's Speeches and Writings* (Madras: Emerald Publishers).

Veeramani, K. (ed.) (1992), *Periyar on Women's Rights, Selected Speeches and Writings of Periyar E. V. Ramasami* (Madras: Emerald Publishers).

Venkataramanam, R. (2011), 'Learning by Rote Prevalent in Top Schools too', *The Hindu*, 16 December.

Verma, Shilp (2011), 'MG-NREGA Assets and Rural Water Security: Synthesis of Field Studies in Bihar, Gujarat, Kerala and Rajasthan', Draft report, International Water Management Institute, Anand.

Vickers, J. and Yarrow, G. (1988), *Privatization: An Economic Analysis* (Cambridge, MA: MIT Press).

Vikas Samvad, Spandan and CDC (2013), 'Towards Building a Comprehensive Community-based Model on Malnutrition', Report of Baseline Survey, Vikas Samvad, Bhopal.

Vir, Sheila C. (2012), 'Mitanin Initiative and Nutrition Security Innovation Chhattisgarh State, India: An Evaluation', project report, State Health Resource Centre, Chhattisgarh.

Visaria, Leela (2000), 'Innovations in Tamil Nadu', *Seminar*, 489.

Vivek, S. (2006), 'A Thriving Anganwadi in Tamil Nadu', in Citizens' Initiative for the Rights of Children Under Six (2006).

Voice for Child Rights Odisha (2012), *A Study on Status of Service Delivery of SNP & Pre Schooling Education under Integrated Child Development Services (ICDS)* (Bhubaneshwar: VCRO).

Wail, B., Said, H. and Abdelhak, K. (2011), 'A New Data Set on Educational Inequality in the World, 1950–2010: Gini Index of Education by Age Group', available at http://www.education-inequality.com/Article/BHK,%202011.pdf

Walker, Maurice (2011), *PISA 2009 Plus Results* (Camberwell, Victoria: Australian Council for Educational Research).

Wang, Shaoguang (2008), 'Double Movement in China', *Economic and Political Weekly*, 27 December.

Weisskopf, Thomas E. (2011), 'Why Worry about Inequality in the Booming Indian Economy?', *Economic and Political Weekly*, 19 November.

Wheatley, Alan (2012), 'Fed Likely to Stay on Sideline on Economy: Economic Outlook', *International Herald Tribune*, 16 July.

WHO Multicentre Growth Reference Study Group (2006), 'Assessment of Differences in Linear Growth Among Populations in the Multicentre Growth Reference Study', *Act Paediatrica*, Suppl. 450.

Wilkinson, R. and Marmot, M. (eds.) (2003), *Social Determinants of Health: The Solid Facts*, 2nd edn. (Geneva: World Health Organization).

Wilkinson, R. and Pickett, K. (2009), *The Spirit Level: Why More Equal Societies Almost Always Do Better* (London: Allen Lane).

Working Group for Children Under Six (2007), 'Strategies for Children Under Six', *Economic and Political Weekly*, 29 December.

Working Group for Children Under Six (2012), *Strategies for Children Under Six: Update and Recommendations for the 12th Plan* (New Delhi: Public Health Resource Network).

Working Group on Human Rights in India and the UN (2012), *Human Rights in India: Status Report 2012*, Report prepared for the second Universal Periodic Review conducted by the United Nations Human Rights Council (New Delhi: WGHR).

World Bank (1980), *World Development Report 1980* (Washington, DC: World Bank).

World Bank (2007), *Whispers to Voices: Gender and Social Transformation in Bangladesh* (Washington, DC: World Bank).

World Bank (2011a), *Perspectives on Poverty in India: Stylised Facts from Survey Data* (Washington, DC: World Bank).

World Bank (2011b), *Social Protection for a Changing India*, 2 vols. (Washington, DC: World Bank).

World Bank (2012), *World Development Indicators 2012* (Washington, DC: World Bank).

World Bank and UNESCO (2000), *Higher Education in Developing Countries: Peril and Promise, Report of the Task Force on Higher Education and Society* (Washington, DC: World Bank).

Yadav, Yogendra (2010a), 'On Remembering Lohia', *Economic and Political Weekly*, 2 October.

Yadav, Yogendra (2010b), 'What is Living and What is Dead in Rammanohar Lohia?', *Economic and Political Weekly*, 2 October.

Yale Center for Environmental Law and Policy and Columbia Center for International Earth Science Information Network (2012), *Environmental Performance Index and Pilot Trend Environmental Performance Index* (New Haven, CT: Yale Center for Environmental Law and Policy).

Yip, W. and Mahal, A. (2008), 'The Health Care Systems of China and India', *Health Affairs*, 27.

Yip, W. C. M., Hsiao, W. C., Wen Chen, Shanlian Hu, Jin Ma and Maynard, A. (2012), 'Early Appraisal of China's Huge and Complex Health-Care Reforms', *The Lancet*, 379.

Young, Katharine G. (2012), *Constituting Economic and Social Rights* (Oxford: Oxford University Press).

Name Index

413

Subject Index

* See also Statistical Appendix.